From the Collections of
Bridwell Library
WITHDRAWN
Perkins School of Theology
Southern Methodist
University

IN RED AND BLACK

by the same author

The Political Economy of Slavery

The World the Slaveholders Made

IN RED AND BLACK

Marxian Explorations in Southern and Afro-American History

Eugene D. Genovese

Pantheon Books
A Division of Random House
New York

 Published in the United States by Pantheon Books, a division of Random House, Inc., New York, and simultaneously in Canada by Random House of Canada Limited, Toronto.

ISBN: 0-394-46792-2

Library of Congress Catalog Card Number: 73-135366

Manufactured in the United States of America
by The Colonial Press Inc., Clinton, Mass.

9 8 7 6 5 4 3 2

FIRST EDITION

By Way of a Dedication . . .

The academic year 1968–1969 will be remembered as the high-water mark of campus frustration and confusion, when a small number of students, encouraged by an even smaller number of professors, who were themselves almost invariably missing during the ensuing rough confrontations, momentarily transformed radical politics into a pseudo-Freudian passion play in which each participant could become his own hero, martyr, and savior. It will take the American Left a while to pick up the pieces.

But now that a great number of leftwing students and faculty members are pulling themselves together, and restoring sanity to the remains of the miscalled and abortive "New Left," it would seem appropriate to recall a few of those on the Left who fought the nihilist perversions and made possible the restoration of a genuine political movement.

This book is dedicated to seven of them:

ALAN ADAMSON,
CHARLES BERTRAND,
SANFORD ELWITT,
A. NORMAN KLEIN,
AILEEN KRADITOR,
JOHN LAFFEY,
and G. DAVID SHEPS.

At Sir George Williams University in Montreal these five American and two Canadian leftwing faculty members faced a difficult problem. A young, conservative, rather unpopular member of the faculty was accused of white racism by some black West Indian students of dubious political connections. (Their black "Maoist" spokesman, for example, was later proved to be a member of the conservative party and a close associate of its most right-wing, anti-Chinese, anticommunist leaders.) The charges were a frame-up. No evidence was ever presented against the accused, for there had never been any to present. The nihilist factions of the Left, including a contingent of agents-provocateurs, *joined the incipient* auto-da-fé: *"Purge the racist university!" "All power to the oppressed black students!" (Most of whom, by the way, subsequently demonstrated their revolutionary commitments by leaving for Trinidad, where they received a hero's welcome from the anticommunist, pro-American regime of Dr. Eric Williams.) "Down with the liberal temporizers!" The liberal temporizers, as one might have guessed, did not deserve this rebuke, for they could hardly wait to announce their support for those students who proceeded to burn the computer center and terrorize the campus.*

Let it be recorded, however, that these and other faculty members said no—no to frame-ups, no to opportunism, no to the demagogic manipulation of the real oppression suffered by black people, and no to reactionary nihilism masquerading as revolutionary action. They insisted, at great personal risk, that the socialist struggle for justice, equality, and freedom must rest on decency, honesty, and principle. In so doing, they defended the socialist movement and helped insure its resurgence. At that moment they were beautiful. Honor to them—and to the thousands of others who, during these painful last few years kept the faith and prevented momentary madness from becoming a permanent condition.

Preface

The essays collected here have all been written during the last five tumultuous years. Like other Americans, especially those connected in one way or another with the campus, I have found that participation in and observation of the incredible onrush of events have led to much re-examination of assumption and interpretation. Most of the essays grew out of the professional commitments attendant upon my work as a historian of slave societies; some had more immediate and political origins. All, in one way or another, reflect a discussed Marxian perspective and in a broad sense, in the first essay, are meant to bear on political concerns. For that reason I have risked opening and closing the volume with two essays that have no direct connection with the subject matter of the rest of the book but that may help the reader to see the rest from the author's perspective.

Part Three should be self-explanatory. The essays are offered in the hope that individually and collectively (if loosely) they provide a way of looking at some important facets of the life of the Old South. By examining the work of some other historians I have tried to comment on the issues being debated by scholars of diverse viewpoints and thereby to clarify my own point of view.

Part Two probably is not self-explanatory, at least not in one important respect. Each of the essays on the black experience, so much of which is also part of the Southern experience and vice versa, has been written by a white man who, whatever his sins, has never tried to tell black people how to be black. Every historian of the United States and especially the South cannot avoid making estimates of the black experience, for without them he cannot make estimates of anything else. When, therefore, I am asked, in the fashion of our insane times, what right I, as a white man, have to write about black people, I am forced to reply in four-letter words.

Ironically, it was only a few years ago that a distinguished clown, who happened to be delivering the presidential address to the American Historical Association, bemoaned the influx of the non-WASP into the historical profession. After all, how could Jews, Italians, and Irishmen possibly understand an American culture that was so profoundly Anglo-Saxon and Teutonic? Putting the two arguments together, I have concluded that I am qualified to write only the history of Italian immigration—a subject I know nothing about. I prefer, however, to wait until I can convince a black graduate student to undertake that task; he will, I think, do it in a more detached way than I, although, not having been raised on pasta, well-wrapped fig trees, and vendettas, he will certainly miss some important parts of the culture. Many white Southerners have graciously decided that perhaps someone raised entirely outside their experience might have something worthwhile to say to them; I see no reason to think that black Southerners will prove less gracious. In some respects, after all, Southerners are Southerners.

But these essays on the black experience are consciously written from the outside in a more radical way than those on the white South. They also represent an attempt to bring a Marxian viewpoint to the black experience without, I hope, imposing some external ideological position on it. Their value, then, if any, must rest precisely on the possibilities and in fact the necessity for writing the history of any people both from within and without.

So many friends have helped me over the years with the individual essays that I could not begin to list them. They will have to forgive me for not trying. I am, in any case, wary of acknowledgments these days. In my last book I decided to have some fun and protest against the absurdity of ritualized acknowledgments by insisting that each of the persons named should be held responsible for my errors. I should have known better. Franklin Knight, among others, has been followed by hostile critics who demand to know how he could possibly have said thus and so. "But," the poor man has been heard to protest, "Genovese said that; I didn't." He is then reminded of what I said in my preface. No more acknowledgments. Not even for Betsey, who put in so much time, effort, and hard criticism. Anyway, she knows.

NOTE:
With the exception of a few minor stylistic changes, all the essays except one appear here as they were published. Where more substantial corrections or reply to criticism seemed in order, I have added introductory notes and postscripts.

Contents

Part One

A POINT OF VIEW

Chapter 1

ON BEING A SOCIALIST AND A HISTORIAN

AFTER A DECADE of legal and extralegal repression, the American Left reemerged during the 1960s and made a considerable impact upon American life. At this writing, as we enter the 1970s, that movement is in crisis. By several reasonable standards of measurement, it has been a tremendous success. Not since the 1850s has so large a portion of the American people been in political motion and been willing to listen to the most fundamental criticisms of our social order. The juxtaposition of this growing constituency and its shrinking organizational base presents a paradox the exploration of which will have to be left for another book, but this one, like the individual essays it contains, necessarily stands within that political context.

This assertion of political engagement may seem strange since many of the essays do not concern politics at all and others do so only tangentially. It may seem especially strange to those who work in the historical profession or who follow leftwing factional debates and have been led to believe that socialist historians like myself stand for the separation of politics and history. In fact, what we stand for is the realization that all historical writing and teaching—all cultural work—is unavoidably political intervention, but that ideologically motivated history is bad history and ultimately reactionary politics. The most technical essay in this book is neither more nor less political than the most directly partisan essay. But this assertion of political content has nothing in common with those demands for a political (a "relevant") approach to history which ring across our campuses today. The assertion, in effect, rests on the belief that every contribution to history and the humanities, to the extent to which it takes a critical stance, helps to defend humanity against the barbarism of our age; and that it therefore constitutes as important a task for socialist intellectuals as opposition to the war in Vietnam. Holding this viewpoint as we do, we do not find it surprising that nihilists and utopians accuse us of deserting the cause and embracing pure scholarship and value-free social science.

Socialists do not advocate pure scholarship and value-free social science because we do not advocate the impossible. But we do insist that the inevitability of ideological bias does not free us from the responsibility to struggle for maximum objectivity. We must confess to other sins as well. We are terribly smug people: We really do believe that our political movement represents the hope of humanity and the cause of the exploited and oppressed of the world. And we are terribly conceited: We are so convinced we are right that we believe we have nothing whatever to fear from the truth about anything. It is our contention, on the contrary, that only ruling classes and the waves of nihilists who regularly arise to entertain these same ruling classes have anything to gain from the ideological approach to history. Our pretensions, therefore, lead us to the fantastic idea that all good (true, valid, competent) history serves our interest and that all poor (false, invalid, incompetent) history serves the interest of our enemies—or at least of someone other than ourselves. So, when we write a methodological essay on the treatment of slaves, or an interpretive essay on Dante's religious views, or a descriptive essay on the organization of the shipbuilding industry in Bordeaux, or an informative essay on anything else of which men and women have ever been a part—when, in other words, we follow our calling or, as it were, do our thing—we think we are meeting at least part of our political responsibility. We hold the strange notion that socialists (and all decent human beings) have a duty to contribute through their particular callings to the dignity of human life, a part of which is necessarily the preservation of the record of all human experience.

But we are not so smug as to think that socialism can guarantee the more humane life for which it has become a prerequisite; nor are we so conceited as to think that, because we are right on the essential question, we shall prevail or even deserve to prevail if we are badly wrong on other questions. We know that a socialist movement capable of winning mass support in the United States must have a philosophy and a program that can reconcile individual liberty with democratic rule, humane learning with mass education, political freedom with social order; a movement that can rest its reconciliation on a defense of the admirable and the solid in the experience of our nation and of Western civilization—not the least of which is precisely the achievement of a rationalist and critical tradition. And we also know that any movement without such a philosophy and program which did achieve political power would bring a catastrophe down on our nation and the world. We see our work as historians, no matter how small the subject investigated, as a modest but necessary contribution to the development of a movement that can meet this moral responsibility.

The radical press has, in recent years, carried a number of articles on the "role" of the radical scholar. Two viewpoints have emerged from this debate. According to the first viewpoint, the scholar must first be a human being—a contention no self-respecting fascist, much less liberal, would dispute. He must therefore march in demonstrations and politicize every professional organization. After all, how can we sit around and discuss medieval France while children are being napalmed in Vietnam? In principle, this is hardly a radical position, for a fascist would certainly agree, as he marched off to a prowar demonstration and worried about the death of our American boys, and a liberal or a conservative might agree and respond one way or the other to the specifics. According to the second viewpoint, our scholarship must be engaged in the struggle—a viewpoint noticeably popular among those who study contemporary affairs or even the history of the last two hundred years but not at all popular among those who study the history of ancient Persia, medieval China, renaissance Italy, or the rise and fall of the Incas, and who somehow get the idea that they are being told to get lost. Unless one means that the writing of history should be the formulation of propaganda, the second viewpoint differs from the first only in suggesting that modern history and a few selected subjects from earlier periods are worthy of a radical's time. Basically, both views rest on the idea that everyone should be a political activist and that history, to be tolerated, must be "relevant" to immediate politics.

The dishonesty of the children-are-being-napalmed argument becomes apparent as soon as we reflect on the continuity of oppression and barbarism throughout history. Probably, the human race has never experienced a single year during which one or another large-scale atrocity has not been committed somewhere. There has certainly not been a single year in the history of the United States during which atrocities have not been committed against black people. The argument, therefore, reduces immediately to the proposition that history is not worth pursuing as a vocation unless it is directly related to the struggle against the latest atrocities.

No one on the Left would deny that every man and woman ought to be politically active. But one does not ask a welder to stop welding in order to become a full-time political organizer. Of course, some welders—those who have the inclination, temperament, opportunity, and talent—may do just that. If someone were to ask the most politically dedicated and revolutionary welder how he could possibly keep welding while children were being napalmed in Vietnam, the man would probably answer with a blank stare. Only intellectuals are subjected to these ravages and, of course, only by other intellectuals. Welders normally have more sense than to torment each other with such stupidity.

Most radical graduate students and many young professors are, however, pulled two ways. On the one hand, they do feel deeply about those children in Vietnam and do ask themselves if they are doing enough to end the war, much less to build a socialist movement. On the other hand, they know that their work as historians is socially necessary and that it is the work they are best suited for. The great problem for radical graduate students is to decide whether to commit themselves to full-time study and to engage in politics as time and circumstances will allow, or to commit themselves to full-time political work and to study history as time and circumstances will allow. Some students try hard to study and do political work in equal amounts. They invariably fail, for each kind of work demands long, often exhausting hours every day. Usually, they also find out that different kinds of talent and temperament are required for each and that it is a rare man who can manifest both for very long.[1]

Being a good historian is full-time work. It is not surprising that our graduate students struggle against admitting this unpleasant truth; there is no good reason that young people should stop asking for everything at once until their own experience teaches them just how much they personally can and cannot achieve. There is, however, less excuse for thirty-five- and forty-year-old professors who, never having been able to reconcile the tendencies warring within them, proclaim their neurotic indecision as a political principle and demand that everyone else adhere to it. Those who think that they can make a contribution to society generally and to the Movement in particular by becoming political organizers have the duty as well as the privilege of doing so, and no one could reasonably insist that such a calling was inferior to that of the academic intellectual. But the reverse is also true. Socialist historians are not the last word in social necessity, but they do have important work to do—as socialists who work at history.

In this introductory essay I propose to discuss the nature of that work and to do what I have heretofore felt ridiculous in doing: to defend the propositions, which in saner times would need no defense, that the "role" of the socialist historian is to be a good historian; that the question of "relevance" is irrelevant to anything of importance beyond the egos of those who prate about it; and that the study of history, and in fact all humane learning, is the major responsibility of those intellectuals who would work for a better society.

The writing of history cannot be done well by those who do not love their work, including the most ordinary and discretely dull portions of it. It cannot be done well by those who consider it a poor supplement to or substitute for the more exciting vocation of street fighting or "organizing." To those who hate their work but stay at it because they have not the will or the opportunity to do something else, we owe sympathy. But we may also respectfully urge them to keep their misery to themselves and not pretend that it represents some deep and admirable moral commitment.

II

THE CASE AGAINST American intervention in Vietnam rests on much more than the killing of civilians and the destruction of villages, for all war, just and unjust, generates the slaughter of the innocent. It rests, rather, on the special character of the American war effort: Since the United States is fighting not merely a nation but a nation in the process of social revolution, the war it wages must necessarily be a war to destroy a people. Mr. Nixon has quite candidly told us that Vietnam is a question of credibility and commitment and that Africa, the Middle East, and Latin America are at stake. Indeed so. If a small nation and a militarily backward people can defeat the greatest power in world history, nothing will quench the fires of peoples' war from one end of the earth to the other. The United States cannot defeat the Vietnamese people in any conventional sense, but it can try to exact a price so high as to discourage other neocolonial peoples from taking the revolutionary path. The destruction of Vietnam, therefore, would qualify as a kind of victory. The inhumanity of this perspective exposes the irrationality of the social system and world order that demand it. The case against the United States in Vietnam is the case against our social system and its political and military exigencies.

When radicals, in contradistinction to liberals, oppose the war, they do so as part of a general critique of the capitalist social order. This is not the place to outline or defend that critique. Suffice it that radicals of all shades agree that there is an increasing degradation of our national culture and see that degradation as part of the same process by which countries like Vietnam are being physically devastated. For radicals the success of imperialism abroad remains inseparable from the success of imperialist-generated moral decay at home. These are the ABC's of any American radicalism. The question of a socialist historian's responsibilities must, accordingly, be discussed within this context.

The study of history can rarely be put to direct political use; the ideologically motivated creation of a desired past can be, but only by rulers and exploiters. The experience of the twentieth century, from Stalinism to revolutionary nationalist mythologies, provides no exceptions. In each case the demand for ideological history, for "class truth," for "partisanship in science," has ended in the service of a new elite, a new oppressor. Nowhere have the people ever benefited from the efforts of those intellectuals who have beneficently lied to them, ostensibly for their own good and in order to provide them with the beliefs necessary to shore up their courage and sustain them in battle. Historians who do not respect historical truth, who sneer at objectivity and fear disorienting the masses by laying bare the complexity, contradiction, and tragedy that define all human experience, can end only by serving the ruling class they think they are opposing or, at best, some new and exploitative elite waiting to ride the waves of revolutionary change.

Lenin and Gramsci, among others, were great intellectuals, but by working primarily as political leaders, they assumed responsibilities different from those confronting academics. One can readily respect such intellectuals, who choose to move decisively from the academy or its equivalent into party work, and one can sympathize with their struggle to maintain their integrity and critical spirit under the most difficult of conditions. Those responsible for the attacks on socialist historians are not, however, party intellectuals; that honor belongs to other radical historians. The real question is whether or not the socialist movement needs people—beyond party intellectuals—who write history and teach in universities instead of working as welders. (We may hope that the opponents of Academia are not about to denounce even welding as bourgeois dilettantism.)

Here we come to the question of the place of the socialist in the university and to the persistent effort of self-proclaimed revolutionaries to hide their politics behind a smoke screen of crowd-pleasing rhetoric. The conditions of life in America during the second half of the twentieth century provide no place outside the university for the great majority of left intellectuals to work effectively. This fact—and it can hardly be denied to be a fact—must shape our attitude toward the university as an institution, and it must be understood to impose certain limits and restrictions (compromises, if you will) on those who seek its protection. What, then, is the excuse for the demand to treat the university as if it were just another corporation, just another part of the military-industrial complex, just another whorehouse? Stupidity, envy, and malice aside—and there has been no shortage of these—the attacks on the university, the contempt for academic freedom, and the foolishness about "relevance" make sense only as part of a certain political estimate—viz., that the country is on the verge of a revolution to which everything else must be subordinated. But even then, there would be no reason to say more than that; there would be no reason, that is, to make virtues out of painful and dangerous necessities.

Few of our declared revolutionaries believe their own cant. If they did believe it, they would quit the campuses for full-time political work. But it is so much easier to proclaim, as one Ivy League full professor did, that we should all support the Weathermen and still continue to teach, live, and collect checks from a privileged sanctuary known as tenure.

Those who wish to spend their lives in the fantasies of a revolutionary apocalypse—of a grand denouement that features the overthrow of the American state by an invincible army of acid-heads and surburbanites—have no need for intellectual work beyond that which informs strategy and tactics. Those, on the other hand, who have lost patience with this cult of perpetual adolescence, who are interested in building a movement to change society and not merely in rebelling against society for the comfort of one's own soul, and who can face the necessity of waging a long, hard struggle to reshape our national culture as well as our national politics, cannot afford to make a single concession to nihilist doctrines. The responsibility of socialist intellectuals, especially those in the universities, is to get on with their work of fashioning a world view appropriate to the movement and society they wish to see born. No intellectual effort, no matter how modest, small, or removed from day-to-day politics, is irrelevant.

In short, an unbridgeable gulf separates socialist intellectuals from the "revolutionaries" who proclaim the arrival of the Day of Judgment and who demand relevance and their own style of engagement. They have nothing of importance in common with each other. No wonder, then, that those naive Establishment historians who lump them together as "radical historians" discover that these crazy radicals can never agree on anything. Precisely so. And for that reason it behooves the esteemed gentlemen of the Establishment to stop making fools of themselves, much as it behooves those on the Left to put an end to the pretense that they are all part of something called "The Movement."

It is the responsibility of all intellectuals to defend and extend the critical spirit, and the special responsibility of historians to bring that spirit to the study of the past—to the record of humanity's struggle to live decently and to become human. The specialist on medieval France cannot readily offer us direct lessons for our own political engagements although, like Marc Bloch, he may be wholly engaged himself, and it would be insolent to demand that he try. But he must tell us, as best he can, how particular human beings solved and did not solve particular problems, adjusted and did not adjust to momentous changes, made and failed to make better lives for themselves and their children, honored and dishonored their God and their community. He must present some chapter of the infinite grandeur of the human spirit—a grandeur no less for the inescapable frailty and evil that must forever go into the making of everything human.

When, therefore, a student asks his professor of medieval history to talk about something "relevant," such as the war in Vietnam, instead of wasting time on dead subjects, the professor might well demand that the student establish his relevance to them. Chaucer and St. Thomas Aquinas have for centuries imparted to humanity pleasure, wisdom, and evidence of man's effort to master his world. Their work tells us, among other things, much about the ways in which art and philosophy have enriched humanity and revealed some of its essential qualities. A student who cannot grasp this simple fact merely provides evidence of the extent to which he has become a victim of the barbarism that his politics ostensibly challenge.

What, then, of those radicals who wish to know how socialists and others can go on with business-as-usual while those children are dying in Vietnam? These people and their argument constitute part of the sickness of our time, not part of the cure. If, as radicals assert, the bourgeois social order has grown corrupt and if the reduction of humane learning to the status of a plaything is one of the measures of the depth of that corruption, then those historians who preach relevance and consider it hypocritical to do business-as-usual are nothing more than the advanced guard of the corruption itself. The defense of humane learning being one front in the war against decadence, those who undermine it further are, whatever their protestations, in the service of the enemy. The business-as-usual of which they so stridently complain happens to be the business of life. The duty of the socialist historian, therefore, is, first and foremost, to develop himself into as good a historian as his talent and circumstances permit and thereby to defend and enrich the historically developed values of humanity by revealing, with increasing precision, the story of man's struggle to conquer both himself and nature.

What separates us from conservatives and liberals in the profession? Our politics. We have a different estimate of the forces that have generated the present crisis in our culture and that threaten those values at least some of which we share with our ideological opponents. There are many conservatives with whom we share little or nothing, but these types are usually just as sharply at war with those conservatives and liberals, who do defend humane values, as they are at war with us. For this reason, among others, socialists must oppose all totalitarian education and insist upon the depoliticization of the universities and the professional organizations. The universities and attendant organizations are precisely the grounds of ideological contention on which we have to advance our point of view. The attempt to take that ground by moral terror, administrative measures, packed meetings, and meaningless statements of policy amounts to nothing more than political suicide. The danger does not arise from the reaction such behavior invariably generates, for all action, good or bad, is likely to engender a reaction. It arises, rather, from the necessity for socialists to make the cause of intellectual freedom and diversity their own—and therefore to defend the universities and professional associations as places of contention—or else condemn themselves to the repudiation of everything in the Western tradition necessary to distinguish socialism from some new collectivist totalitarian nightmare. An American people who have witnessed the degeneration of the Russian revolution into Stalinism and who have seen socialism arise only in countries without an effective democratic tradition will turn anywhere and to anything before they turn to a socialism that promises to go down the same road. We will never develop a socialist theory and perspective adequate to the needs of our people and our nation unless we are prepared to meet respectfully and fully the intellectual challenge of our honest opponents—a challenge which, we may as well admit, contains all the questions we have not yet been able to answer satisfactorily and which we shall have to answer if we are ever to build a movement of our own.

Socialists are also separated from their liberal and conservative colleagues by the philosophical point of view they bring to history—a point of view that intersects with their politics at almost every point and yet, whatever partisan ideologues may say, is not entirely inseparable from it. That point of view is Marxism, for no other coherent radical interpretation of history has arisen. Our work as historians is, among other things, our way of trying to establish Marxism's claims. But, of course, there are Marxists and Marxists, and these days it sometimes appears that everyone on the campuses who does not like Spiro Agnew finds it necessary to be "a bit of a Marxist" in order to get students to listen to him. More seriously, there are socialist historians who are not Marxists, and there are historians who bring a Marxian interpretation to their history, whether or not they choose to admit it, but who are not socialists. Marxism itself is a process, not the religious dogma most of its detractors and some of its exponents make it out to be, and we can no longer easily decide who is who. Nor need we worry about it.

By not worrying about it—by refusing to make the rigid separation of socialist from other historians a test of ideological and political acceptability—we may avoid what has been our greatest embarrassment. Socialists have generally been arrogant about their ostensibly superior intellectual qualities. There is hardly a publication of the Old Left or the New that does not take it for granted that we are simply smarter than our enemies, closer to the truth, more honest, and in a word, morally and intellectually superior. Hence, the embarrassment. If so, how is it that we have so little to produce as intellectual evidence? With the exception of William Appleman Williams, no socialist historian of the United States could be mentioned in the same breath with C. Vann Woodward or Richard Hofstadter, to mention only two of the outstanding men now under attack from the Left. How strange that people who claim for themselves moral and intellectual superiority and a more scientific viewpoint than others possess do not do work anywhere near as good. There are reasons for the slow arrival of an adequate Marxism in American historiography, some of which should embarrass us deeply and some of which flow from the political repression to which our comrades, especially in the 1950s, have been subjected. But the generation that arose in the 1960s has made a good start toward establishing a point of view and a tradition of radical historical criticism on which a future generation may build. The rapid increase in able graduate students and young scholars suggests that the best is yet to come, provided, of course, that no concessions are made to the profession's nihilist goon squad.

We need not be embarrassed because of our sense of responsibility as socialists who are historians does not divide us too sharply from many of our conservative and liberal colleagues. I was delighted to find that many of the thoughts Christopher Lasch put forward in an article in the *New York Review of Books* on the crisis in the universities had close parallels in an article published in *National Review* by the conservative, Catholic historian, Stephen Tonsor. I see no reason to regret that Eric Weil (*Daedalus,* Spring 1970) and J. H. Plumb (*The Death of the Past*) have recently written in defense of the humanities and of the pursuit of history with far greater learning and power than I could possibly bring to these pages. If we take our socialism seriously, we shall have to accept the challenge of Tonsor's viewpoint, which locates the roots of the contemporary crisis in education far from where Lasch and I suggested they should be located; and we shall have to demonstrate, in the face of the contrary views of the Weils and Plumbs, that we are justified in claiming that only a socialist reconstruction of society can reverse the barbarous trend against which they are also fighting. But socialist intellectuals cannot meet these challenges by their political activity although, as citizens, they have a responsibility to participate in political activity to the fullest extent possible; they can only meet them by their creative work as intellectuals.

It is preposterous to think that we can claim for socialism the historical task of defending our national culture, and simultaneously abandon cultural work for other forms of action. On the contrary, the decadence that imperialism has brought down on our people would proceed the more rapidly if intellectuals allowed themselves to accept the reactionary, not to say fascist, viewpoint that humane learning is a trival pursuit, a pastime for effete snobs, a matter of little importance to the struggle for a better life. The slogan "Action first, doctrine later," we would do well to recall, was Mussolini's. That is precisely the trap that imperialism, understood as an objective process and not a conspiracy of evil men, has laid for us, and those "radicals" who madly hurl themselves into it are part of that objective process of national degradation. The grim experiences of Russia, China, and other undemocratic socialist countries—whose revolutions and social systems we support in principle—ought to be enough to convince us that one of our major responsibilities is to guarantee that our own movement embody those great and living traditions of free and critical thought which are the glory of Western civilization and without which we have nothing to offer the American people or our comrades in the socialist countries who are today fighting with genuine heroism to humanize their own societies.

III

I HAVE TAKEN a long and circuitous road to introduce essays on subjects far removed from the subject matter of the preceding pages, but I have gambled that anyone willing to read a collection of loosely connected, previously published essays will stand for anything. Having gone this far, perhaps I may be permitted to anticipate some misunderstandings.

I began by asserting that the essays were intended as political intervention. It ought by now to be clear that the assertion covers the most technical of them—for example, the discussion of the treatment of slaves—as well as the most politically engaged. What I have not included in this book are a number of specifically political essays, most of which were published in leftwing journals. I have been tempted to reprint one or two of the pieces I wrote in the mid-1960s, when briefly I was enjoying the favor of the New Left, for they would show clearly enough that the position I have advanced here was the position I held then. My wife and my publisher have forbidden this particular self-indulgence. Those pieces would be out of place because they are about politics, not about the writing or teaching of history. So, I have included only those political essays that have been inseparable from my work as a historian—that I could not have written had I been engaged in some other vocation. For the most part, however, the essays are not about politics at all. Their political aspect manifests itself only in the broader terms for which I have been arguing here. I would hope therefore—but certainly do not expect—that I shall be spared reviews such as that by a well known Marxist economist who said of my *Political Economy of Slavery* that it was just great on the questions to which it addressed itself but that it should have addressed itself to more recent and pressing problems.

As part of a growing group of leftwing historians, I have tried in these essays and elsewhere to contribute, as best I can, to the development of a Marxian interpretation of history—specifically, Southern and Afro-American history. It is fashionable in Establishment circles to say of a Marxist that his work is good in spite of his Marxism or, conversely, that it is poor because of his Marxism. One is tempted to turn this patronizing around and to claim that good work by a Marxist is good because of his Marxism and that poor work is poor in spite of his Marxism. Certainly, there is as much value in the one set of claims as in the other. But Marxists, like non-Marxists, are whole human beings, who cannot be so easily compartmentalized. A historian's philosophy informs his work and is inseparable from it. For better or worse, it will have to be swallowed whole.

The Marxian interpretation of history constitutes a way—the most fruitful way, in my experience—of seeing history as a process and of binding the past to the future: not in the sense of providing a basis for prediction (we may leave that to astrologers), but in the sense of suggesting the contours both of that which is possible and of disasters to be avoided. By discovering the limits of social action as well as the potentialities inherent in human effort, it can help guide constructively the actions of men and women who make their own history.

Marxism maintains that the root of the great qualitative leaps in social development are to be sought in the rise, development, and confrontation of social classes. This assertion contains no few difficulties, as Marxists well know, but my purpose is to provide a context for a specific body of essays, not to write a philosophical tract or an elaboration of a theory of history. In *The Political Economy of Slavery* (1965), I tried to test this hypothesis by examining the crisis of one social class (the slaveholders) and the society it ruled (the Old South). In *The World the Slaveholders Made* (1969), I tried to extend that analysis through a comparative study of the slaveholders of various New World societies. In both, but especially in the second, it became increasingly necessary to confront the complexity that is "class" itself.

In the beginning life was simple and everything clear. Social classes were neatly defined by the relationship of people to the means of production, and shifts in class power constituted the motor force of historical change. Later, life grew complicated, and things began to get murky. Are all important historical changes the outcome of class confrontations? Obviously not. Well, if we then say that the great revolutionary changes are, do we not fall into a tautology, for revolutionary changes are by definition changes in class power? Not necessarily—not if we can demonstrate that these changes have been, in some meaningful sense, decisive for the history of mankind. But we can do this—if indeed it can be done at all—only by proceeding with the knowledge that we are armed with the best possible hypothesis we can derive from what we already know. Let that hypothesis become a dogma, to be "applied" or "defended" or "justified," and we have failed, whatever the pretensions or presumed political advantages. Our Marxism, therefore, is itself a process of labor, which binds us to nothing that cannot be verified or maintained as the most plausible explanation of the facts at our disposal.

This part of our effort leads us to the problem of a meaningful and flexible idea of "class." All Marxian history may, from one point of view, be judged good or poor by the extent to which it contributes to our understanding of class. If, for example, the analyses in my two previous books are judged to have added nothing of value to an understanding of class, then their author has failed to accomplish what he set out to do, no matter how gracious his critics may wish to be about other facets of the work. The problem plaguing him has always been the crudeness of the tool and especially its tendency toward economic determinism, which naturally tempts anyone who begins with "relations of production."

The difficulty cannot be resolved by shibboleths about how the "superstructure reflects the base" (i.e., how ideas and institutions are derived from economic relations). Marx, despite some awkward moments, knew too much of the world to peddle such nonsense. Taken straight, such a formulation denies the very dialectics that are at the heart of that interpretation of history which his work began to formulate and which now bears his name.

The problems inherent in the idea of class and its historical centrality left their marks on my first two books, and they are greatly complicating the writing of another, which has been under way for almost ten years—a study of the lives of Afro-American slaves. That as-yet-unwritten book, more clearly than its predecessors, compels a direct attack on those problems, for it treats the history of a class in a much less abstract way than its predecessors. While reflecting upon the results of that research and while re-examining and reconsidering the lives of the slaveholding and non-slaveholding whites, I have had to face two interrelated challenges—the question of nationality and the question of culture. In so doing, I have had to abandon the dogmatic assertion with which I saddled *The Political Economy of Slavery,* that the Old South could not generate a separate nationality. That question now looks far more complicated than I had made it seem. More to the point, I have had to admit, not without misgivings that now seem a bit foolish, that black Americans themselves embrace genuine ingredients of a separate nationality, even as they form part of a general American nationality—a duality that drives to distraction all who attempt to bring coherence to the history of the United States and of Afro-America. In any case, it is no longer possible to believe that a class can be understood apart from its culture, or that most modern classes can be understood apart from their nationality.

Far from leading away from a class interpretation of history, this shift has given it new meaning. It is impossible to make sense out of nationalism apart from national culture, and it is impossible to make sense out of either national culture or national interest apart from the particular confrontation of the class elements that determine them. In the case of the abortive Southern nationality that disintegrated after 1865, and especially in the case of the unique nationality of Afro-America, the class dimension causes embarrassments. Many Southerners do not enjoy the thought that the fundamental thrust of their early national strivings came from slaveholders. And most assuredly, many blacks express uneasiness at the thought that so much of their cultural distinctiveness arose from or was tempered in slave quarters. In time, however, whatever the judgment on an abortive Southern nationality that has ceased to be a factor, the judgment of a growing Afro-American nationality will, I am convinced, come to rest on a positive estimate of the genius displayed by black people under the ultimate test of bondage.

Elaboration and defense of these formulations will have to await future books, and an adequate theoretical statement of the historical relationship of class and national culture will have to await a more learned and intellectually rigorous mind. What I have tried to do in these essays is to probe some of the lower- and middle-range problems that have to be solved along the way to a proper synthesis. Naturally, I hope that they are worth reading as limited comments on limited subjects, but their ultimate justification—and certainly the justification for their combination here—will have to rest on their claims to being useful contributions to the solution of larger problems.

NOTE

1. For an account of one historian's personal struggle with a variation of this problem, see Martin Duberman's, "On Becoming a Historian," in *The Uncompleted Past* (New York, 1969), pp. 335-356. However much one may disagree with Duberman's formulations or regret his choices, it is impossible not to be moved by his insight and frankness, his defense of cultural work despite his disillusionment with his own career as a historian, and his refusal to try to turn a personal dilemma into an assertion of moral superiority.

Chapter 2

MATERIALISM AND IDEALISM IN THE HISTORY OF NEGRO SLAVERY IN THE AMERICAS

THE STUDY OF Negro slavery in the United States is verging on a new and welcome development as historians begin to appreciate the need for a hemispheric perspective. In 1950 Allan Nevins entitled the appropriate chapter of his *Emergence of Lincoln* "Slavery in a World Setting," and in 1959 Stanley M. Elkins rescued the work of Frank Tannenbaum from an undeserved obscurity. It was Tannenbaum's remarkable essay, *Slave & Citizen* (1947) that first demonstrated the sterility of treating Southern slavery in national isolation, although the point had been made previously. Oliveira Lima, as early as 1914, had discussed the profound differences between Brazilian and North American race relations and historical experiences with slavery, and Gilberto Freyre has been offering suggestive comparisons since the 1920s.[1] Without making unreasonable claims for Tannenbaum's originality, we may credit him with having been the first to show that only a hemispheric treatment could enable us to understand the relationship between slavery and race relations and the social and political dynamics of the transition from slavery to freedom. Simultaneously, the questions Tannenbaum posed and the method he suggested wiped out the line between history and the social sciences. Elkins's controversial book illustrates how quickly the discussion must pass into considerations of psychology and anthropology. The improved prospects for compartive analysis derive in part from the advances being made by Spanish American and especially Brazilian historians, sociologists, and anthropologists and in part, as Magnus Mörner suggests, from the excellent work done recently on slavery in the Iberian peninsula itself.[2]

Under the circumstances it is appropriate that the first sweeping assault on Tannenbaum's thesis should come from Marvin Harris, an anthropologist, and equally appropriate that the assault implicitly should accept Tannenbaum's main point—that slavery and race relations must be studied hemispherically.[3] The argument has been joined on two levels: on such specific questions as the significance of different slave codes, the degree of paternalism in the social system, and the daily treatment of slaves; and on such general questions of method and philosophy as reflect the age-old struggle between idealist and materialist viewpoints. The specific questions will hopefully be settled in due time by empirical research; the second are likely to stay with us. Since empirical research will necessarily be conditioned by contending viewpoints, we must make every effort to clarify the methodological and philosophical issues or risk wasting a great deal of time and effort talking past each other and chasing solutions to spurious problems. The value of Harris's book, apart from specific contributions to our knowledge, is that it extends the discussion to a fruitful way. Presumably, its deficiencies of style will not deny it a hearing. Unlike Harris's *The Nature of Cultural Things,* which comes close to being unreadable, *Patterns of Race in the Americas,* despite lapses into unnecessary jargon and some regrettable rhetoric, is straightforward and vigorous. Unfortunately, it is marred by savage polemical excursions. Harris appears to be a man of strong and, to me, admirable social views, but I fear that he is among those who confuse ideological zeal with bad manners. As a result, his harsh attacks on opposing scholars, some of whom are deservedly respected for their fairness and generosity to others, often result in unjust and arbitrary appraisals of their work and, in any case, leave the reader with a bad taste.

I propose to discuss Harris's demand for a materialist alternative to the idealist framework of Tannenbaum, Freyre, and Elkins and to avoid, so far as possible, discussions of specific differences about data. Those differences may be left to specialists and will not be resolved without much more work by scholars in several disciplines. I propose, too, to ignore Harris's illuminating work on the highland Indian societies. Since the book has much to offer on these and other themes it should be understood that no balanced review is intended here. Even if it suffers from as grave weaknesses of method and assumption as I believe, it would retain considerable value on other levels and may properly be evaluated more fully elsewhere.

Tannenbaum divides the slave systems of the western hemisphere into three groups—Anglo-Saxon, Iberian, and French. The Anglo-Saxon group lacked an "effective slave tradition," a slave law, and religious institutions concerned with the Negro; the Iberian had a slave tradition and law and a religious institution imbued with the "belief that the spiritual personality of the slave transcended his slave status"; the French shared the religious principles of the Iberian but lacked a slave tradition and law.[4] Tannenbaum, to his cost, ignores the French case and does not, for example, discuss the *Code Noir*. Were he to do so, he might reflect further on the significance of the Iberian codes, for the *Code Noir* was notoriously a dead letter in Saint-Domingue.

The burden of Tannenbaum's argument rests on his estimate of the strength of the Catholic Church in relation to the landowners and of the extent to which the law could be or was enforced. He undoubtedly takes too sanguine a view of

Brazilian slavery and simultaneously greatly underestimates the force of community pressure and paternalism in reducing the harshness of the Southern slave codes. He risks broad generalizations and necessarily sacrifices much in the process; many of his generalizations, with qualifications, nonetheless obtain. The essential point is not that Brazilian slaves received kinder treatment, but that they had greater access to freedom and once free could find a secure place in the developing national culture. Tannenbaum, accepting the authority of Gilberto Freyre, does suggest a correlation between class mobility, the absence or weakness of racism, and kind treatment, but he does so tentatively, and it forms no essential part of his argument.

Tannenbaum demonstrates that the current status of the Negro in the several societies of the New World has roots in the attitude toward the Negro as a slave, which reflected the total religious, legal, and moral history of the enslaving whites. From this assertion he proceeds to a number of theses of varying value. When, for example, he relates the acceptance of the "moral personality" of the Negro to the peaceful quality of abolition, we may well wonder about Haiti, or about Brazil, where the peaceful abolition followed decades of bloody slave insurrections and social disorders,[5] or about the British islands, where peaceful abolition followed a denial of that moral personality. We may, accordingly, take the book apart; it was intended to open, not close, the discussion of an enormously complicated subject. The essentials of the viewpoint remain in force: (1) Slavery was a moral as well as a legal relationship; (2) where tradition, law, and religion combined to recognize the moral personality of the slave, the road to freedom remained open, and the absorption of the freedmen into the national culture was provided for; (3) the recognition of moral personality flowed from the emergent slaveholders' legal and religious past, the extent and nature of their contact with darker peoples, and their traditional view of man and God— of their total historical experience and its attendant world view. Tannenbaum draws the lines much too tightly. As David Brion Davis shows, the duality of the slave as man and thing always created problems for enslavers, who rarely if ever were able to deny the slave a moral personality.[6] We may nonetheless note a wide range of behavior and attitude within such recognition, and Tannenbaum's problem therefore remains with us.

The great weakness in Tannenbaum's presentation is that it ignores the material foundations of each particular slave society, especially the class relations, for an almost exclusive concern with tradition and cultural continuity. Tannenbaum thereby avoids essential questions. How, for example, did the material conditions of life in the slave countries affect their cultural inheritance? Tannenbaum implies the necessary victory of the inheritance over contrary tendencies arising from immediate material conditions. Thus, Harris can label his viewpoint idealist and insist, as a materialist, that material conditions determine social relations and necessarily prevail over countertendencies in the historical tradition. The special usefulness of Harris's book lies in the presentation of an alternative, materialist interpretation and the concomitant attention paid to many problems that Tannenbaum avoids or obscures. Unfortunately, his materialism, like that of such earlier writers as Eric Williams, is generally mechanical and soon reveals itself as a sophisticated variant of economic determinism. It is, in short, ahistorical.

Harris vigorously attacks Freyre for asserting that Brazil has been a virtual "racial paradise," but his discussion actually reinforces Freyre's argument. Harris, like Charles Wagley,[7] insists on a close relationship between class and race and insists that Brazilian Negroes have always faced intense discrimination because of their lower-class status. Brazil's racial paradise, he argues, is occupied only by "fictional creatures"; the real Negroes of Bahia and elsewhere suffer immensely as members of the lower classes in a country in which the rule of thumb alleges a correlation between class and race.[8]

Harris slips into a position that Wagley largely avoids. Wagley, too, attacks Freyre by drawing attention to the class dimension of race relations. He denies the absence of racism and refers to the "widely documented color prejudice in almost every part of the nation."[9] Yet, Wagley properly adds that despite prejudice and discrimination Brazilian racial democracy is no myth. Brazilians happily do not usually put their racial talk into practice: Continuing miscegenation undermines racial lines, and the doctrine that "money whitens the skin" prevails. In these terms, so different from those which might be applied to the United States, we may look at Brazilian racial democracy as a reality relative to other societies, or as myth relative to national standards and pretensions and fully appreciate the force of Octavio Ianni's reference to "the intolerable contradiction between the myth of racial democracy and the actual discrimination against Negroes and mulattoes."[10]

The admirable work of C. R. Boxer at first glance supports Harris against Freyre, but that glance proves deceptive. Boxer dismisses as "twaddle" the notion that no color bar exists in the Portuguese-speaking world and brings us back to earth from Freyre's flights of romantic fancy, but he does not overthrow the essentials of Freyre's argument.[11] What Boxer does show is how painful a struggle has had to be waged and how much racism has persisted. The strides toward racial democracy that he describes in *Race Relations in the Portuguese Colonial Empire, Portuguese Society in the Tropics, The Golden Age of Brazil,* and elsewhere remain impressive when considered against Anglo-Saxon models. The question is what accounts for the greater "plasticity" (to use Freyre's word) of the Portuguese. The economic and demographic features of colonization, stressed almost exclusively by Harris, played a great role, but the careful research of so skeptical and cautious a historian as Boxer shows the force of legal, moral, religious, and national traditions. Viewed polemically, Boxer's work destroys the propagandistic nonsense of Dr.

Salazar's court historians but only qualifies the main lines of argument in Freyre and Tannenbaum.

In asserting a racial paradise all Freyre could possibly mean is that considerable racial mobility exists and that discrimination is held within tolerable bounds. The criticisms of Wagley, Harris, Boxer, and others demonstrate the existence of an acute class question with a racial dimension; they do not refute Freyre's main claim that society is not, by the standards of the Anglo-Saxon countries, racially rent. Freyre is undoubtedly open to criticism, for he slides impermissibly from race to class. He insists that miscegenation "never permitted the endurance in absolute antagonisms of that separation of men into masters and slaves imposed by the system of production. Nor the exaggerated development of a mystique of white supremacy nor of nobility."[12] When he writes that miscegenation negated the class antagonism of master and slave, he talks nonsense; but when he writes that it inhibited—he does not say prevented—a mystique of white supremacy, he is surely correct.

Freyre, possibly in response to criticism of his earlier exaggerations, tries to qualify his lyrical praise of Luso-Brazilian racial attitudes and practices. Sometimes, although by no means consistently even in his most recent work, his evaluations are so well balanced as virtually to accept the criticisms and qualifications offered on all sides:

> Not that there is no race or color prejudice mixed with class prejudice in Brazil. There is. . . . But no one in Brazil would think of laws against interracial marriage. No one would think of barring colored people from theatres or residential sections of a town.[13]

The main point for Freyre is not that race prejudice has been absent but that "few Brazilian aristocrats were as strict about racial impurity as the majority of the Anglo-Saxon aristocrats of the Old South were"[14] and that the Brazilian Negro "has been able to express himself as a Brazilian and has not been forced to behave as an ethnic and cultural intruder."[15] Harris writes: "Races do not exist for Brazilians. But classes do exist both for the observer and *for* the Brazilians."[16] With these words he surrenders the argument.

Law, Church, and cultural tradition are not viewed by Tannenbaum, or even Freyre, as unambiguous forces for racial equality. Both men appreciate the internal conflicts and are concerned with the different outcomes of these conflicts in different cultures. "The colonial governments, the Spaniards, and the *criollos* treated the mestizo as an inferior human being."[17] Much race prejudice, Tannenbaum adds, existed and exists against Indians and Negroes throughout Latin America. He notes too, in a striking comment on class and race, that United States Negroes can and do advance themselves personally in the economic, social, and political arenas with greater ease than do Latin American Negroes, for whom class rigidities and the economic backwardness of society present severe limitations.[18] The distance between rich and poor, cultured and uncultured in Latin America "is obviously not racial, not biological, nor based on color of skin or place of origin, but it is perhaps even more effective as a dividing line, and perhaps more permanent. It is an ingrained part of the total scheme of things."[19]

Harris rejects, on principle, the idea that Portuguese tradition, law, and religion could overcome the counterpressures inherent in Brazilian slavery. He makes some strange assumptions in his often admirable discussion of political relations of Church, state, and landowner in highland and lowland America. He properly portrays each as a separate entity, struggling for control of material resources, but he portrays them as only that. Apart from a grudging phrase here and there (and we find a touch of sarcasm even there), he leaves no room for landowners who on many matters would follow the advice and teaching of the Church simply out of religious commitment, nor for a state apparatus deeply infused with

Catholic ethics, nor for a Church with a genuine sense of responsibility for the salvation of souls. Instead, he offers us three collective forms of economic man. Harris repeatedly dismisses as romantic nonsense and the like arguments appealing to Catholic sensibility or inherited values. He misses much of Tannenbaum's implicit schema of a society resting on a balance of power between state, church, and family-based economic interests, and he misses Elkins's acute restatement of Tannenbaum's schema as descriptive of a precapitalist society in which minimal room is provided for unrestricted economic impulse.

The burden of Harris's criticism lies in his badly named chapter, "The Myth of the Friendly Master." He begins by asserting that "Differences in race relations within Latin America are at root a matter of the labor systems in which the respective subordinate and superordinate groups become enmeshed. . . . A number of cultural traits and institutions which were permitted to survive or were deliberately encouraged under one system were discouraged or suppressed in the other. . . ."[20] He contrasts his view with those of Tannenbaum and Freyre: "It is their contention that the laws, values, religious precepts, and personalities of the English colonists differed from those of the Iberian colonists. These initial psychological and ideological differences were sufficient to overcome whatever tendency the plantation system may have exerted toward parallel rather than divergent evolution."[21] Tannenbaum and Freyre may be read this way but need not be. Harris has reduced their position to its most idealistic and superficial expression. Harris is not alone among social scientists of deserved reputation in caricaturing their ideas. K. Oberg, for example, hails *Patterns of Race in the Americas* for having demolished the supposedly prevalent notion that these patterns could be traced to "the Iberian soul or the inherent racism of the Anglo Saxon."[22] For polemical purposes this reading scores points, but it does not get us very far. Tannenbaum and Freyre may be—and in my opinion ought to be—read another way, for each in effect describes the historical formation of slaveholding classes.

It is easy but unenlightening to dismiss discussions of psychology and ideology as if they were mere prejudices of romantics when laid against material interests. Harris, like every sensible man, rejects "simplistic economic determinism" and single-factor explanations,[23] but on close inspection he rejects the simplistic rather that the economic determinism. "From the standpoint of an evolutionary science of culture," he writes, "it matters not at all if one starts first with changes in the techno-environmental complex or first with changes in the institutional matrix; what matters is whether or not there is a correlation."[24] For him, however, the correlation reduces itself to an ideological reflection of the material reality. What Harris's materialism, in contradistinction to Marxian materialism, fails to realize is that once an ideology arises it alters profoundly the material reality and in fact becomes a partially autonomous feature of that reality. As Antonio Gramsci says about Marx's more sophisticated and useful comments on the role of ideas in history:

> The analysis of these statements, I believe, reinforces the notion of "historical bloc," in which the material forces are the content and ideologies the form—merely an analytical distinction since material forces would be historically inconceivable without form and since ideologies would have to be considered individual dabbling without material forces.[25]

This understanding of ideology and economics as reciprocally influential manifestations of particular forms of class rule may be contrasted with Harris's mechanistic and economistic view. He replies to a friendly critic who seeks to defend him against the charge of economic determinism by embracing it proudly: "I share with all economic determinists the conviction that in the long run and in most cases ideology is swung into line by material conditions—by the evolution of techno-environmental and production relationships."[26] Psychology and ideology are, however, as much a part of class formation as economic interest. Harris implies that ideology simply reflects material interests, which fluctuate sharply, but the ideology of a ruling class ought to be understood as its world view—the sum of its interests and sensibilities, past and present. An essential function of the ideology of a ruling class is to present to itself and to those it rules a coherent world view that is sufficiently flexible, comprehensive, and mediatory to convince the subordinate classes of the justice of its hegemony. If this ideology were no more than a reflection of immediate economic interests, it would be worse than useless, for the hypocrisy of the class, as well as its greed, would quickly become apparent to the most abject of its subjects.[27]

Harris admits that the Portuguese in Portugal exhibited little race prejudice but adds that "This datum can only be significant to those who believe that discrimination is caused by prejudice, when the true relationship is quite the opposite."[28] He argues, especially for Brazil, along the lines that the Marxists, Eric Williams and C. L. R. James, have argued for the Caribbean and that American Marxists and non-Marxists like Herbert Aptheker and the Handlins have argued for the United States.[29] Unhappily, Harris asserts what needs to be proven, and the assertion exposes the fundamental weakness in his ideological armor: He insists, on principle, that the relationship must be one way and makes the case for materialism rest on this dogma. "If, as asserted, the Iberians initially lacked any color prejudice, what light does this shed upon the Brazilian and other lowland interracial systems?"[30] According to this view, the past plays no vital role in the present except for transmitted technology. If the case for materialism rests on a denial of the totality of human history and on the resurrection of an economic determinism brought to a higher level of sophistication, materialism has poor prospects.

It is easy to dismiss as idealism or subjectivity the view that prejudice existed prior to discrimination, but the tenacious defense of this position by such sober and diverse scholars as Carl Degler, Juan Comas, Arnold A. Sio, and David Brion Davis ought to give us pause. Davis recounts the various origins of anti-Negro prejudice in Europe. "The fact that Africans had traditionally been associated with Noah's curse of Canaan," he notes for example, "may have disposed some Europeans to regard them as suitable for bondage."[31] Winthrop D. Jordan has made a simple point to present us with a complex reality. He has convincingly traced the origins of anti-Negro prejudice in New England to the prior existence of slavery, discrimination, and racism in Barbados.[32] Thus, we may obediently agree on the materialist formula—exploitation →discrimination→prejudice—and find ourselves nowhere except with the further ahistorical assumption that ideas, once called into being, have no life of their own.[33] As M. I. Finley observes:

> For most of human history labor for others has been involuntary . . . . Slavery in that context must have different overtones from slavery in a context of free labor. The way slavery declined in the Roman Empire . . . illustrates that. Neither moral values nor economic interests nor the social order were threatened by the transformation of slaves and free peasants together into tied serfs. They were—or at least many powerful elements in society thought they were—by proposals to convert slaves into free men.
>
> What sets the slave apart from all other forms of involuntary labor is that in the strictest sense, he is an outsider. He is brought into a new society violently and traumatically; he is cut off from all traditional human ties of kin and nation and even his own religion; he is prevented from creating new ties, except to his masters, and in consequence his descendants are as much outsiders, as unrooted, as he was . . . .
>
> Dr. [Eric] Williams holds that "slavery was not born of racism, rather racism was the consequence of slavery." One wishes profoundly that one could believe that. However, the slave-outsider formula argues the other way, as does the fact

that as early as the 1660s southern colonies decreed that henceforth all Negroes who were imported should be slaves, but whites should be indentured servants and not slaves. The connection between slavery and racism has been a dialectical one, in which each element reinforced the other.[34]

The most balanced and suggestive statement on the Portuguese remains Boxer's:

> One race cannot systematically enslave members of another on a large scale for over three centuries without acquiring a conscious or unconscious feeling of racial superiority.[35]

The good sense of this observation enables us to grasp the necessarily racist influence of Negro slavery on European cultures without destroying our ability to distinguish between levels of influence and without compelling us to turn our backs on either historical-traditional or ecological processes.[36] The work of the distinguished Brazilian Marxian scholar, Caio Prado, Jr., may be cited as an illustration of the way in which the force of the historical inheritance can be taken into account in a materialist analysis. For Prado the historical conditioning stressed by Freyre and Tannenbaum played its part precisely because the material basis of life and especially the class relationships provided room for it to breathe, but, given this room, it seriously affected that basis and those relationships.[37]

Harris's failure to grasp the historical and class nature of Tannenbaum's argument appears most strikingly in his reference to English law. Tannenbaum notes that slavery and a slave code had long disappeared in England, which therefore had no legal tradition to humanize the practice of colonial slavery. "Why this legal lacuna should have been significant for the course run by slavery in the United States is quite obscure."[38] There is nothing obscure about it, and Harris could find the answer in Elkins's discussion of a slave system's rise amidst an "uncontrolled capitalism." Here again, idealists or no, Tannenbaum and Elkins have greatly deepened our understanding of the processes by which specific slaveholding classes were formed, and those processes are, or ought to be, the central concern of a materialist interpretation of history.

"At one point, and one point only," Harris writes, "is there a demonstrable correlation between the laws and behavior, the ideal and the actual, in Tannenbaum's theory: the Spanish and Portuguese codes ideally drew no distinction between the ex-slave and the citizen, and the actual behavior followed suit."[39] This one point kills Harris's argument since Tannenbaum set out to explain the absorption of former slaves into the national culture in Brazil and the extreme difficulties in the United States. Harris has much to offer to complement the work of Freyre and Tannenbaum. In particular, he is strong on the economic and material exigencies of colonial Brazil and their influence in promoting race patterns. Instead of seeing a twofold process within which colonial conditions reinforced tradition and allowed it to expand and within which tradition altered, however secondarily, material conditions, he insists dogmatically on either/or. "One can be certain that if it had been materially disadvantageous to the Latin colonists, it would never have been tolerated—Romans, *Siete Partidas* and the Catholic Church notwithstanding."[40] Harris may be certain; others may be permitted some doubt. Had such a divergence occurred, the outcome would have been determined by the strength of the contending forces, with Church and state opposing slaveholders and with the conscience and consciousness of the slaveholders split among various commitments. Harris's crystal-ball-gazing constitutes not materialism but fatalism, not history but a secular equivalent of theology.

Harris misunderstands and misrepresents Tannenbaum as arguing that Negro slaves were better treated in Brazil than in the United States. Tannenbaum does express such an opinion, but he merely accepts Freyre's probably erroneous judgment; it forms no essential part of his thesis. Tannenbaum could live comfortably with evidence that Brazilian slaves were treated more harshly than American, for his case rests on the degree of class and race mobility. Harris, by identifying Tannenbaum with Freyre here and by merging two separate theses in Freyre, confuses the issues. Elkins argues quite sensibly that Hispanic slaves could have been more severely mistreated than American "without altering the comparison." Harris replies, in one of his most inexcusable polemical outbursts, with sarcasm and personal abuse, but he does not reply to the argument.[41]

Harris's discussion of demographic and economic forces in the formation of a mulatto population and a class of free blacks is a solid contribution, notwithstanding some statistical juggling, but the methodological difficulties reappear. He insists that Brazilian slaveholders "had no choice but to create a class of half-castes" to function as soldiers, cattlemen, food growers, and intermediaries of various kinds.[42] Unlike the United States, he notes, Brazil lacked a white population large enough to serve as a middle class and to provide a political and military establishment. Brazilian slaveholders consequently smiled on the elevation of the mulattoes. Winthrop D. Jordan also questions the emphasis on national characteristics by pointing out that in the British West Indies, where conditions similar to those in Brazil existed, Anglo-Saxon hostility toward miscegenation was much softened and a much greater respect for the mulatto emerged.[43] Yet, the juxtaposition of the British West Indies, the United States, and Brazil favors a qualified version of Tannenbaum's argument, for what emerged in the islands was not the Brazilian pattern but a compromise: a three-caste system in which "coloreds" were set apart from both whites and blacks. The material conditions of life had indeed prevailed over the purely ideological-institutional inheritance, as materialists would expect, but that inheritance significantly shaped and limited the force of those conditions.

Harris cites the work of Fernando Ortiz to show that law and tradition fared badly in Cuba againt economic pressure. Here again, however, he assumes a fatalistic stance. Sidney W. Mintz also cites the Cuban case as especially instructive, but he does so with greater perception and caution: Cuba, he writes, shows what happens to "those rosy institutional arrangements which protected the slave, once slavery became part of the industrial plantation system . . . . Institutional restrictions may have hampered the maturation of slave-based agricultural capitalism in Cuba; but . . . could not prevent it. In the mid-nineteenth century, Cuban slavery dehumanized the slaves as viciously as had Jamaican or North American slavery." Mintz notes that Tannenbaum and Elkins "circumvent critical evidence on the interplay of economic and ideological forces." Elsewhere he writes that the way men were treated in colonial Caribbean societies was "determined much more by the level of economic development than by the ideologies of the different metropolitan powers."[44] The words "much more than" leave considerable room for the autonomous force of ideology. If Harris were to restrict himself within the limits of Mintz's critique, he might help develop the work of Freyre, Tannenbaum, and Elkins along materialist lines, but instead he declares ideological war. Mintz's remarks on the intersection of ideology and economics constitute the beginning of a new departure, although I should prefer to subsume both within a synthetic analysis of social classes that avoids compartmentalizing their constituent human beings. Social classes have historically formed traditions, values, and sentiments, as well as particular and general economic interests. Harris, like Mintz, Eric Williams, and others, refers to the components of the slaveholders' world view and the possible divergence between economic interests and traditional commitments. The solution of these problems awaits empirical research. A materialist interpretation must account for the full range of possibilities, but it can do so only if it eschews economic determinism and a narrow ecology for a concern with the historical formation of class interests and antagonisms under specific geographic and technological conditions.[45]

Harris makes much of the philosophical idealism of Freyre, Tannenbaum, and Elkins but does not analyze it. Since Freyre has written at some length on his method and viewpoint, Harris ought to examine them specifically instead of contenting himself with the application of labels. That Freyre, Tannenbaum, and Elkins may be safely classed as idealists I do not deny, but their superb work ought to warn their philosophical opponents that the subject matter resists simplistic materialist schemata. A review of Freyre's methodological comments will lay bare the weakness of idealist interpretations and also the elusiveness of the reality which makes such interpretations possible and even enormously helpful.

Freyre's critique of historical materialism is especially suggestive, for he rejects it without hostility and indeed with considerable appreciation. "However little inclined we may be to historical materialism," he writes, "which is so often exaggerated in its generalizations—chiefly in the works by sectarians and fanatics—we must admit the considerable influence, even though not always a preponderant one, exerted by the technique of economic production upon the structure of socities and upon the features of their moral physiognomies. It is an influence subject to the reaction of other influences, yet powerful as no other . . . ."[46] Freyre's words strike sharply at economic determinism, which has roots in Marxism where it clutters up rich fields, and at certain schools of ecology, but they are generally consistent with a properly understood dialectical materialism. What is primarily missing in Freyre's organic view of society is a suitable concern for class antagonisms as the historical motor force, but that is precisely what is missing from Harris's materialism.

Freyre's objections to historical materialism rest largely on his narrow economic reading of Marxian theory. In *The Mansions and the Shanties* he refers to an essay by Lefebvre des Noëttes in which it is asserted that moral suasion proved helpless against slavery until technological developments gave it room to expand. Freyre asks if this means "the absolute dependence of moral progress on material progress, as narrowly sectarian 'historical materialists' claim . . . ?"[47] He answers negatively, citing the United States as proof that slavery and technological progress could coexist. I doubt that the United States would offer him much evidence to refute even vulgar Marxism on this point, but we need not discuss the specific questions now. The main point is that he sees Marxism as an economic and technological determinism; in effect, he describes it in terms much more appropriate to certain schools of ecology. If it is Marxism, then certainly it is the kind that once drove Marx to protest, *"Je ne suis pas un marxiste."* The class element has somehow disappeared, but without it historical materialism is a senseless abstraction.

If historical materialism is not a theory of class determinism, it is nothing, but to be a theory of class determinism it must accept two limitations. Certain social classes can only rise to political power and social hegemony under specific technological conditions. The relationship of these classes, from this point of view, determines the contours of the historical epoch. It follows, then, that changes in the political relationship of classes constitute the essence of social transformations; but this notion comes close to tautology, for social transformations are defined precisely by changes in class relationships. What rescues the notion from tautology is the expectation that these changes in class relationships determine —at least in outline—the major psychological, ideological, and political patterns, as well as economic and technological possibilities, that changes in class structure constitute the most meaningful of all social changes. To argue that they constitute the only meaningful changes is to reduce historical materialism to nonsense and to surrender its dialectical essence.

Freyre's idealism appears most crudely in his discussion of Portuguese colonization. He refers to the "task" of colonization as being "disproportionate to the normal resources of the population, thereby obliging the people to maintain themselves in a constant state of superexcitation, in the interests of large-scale procreation."[48] Lapses into teleology and mysticism abound in his writings, and one could, if one wished, put them side by side to prove him quaint or foolish. He who wastes time doing so will be the loser, for Freyre's thought is too rich for us to focus on its weak side. To see where Freyre is going we need to analyze his notion of the "creative image."

In writing of Brazilian patriarchal society and of the intersection of Indian, Negro, and European cultures Freyre "was trying to accomplish a pale equivalent of what Picasso has masterfully accomplished in plastic art: the merging of the analytic and the organic approaches to man: what one of his critics has called 'a creative image.' "[49] Freyre seeks to use methods and data of the physical, biological, and social sciences to assist in what is essentially an artistic project, for only through artistic image can the wholeness of man and his world be glimpsed. He admits the large role assigned to intuition in his work.[50] In a passage, which seems to me to reflect a strong Sombartian influence, he writes, "The truth really seems to be that only 'within' the living whole of human development can the relations between what is arbitrarily considered rationality and irrationality in human behavior, or between different human cultures, be fully understood."[51] Properly disciplined, this concern with getting "within" a society should mean a concern with its spirit—its dominant ideology, system of values, and psychological patterns. Freyre's effort can and should be assimilated into a historical view of social classes, for it is essentially an attempt to grasp the wholeness of a society's world view, including its self-image. Only two steps are required to place Freyre's viewpoint on materialist ground. The first takes us to the realization that society's world view must necessarily be essentially the view of its ruling class; the second to the realization that, in order to rule, a ruling class must be sufficiently wise and flexible to incorporate much from the manners and sentiments of the classes being ruled.

Freyre is therefore not toying with us when he writes that he endeavors to be "almost entirely objective" but that at certain points he introduces an "objective-introspective" method. His purpose is to be able to feel life as lived by his long-dead subjects in all its "sensual fullness of outline."[52] This attempt at psychological reconstruction, he wisely observes, depends less on "the strictly psychological approach of academic psychologists than that of novelists who have found it necessary to add a psychological time to the conventional chronological one, in novels otherwise historical in their substance . . . ."[53] In this spirit he constructs, for example, a historical-psychological model of Indian and African personality traits, as absorbed into Brazilian culture.[54] So far as possible, he strives to discover the roots of these divergent patterns in social and technical modes of life. The problem lies in the elusiveness of a full explanation. The mechanisms and the extent of the inheritance of acquired group characteristics continue to elude us and may to some degree always do so. Recognition of this elusiveness and of how few definite, scientifically demonstrated conclusions we can borrow from psychologists or from other social and biological scientists throws Freyre and the rest of us back on our own fragile ability as social historians to reach for everything at once. Poetry, for us as well as for the ancient Greeks, remains truer than history. As Freyre reminds us:

> The human being can only be understood—in so far as he can be understood—in his total human aspect; and understanding involves the sacrifice of a greater or lesser degree of objectivity. For in dealing with the human past, room must be allowed for doubt, and even for mystery. The history of an institution, when undertaken or attempted in keeping with a sociological criterion which includes the psychological, inevitably carries

> us into zones of mystery where it would be ridiculous for us to feel satisfied with Marxist interpretations or Behaviorist or Paretist explanations, or with mere description similar to those of natural history.[55]

Freyre's willingness to speak approvingly of intuition, "mystery," and the sacrifice of objectivity opens him to attack and even ridicule from those who are content to ignore the challenge. Yet Freyre's intuition, like the passionate opposition to racial and social injustice that informs all of Harris's work, has its place. As Gramsci observes, "Only passion sharpens the intellect and cooperates to render intuition clearer."[56] Freyre, sensing the elusiveness of historical truth and the dangers of strict rationalism, has raised serious objections to materialist theory, and only superficial mechanists could fail to realize as much. Since a full reply would entail an effort beyond the reader's patience, I should like to restrict myself to a few observations.

The strength of Marxian materialism, relative to other materialisms, is its dialectic, which gives it, or ought to give it, the flexibility and wholeness Freyre demands. The principle of interrelatedness is fundamental to Hegelian and Marxian dialectics and cannot be sacrificed to convenient notions of simple causation. If dialectical materialism is taken seriously, it must assert historical continuity as well as discontinuity. Every historical event necessarily embraces the totality of its components, each of which brings to that event the product of its total historical development. For this reason alone, a failure to respect the force of a people's tradition and historically developed sensibility will always prove fatal to materialist thought and betray it into mechanism. The task of those who would confront Freyre's idealism with a convincing materialism is to account for the complexity of societies in their historical uniqueness and for the special manifestations of the human spirit embodied in each such society.

Freyre's recourse to an idealist stance results from an

irresponsible attitude toward the complex reality he seeks to explain. In his methodological preface to his study of post-monarchical Brazil, he identifies his subject as a society entering the modern world with a persistent tradition of patriarchalism; and he identifies his method as less the historical than the anthropological and psychological.[57] Life, he insists, is a process of development of values and lends itself only partially to scientific analysis.[58] Perhaps so, but as Marx, Freud, and Weber, among others, have argued, it is both necessary and possible to deal rationally with the irrational and to develop, at least in approximation, a disciplined approach to a reality so rich that we shall certainly never fully grasp it. The most attractive inheritance of Marxism from the Hegelian dialectic is the simultaneous assertion of progress toward essential knowledge and yet the ultimate elusiveness of the whole. It is this inheritance that makes Marxian philosophy, when it is not trampled on by political imbeciles, enthusiastically embrace the experimental sciences without fear of losing its dogmatic virginity. Freyre's weakness lies in his unwillingness to try to discipline his many-sided viewpoint. I do not suggest that he ought to tell us which "factor" in the social organism he analyzes is "primary." I cannot imagine what a "historical factor" is, and the assignment of primacy would do violence to the spirit of his work. I do suggest that we need some clue to the motor force of social change. Freyre fails us here; hence the sharpness of Harris's critique.[59]

Freyre's failure—like Harris's—emerges most clearly from his friendly reply to an author who "would place responsibility for the principal defects in our social, economic, and moral development upon slavery . . . where I am inclined to put the blame upon monoculture and the latifundia . . . ."[60] The difference, Freyre argues, is one of emphasis, and each emphasis does fall on the material conditions of life. Ironically, Harris's position is close to Freyre's although more rigid, for Freyre himself often slides into a narrow mechanism when he discusses specific historical problems rather than theoretical and methodological ones. He does not, for example, pay nearly enough attention to the feudal-Catholic tradition in his discussions of morality, sexual relations, sadism in pedagogy, and some other matters.[61] The advantage of emphasizing slavery rather than monoculture lies not in the superior virtue of one "factor" over the other, but in the focus on human relationships. The special quality of master-slave relationships in Brazilian slavery lies in their being a special case in a broad pattern of quasi-feudal, paternalistic relationships brought from Portugal and reinvigorated on the virgin soil of Bahia and Pernambuco. Freyre himself contributes much toward such an analysis in at least two ways: (1) by treating the slave plantation as an integrated community and (2) by seeing that community as a projection of the traditional family unit. Tannenbaum's early formulation of the problem remains one of the best:

> It is better to speak of a slave society rather than of slavery, for the effects of the labor system—slave or free—permeate the entire social structure and influence all of its ways. If we are to speak of slavery, we must do it in its larger setting, as a way of life for both master and slave, for both the economy and the culture, for both the family and the community.[62]

What needs to be explored is the relationship between this peculiar class structure and the prevalent psychological and ideological patterns in society.

A parallel weakness in Freyre's attempt at synthetic analysis may be found in his discussion of the economic ills of monoculture. These surely were not absolute. If they crippled society at a certain point, they did so because they badly compromised the ruling class and hampered its ability to rule with that evenhandedness without which the successful exercise of social hegemony would be impossible. Whether slavery or monoculture caused soil exhaustion is not an especially useful question, for they were functionally related. More to the point, they represented social and economic aspects of a specific form of class rule. In economic experience, as in the psychology of the leading strata, the relationship of master to slave proved decisive: it set limits to labor productivity, the flexibility of organization, the growth of the home market, and the accumulation of capital. It determined, in essential respects, the sensibilities of those who could and did place their imprint on society.[63]

Of the planters Freyre writes that they "represented, in the formation of Brazilian society, the most typical of Portuguese tendencies: namely, settledness, in the sense of patriarchal stability. A stability based upon sugar (the plantation) and the Negro (the slave hut) . . . . I would merely set alongside the purely material or Marxist aspect of things or, better, tentencies of the psychologic aspect. Or the pscho-physiologic."[64] Harris has not yet answered this challenge satisfactorily. We need not choose between Freyre's eclecticism and Harris's version of materialism. The historical task, to which a properly understood materialism seems to me to offer the best solution, is twofold: to relate satisfactorily the psychological, "material," and other aspects of a society to each other in such a way as to present reality as integrated social process; and to avoid a sterile functionalism by uncovering the fundamental pattern of human relationships conditioning both material and spiritual life. To fulfill this task we need to examine historical continuity, with its cumulative traditions and ways of thought, as well as ecology, more narrowly understood. Freyre's idealism may, as Harris alleges, weaken his work, but neither Freyre nor any of us could be expected to do better by rejecting a concern for the whole man in a social setting that links past to present. At his best Freyre is marvellously dialectical, as in his pregnant remarks on the Brazilian adaptation of the Portuguese language,[65] or in his discussion of the psychology of the Portuguese colonizer, which he relates to the "intimate unity" of Portuguese culture as "a consequence of the processes and of the conditions of Portuguese colonization."[66]

The sad part of Harris's book, which is so impressive in many of its particular analyses, is the implicit conflict between his denigration of ideas, ideals, and values and his passionate plea for racial and social justice. How ironical that he should end his book with an exhortation— to whom and to do what is not clear:

> The backwardness of vast multitudes of the New World peasantry, illiterate, unskilled, cut off from the twentieth century and its brilliant technological advances did not simply happen by itself. These millions, about whose welfare we have suddenly been obliged to concern ourselves, were trained to their role in world history by four centuries of physical and mental conditioning. They were deliberately bottled up. Now we must either pull the cork or watch the bottle explode.[67]

In the context of his book these words are puzzling and might easily be dismissed, were it not for the obvious personal sincerity and social urgency they suggest. One is tempted to reply to Harris in the words Tannenbaum used many years ago to reply to Eric Williams:

> It is hard to be a child of the Renaissance and a high priest of economic interpretation. If slavery was merely economic, and if economic forces are the only conditioning factor in shaping human institutions, then why all the indignation and the sarcasm? Why the appeal to moral forces, to justice, and to humanity?[68]

Harris, by attempting to construct a materialism that bypasses the ideological and psychological elements in the formation of social classes, passes over into a variant of vulgar Marxism. In so doing, he ranges himself much further away from a consistent and useful materialism than do the idealists themselves, for he turns from everything living in modern materialism—its dialectics and sense of historical process—and offers us the dead bones of a soulless mechanism.

NOTES

1. Allan Nevins, *The Emergence of Lincoln,* 2 vols. (New York, 1950); Frank Tannenbaum, *Slave & Citizen: The Negro in the Americas* (New York, 1947); Manoel de Oliveira Lima, *The Evolution of Brazil Compared with that of Spanish and Anglo-Saxon America* (Stanford, 1914); Roy Nash, *The Conquest of Brazil* (New York, 1926); Gilberto Freyre, "Social Life in Brazil in the Middle of the Nineteenth Century," *Hispanic American Historical Review,* 5 (Nov. 1922), 597–628.

2. Magnus Mörner, "The History of Race Relations in Latin America: Comments on the State of Research," *Latin American Research Review,* 1 (1966), 17–44. Pages 35–44 contain an excellent bibliography.

3. Marvin Harris, *Patterns of Race in the Americas* (New York, 1964). Since Harris published, David Brion Davis has brought out his splendid *The Problem of Slavery in Western Culture* (New York, 1966), which takes up a critical stance toward Tannenbaum. His criticisms, which will be noted briefly below, are tangential to the main task of his book. Harris's book is, so far, the only attempt to replace the full burden of Tannenbaum's argument.

4. Tannenbaum, p. 65, n. 153.

5. Richard Graham, "Causes of the Abolition of Slavery in Brazil: An Interpretive Essay," *Hispanic American Historical Review,* 46 (May 1966), 123–137.

6. Davis, *passim.* This point is one of the leading theses of Davis's book.

7. Charles Wagley, *An Introduction to Brazil* (New York, 1963), p. 132.

8. Harris, p. 64.

9. Wagley, p. 238; cf. pp. 140–142.

10. Octávio Ianni, *Raças e classes sociais no Brasil* (Rio de Janiero, 1966), p. 15.

11. C. R. Boxer, *Salvador de Sá and the Struggle for Brazil and Angola, 1602–1686* (London, 1952), p. 235.

12. Gilberto Freyre, *O Mundo que o portugues criou & Uma Cultura ameaçada: A Luso-Brasileira* (Lisbon, 1940), p. 41.

13. Gilberto Freyre, *New World in the Tropics: The Culture of Modern Brazil* (New York, 1963), p. 8. At that, he underestimates the extent of prejudice and discrimination. See *e.g.,* the important socio-

logical studies of Fernando Henrique Cardoso and Octávio Ianni, *Côr e mobilidade social em Florianópolis* (São Paulo, 1960); and Roger Bastide and Florestan Fernandes, *Brancos e negros em São Paulo,* 2ª ed. (São Paulo, 1959).

14. Freyre, *New World,* p. 82.

15. Ibid., p. 144.

16. Harris, p. 64. Original emphasis.

17. Frank Tannenbaum, *Ten Keys to Latin America* (New York, 1965), p. 43.

18. Ibid., pp. 49–51.

19. Ibid., p. 52. Similarly Elkins draws attention to Hispanic race prejudice and discrimination against Negroes. "Was there squalor, filth, widespread depression of the masses? Much more so than with us—but there it was the class system and economic 'underdevelopment,' rather than the color barrier, that made the difference" (*Slavery: A Problem in American Institutional and Intellectual Life* [Chicago, 1959], p. 79).

20. Harris, p. 65.

21. Ibid., pp. 65–66.

22. K. Oberg, Comment on Harris's article, "The Cultural Ecology of India's Sacred Cattle," *Current Anthropology,* 7 (Feb. 1966), 62.

23. Cf., Marvin Harris, "The Economy Has No Surplus?" *American Anthropologist,* 61 (April 1959), 188.

24. Harris, "The Economy Has No Surplus?" p. 194.

25. Antonio Gramsci, *Il Materialismo storico e la filosofia di Benedetto Croce* (Turin, 1949), p. 49.

26. Marvin Harris, Reply to Criticism, appended to his article, "The Cultural Ecology of India's Sacred Cattle," *Current Anthropology,* 7 (Feb. 1966), 64.

27. The most suggestive discussions of the problem from a Marxian point of view are to be found in Gramsci's *Opere,* but see also John M. Cammett's excellent introduction to Gramsci's life and thought, *Antonio Gramsci and the Origins of Italian Communism* (Stanford, 1967).

28. Harris, *Patterns of Race,* p. 67.

29. Cf., Eric Williams, *Capitalism & Slavery* (New York, 1961) and *The Negro in the Caribbean* (Manchester, England, 1942); Herbert Aptheker, *American Negro Slave Revolts* (New York, 1943); Oscar and Mary F. Handlin, "Origins of the Southern Labor System," *William and Mary Quarterly,* 3rd Series, 7 (April 1950), 199–222; C. L. R. James, *The Black Jacobins: Toussaint L'Ouverture and the San Domingo Revolution,* 2nd ed. (1963).

30. Harris, *Patterns of Race,* p. 68.

31. Davis, p. 281.

32. Carl Degler, "Slavery and the Genesis of American Race Prejudice," *Comparative Studies in Society and History,* 2 (Oct. 1959), 49–66; Juan Comas, "Recent Research on Racial Relations—Latin America," *International Social Science Journal,* 13, no. 2 (1961), 271–

299, esp. 291; Arnold A. Sio, "Interpretations of Slavery: The Slave Status in the Americas," *Comparative Studies in Society and History,* 7 (April 1965), 289–308; Winthrop D. Jordan, "The Influence of the West Indies on the Origins of New England Slavery," *William and Mary Quarterly,* 3rd series, 18 (April 1961), 243–250.

33. Since this essay was originally published Jordan has brought out his stimulating and learned book *White Over Black* (Chapel Hill, 1968).

34. M. I. Finley, review of Davis, *The Problem of Slavery* in *New York Review of Books,* 8 (Jan. 26, 1967), 10.

35. C. R. Boxer, *Race Relations in the Portuguese Colonial Empire, 1415–1825* (Oxford, 1963), p. 56.

36. Regrettably, even Boxer slights the historical dimension. It is noteworthy that he begins his survey, *Race Relations,* with the conquest of Ceuta in 1415 and leaves aside the racial conditioning of Portuguese life that preceded it. For an excellent statement of the intersection of tradition and economic milieu in the formation of Brazilian attitudes see Roger Bastide, "Race Relations in Brazil," *International Social Science Bulletin,* 9, no. 4 (1957), 495–512, esp. 495–496.

37. Caio Prado Júnior, *Formação do Brasil contemporâneo: Colonia,* 7ª ed. (São Paulo, n. d.), pp. 103–104; *Evolução política do Brasil e outros estudios,* 4ª ed. (São Paulo, n.d.), pp. 46–47.

38. Harris, *Patterns of Race,* p. 70.

39. Ibid., p. 79.

40. Ibid., p. 81.

41. Elkins, p. 77; Harris, *Patterns of Race,* p. 75.

42. Harris, *Patterns of Race,* p. 86.

43. Winthrop D. Jordan, "American Chiaroscuro: The Status and Definition of Mulattoes in the British Colonies," *William and Mary Quarterly,* 3rd series, 19 (April 1962), 183–200.

44. Sidney W. Mintz, review of Elkins's *Slavery* in *American Anthropologist,* 63 (June 1961), 579–587; "Labor and Sugar in Puerto Rico and in Jamaica, 1800–1850," *Comparative Studies in Society and History,* 1 (March 1959), 273–283, quote from p. 283. On the effects of commercialization see Sio, *Comparative Studies in Society and History,* 7 (April 1965), 298–308.

45. The limits of the ecological viewpoint are brought out with great skill by Clifford Geertz. Several passages from his book, *Agricultural Involution: The Processes of Ecological Change in Indonesia* (Berkeley, 1963) are especially useful:

> How much of the past growth and the present state of Indonesian culture and society is attributable to ecological processes is something to be determined, if at all, at the end of inquiry, not at the beginning of it. And as political, stratificatory, commercial, and intellectual developments, at least, seem to have acted as important ordering processes in Indonesian history, the final awarding of pre-

potency to ecological developments seems no more likely than that they will turn out to have been inconsequential (p. 11).

On the contrast between Japanese and Javanese society:

Given, then, all the admittedly background differences, one can hardly forbear to ask when one looks at these two societies: "What has happened in the one which did not happen in the other?" A satisfactory answer to such a question would involve the whole economic, political and cultural history of the two civilizations . . . (p. 131).

A search for the true diagnosis of the Indonesian malaise takes one, thus, far beyond the analysis of ecological and economic processes to an investigation into the nation's political, social, and cultural dynamics (p. 154: the last sentence in the book).

46. Gilberto Freyre, *The Masters and the Slaves: A Study in the Development of Brazilian Civilization,* 2nd English language ed. (New York, 1956), p. xxvii.

47. Gilberto Freyre, *The Mansions and the Shanties: The Making of Modern Brazil* (New York, 1963), p. 305.

48. Freyre, *Masters and Slaves,* p. 262.

49. Ibid., p. xxi.

50. Ibid., p. xxi.

51. Ibid., p. xxii.

52. Ibid., p. lviii.

53. Ibid., p. lxix. Perhaps the most straightforward illustration of Freyre's method is, appropriately, *Mother and Son: A Brazilian Tale* (New York, 1967), which he describes as a semi-novel and in which fictional situations are meant to represent historical and social reality, apparently on the principle of *se non e vero, e ben' trovato.* As the narrator writes of a character about whom he planned to write and who suddenly appears before him in real life (p. 4): "I must be aware that she had existed before I had imagined her; if she had not, I would not have tried to conjure her up."

54. Freyre, *Masters and Slaves,* pp. 284–285.

55. Freyre, *Mansions and Shanties,* p. xxix.

56. Quoted by Cammett, *Antonio Gramsci,* p. 197.

57. Gilberto Freyre, *Ordem e progresso: Processo de disintegração das sociedades patriarcal e semipatriarcal no Brasil sob o regime do trabalho livre* . . . , 2 vols. (Rio de Janeiro, 1962), p. xxiv. I deliberately pass over Freyre's extension of his psychological method in his theory of Luso-Tropicalism. This extension raises a different set of problems, beyond the scope of this paper. See Freyre, *The Portuguese and the Tropics* (Lisbon, 1961), esp. p. 9.

58. Freyre, *Ordem e progresso,* pp. xxxii–xxxiii. It is only a short step from this attitude to a romanticization of the Brazilian past. Stanley J. Stein is harsh but not unjust when he rebukes Freyre for transforming hypotheses advanced in the *Masters and Slaves* into "facts"

simply by restating them in later books. See Stein, "Freyre's Brazil Revisited: A review of *New World in the Tropics: The Culture of Modern Brazil,*" *Hispanic American Historical Review,* 41 (Feb. 1961), 113.

59. There is also, apparently, a political and ideological component to this sharpness. Freyre's writings on Angola and Moçambique have come close to apologetics for Dr. Salazar's imperialist policies. Harris sees a direct line between Freyre's point of view on Brazilian colonization and his recent political pronouncements. As one who has seen the ravages of Portuguese imperialism first hand and who has done good work in exposing them, Harris is incensed. I agree that there is a direct line between the two sets of views, but I also think that Freyre's polite criticisms of Portuguese racial policies as "un-Portuguese" ought to be given due weight. His views of past and present can be related to a general ideological commitment that looks to me—he would probably deny it—as a sophisticated greater-Brazilian nationalism. In any case, we dare not permit criticisms of Freyre's politics to blind us to the value of his contributions to history and sociology. His formulations on Brazilian history and culture must be examined strictly on their merits.

60. Freyre, *Masters and Slaves,* pp. 64–65, n. 176; cf., *O Mundo que o português criou,* p. 108.

61. Cf., *Masters and Slaves,* pp. 368, 401, 416–417, n. 34.

62. Frank Tannenbaum, "A Note on the Economic Interpretation of History," *Political Science Quarterly,* 61 (June 1946), 248.

63. The most suggestive starting point for a psychology of slaveholding may be found in G. W. F. Hegel, *The Phenomenology of Mind,* 2 vols. (London, 1910), 1:183 ff. I have tried to sketch, in a preliminary way, the slaveholding experience in the United States: *The Political Economy of Slavery* (New York, 1965), pp. 31–34.

64. Freyre, *Masters and Slaves,* p. xl.

65. Ibid., p. 348.

66. Freyre, *O Mundo que o português criou,* p. 39; *New World in the Tropics,* p. 54.

67. Harris, *Patterns of Race,* p. 99.

68. Tannenbaum, *Political Science Quarterly,* 61 (June 1946), 252.

Part Two

BLACK EXPERIENCE/ WHITE HISTORY

Chapter 3

CLASS AND NATIONALITY IN BLACK AMERICA

UNTIL RECENTLY, American Marxists like many others viewed racism as simply a class question. They regarded racial discrimination as a "mask for privilege"—a technique by which the ruling class exploits minorities and divides the working class. According to this view, capitalism generated slavery, and slavery generated racism; but the destruction of slavery did not end the economic exploitation of black people that racism justified and perpetuated. As an oppressed proletariat, the blacks had class interests identical with those of the white working class and a clear duty to join with their white brothers in bringing down the capitalist system: "Black and white, unite and fight!"

These formulations are not so much untrue as schematic and one-dimensional; accordingly, they lead to serious polit-

This essay was originally prepared as a speech to the Boston-Cambridge SDS in 1968. It was revised by Christopher Lasch when we thought of using it in a book we intended to write together.

I am indebted to Professor Lasch for his help and for his agreement to include the essay here.

ical miscalculations and mistakes. It is true that slavery bred racism. As C. R. Boxer has observed, no people can systematically enslave another for several hundred years without developing racism in some form. But racial prejudice in the New World arose from a variety of sources; various subtle influences had already conditioned Europeans for their negative view of the black man long before the development of slavery in the western hemisphere. Racism, understood as a developed theoretical justification for a system of discrimination and ethnic exploitation, is a distinctly European contribution to world civilization. The slave systems of the New World generated a great many varieties of racism. Brazilian slavery generated a milder form of racism than did American, although the recent onset of industrialism in Brazil, which has thrown black workers into competition with immigrant Europeans, has already led to a deterioration in race relations. The Spanish variant of racism was generally milder than the Dutch, but great variations developed within the Spanish colonies themselves. The considerable variations among the New World slave systems as a whole lead to the conclusions, first, that although slavery produced racism by its very nature, the quality and intensity of racism varied according to the national, religious, and ethnic traditions of the enslavers; and second, that these original variations deriving from the European background of colonization tended in time to grow weaker (although not to disappear) as commercialization developed and with it the possibility of large-scale plantations with factory-like discipline.

In the United States a peculiar combination of circumstances produced a peculiarly virulent and dangerous form of racism. The American colonists suffered from what appears to be special, historically conditioned Anglo-Saxon susceptibility to racial prejudice in extreme forms. Worse, population structure reinforced this tendency. Whereas blacks in the British West Indies made up the overwhelming majority of the population and the coloreds (mixed) constituted, of necessity, a middle class as well as a middle stratum, the blacks and coloreds of the American South were a minority of the total population. It was not necessary to distinguish between the two—every man who was part black was a nigger—and it was not necessary to rely on slaves or free coloreds for much more than manual labor. Thus the circumstances that elsewhere set limits to racist ideology were much weaker in the South than elsewhere. Slavery produced racism everywhere, but in the United States it gave rise to the most viciously racist society of all. We dwell on this point because American Marxists, as well as Americans generally, have greatly underestimated the depth of American racism, failing to understand its roots in a long historical past, and have therefore underestimated the difficulty of destroying racist attitudes and institutions.

The complexity and difficulty of the race problem are further obscured by the tendency to see black people in America simply as an exploited class or, even more confusingly, as one of a number of ethnic groups all of which capitalism has oppressed in various ways. American blacks constitute not so much a class as a nation, and their experience in the United States has been unique. Nor is the relation between capitalism and racism as clear and direct as many leftist critics assume. For one thing, the American North, like the South itself, was racist before its capitalism matured. Capitalism in the North did not depend for its growth and development on the forced labor of blacks, although it indirectly profited from the slave trade and from Southern slave labor. Until the first World War, black people were a small minority of the population. Thereafter, mechanization of agriculture in the South sent them northward in growing numbers, but they did not simply blend into Northern city life as one more ethnic group within the exploited working class. Instead, the declining importance of unskilled and semiskilled labor in Northern industry rendered large numbers of them economically superfluous or peripheral. Certain ultra-leftists, in order to assimilate this history to a simple-minded class analysis, have argued that blacks have been victims of "super exploitation"—that is, of systematic exploitation well beyond the normal rate of extracting surplus value. But this interpretation in itself implies imperialist oppression of a separate nationality and ought to lead logically to the position that blacks have the right to national self-determination.

Blacks are Americans and yet a people apart. Unlike Italians, Poles, Irish, and others, Africans came involuntarily to America, where they were enslaved, deprived of constitutional rights, and subjected not merely to prejudice and ethnic discrimination but to an atrocious racism that declared them virtually subhuman. In order to survive in the face of these appalling conditions, the black community over the centuries has had to develop an inner cohesiveness and culture of its own. Black nationality arises from two sources: a community of interest in a virulently racist society; and a particular culture that has itself been a mechanism for survival as well as for resistance to racist oppression. At the same time, blacks live among whites, and share in the general American national culture. They are, in short, both part of and yet apart from the American nation. The notion of "a nation within a nation," which has intermittently been popular within the black community, expresses this duality. The position of black people in America represents a conjuncture of class and national oppression, both of which become partly obscured when subsumed by the category "race."

If there was no direct causal connection between the development of American capitalism and the growth of racism, it remains true that capitalism contributed immensely to racism, first by spawning slave systems and then by introducing or encouraging a variety of specific practices. Historical conditioning, together with the direct influence of a slaveholders' culture in the South, combined to produce a racist society in the ante-bellum North. The ensuing sectional war only slightly modified Northern sentiment and practice. During Reconstruction new opportunities for racial reconciliation presented themselves, but these were lost in the subsequent reaction. During and after Reconstruction American capitalism passed quickly into a monopolistic and then an imperialist phase. Neither development provided the slightest check to the racist tendencies in American life; on the contrary, both enormously stimulated those tendencies. The great corporations' conquest of American society required the political support of a solid South, and racism formed the cornerstone of this sectional bargain. The concentration of capital both in the North and in the South required the suppression of the demand for "40 acres and a mule," which envisioned the emergence of an independent black yeomanry in the South and which would have strengthened the white middle class against oligopolistic encroachments. Monopoly capital was inherently opposed to the interests of black people and therefore racist, in the objective sense that it prevented the enactment of those socioeconomic measures which would have enabled the blacks to repel racist aggression. In the nineties, when American capitalism entered its imperialist phase, racism became virtually an official national ideology.

Since the First World War, the relationship between capitalism and racism has by no means been so clear. American society in the last half-century has reflected a number of important antiracist influences: the militancy of the blacks themselves; the belated discovery of social scientists that racism is an intellectual fraud; the rise of an independent Africa and Asia; and perhaps even a greater sensitivity and decency among substantial numbers of white Americans who experienced the political and ideological currents of the war against fascism. With the decline of sharecropping and tenancy in the South, with urbanization, and with substantial structural changes in the economy, American capitalism no longer needs or generates in the old way racial discrimination as an organized form of class rule. Since the blacks today are prepared to exact a high price for the conditions to which they are subjected, there is good reason to believe that the capitalists as a class and capitalism as a system would purge themselves of racism if they could. Racism, however, is so deeply rooted in American society that it cannot be torn up without fundamental changes in capitalism itself.

In the first place, the blacks will no longer be satisfied with doles, poverty programs, welfare checks, and other brutal and barbarous offerings of peace. Not that they were docile and meekly submissive before. As slaves, American blacks did not develop a tradition of armed resistance or mount insurrections on the scale of slave rebellions in Brazil, Jamaica, or Saint-Domingue; but neither did they meekly submit. The heroism of the blacks against slavery was largely the heroism of individual action and of collective cultural effort for sheer survival. Unable as slaves to establish specifically political organizations, they found it difficult to defend themselves, both as slaves and as free men following emancipation, against a highly paternalistic system well calculated to undermine their collective self-confidence. During the period between Reconstruction and the Second World War, the chief characteristics of black response to racism were neither docility nor lack of militancy nor even simple accommodation but, rather, dependence on white allies and leadership, lack of independent organization and program, and individual antisocial acts that showed an unwillingness to accept the status quo but little sense of an alternative. These circumstances perpetuated the racist illusion that blacks were docile and submissive and that all those not fitting this stereotype could be dismissed as a criminal element and treated accordingly. Racism has ended in a grim joke on the racists. The emergence of an organized and disciplined movement among black people has caught white America by surprise, without institutional mechanisms for dealing with it. Since the demands of the blacks are old ones, the notion that they can possibly agree to slow down the pace of their realization is absurd. The demands have been pressed for more than a century, and seem new and even extreme only because until recently white Americans never had to listen to them or to take them seriously. They seem old and moderate to people who have been crying out for justice as long as the American nation has existed.

The impatience of the blacks and the mixture of surprise, alarm, and guilt that it elicits from whites make it difficult for the capitalists to respond rationally and with dispatch to black demands. There are other difficulties as well. The sharp clash between blacks and first- and second-generation working-class whites has a long history and is firmly rooted in economic rivalry. The racism of Polish, Irish, Italian, and other American workers—a racism for the most part born among them in the United States rather than imported from Catholic Europe—has had a long time to grow. Economic competition not only remains but grows worse. If the blacks are to receive a share in the existing economic capacity of the United States, someone else must move over; and these groups, as noted above, are the groups most immediately exposed. American capitalism might be able to solve this problem temporarily through an accelerated rate of growth, but increased growth unaccompanied by a corresponding rearrangement of domestic priorities would have no lasting effects.

In any case, American capitalism apparently no longer has the capacity to sustain a sufficiently high growth rate. The war in Vietnam has further weakened the American economy, relative to those of Western Europe and Japan, by imposing enormous additional burdens on both the private and the public sectors of the economy. Drastic measures are necessary in order to improve the competitive position of the United States in the world market—reduction of costs, rationalization of industrial operations, and a more stringent allocation of resources. Even these may fail in the long run, and in the meantime they are the very measures that will widen the gap between blacks and whites and thus militate against the absorption of blacks, as equals, into the industrial system. The rationalization of industry requires, among other things, a further reduction of the system's dependence on unskilled and semi-skilled workers. The black community already suffers from acute unemployment; such a program would only make matters worse.

The blacks demand and need more than jobs. They need subsidized education, housing, community services, and in general a redefinition of priorities in favor of social programs as against the maintenance of existing rates of profit. The economy must be reorganized to permit the retraining of a whole people, under conditions of equality and in ways consistent with their own sense of dignity, even at the cost of a temporarily lower rate of growth. In other words, the competitive position of American capitalism in the world market must cease to be a matter of importance and therefore capitalism itself must cease to be a matter of importance. Meanwhile broad social and economic guarantees will be needed to allay the fears of the white working class and new middle class, at the very moment that a national effort is raising the economic level of the blacks and poor whites. These measures, together with the reorganization of the political process to assure genuine participation from below and the reorganization of communications to make possible a broad-based ideological struggle against racism in every form, strike at the very basis of the existing social system. No half-hearted reformist solutions will produce anything more than another dose of demagogy and disillusionment.

American capitalism, then, cannot deal with the race question. It is not so much that capitalism any longer deliberately stimulates racism or needs it to insure political stability, as that racism has struck roots so deep in our social, political, and economic life that nothing short of a total restructuring of American society can remove it. The competitive position of American capitalism demands measures that will undermine efforts to deal with racism, and the imperialist foreign policy of the United States, which increasingly draws it into open conflict with people of other races, makes it doubly difficult to mount an attack on racism at home. The war in Vietnam has exposed anew the link between racism and imperial pretensions. So long as the United States government is throttling colored peoples abroad, it will find itself unable to undertake a nationally coordinated attack on white racism. We need not doubt the sincerity of American leaders who denounce racism while supporting the war, or point to the performance of black troops as proof of national solidarity. These arguments raise questions not about their sincerity but about their intelligence and knowledge. Black men have fought bravely in all American wars, have been promised a new day for their efforts, and have returned to face lynch mobs or indifference. If they return to something better now, it is because they give evidence of a willingness to use the guns that have been placed in their hands. Meanwhile the policies of the United States in Vietnam, Africa, Indonesia, and elsewhere, unavoidably reinforce the primitive reactions of a white-supremacist people. Although American leaders officially condemn racism, even now they are slyly invoking the spectre of the yellow peril.

If there is no reason to believe that the race problem can be resolved within the capitalist system, there is even less reason to believe that the black liberation movement can long sustain itself without an anti-capitalist ideology. Stokely Carmichael, once regarded as a leftwing black militant, has declared that the black revolt has nothing to do with capitalism or socialism and that it is a colonial revolution. It is precisely the question of socialism or capitalism, however, that faces the new nations; and it is this same question, at bottom, that faces the black "colony" in the United States.

Historically, black opposition to racial oppression in the United States has taken two forms, separatist and integrationist. Both strains have a long history. In general, the integrationist and civil rights tendency has prevailed during periods in which whites were more receptive than usual to black demands—for example, during Reconstruction or, again, in the 1940's and 1950's. The nationalist and separatist tendency has flourished, on the other hand, during periods of severe white racism and the defeat of integrationist hopes. In the intensely racist years from the 1890's to the First World War, the black community by and large followed Booker T. Washington, whose thought and program ironically contributed to the nationalist tradition. Today, when disillusionment with integrationism is bitter and deep, the separatist tendency is once again ascendant.

In the face of repeated defeats, it is perhaps remarkable that integrationism has survived at all. Its persistence suggests that black Americans know that they are American, not displaced Africans, and that they have always understood, on one or another level of consciousness and sophistication, that their fate is bound up with the fate of the United States. Afro-American culture is part of American culture. There is no South, no Southern culture, no Southern sensibility, not even that vaunted Southern cooking, that does not depend on the contribution of blacks. Whites and blacks in the South, and in America generally, represent two versions of a single people, and although both may cry out in protest, they are condemned to this historical fate. In any case, there is no place to which the black masses can practicably escape. The persisting strength of the integrationist tendency suggests that the black masses know as much, and that their stubborn realism sets definite limits to the separatist appeal.

The separatist tendency cannot, however, be regarded as the creation of a few fanatics. So long as white racism persists, separatism will command respectful attention. Far more than the integrationist tendency, black nationalism has expressed the need to overcome a slave psychology and to repudiate all forms of white paternalism, no matter how indirect or subtle. In these respects it shows more direct response to the sources of black degradation, particularly in the Northern ghettos, than the civil rights tendency has shown.

Black nationalism reflects, more accurately than integrationism, the historical uniqueness of the black experience in America. In its negative and reactive aspect it expresses the intrinsic limits set by white racism to integrationist advance. In its positive and assertive aspect, it rests on the cultural distinctiveness of the American blacks. Thus, it encompasses elements of the black experience that are ignored or imperfectly reflected by the civil rights movement.

Black nationalists have not, however, been able to formulate plausible political demands and to translate cultural nationalism into a program. The demand for five wholly-black states in the South cannot be taken seriously; it is particularly pointless at a time when blacks are a declining portion of the Southern population. The demand for a separate economy likewise ignores economic realities. In the age of oligopoly, the hope that the black community can create its own industrial-financial bourgeoisie represents the height of utopianism. Corporate capitalism long ago crushed the white middle class—defined as owners of property and not as an income or vocational stratum—and reduced its members to the status of retainers and servants of big business. More than fifty years ago, Dr. Du Bois exposed the absurdity of the theory that capital would be forthcoming to establish a separate black economy based on black-capitalist leadership and black-capital accumulation. The reappearance of this idea today suggests, not that changing conditions have made it more tenable—the exact opposite is the case—but that the Left in general, and until recently black intellectuals in particular, have failed to develop an analysis that does justice to the duality of black life in America. Thus, although integrationism has not been able to deliver the promised victory, separatism still remains politically feeble.

The Black Power movement, which today takes new

forms and looks for a new name, is an attempt to overcome precisely this contradiction, to combine the more realistic elements of both integrationism and separatism, and to strike out for a new and practical solution. On the one hand, it calls for local black autonomy—for separate political representation and even for new political institutions, and for black control of schools, police, local businesses, and cultural organs. On the other hand, it demands a fair share of the national economy. To risk oversimplification, it combines cultural nationalism with economic demands that implicitly take integrationist ground. Black Power thus represents in its essence an ingenious compromise, with decent prospects. Black-controlled cultural "enclaves" can reshape the consciousness of the black community, wipe out the legacy of slavery and degradation, and serve as the cultural and political base from which to demand and win a greater share of the national wealth.

The economic side of Black Power requires two things: greater investment in the ghetto itself, and black access to jobs outside the ghetto. The advocates of Black Power have begun to push these demands, but within a basically bourgeois framework. Thus, the corporations are urged to invest in the ghettos, and many spokesmen of the corporations and foundations have themselves taken up the cry. It is extremely doubtful—to say the least—that such measures will eliminate unemployment among blacks. They imply a socially directed relocation of capitalist industry on a vast scale. Even if the corporations were capable of such an effort, the result in any case would merely perpetuate the colonial status of the ghetto. Owned by outside white capitalists or by black capitalists mortgaged to whites, black enterprises would be no more autonomous than capitalist enterprises in undeveloped countries. Outside investment in the ghetto would have a liberating effect only if control of the local economy were lodged in black hands. In the absence of a class of black capitalists, this control could be achieved only through socialized or cooperative community ownership—a new thing for the United States on the scale required to make self-determination a reality.

Even then, most black people would still have to work outside the ghetto. The emergence of a powerful, decentralized, socialist sector has to be accompanied by the socialization of the economy as a whole. If not, the employment of black people in industry would recreate existing patterns of discrimination in new forms. In order for black people to achieve equality in industrial employment, they will have to achieve a share in industrial decision-making. Any such control will have to be exercised at the political level because it implies the socialization of the great corporations. When we add to these problems those mentioned earlier—the need to retrain and to train for the first time millions of people to participate in a modern economy—it is clear, once again, that the economic needs of the black community demand a general restructuring of the entire economy. The Black Power position must either lapse back into a lower-middle-class black nationalism, no more capable than its predecessors of solving the problems it set out to solve, or it must move forward to a socialist position on the nature of American society.

The ultimate success of Black Power depends on the emergence of a mass socialist movement among whites. The blacks cannot make a revolution by themselves, and those whites who look to blacks as a revolutionary vanguard or as leaders of revolutionary change harm both themselves and the black people they claim to befriend. The white Left, like American society as a whole, has had a long history of paternalism toward the black man. White radicals, both in the Old Left and in the New, have professed to defer to blacks as the vanguard of revolutionary change while hoping to use the black movement for their own purposes. The black movement, moreover, has been historically a refuge for the white radicals with escapist tendencies, who seek in the companionship of black people the illusion of revolutionary solidarity as well as a release from bourgeois inhibitions. Black

Power represents, among other things, a revolt against parasitical white radicals who seek in the black movement an ethos, a revolutionary *élan,* and a program they have failed to create in their own movement.

There can be no question that a predominantly white socialist movement will encounter many difficulties in its efforts to effect a coalition with the black liberation movement, especially if the nationalists remain ascendant. In the past, the white Left wittingly or unwittingly tried to use the black movement for its own ends, and certain radical groups continue to try, but the relationship is rapidly being reversed. Today black militants generally show much more talent in manipulating opportunist and naive white Leftists than vice versa. This reversal is, one supposes, some kind of progress, but it can hardly accomplish much for either party. The only proper terms for an alliance between white socialists and black nationalists are those of equality and mutual interest. Since socialists and nationalists have overlapping but not identical interests any coalition must be partial, tentative, and based on specific issues.

The campuses today provide an excellent illustration of the problems besetting those who blithely assert an identity of interests and insist that white radicals should support all black demands. Socialists must champion the institutional autonomy of the university and the cause of academic freedom, if the Left is to have a future. Many black professors and students fully share these goals, whether they are socialists or not, but important sections of the black liberation movement on the campuses do not. The demand for autonomy and student control of black studies programs and the more recent attempts to coordinate all black studies programs from a single extra-university political center do violence to the spirit and letter of university autonomy and academic freedom. The demand that the university be made responsive to the "black community"—although a perfectly reasonable extension of the disgraceful liberal principle of responsiveness to government, business, and the war machine—is in direct conflict with the needs of a socialist program for the campuses. Certainly, these extreme and unreasonable black demands reflect something other than perversity or an irresponsible thirst for power. Those blacks who wish to build their own universities —that is, universities committed to the development of a nationalist intelligentsia and not merely universities for black people—have been frustrated by the hostility and indifference of those with the money and power necessary to support them. Their actions on predominantly white campuses represent a desperate attempt at a flanking movement.

In principle, the resultant tension between white socialists who defend the traditional university and black nationalists who have (for them) more important things on their minds could be resolved by a joint campaign to establish one or more financially secure universities under black control. But the white Left is too weak to have its support for such a project count for anything, and so the blacks are understandably unimpressed by such proposed alliances.

In practice, white socialists are forced to choose sides on issues not of their own making and not in their own interests. In this case we believe they must be prepared to oppose black demands for autonomy or outside control. But however one feels about this issue, it ought to be clear that divisions between socialists and any kind of nationalists are bound to occur. In the long run the only way that the white Left could establish a principled and viable alliance with a generally nationalistic black-liberation movement would be to build its own base; in order to build that base, however, it will have to consult its own interests and ally with or oppose specific black demands on their merits.

The commitment to black self-determination must be firm, but it does not imply acceptance of any interpretation or strategy that happens to be popular in black circles. When, for example, blacks seek to control their local schools, as during the Ocean Hill-Brownsville struggle in New York City, they deserve full support, but when they—as they must—call for reorganization of the school system in the city as a whole, then each demand must be judged separately and with full respect for the just claims of white working-class and middle-class communities.

Until the white Left gets itself together behind a constructive and practicable program for change, instead of attempting to ride the coattails of the black movement, black people will be understandably suspicious of interracial alliances. Nor will they be attracted to socialism until socialists can offer a program that addresses itself to the specific needs of the ghetto. So long as socialism identifies itself with centralized power and with schemes for nationalization based on the social conditions of a hundred years ago, it will have no more to offer black people than it has to offer the working class. What we have said about the socialist implications of Black Power, therefore, should not be construed as a reproach to black intellectuals for not developing a socialist theory. Rather, it is a reproach to white socialists who have sought to use the black movement as a short-cut to power while neglecting their real duties: to combat white racism among workers and the new middle class; to create a socialist theory that speaks to the need of blacks as well as of whites for political decentralization and cultural self-determination; and to build a movement capable of transforming American society.

If the main lines of this analysis are correct, certain points may be summarized and extended.

1) Racism in America has grown out of a complex conjunction of historical forces and cannot be viewed as a class question except in a special sense—namely, that its destruction demands the destruction of bourgeois hegemony over the American people.

2) The distinctive history of the blacks in America has made them at once a separate nation and a part of the American nation. Given the element of separate nationality, black people's right to self-determination must be respected. We do

not advocate separation. Among whites, only racists can advocate separation, for it is clear that the reason blacks wish to separate, even when they wish to develop their distinctiveness as a matter of pride and sensibility, is that they cannot now live decently among white people. Whites who oppose racism have the duty to make America the kind of country from which blacks would have no desire to separate, even if they wished to cultivate a large measure of ethnic distinctiveness. Blacks, however, retain the right to do so under any conditions, and this right must be strictly respected.

3) Since total integration or complete separation appear equally utopian, it seems likely that the Black Power movement will coalesce around a program that avoids the pitfalls of both and combines national consciousness and limited separation with a new approach to integration at the economic level. To repeat: this is not "our" program for black America, which has not asked our advice; it is our estimate of the direction of events.

4) If, as seems probable, black Americans will find that it is impossible to destroy racism within a bourgeois framework, they will find their own road to socialism. The only way whites can or should influence this process is to build a socialist movement in white America. American radicals must give up their unrequited affair with the black liberation movement. They must abandon all illusions that the black movement will lead the white working class to victory against the capitalist system. Whites cannot expect black people to solve their problems, nor vice versa. The problems overlap and require in part the same general solution, but they remain distinct.

5) The task of American socialists is to build a socialist movement that will be free of the hidden racism that has so often characterized radical movements in the United States. Specifically, it is to win the white middle and working classes to a sympathetic understanding of the two-fold nature of black demands, by demonstrating that the demands are not only just but can be realized without threatening the social

and economic gains of the white community. Whites retain a good deal of good will toward blacks, together with a bad conscience. But they are wracked with fear. What has to be insisted on is that the cost of realizing black demands need not and should not be charged to the lower and middle sections of the white population. The working and middle classes will have to pay only if bourgeois priorities continue to be adhered to. In the coming years, capitalism's incapacity to destroy racism and to provide just solutions to the problems it created will furnish another and particularly ugly proof of its bankruptcy.

Chapter 4

REBELLIOUSNESS AND DOCILITY IN THE NEGRO SLAVE A Critique of the Elkins Thesis

DESPITE THE HOSTILE RECEPTION given by historians to Stanley M. Elkins's *Slavery: A Problem in American Institutional and Intellectual Life*,[1] it has established itself as one of the most influential historical essays of our generation. Although Elkins ranges widely, we may restrict ourselves to his most important contribution, the theory of slave personality, and bypass other questions, such as his dubious theory of uncontrolled capitalism in the South. His psychological model would fit comfortably into other social theories and may, up to a point, be analytically isolated.

Elkins asserts that the Sambo stereotype arose only in the United States. He attempts to explain this allegedly unique personality type by constructing a social analysis that contrasts a totalitarian plantation South with a feudal Latin America in which church, state, and plantation balanced one another. To relate this ostensible difference in social structure to the formation of slave personality he invokes an analogy to Nazi concentration camps to demonstrate the possibility of mass infantilization and proceeds to apply three theories of person-

This essay was originally published in *Civil War History*, 13, Dec. 1966, pp. 293–314.

ality: (1) the Freudian, which relates the growth of a personality to the existence of a father figure and which accounts for the identification of a tyrannized child with a tyrannical father; (2) Sullivan's theory of "significant others," which relates the growth of a personality to its interaction with individuals who hold or seem to hold power over its fortunes; and (3) role theory, which relates the growth of a personality to the number and kinds of roles it can play.[2] Elkins assumes that Sambo existed only in the United States and that our task is to explain his unique appearance in the Old South. I propose to show, on the contrary, that Sambo existed wherever slavery existed, that he nonetheless could turn into a rebel, and that we need to discover the conditions under which the personality pattern could become inverted and a seemingly docile slave could suddenly turn fierce.

Elkins asserts that the United States alone produced the Sambo stereotype—"the perpetual child incapable of maturity." He does not, as so many of his critics insist, equate childishness with docility, although he carelessly gives such an impression. Rather, he equates it with dependence and, with a subtlety that seems to elude his detractors, skillfully accounts for most forms of day-to-day resistance. His thesis, as will be shown later, is objectionable not because it fails to account for hostile behavior, but because it proves too much and encompasses more forms of behavior than can usefully be managed under a single rubric.

Elkins's assumption that the existence of a stereotype proves the reality behind it will not stand critical examination either as psychological theory or as historical fact. As psychological theory, it is at least open to question. John Harding and his collaborators have argued that stereotypes, under certain conditions, may in fact be without foundation;[3] this side of the problem may be left to specialists and need not alter the main lines of the argument. Historically, Sambo was emerging in the United States at the same time he was emerging in the French colonies. Negroes, if we would believe the French planters, were childlike, docile, helpless creatures up until the very moment they rose and slaughtered the whites. Accordingly, I have a sporting proposition for Elkins. Let us substitute French Saint-Domingue for the United States and apply his logic. We find a Sambo stereotype and a weak tradition of rebellion. True, there was a century of maroon activity, but only the efforts of Mackandal constituted a genuine revolt. Those efforts were, in the words of C. L. R. James, "the only hint of an organized attempt at revolt during the hundred years preceding the French Revolution."[4] Boukman's revolt ought properly to be regarded as the first phase of the great revolution of 1791 rather than a separate action. In short, when the island suddenly exploded in the greatest slave revolution in history, nothing lay behind it but Sambo and a few hints. Now, let us rewrite history by having the French Jacobins take power and abolish slavery in 1790, instead of 1794. With the aid of that accident the slaves would have been freed as the result of the vicissitudes of Jacobin-Girondist factionalism and not by their own efforts. We would then today be reading a Haitian Elkins whose task would be to explain the extraordinary docility of the country's blacks. As the rewriting of history goes, this excursion requires little effort and ought to make us aware of how suddenly a seemingly docile, or at least adjusted, people can rise in violence. It would be much safer to assume that dangerous and strong currents run beneath that docility and adjustment.

Reaching further back into history, we find an identification of Negroes, including Africans, with a Sambo-like figure. As early as the fourteenth century—and there is no reason to believe that it began that late—so learned and sophisticated a scholar as Ibn Khaldun could write:

> Negroes are in general characterized by levity, excitability, and great emotionalism. They are found eager to dance whenever they hear a melody. They are everywhere described as stupid . . . . The Negro nations are, as a rule, submissive to

> slavery, because (Negroes) have little (that is essentially) human and have attributes that are quite similar to those of dumb animals.[5]

In 1764, in Portugal, a pamphlet on the slavery question in the form of a dialogue has a Brazilian slaveowning mine operator say: "I have always observed that in Brazil the Negroes are treated worse than animals . . . . Yet, withal the blacks endure this." The conclusion drawn was that this submissiveness proved inferiority.[6]

Sambo appears throughout Brazilian history, especially during the nineteenth century. In the 1830s the ideologues of Brazilian slavery, significantly under strong French influence, assured planters that the black was a "man-child" with a maximum mental development equivalent to that of a white adolescent. This and similar views were widespread among planters, particularly in the highly commercialized southern coffee region.[7] Brazilian sociologists and historians accepted this stereotype well into the twentieth century. Euclides da Cunha, in his masterpiece, *Rebellion in the Backlands,* described the Negro as "a powerful organism, given to an extreme humility, without the Indian's rebelliousness."[8] Oliveira Lima, in his pioneering comparative history of Brazil and Spanish and Anglo-Saxon America, described the Negro as an especially subservient element.[9] João Pandía Calógeras, in his long standard *History of Brazil,* wrote:

> The Negro element in general revealed a perpetual good humor, a childish and expansive joy, a delight in the slightest incidentals of life . . . . Filled with the joy of youth, a ray of sunshine illumined his childlike soul. Sensitive, worthy of confidence, devoted to those who treated him well, capable of being led in any direction by affection and kind words, the Negro helped to temper the primitive harshness of the Portuguese colonists.[10]

One of the leading interpretations in Brazil today regards the blacks as having been subjected to a regime designed to produce alienation and the destruction of the personality by means of the exercise of the arbitrary power of the master. The account given in Kenneth M. Stampp's *The Peculiar Institution* of the efforts to produce a perfect slave has a close parallel in Octávio Ianni's *As Metamorfoses do Escravo*, which analyzes southern Brazil during the nineteenth century.[11]

Nor did Sambo absent himself from Spanish America. The traditional advocacy of Indian freedom often went together with a defense of Negro slavery based on an alleged inferiority that suggests a Sambo stereotype.[12] In 1816, Simón Bolívar wrote to General Jean Marión of Haiti:

> I have proclaimed the absolute emancipation of the slaves. The tyranny of the Spaniards has reduced them to such a state of stupidity and instilled in their souls such a great sense of terror that they have lost even the desire to be free!! Many of them would have followed the Spaniards or have embarked on British vessels [whose owners] have sold them in neighboring colonies.[13]

Elkins cites evidence that the Spanish regarded the Indians as docile and the Negroes as difficult to control, but evidence also exists that shows the reverse. The view of the Indian or Negro as docile or rebellious varied greatly with time, place, and circumstance.[14] Sidney Mintz, with one eye on Cuba and Puerto Rico and the other eye on Brazil, has suggested that, regardless of institutional safeguards, the more commercialized the slave system the more it tended to produce dehumanization. This thesis needs considerable refinement but is at least as suggestive as Elkins's attempt to construct a purely institutional interpretation.[15]

On close inspection the Sambo personality turns out to be

neither more nor less than the slavish personality; wherever slavery has existed, Sambo has also.[16] "Throughout history" David Brion Davis has written, "it has been said that slaves, though occasionally as loyal and faithful as good dogs, were for the most part lazy, irresponsible, cunning, rebellious, untrustworthy, and sexually promiscuous."[17] Only the element of rebelliousness does not seem to fit Sambo, but on reflection, even that does. Sambo, being a child, could be easily controlled but if not handled properly, would revert to barbarous ways. Davis demonstrates that by the fifth century B.C. many Greeks had come to regard the submission of barbarians to despotic and absolute rulers as proof of inferiority.[18] By the end of the eighteenth century, America and Europe widely accepted the image of the dehumanized black slave, and even Reynal believed that crime and indolence would inevitably follow emancipation.[19]

Sambo has a much longer pedigree and a much wider range than Elkins appreciates. Audrey I. Richards, in 1939, noted the widespread existence of "fatal resignation" among primitive peoples in Africa and suggested that their psychological and physical sluggishness might be attributable in a large part to poor diet and severe malnutrition.[20] Josué de Castro, former head of the United Nations Food and Agriculture Organization, has made the same point about Brazilian slaves and about people in underdeveloped countries in general.[21] As Jean-Paul Sartre has suggested, "Beaten, undernourished, ill, terrified—but only up to a certain point—he has, whether he's black, yellow, or white, always the same traits of character: he's a slyboots, a lazybones, and a thief, who lives on nothing and who understands only violence."[22] By constructing a single-factor analysis and erroneously isolating the personality structure of the Southern slave, Elkins has obscured many other possible lines of inquiry. We do not as yet have a comparative analysis of slave diets in the United States, Brazil, and the West Indies, although it might tell us a great deal about personality patterns.

It is generally believed that Elkins merely repeated Tannenbaum when he declared Sambo to be a native of the Old South; in fact, the assertion is, for better or worse, entirely his own. I would not dwell on this point were it not that I cannot imagine Tannenbaum's taking so one-sided a view. I intend no disrespect to Elkins by this observation, for, as a matter of fact, his single-mindedness, even when misguided, has helped him to expose problems others have missed entirely. Elkins's greatest weakness, nonetheless, is his inability to accept the principle of contradiction, to realize that all historical phenomena must be regarded as constituting a process of becoming, and that, therefore, the other-sidedness of the most totalitarian conditions may in fact represent the unfolding of their negation. If Sambo were merely Sambo, then Elkins must explain how an overseer could publicly defend his class, without challenge, for having "to punish and keep in order the negroes, at the risk of his life."[23]

Elkins recognizes a wide range of institutional factors as having contributed to the contrast between the Latin and Anglo-Saxon slave systems, but he places special emphasis on the system of law in relation to the structure and policies of Church and Crown.[24] Although in this way Elkins follows Tannenbaum, he necessarily must go well beyond him, and therein lies his greatest difficulty. Tannenbaum's well known thesis need not be reviewed here, but we might profitably recall his suggestive comment on *Las Siete Partidas:*

> *Las Siete Partidas* was formed within the Christian doctrine, and the slave had a body of law, protective of him as a human being, which was already there when the Negro arrived and had been elaborated long before he came upon the scene.[25]

The essential point of Tannenbaum's contrast between this legal tradition and that of Anglo-Saxon lies in its bearing on the problem of emancipation. Whereas the Hispanic tradition favored and encouraged it, the Anglo-Saxon blocked it.[26]

So long as a general contrast can be demonstrated, Tannenbaum's thesis obtains, for he is primarily concerned with the social setting into which the Negro plunged upon emancipation. His thesis, therefore, can absorb criticism such as that of Arnold A. Sio, who argues that the Romans assimilated the rights of their slaves to property despite a legal code which respected the moral personality of the slave. Sio finds evidence of a similar tendency in Latin as well as Anglo-Saxon America.[27] Tannenbaum's thesis would fall only if the tendency were equally strong everywhere; but obviously it was not.[28] Elkins, however, cannot absorb such qualifications, for he necessarily must demonstrate the uniqueness of the southern pattern as well as the absoluteness of the contrast with Latin America. If the contrast could be reduced to a matter of degree, then we should be left with more American than Latin American Sambos, but Elkins's notion of a special American personality pattern and problem would fall.

Elkins, like Tannenbaum, ignores the French slave colonies, but nowhere was the gap between law and practice so startling. The *Code Noir* of 1685 set a high standard of humanity and attempted to guarantee the slaves certain minimal rights and protection. It was treated with contempt in the French West Indies, especially when the islands began to ride the sugar boom. It was enough to quote a governor of Martinique, one of the men charged with the enforcement of these laws: "I have reached the stage of believing firmly that one must treat the Negroes as one treats beasts."[29] On the eve of the Haitian Revolution probably not one of the protective articles of the *Code Noir* was being enforced.[30]

Elkins offers Brazil as a counterpoint to the Old South and invokes the Iberian legal tradition, together with the power of Church and Crown. Yet, even Gilberto Freyre, on whom Elkins relies so heavily, writes of the widespread murders of slaves by enraged masters.[31] As late as the nineteenth century, slaves were being whipped to death in the presence of all hands. The law might say what it would, but the *senhores* controlled the police apparatus and supported the doctors who falsified the death certificates.[32] The measures designed to prevent wanton killing of slaves do not seem to have been better in Latin America than in Anglo-Saxon America.[33] If Brazilian slaves went to the police to complain about unjust or illegally excessive punishment, the police would, in Freyre's words, give them a double dose.[34] If the law mattered much, we need to know the reason for the repeated re-enactment of legislation to protect slaves. The famous Rio Branco Law of 1871, for example, granted slaves rights they were supposed to have enjoyed for centuries, and these too remained largely unrespected.

The Portuguese Crown could legislate in any manner it wished, and so later could the Emperor of Brazil; local power resided with the senhores, as the emissaries of the Crown learned soon enough. We may imagine conditions in the first three centuries of colonization from Freyre's succinct comment on conditions in the middle of the nineteenth century: "The power of the great planters was indeed feudalistic, their patriarchalism being hardly restricted by civil laws."[35] Not until that time did a strong central government arise to challenge effectively the great planters.[36] That the contrast with the Old South might have been the reverse of what Elkins thinks is suggested by the diary of an ex-Confederate who fled to Brazil after the war. George S. Barnsley, formerly a Georgia planter and Confederate army surgeon, complained as late as 1904 of the lack of government and the prevalence of virtually feudal conditions.[37]

Las Siete Partidas constituted a theoretical work and standard of values, the importance of which ought not to be minimized, but it had little to do with the actual practice on which Elkins's thesis depends.[38] The kind of protection that transcended the theoretical and might have conditioned decisively the personality development of the slave population as a whole probably did not appear until the *Real Cédula* of 1789. As Davis suggests, "There are many indications, moreover, that Spanish planters paid little attention to the law."[39]

Elkins assumes that the strongly centralized Spanish state could and did prevail over the planters. No doubt it did in matters of prime importance to its survival and income. In most matters, notwithstanding its best efforts at institutional control, the planters continued to have their way on their own estates. The Spanish court promulgated humane legislation to protect the natives of the Canary Islands, but attempts at enforcement so far from home proved futile. The problem swelled enormously when transferred to the West Indies, not to mention to the mainland.[40] The fate of the protective features of the Laws of Burgos (1512) and of similar legislation is well known.[41] The British and other foreigners who did business in Spanish America ridiculed the mass of laws and the clumsy administrative apparatus designed to enforce them. As the agent of the South Sea Company at Jamaica noted in 1736, he who wants to deal illegally with the Spanish officials needs only the cash necessary to bribe them.[42] The lot of the slaves could, under such conditions, hardly reflect other than the disposition of the masters. A case study by Jaime Jaramillo Uribe of the judicial system of New Grenada shows that even the reform laws of the eighteenth century could not reach down into the plantations to protect the slaves.[43]

Much of Elkins's treatment of Spanish law deals with Cuba and flows from the work of Herbert Klein.[44] Without attempting a close examination of the intricacies of the Cuban case, we ought to note that it presents a striking picture of a bitter struggle between planters and state officials. The planters, there too, usually won the day. The liberal Governor Concha finally admitted that the resistance of the slaveowners to government intervention was justified by the necessity for controlling the blacks and avoiding any ambiguity in authority. In 1845 the government did seriously challenge the masters' power, but the uproar proved so great that the militant officials had to be removed.[45]

The fate of the law during the sugar boom requires more attention than Elkins and Klein have given it. In its earlier phases Cuban slavery was exceptionally mild and fit much of Elkins's schema. When the Haitian Revolution removed the Caribbean's leading sugar producer from the world market, Cuba entered into a period of wild expansion and prosperity. The status of the slave declined accordingly. The old institutional arrangements did not disappear, but their bearing on the life of the great mass of slaves became minimal or nonexistent.[46]

The legal and political structure of Spanish America in general and of Cuba in particular helped ease the way to freedom by providing a setting in which the slave might be abused brutally but retained a significant degree of manhood in the eyes of society. For Tannenbaum's purpose, this distinction establishes the argument: the slave was abused as a slave but only incidentally as a Negro. The master might rule with absolute authority, but only because he could get away with it, not because it was, by the standards of his own class, church, and society, just and proper. Tannenbaum and Freyre do make too much of this argument. The persistence and depth of racial discrimination and prejudice in twentieth century Brazil and Cuba ought to remind us that the enslavement of one race by another must generate racist doctrines among all social classes as well as the intelligentsia. Qualitative and quantitative distinctions nonetheless obtain, and Tannenbaum's argument requires correction and greater specificity, not rejection. For Elkins, Tannenbaum's distinction, however qualified, is not enough. If, as seems likely, the great majority of the slaves labored under such absolutism, theoretical or not, their personalities would have been shaped in response to conditions equivalent to those he describes for the United States.

In the United States, as in the British West Indies and everywhere else, custom and conventional moral standards had greater force than the law, as Ulrich B. Phillips long ago argued. Just as the vast range of rights granted the slaves in Latin America usually proved unenforceable in a society in which power was largely concentrated in local planter oligarchies, so in Anglo-Saxon America the quasi-absolute power of the master was tempered by the prevailing ethos. Tannenbaum, and especially Elkins, go much too far in denying that English and American law recognized the moral personality of the slave. As Davis has demonstrated, the double nature of the slave as thing and man had to be, and in one way or another was, recognized in law and custom by every slave society since ancient times. As a result, every southern planter knew intuitively the limits of his power, as imposed by the prevailing standards of decency. If he exceeded those limits, he might not suffer punishment at law and might even be strong enough to prevent his being ostracized by disapproving neighbors. For these reasons historians have dismissed community pressure as a factor. In doing so, they err badly, for the point is not at all what happened to a violator of convention but the extent to which the overwhelming majority of slaveholders internalized conventional values. In this respect the legal structures of Brazil and the United States were important in conditioning those conventional values. Once again, the difference between the two cases suffices for Tannenbaum's thesis but not for Elkins's, which depends entirely on the experience of absolute power by the slave.

Elkins follows Tannenbaum in ascribing a special role to the Catholic Church in the development of Ibero-American slave societies. The Church defended the moral personality of the slave from a position of independent institutional strength, whereas in the Anglo-Saxon world the separation of church and state, the bourgeois notion of property rights, and the divisions within the religious community largely excluded the churches from the field of master-slave relations. The religious as well as the legal structure helped generate a particular climate of moral opinion into which the Negro could fit as a free man. The difference in structure and result satisfies Tannenbaum's argument; it does not satisfy Elkins's argument, which turns on the specific role played by the priesthood in the life of the slave.

Since Brazil, as the largest Catholic slaveholding country, ought properly to serve as a test case, we might profitably begin with a consideration of developments in Angola, which supplied a large part of its slaves. The clergy, including Jesuits and Dominicans, participated in every horror associated with the slave trade; there is little evidence of its having played a mediating role.[47] By the middle of the seventeenth century Catholic proselytism in the Congo and Angola had spent its force. Contemporary Catholic sources admitted that much of the failure was due to the greed of the clergy in pursuing slave-trade profits and to the generally venal character of priests, secular officials, and laymen.[48] The governor of Angola, the troops, the bishop, and the entire staff of civil and ecclesiastical officials drew their salaries from the direct and indirect proceeds of the slave trade. The Holy House of Mercy [*Misericórdia*] at Luanda, as well as the Municipal Council [*Camara*] lived off the trade. Since the *Junta das missoẽs,* the chief missionary agency, was supported by these proceeds we need not be surprised that it accomplished little.[49]

In Brazil itself the decisive questions concern the number, character, and relative independence of the priests.[50] We have little data on numbers, but in the mid-twentieth century, Brazil, with a population of fifty million, of whom ninety-five per cent were nominal Catholics, had, according to Vianna Moog, only six thousand priests.[51] We may, nonetheless, assume for a moment that a high ratio of priests to slaves existed. There is good reason to believe that a significant percentage of the priests who ventured to the colonies had questionable characters and that many of good character succumbed to the indolence, violence, and corruption that marked their isolated, quasi-frontier environment. It is no insult to the Church to affirm this state of affairs, for the

Church has had to struggle for centuries to raise the quality of its priests and to maintain high standards of performance. Like other institutions of this world it has consisted of men with all the weaknesses of men, and in the difficult circumstances of colonial life the adherence of its men to the high standards of the Church Militant proved erratic and uncertain.

Even if we grant the Brazilian clergy a higher quality than it probably deserved, we confront the question of its relationship to the master class. The local chaplain depended on and deferred to the planter he served more than he depended on his bishop. The Brazilian Church never achieved the strength and cohesion of the Church in Spanish America. The typical sugar planter, in Freyre's words, "though a devout Catholic, was a sort of Philip II in regard to the Church: he considered himself more powerful than the bishops or abbots." Under these conditions the interposition of priest between master and slave was probably little more significant than the interposition of the mistress on a plantation in Mississippi. The analogy assumes particular force when we consider that, increasingly, the Brazilian priesthood was recruited from the local aristocracy.[52] In coffee-growing southern Brazil, in which slavery centered during the nineteenth century, few priests resided on plantations at all and visits were possibly less common than in the United States. The large number of Africans imported during 1830–1850 received little attention from the Church.[53]

The situation in Spanish America worked out more favorably for Elkins's argument because the Church there came much closer to that independence and crusading spirit which has been attributed to it. Even so, the ruthless exploitation of Indians and Negroes by large sections of the clergy is well documented. The position of the Church as a whole, taken over centuries, demonstrates its growing subservience to state and secular power in respects that were decisive for Elkins's purposes. The bulls of Popes and the decrees of kings proved inadequate to temper the rule of the great planters of the New World, although they did play a role in shaping their moral consciousness.[51] In Cuba the clergy acted more boldly and, according to Klein, had a numerical strength adequate to its tasks. However, the effective interposition of even the Cuban clergy during the sugar boom of the nineteenth century has yet to be demonstrated, and if it were to be, Cuba would stand as an exception to the rule.

That more Brazilian and Cuban slaves attended religious services than did Southern is by no means certain, the law to the contrary notwithstanding. That the Catholic clergy of Latin America interposed itself more often and more effectively than the Protestant clergy of the South cannot be denied. On balance, Tannenbaum's case is proven by the ability of the Catholic Church to help shape the ethos of slave society and the relative inability of the Protestant to do the same. But Elkins's case falls, for the difference in the potentialities for and especially the realities of personal interposition remained a matter of degree.

Despite the efforts of law and Church in Latin America it is quite possible that as high or higher a percentage of Southern slaves lived in stable family units than did Latin American. The force of custom and sentiment generally prevailed over the force of law or institutional interference. In Brazil, as in the Caribbean, male slaves greatly outnumbered female; in the United States the sexes were numerically equal. This factor alone, which derived primarily from economic and technological conditions, encouraged greater family stability in the United States and therefore casts great doubt on Elkins's thesis. To the extent that participation in a stable family life encouraged the development of a mature personality, the slaves of the South probably fared no worse than others. Elkins argues that the Latin American families could not be broken up because of Church and state restrictions. In fact, they often were broken up in open defiance of both.

The greatest guarantee against sale existed not where the law forbade it, but where economic conditions reduced the necessity.

The attendant argument that Latin American slaves could function in the roles of fathers and mothers, whereas Southern slaves could not, is altogether arbitrary. The feeling of security within the family depended on custom and circumstance, not law, and a great number of southern slaves worked for masters whose economic position and paternalistic attitudes provided a reasonable guarantee against separate sales. In any case, all slaves in all societies faced similar problems. When a slaveowner beat or raped a slave woman in Brazil or Cuba, her husband was quite as helpless as any black man in Mississippi. The duties, responsibilities, and privileges of fatherhood were, in practice, little different from one place to another.

The point of Elkins's controversial concentration camp analogy is not altogether clear. Sometimes he seems to wish to demonstrate only the possibility of mass infantilization, but if this were all he intended, he could have done so briefly and without risking the hostile reaction he brought down on himself. At other times he seems to intend the analogy as a direct device. Although he denies saying that slavery was a concentration camp or even "like" a concentration camp, he does refer to concentration camps as perverted patriarchies and extreme forms of slavery; he finds in them the same total power he believes to have existed on the Southern plantations. In the first, restricted, sense the analogy, used suggestively, has its point, for it suggests the ultimate limits of the slave experience. In the second, and broader, sense it offers little and is generally misleading. Unfortunately, Elkins sometimes exaggerates and confuses his device, which only demonstrates the limiting case, with the historical reality of slavery. His elaborate discussion of detachment offers clues but is dangerously misleading. The process did not differ for slaves bound for different parts of the New World; only the post-shock experience of the slave regimes differed, so that we are led right back to those regimes. No doubt Elkins makes a good point when he cites concentration camp and slave trade evidence to show that many participants were spiritually broken by the process, but he overlooks the contribution of newly imported Africans to slave disorders. Everywhere in the Americas a correlation existed between concentrations of African-born slaves and the outbreak of revolts. The evidence indicates that creole slaves were generally more adjusted to enslavement that those who had undergone the shock and detachment processes from Africa to America.[55]

The fundamental differences between the concentration camp and plantation experience may be gleaned from a brief consideration of some of the points made in Bruno Bettelheim's study, on which Elkins relies heavily.[56] Prisoners received inadequate clothing and food in order to test their reaction to extremities of inclement weather and their ability to work while acutely hungry. Slaves received clothing and food designed to provide at least minimum comfort. Slaves suffered from dietary deficiencies and hidden hungers, but rarely from outright malnutrition. In direct contrast to prisoners, slaves normally did not work outdoors in the rain or extreme cold; usually, they were deliberately ordered to stay indoors. Pneumonia and other diseases killed too many slaves every winter for planters not to take every precaution to guard their health. Therein lay the crucial differences: prisoners might be kept alive for experimental purposes, but slaves received treatment designed to grant them long life. Prisoners often did useless work as part of a deliberate program to destroy their personality; slaves did, and knew they did, the productive work necessary for their own sustenance. Prisoners were forbidden to talk to each other much of the day and had virtually no privacy and no social life. Slaves maintained a many-sided social life, which received considerable encouragement from their masters. The Gestapo deliberately set out to deny the individuality of prisoners or to permit distinctions among them. Planters and overseers made every effort to take full account of slave individuality and even to encourage it up to a point. Prisoners were deliberately subjected to torture and arbitrary punishment; those who followed orders endured the same indignities and blows as those who did not. Slaves, despite considerable arbitrariness in the system, generally had the option of currying favor and avoiding punishment. As Hannah Arendt has so perceptively observed: "Under conditions of total terror not even fear can any longer serve as an advisor of how to behave, because terror chooses its victims without reference to individual actions or thoughts, exclusively in accordance with the objective necessity of the natural or historical process."[57] Concentration camp prisoners changed work groups and barracks regularly and could not develop attachments. Slaves had families and friends, often for a lifetime. The Gestapo had no interest in indoctrinating prisoners. It demanded obedience, not loyalty. Masters wanted and took great pains to secure the loyalty and ideological adherence of their slaves. In general, the slave plantation was a social system, full of joys and sorrows and a fair degree of security, notwithstanding great harshness and even brutality, whereas the concentration camp was a particularly vicious death cell. They shared a strong degree of authoritarianism, but so does the army or a revolutionary party, or even a family unit.

With these criticisms of data we may turn to Elkins's discussion of personality theory. His use of Sullivan's theory of "significant others" breaks down because of his erroneous notion of the absolute power of the master. In theory the master's power over the slave in the United States was close to absolute; so in theory was the power of Louis XIV over the French. In practice, the plantation represented a series of compromises between whites and blacks. Elkins's inability to see the slaves as active forces capable of tempering the authority of the master leads him into a one-sided appraisal.[58]

According to Elkins, the Latin American slave could relate meaningfully to the friar on the slave ship; the confessor who made the plantation rounds; the zealous Jesuit who especially defended the sanctity of the family; the local magistrate who had to contend with the Crown's official protector of the slaves; and any informer who could expect to collect one-third of the fines. In general, it would not be unfair to say that, notwithstanding all these institutional niceties, the Latin American slaveowners, especially the Brazilian, ruled their plantations as despotically as any Southerner. Priest, magistrate, and anyone careless enough to risk his life to play the informer came under the iron grip of the plantation owners' enormous local power.

Various other persons did affect meaningfully the lives of slaves in all systems. The plantation mistress often acted to soften her husband's rule. The overseer did not always precisely reflect the master's temperament and wishes, and slaves demonstrated great skill in playing the one against the other. The Negro driver often affected their lives more directly than anyone else and had considerable authority to make their lives easy or miserable. Slaves who found it difficult to adjust to a master's whims or who feared punishment often ran to some other planter in the neighborhood to ask for his intercession, which they received more often than not. Elkins ignores these and other people because they had no lawful right to intervene; but they did have the power of persuasion in a world of human beings with human reactions. To the vast majority of slaves in all systems, the power of the master approached the absolute and yet was tempered by many human relationships and sensibilities. To the extent that slavery, in all societies, restricted the number of "significant others," it may well have contributed toward the formation of a slavish personality, but Latin America differed from the South only in permitting a somewhat larger minority to transcend that effect.

Similar objections may be made with reference to the application of role theory. The Latin American slave could ordinarily no more act the part of a husband or father than could the Southern. The typical field hand had roughly the same degree of prestige and authority in his own cabin in all societies. Legal right to property did not make most Latin American slaves property owners in any meaningful sense, and many Southern slaves were de facto property owners of the same kind. The theoretical right of the one and the mere privilege of the other did not present a great practical difference, for the attitude of the master was decisive in both cases. For Tannenbaum's social analysis the significance of the difference stands; for Elkins's psychological analysis it does not.

The theory of personality that Elkins seems to slight, but uses to greatest advantage, is the Freudian, perhaps because it offers a simple direct insight quite apart from its more technical formulations. We do not need an elaborate psychological theory to help us understand the emergence of the slaveowner as a father figure. As the source of all privileges, gifts, and necessaries, he loomed as a great benefactor, even when he simultaneously functioned as a great oppressor. Slaves, forced into dependence on their master, viewed him with awe and identified their interests and even their wills with his. Elkins's analogy with concentration camp prisoners who began to imitate their SS guards indicates the extreme case of this tendency. All exploited classes manifest something of this tendency —the more servile the class the stronger the tendency. It is what many contemporary observers, including runaway slaves and abolitionists, meant when they spoke of the reduction of the slave to a groveling creature without initiative and a sense of self-reliance. Elkins, using Freudian insight, has transformed this observation into the politically relevant suggestion that the slave actually learned to see himself through his master's eyes.

Elkins has often been criticized for failing to realize that slaves usually acted as expected while they retained inner reservations, but he did recognize this possibility in his discussion of a "broad belt of indeterminacy" between playing a role and becoming the role you always play. The criticism seems to me to miss the point. The existence of such reservations might weaken the notion of total infantilization but would not touch the less extreme notion of a dependent, emasculated personality. The clever slave outwitted his master at least partly because he was supposed to. Masters enjoyed the game: it strengthened their sense of superiority, confirmed the slaves' dependence, and provided a sense of pride in having so clever a man-child. On the slave's side it made him a devilishly delightful fellow but hardly a man. The main point against Elkins here is the same as elsewhere—when he is sound he describes not a southern slave but a slave; not a distinctly Southern Sambo personality but a slavish personality.[59]

Elkins's general argument contains a fundamental flaw, which, when uncovered, exposes all the empirical difficulties under review. In his model a regime of total power produces a Sambo personality. Confronted by the undeniable existence of exceptions, he pleads first things first and waves them aside as statistically insignificant. Even if we were to agree that they were statistically insignificant, we are left with a serious problem. Elkins did not construct a model to determine probabilities; he constructed a deterministic model, which he cannot drop suddenly to suit his convenience. The notion of "total power" loses force and usefulness and indeed approaches absurdity in a world of probabilities and alternatives. If Elkins were to retreat from this notion and consequently from his determinism, he could not simply make an adjustment in his model; he would have to begin, as we must, from different premises, although without necessarily sacrificing his remarkable insights and suggestions. If the basic personality pattern arose from the nature of the regime, so did the deviant patterns. It would be absurd to argue that a regime could be sufficiently complex to generate two or more such patterns and yet sufficiently simple to generate them in mutual isolation. The regime threw up all the patterns at once, whatever the proportions, and the root of every deviation lay in the same social structure that gave us Sambo.

This range of patterns arose from the disparity between the plantations and farms, between resident owners and absentees, and above all between the foibles and sensibilities of one master and another. They arose, too, within every slaveholding unit from the impossibility of absolute power—from the qualities, perhaps inherited, of the particular personalities of slaves as individuals; from the inconsistencies in the human behavior of the severest masters; from the room that even a slave plantation provides for breathing, laughing, crying, and combining acquiescence and protest in a single thought, expression, and action. Even modern totalitarian regimes, self-consciously armed with unprecedented weapons of terror, must face that opposition inherent in the human spirit to which Miss Arendt draws attention. The freedom of man cannot be denied even by totalitarian rulers, "for this freedom—irrelevant and arbitrary as they may deem it—is identical with the fact that men are being born and that therefore each of them *is* a new beginning, begins, in a sense, the world anew."[60] We need not pretend to understand adequately that remarkable process of spiritual regeneration which repeatedly unfolds before our eyes. The evidence extends throughout history, including the history of our own day; its special forms and content, not its existence, constitute our problem. Miss Arendt therefore concludes her analysis of terror wisely: "Every end in history necessarily contains a new beginning . . . . Beginning, before it becomes a historical event, is the supreme capacity of man; politically, it is identical with man's freedom . . . . This beginning is guaranteed by each new birth; it is indeed every man."[61]

Sambo himself had to be a product of a contradictory environment, all sides of which he necessarily internalized. Sambo, in short, was jarred from within or without; he might then well have become Nat Turner, for every element antithetical to his being a Sambo resided in his nature. "Total power" and "Sambo" may serve a useful purpose in a theoretical model as a rough approximation to a complex reality, provided that we do not confuse the model with the reality itself. Neither slavery nor slaves can be treated as pure categories, free of the contradictions, tensions, and potentialities that characterize all human experience.

Elkins, in committing himself to these absolutist notions, overlooks the evidence from his own concentration camp analogy. Bettelheim notes that even the most accommodating, servile, and broken-spirited prisoners sometimes suddenly defied the Gestapo with great courage. Eugen Kogon devotes considerable space in his *Theory and Practice of Hell* to the development and maintenance of resistance within the camps.[62] In a similar way the most docile field slaves or the most trusted house slaves might, and often did, suddenly rise up in some act of unprecedented violence. This transformation will surprise us only if we confuse our theoretical model with the reality it ought to help us to understand.

Elkins has not described to us the personality of the Southern slave, nor by contrast, of the Latin American slave; he has instead demonstrated the limiting case of the slavish personality. Every slave system contained a powerful tendency to generate Sambos, but every system generated countervailing forces. Elkins, following Tannenbaum, might properly argue that differences in tradition, religion, and law guaranteed differences in the strength of those countervailing forces; he cannot prove and dare not assume that any system lacked them.

Elkins accounts for such forms of deviant behavior as lying, stealing, and shirking by absorbing them within the general framework of childish response. He is by no means completely wrong in doing so, for very often the form of a particular act of hostility degraded the slave as much as it irritated the master. Elkins's approach is not so much wrong as it is of limited usefulness. Once we pass beyond the insight that the form of rebelliousness might itself reveal accommodation, we cannot go much further. If all behavior short of armed revolt can be subsumed within the framework of childishness and dependence, then that formulation clearly embraces too much. Our historical problem is to explain how and under what conditions accommodation yields to resistance, and we therefore need a framework sufficiently flexible to permit distinctions between accommodating behavior that, however slightly, suggests a process of transformation into opposite qualities; such a framework must, moreover, be able to account for both tendencies within a single human being and even within a single act.

It has become something of a fashion in the adolescent recesses of our profession to bury troublesome authors and their work under a heap of carping general and specific complaints; it is no part of my purpose to join in the fun. Elkins's book has raised the study of Southern slavery to a far higher level than ever before, and it has done so at a moment when the subject seemed about to be drowned in a sea of moral indignation. It has demonstrated forcefully the remarkable uses to which psychology can be put in historical inquiry. It has brought to the surface the relationship between the slave past and a wide range of current problems flowing from that past. These are extraordinary achievements. To advance in the direction Elkins has pointed out, however, we shall first have to abandon most of his ground. We cannot simply replace his psychological model with a better one; we must recognize that all psychological models may only be used suggestively for flashes of insight or as aids in forming hypotheses and that they cannot substitute for empirical investigation. As the distinguished anthropologist, Max Gluckman, has observed, respect for psychology as a discipline requiring a high degree of training in the acquisition and interpretation of data forces us to bypass psychological analyses whenever possible.[63] Or, to put it another way, if we are to profit fully from Elkins's boldness, we shall have to retreat from it and try to solve the problems he raises by the more orthodox procedures of historical research.

NOTES

1. Stanley M. Elkins, *Slavery: A Problem in American Institutional and Intellectual Life* (Chicago, 1959). For a brief critique of the book as a whole see Genovese, "Problems in Nineteenth Century American History," *Science & Society*, 25 (1961). This present paper shall, so far as possible, be limited to questions of method and assumption. A much shorter version was read to the Association for the Study of Negro Life and History, Baltimore, Maryland, Oct., 1966, where it was incisively criticized by Professor Willie Lee Rose of the University of Virginia. Mrs. Rose was also kind enough to read and criticize the first draft of this longer version. I do not know whether or not my revisions will satisfy her, but I am certain that the paper is much better as a result of her efforts.

2. Elkins, *Slavery*, pp. 115–133 and the literature cited therein.

3. John Harding, *et al.*, "Prejudice and Ethnic Relations," *Handbook of Social Psychology*, ed. Gardner Lindzey (Cambridge, 1954), 2, 1021–1062, esp. 1024.

4. C. L. R. James, *The Black Jacobins: Toussaint L'Ouverture and the San Domingo Revolution* (Vintage ed., New York, 1963), p. 21.

5. Ibn Khaldun, *The Muqaddimah*, trans. Franz Rosenthal (New York, 1958), 1: 174, 301; the parentheses were inserted by the translator for technical reasons. David Brion Davis maintains that as Muslims extended their hegemony over Africa, they came to regard black Africans as fit only for slavery: *The Problem of Slavery in Western Culture* (Ithaca, 1966), p. 50. Cf. Basil Davidson, *Black Mother* (Boston, 1961), pp. xvii, 7, 45, 92–93 for Sambo's appearance in Africa.

6. C. R. Boxer, ed., "Negro Slavery in Brazil" [trans. of *Nova e Curiosa Relação (1764)*], *Race*, 5 (1964), 43.

7. Stanley J. Stein, *Vassouras: A Brazilian Coffee County, 1850–1900* (Cambridge, Mass., 1957), p. 133.

8. Euclides da Cunha, *Rebellion in the Backlands (Os Sertoẽs)*, trans. Samuel Putnam (Chicago, 1944), p. 71; for a critical review of some of this literature see Arthur Ramos, *The Negro in Brazil* (Washington, 1939), pp. 22–24.

9. Manoel de Oliveira Lima, *The Evolution of Brazil Compared with That of Spanish and Anglo-Saxon America* (Stanford, 1914), p. 122.

10. João Pandía Calógeras, *A History of Brazil* (Chapel Hill, 1939), p. 29. Even today, when Negroes face discrimination in Brazil, whites insist that it is a result of their own incapacities and sense of inferiority. See Fernando Henrique Cardoso and Octávio Ianni, *Côr e mobilidade em Florianópolis* (São Paulo, 1964), p. 231.

11. Kenneth M. Stampp, *The Peculiar Institution* (New York, 1956), p. 148:

> "Here, then, was the way to produce the perfect slave: accustom him to rigid discipline, demand from him unconditional submission, impress upon him his innate inferiority, develop in him a paralyzing fear of white men, train him to adopt the master's code of good behavior, and instill in him a sense of complete dependence. This at least was the goal."

Octávio Ianni, *As Metamorfoses do Escravo* (São Paulo, 1962), pp. 134–135:

> "Essential to the full functioning of the regime [was] a rigorous, drastic system of control over the social behavior of the enslaved laborer; . . . mechanisms of socialization appropriate to the dominant social strata . . .; the impossibility of vertical social mobility; . . . rules of conduct ordered according to a standard of rigid obedience of the Negroes in front of white men, whether masters or not."

See also Fernando Henrique Cardoso, *Capitalismo e Escravidão no Brasil Meridional* (São Paulo, 1962), pp. 312–313. Davis follows Ianni and others and speaks of Brazilian slaves as having been reduced "to a state of psychic shock, of flat apathy and depression, which was common enough in Brazil to acquire the special name of *banzo*." *Problem of Slavery,* p. 28; cf. Ramos, *Negro in Brazil,* pp. 22, 135–136.

12. Davis, *Problem of Slavery,* p. 171.

13. *Selected Writings of Bolivar,* I (New York, 1951), 131.

14. For an interpretation of the Spanish slave law as holding Negroes to be an especially revolutionary people see Augustín Alcalá y Henke, *Esclavitud de los negros en la América española* (Madrid, 1919), p. 51. For a view of Brazilian Indians that sounds much like Sambo see the comments of the famous Dutch sea captain, Dierck de Ruiter, as reported in C. R. Boxer, *Salvador de Sá and the Struggle for Brazil and Angola* (London, 1952), p. 20.

15. Sidney Mintz, review of Elkins's *Slavery, American Anthropologist,* 63 (1961), 585.

16. "Slavery is determined 'pas par l'obeissance, ni par rudesse des labeurs, mais par le statu d'instrument et la réduction de l'homme a l'état de chose.'" François Perroux, *La Coexistence pacifique,* as quoted by Herbert Marcuse, *One-Dimensional Man: Studies in the Ideology of Advanced Industrial Society* (Boston, 1964), pp. 32–33.

17. Davis, *Problem of Slavery,* pp. 59–60.

18. *Ibid.,* pp. 66–67.

19. *Ibid.,* p. 420.

20. Audrey I. Richards, *Land, Labour and Diet in Northern Rhodesia: An Economic Study of the Bemba Tribe* (London, 1939), p. 400.

21. Josué de Castro, *The Geography of Hunger* (Boston, 1952), *passim.*

22. Jean-Paul Sartre, preface to Frantz Fanon, *The Wretched of the Earth* (New York, 1965), p. 14.

23. Quoted from the *Southern Cultivator,* 7 (Sept., 1849), 140, by William K. Scarborough, "The Southern Plantation Overseer: A Reevaluation," *Agricultural History,* 38 (1964), 16.

24. See his explicit summary statement, "Culture Contacts and Negro Slavery," *Proceedings of the American Philosophical Society,* 107 (1963), 107–110, esp. 107.

25. Frank Tannenbaum, *Slave & Citizen: The Negro in the Americas* (New York, 1946), p. 48.

26. *Ibid.,* pp. 65, 69, and *passim.*

27. Arnold A. Sio, "Interpretations of Slavery: The Slave Status in the Americas," *Comparative Studies in Society and History,* 7 (1965), 303, 308. For a fresh consideration of the problem of slave law in the islands see Elsa V. Goveia "The West Indian Slave Laws in the Eighteenth Century," *Revista de Ciencias Sociales* (1960), 75–105.

28. Marvin Harris has counterposed an economic viewpoint to Tannenbaum's. Despite considerable exaggeration and one-sidedness, he does demonstrate the partial applicability of an institutional approach. For a critical analysis of Harris's polemic and the literature it touches see Genovese, "Materialism and Idealism in the History of Negro Slavery in the Americas," *Journal of Social History,* 1 (Summer 1968), 371–394.

The experience of the Dutch demonstrates how much religious and national attitudes gave way before the necessities of colonial life. The Dutch experience in Surinam, New Netherland, Brazil, etc. varied enormously. See, e.g., C. R. Boxer, *The Dutch in Brazil* (Oxford, 1957), esp. p. 75; Edgar J. McManus, *A History of Negro Slavery in New York* (New York, 1966), chap. 1.

29. Quoted by James, *Black Jacobins,* p. 17.

30. *Ibid.,* p. 56; Davis, *Problem of Slavery,* p. 254 and the literature cited therein.

31 Gilberto Freyre, *The Masters and the Slaves: A Study in the Development of Brazilian Civilization,* 2nd English language ed. rev. (New York, 1956), p. xxxix.

32. Stein, *Vassouras,* p. 136.

33. See, e.g., the discussion of the law of 1797 in Antigua in Elsa V. Goveia, *Slave Society in the British Leeward Islands at the End of the Eighteenth Century* (New Haven, 1966), p. 191.

34. Gilberto Freyre, *The Mansions and the Shanties: The Making of Modern Brazil* (New York, 1963), p. 226.

35. Gilberto Freyre, "Social Life in Brazil in the Middle of the

Nineteenth Century,"*Hispanic American Historical Review,* 5 (1922), 597–628; see also, Freyre, *Masters,* pp. xxxiii, 24, 42; *New World in the Tropics: The Culture of Modern Brazil* (New York; Vintage ed., 1963), p. 69.

36. Alan A. Manchester describes 1848 as the turning point. See *British Pre-Eminence in Brazil* (Chapel Hill, 1933), pp. 261–262.

37. George S. Barnsley MS Notebook in the Southern Historical Collection, University of North Carolina, Chapel Hill.

38. For a penetrating discussion of these two sides of *Las Siete Partidas* see Davis, *Problem of Slavery,* pp. 102–105.

39. *Ibid.,* p. 240.

40. Arthur Percival Newton, *The European Nations in the West Indies, 1493–1688* (London, 1933), p.3.

41. For a useful recent summary discussion of the literature see Harris, *Patterns of Race,* pp. 18–20.

42. Cf., Arthur S. Aiton, "The Asiento Treaty as Reflected in the Papers of Lord Shelburne," *Hispanic American Historical Review,* 8 (1928), 167–177, esp. p. 167.

43. Jaime Jaramillo Uribe, "Esclavos y Señores en la sociedad colombiana del siglo XVIII," *Anuario colombiano de hístoria social y de cultura,* 1 (1963), 1–22.

44. Herbert Klein, "Anglicanism, Catholicism and the Negro," *Comparative Studies in Society and History,* VIII (1966), 295–327; *Slavery in the Americas: A Comparative Study of Cuba and Virginia* (Chicago, 1967).

45. See H. H. S. Aimes, *A History of Slavery in Cuba, 1511 to 1868* (New York, 1907), pp. 150–151, 175–177.

46. On this point see Sidney Mintz, foreword to Ramiro Guerra y Sánchez, *Sugar and Society in the Caribbean* (New Haven, 1964), and his review of Elkins's book in the *American Anthropologist,* 63 (1961), 579–587. Klein, Tannenbaum and Elkins make much of the practice of *coartación.* For a critical assessment see Davis, *Problem of Slavery,* pp. 266–267.

47. Boxer, *Salvador de Sá,* p. 279.

48. C. R. Boxer, *Race Relations in the Portuguese Colonial Empire,* 1415–1825 (Oxford, 1963), pp. 7–8, 11–12, 21.

49. C. R. Boxer, *Portuguese Society in the Tropics: The Municipal Councils of Goa, Macao, Bahia, and Luanda, 1510–1800* (1965), pp. 131–132, Davidson, *Black Mother,* p.158.

50. Elkins certainly errs in ascribing a protective role to the Jesuits, whose efforts on behalf of the Indians were not repeated with the Negroes. Jesuit treatment of those Negroes within their reach does not constitute one of the more glorious chapters in the history of the order. The literature is extensive; for a good, brief discussion see João Dornas Filho, *A Escravidão no Brasil* (Rio de Janeiro, 1939), p. 105.

51. Vianna Moog, *Bandeirantes and Pioneers* (New York, 1964), p.

209. Cf., Percy Alvin Martin, "Slavery and Abolition in Brazil," *Hispanic American Historical Review,* 13 (1933), 168: "On most plantations the spiritual life of the slaves received scant attention. Priests were found only on the larger estates."

52. Freyre, *New World in the Tropics,* pp. 70–71, 87–88; *Mansions,* p. 244.

53. Stein, *Vassouras,* pp. 196–199.

54. Cf., Rene Maunier, *The Sociology of Colonies,* 1 (London, n.d.), 293–294.

55. Elkins seems troubled by this—see p. 102—but he does not pursue it. K. Onwuka Dike points out that Guineans brought to the trading depots of the Niger Delta had already been prepared psychologically for slavery by the religious indoctrination accompanying the cult of the Aro oracle. See "The Question of Sambo: A Report of the Ninth Newberry Library Conference on American Studies," *Newberry Library Bulletin,* 5 (1958), 27, and Dike's *Trade and Politics in the Niger Delta, 1830–1885* (Oxford, 1956), chap. 2.

56. Bruno Bettelheim, "Individual and Mass Behavior in Extreme Situations," *Journal of Abnormal and Social Psychology,* 38 (1943), 417–452. On the general problem of the concentration camp analogy see the remarks of Daniel Boorstin as reported in the *Newberry Library Bulletin,* 5 (1958), 14–40 and Earle E. Thorpe, "Chattel Slavery & Concentration Camps," *Negro History Bulletin,* 25 (1962), 171–176. Unfortunately, Mr. Thorpe's thoughtful piece is marred by a clumsy discussion of the problem of wearing a mask before white men.

57. Hannah Arendt, "Ideology and Terror: A Novel Form of Government," *Review of Politics,* 15 (1953), 314. I am indebted to Professor Daniel Walden of the Pennsylvania State University for calling this illuminating article to my attention and for suggesting its relevance to the subject at hand.

58. For a perceptive and well-balanced discussion of this side of plantation life see Clement Eaton, *The Growth of Southern Civilization* (New York, 1961), p. 74 and *passim.*

59. Brazilian slaves saw their masters as patriarchs and, in Freyre's words, "almighty figures." Freyre, *Mansions,* p. 234. See also Celso Furtado, *The Economic Growth of Brazil* (Berkeley, 1963), pp. 153–154.

60. Arendt, *Review of Politics,* 15 (1953), 312.

61. *Ibid.,* 327.

62. Bettelheim, *Journal of Abnormal and Social Psychology,* 38 (1943), 451; Eugen Kogon, *The Theory and Practice of Hell* (New York, 1950), esp. chaps. 20, 31.

63. Max Gluckman, *Order and Rebellion in Tribal Africa* (New York, 1963), pp. 2–3.

Chapter 5

AMERICAN SLAVES AND THEIR HISTORY

THE HISTORY OF the lower classes has yet to be written. The ideological impact of the New Left, the intellectual exigencies of the black liberation movement, and the developing academic concern for the cultural dimension of politics and history have converged to produce the expectation that it will be. If one per cent of the hosannas heaped upon E. P. Thompson's *The Making of the English Working Class* could be translated into disciplined effort to extend its achievement, the future would be bright. And indeed, good work is finally being done, although precious little of it by those who regularly pontificate on the need to rewrite history "from the bottom up."

History written from the bottom up is neither more nor less than history written from the top down: It is not and cannot be good history. To write the story of a nation without taking into consideration the vicissitudes of a majority of its

This essay was originally published in *New York Review of Books*, Dec. 3, 1970, pp. 34–43.

people is simply not a serious undertaking. And yet, it is preposterous to suggest that there could conceivably be anything wrong with writing a book about the ruling class alone, or about one or another elite, or about any segment of society no matter how small. No subject is too small to treat. But a good historian writes well on a small subject while taking account (if only implicitly and without a single direct reference) of the whole, whereas an inferior one confuses the need to isolate a small portion of the whole with the license to assume that that portion thought and acted in isolation. One may, for example, write Southern history by focusing on either blacks or whites, slaves or masters, tenant farmers or landlords; it will be good or bad history if, among other things, the author knows that the one cannot be discussed without a deep understanding of the other. The fate of master and slave was historically intertwined and formed part of a single social process; each in his own way struggled for autonomy—struggled to end his dependence upon the other—but neither could ever wholly succeed. The first problem in the writing of social history lies in this organic antagonism: We tend to see the masters in their own terms, without acknowledgment of their dependence upon the slaves; but we also tend to see the slaves in the masters' terms, without acknowledgment of the extent to which the slaves freed themselves from domination.

There cannot be, therefore, any such thing as "history from the bottom up." A good study of plantation architecture, apart from its contribution to aesthetics, would be one that grasped the social link between the culture of the Big House and that of both the slave quarters and small nonslaveholding farmhouses, for the Big House, whatever else it did, served to impress the humbler men in and out of its orbit. Such a study need never mention the quarters of the farmhouses, but if the essential insight fails or remains undeveloped and abstract, then the entire effort must remain limited. Should it succeed, then it must be ranked as a valuable contribution to the history of Southern society and its constituent races and classes. To consider such a study "elitist" because it concerns itself with upper-class life or eschews moralistic pronouncements is a modern form of absurdity.

There is much to be said for the current notion that blacks will have to write their own history: Black people in the United States have strong claims to separate nationality, and every people must interpret its own history in the light of its own traditions and experience. At the same time, the history of every people must be written from without, if only to provide a necessary corrective in perspective; sooner or later the history of every people must flow from the clash of viewpoints and sensibilities that accompanies both external and internal confrontation. But for the South there is a more compelling reason for black and white scholars to have to live with each other. There is simply no way of learning about either blacks or whites without learning about the other. If it is true, as I suspect, that the next generations of black scholars will bring a special viewpoint to Southern history, then their success or failure will rest, in part, on their willingness to teach us something new about the masters as well as the slaves. He who says the one, is condemned to say the other.

I should like to consider some debilitating assumptions often brought by social historians to the study of the lower classes, and to suggest a way of avoiding the twin elitist notions that the lower classes are generally passive or generally on the brink of insurrection. We have so many books on slavery in the Old South that specialists need to devote full time merely to keeping abreast of the literature. Yet, there is not a single book and only a few scattered articles on life in the quarters —except of course for such primary and undigested sources as the slave narratives and plantation memoirs. A good student might readily be able to answer questions about the economics of the plantation, the life of the planters, the politics of slavery expansionism, or a host of other matters, but he is not likely to know much about slave life, about the relationship of field to house slaves, or about the relationship between the slave driver or foreman and other slaves. To make matters worse, he may well think he knows a good deal, for the literature abounds in undocumented assertions and plausible legends.

The fact remains that there has not been a single study of the driver—the most important slave on the larger plantations—and only a few sketchy and misleading studies of house slaves. So far as the life of the quarters is concerned, it is enough to note that the notion persists, in the face of abundant evidence, that slaves had no family life to speak of. Historians and sociologists, both white and black, have been guilty of reasoning deductively from purely legal evidence—slave marriages were not recognized by law in the United States—and have done little actual research.

I do not propose to discuss the family in detail here, nor house slaves and drivers for that matter, but I should like to touch on all three in order to illustrate a larger point. We have made a great error in the way in which we have viewed slave life, and this error has been perpetuated by both whites and blacks, racists and antiracists. The traditional proslavery view and that of such later apologists for white supremacy as U. B. Phillips have treated the blacks as objects of white benevolence and fear—as people who needed both protection and control—and devoted attention to the ways in which black slaves adjusted to the demands of the master class. Abolitionist propaganda and the later, and now dominant, liberal viewpoint have insisted that the slave regime was so brutal and dehumanizing that blacks should be seen primarily as victims. Both these viewpoints treat black people almost wholly as objects, never as creative participants in a social process, never as half of a two-part subject.

True, abolitionist and liberal views have taken account of the ways in which slaves resisted their masters by shirking their work, breaking tools, or even rebelling, but the proslavery view generally noted that much too, even if within the context of a different interpretation. Neither has ever stopped to consider, for example, that the evidence might reflect less a deliberate attempt at sabotage or alleged Negro inferiority than a set of attitudes toward time, work, and leisure which black people developed partly in Africa and partly in the slave quarters—a set of attitudes which constituted a special case in a general pattern of behavior associated with preindustrial cultures. Preindustrial peoples knew all about hard work and discipline, but their standards were those of neither the factory nor the plantation and were embedded in a radically different culture. Yet, even such sympathetic historians as Kenneth Stampp who give some attention to slaves as subjects and actors, have merely tried to show that slaves exercised some degree of autonomy in their responses to the blows or cajoling of their masters. We have yet to receive a respectful treatment—apart from some brief but suggestive passages in the work of W. E. B. Du Bois, C. L. R. James and perhaps one or two others—of their attempts to achieve an autonomous life within the narrow limits of the slave plantation.[1] We have yet to have a synthetic record of their incessant struggle to escape from the culture as well as the psychological domination of the master class.

In commenting briefly on certain features of family life, house slaves, and drivers, I should like to suggest some of the rich possibilities inherent in an approach that asks much more than "What was done to the slaves?" and, in particular, asks, "What did the slaves do for themselves and how did they do it?" In a more leisurely presentation it would be possible and, indeed, necessary to discuss slave religion, entertainment, songs and dances, and many other things. But perhaps we may settle for a moment on one observation about slave religion.

We are told a great deal about the religious instruction of the slaves, by which it meant the attempt in inculcate a version of Protestant Christianity. Sometimes this instruction is interpreted as a good thing in itself and sometimes as a kind of brainwashing, but we may leave this question aside. Recently, Vincent Harding, following the suggestive probing in Du Bois's work, has offered a different perspective and suggested that the slaves had their own way of taking up Christianity and forging it into a weapon of active resistance.[2] Certainly, we must be struck by the appearance of one or another kind of messianic preacher in almost every slave revolt on record. Professor Harding therefore asks that we look at the slaves as active participants in their own religious experience and not merely as objects being worked on by slaveholding ideologues. This argument may be carried further to suggest that a distinctly black religion, at least in embryo, appeared in the quarters and played a role—the extent and precise content of which we have yet to evaluate—in shaping the daily lives of the slaves. In other words, quite apart from the problem of religion as a factor in overt resistance to slavery, we need to know how the slaves developed a religious life that enabled them to survive as autonomous human beings with a culture of their own within the white master's world.

One of the reasons we know so little about this side of the story—and about all lower-class life—is that it is undramatic. Historians, white and black, conservative, liberal, and radical, have a tendency to look for the heroic moments, either to praise or to excoriate them, and to consider ordinary daily life as so much trivia. Yet, if a slave helped to keep himself psychologically intact by breaking his master's hoe, he might also have achieved the same result by a special effort to come to terms with his God, or by loving a woman who shared his burdens, or even by aspiring to be the best worker on the plantation. We normally think of someone who aspires to be a good slave as an Uncle Tom, and maybe we should. But human beings are not so simple. If a slave aspires to a certain excellence within the system, and if his implicit trust in the generous response of the master is betrayed—as often it must be in such a system—then he is likely to be transformed into a rebel. And if so, he is likely to become the most dangerous kind of rebel, first because of his smashed illusions and second because of the skills and self-control he taught himself while appearing on the scene as an Uncle Tom. The historical record of slavery is full of people who were model slaves right up until the moment they killed their overseer, ran away, burned down the Big House, or joined an insurrection.

So what can be said about the decidedly non-Christian element in the religion of the slave quarters? The planters tell us repeatedly that every plantation had its conjurer, its voodoo man, its witch doctor. To the planters this meant a residue of African superstition, and it is, of course, possible by the 1830s all that remained in the slave quarters were local superstitions rather than a continuation of the highly sophisticated religions originally brought from Africa. But the evidence suggests the emergence of an indigenous and unique combination of African and European religious notions, adapted to the specific conditions of slave life by talented and imaginative individuals, which represented an attempt to establish a spiritual life adequate to the task of linking the slaves with the powerful culture of the masters and yet providing them with a high degree of separation and autonomy.

When we know enough of this story we shall know a good deal about the way in which the culture of an oppressed people develops. We often hear the expression "defenseless slaves," but, although any individual at any given moment may be defenseless, a whole people rarely, if ever, is. It may be on the defensive and dangerously exposed, but it almost invariably finds its own ways to survive and fight back. The trouble is that we keep looking for overt rebellious actions—the strike, the revolt, the murder, the arson, the tool-breaking—and often fail to realize that, in given conditions and at particular times, the wisdom of a people and their experience in struggle dictates a different course and an emphasis on holding together both individually and collectively. From this point of view, the most ignorant of the field slaves who followed the conjurer on the plantation was saying no to the boss and seeking an autonomous existence. That the conjurer may, in any one case, have been a fraud and even a kind of extortionist and, in another case, a genuine popular religious leader is, from this point of view, of little importance.

Let us take the family as an illustration. Slave law refused to recognize slave marriages and family ties. In this respect United States slavery was far worse than Spanish American or Luso-Brazilian. In those Catholic cultures the Church demanded and tried to guarantee that slaves be permitted to marry and that the sanctity of the slave family be upheld. As a result, generations of American historians have concluded that American slaves had no family life and that Cuban and Brazilian slaves did. This judgment will not bear examination. The slave trade to the United States was closed early: no later than 1808, except for statistically insignificant smuggling, and, in fact, for most states it ended decades earlier. The rise of the Cotton Kingdom and the great period of slavery expansion followed the closing of the slave trade. Slavery, in the numbers we are accustomed to thinking of, was a product of the period following the end of African importations. The slave force that was liberated during and after the War for Southern Independence was overwhelmingly a slave force born and raised in this country. We have good statistics on the rate of increase of that slave population, and there can be no doubt that it compared roughly to that of the whites—apart from the fact of imigration—and that furthermore, it was unique among New World slave classes. An early end to the slave trade, followed by a boom in cotton and plantation slavery, dictated a policy of encouraging slave births. In contrast, the slave trade remained open to Cuba and to Brazil until the second half of the nineteenth century; as a result, there was little economic pressure to encourage family life and slave-breeding. In Brazil and Cuba, far more men than women were imported from Africa until late in the history of the respective slave regimes; in the Old South, a rough sexual parity was established fairly early. If, therefore, religion and law militated in favor of slave families in Cuba and Brazil and against them in the Old South, economic pressure worked in reverse. The result was a self-reproducing slave force in the United States and nowhere else, so far as the statistics reveal.

It may immediately be objected that the outcome could have reflected selective breeding rather than family stability. But selective breeding was tried in the Caribbean and elsewhere and never worked; there is no evidence that it was ever tried on a large scale in the South. Abolitionists charged that Virginia and Maryland deliberately raised slaves—not merely encouraged, but actually fostered slave-breeding. There is no evidence. If slave-raising farms existed and if the planters were not complete fools they would have concentrated on recruiting women of childbearing age and used a relatively small number of studs. Sample studies of major slave-exporting countries in Virginia and Maryland show no significant deviations from the parallel patterns in Mississippi or other slave-buying regions.

Now, it is clear that Virginia and Maryland—and other states as well—exported their natural increase for some decades before the war. But this was a process, not a policy; it reflected the economic pressures to supplement a waning income from agriculture by occasional slave sales; it was not incompatible with the encouragement of slave families and, in fact, reinforced it. Similarly, planters in the cotton states could not work their slaves to death and then buy fresh ones, for prices were too high. They had been too high from the very moment the Cotton Kingdom began its westward march, and therefore a tradition of slave-killing never did take root. As time went on, the pressures mounted to provide slaves with enough material and even psychological satisfaction to guarantee the minimum morale needed for reproduction. These standards of treatment—so much food, living space, time off, etc.—became part of the prevailing standard of decency, not easily violated by greedy slaveholders. In some respects the American slave system may have been the worst in the world, as so many writers insist. But in purely material terms, it was probably the best. American slaves were generally fed, clothed, housed, and worked better than those of Cuba, Jamaica, or Brazil.

But the important thing here is that the prevailing standard of decency was not easily violated because the slaves had come to understand their own position. If a master wished to keep his plantation going, he had to learn the limits of his slaves' endurance. If, for example, he decided to ignore the prevailing custom of giving Sunday off or of giving an extended Christmas holiday, his slaves would feel sorely tried and would certainly pay him back with one or another form of wrecking. The slaves remained in a weak position, but they were rarely completely helpless, and by guile, brute courage and a variety of other devices they taught every master just where the line was he dared not cross if he wanted a crop. In precisely this way, slaves took up the masters' interest in their family life and turned it to account. The typical plantation in the South was organized by family unit. Man and wife lived together with children, and within a considerable sphere the man was in fact the man in the house.

Whites violated black family life in several ways. Many families were disrupted by sales, especially in the upper South, where economic pressures were strong. White men on the plantations could and often did violate black women. Nothing can minimize these injustices. The frequency of sales is extremely hard to measure. Many slaves were troublesome and sold many times over; this inflated the total number of sales but obscured the incidence of individual transfers. The crimes against these black people are a matter of record, and no qualifications can soften their impact. But it is not at all certain that most slaves did not live stable, married lives in the quarters despite the pressures of the market. I do not wish to get into the vexing question of the violation of black women here, but certainly there was enough of it to justify the anger of those who condemned the slave regime on this ground alone.

The evidence, however, does not warrant the assumption that a large percentage of black plantation women were so violated. In other words, for a judgment on the moral quality of the regime, this subject is extremely important; for an assessment of the moral life of the slaves, it is much less so.

What the sources show—both the plantation books and letters of the masters, and also the reports of runaway slaves and ex-slaves—is that the average plantation slave lived in a family setting, developed strong family ties, and held the nuclear family as the proper social norm. Planters who often had to excuse others, or even themselves, for breaking up families by sale, would sometimes argue that blacks did not really form deep and lasting attachments, that they lacked strong family sense, that they were naturally promiscuous, and so forth. Abolitionists and ex-slaves would reinforce the prevalent notion by saying that slavery was so horrible, no real family tie could be maintained. Since planters, abolitionists, and ex-slaves all said the same thing, it has usually been taken as the truth. Only it was not.

In the first place, these various sources also say opposite things, which we rarely notice. Planters agonized over the breakup of families and repeatedly expressed regrets and dismay. Often, they went to great lengths to keep families together at considerable expense, for they knew how painful it was to enforce separations. Whether they were motivated by such material considerations as the maintenance of plantation morale or more lofty sentiment is neither here nor there. They often demontrated that they knew very well how strong the family ties were in the quarters. Planters did everything possible to encourage the slaves to live together in stable units; they recognized that a man was easier to control if he had a wife and children to worry about. The slaves, on their side, behaved variously, of course. Many were, indeed, promiscuous although much of the charge of promiscuity stemmed not so much from actual promiscuity as from sequential polygamy. They did change partners more often than Victorian whites could stomach. (In this respect, they might be considered the great forerunners of the white, middle-class sexual morality of the 1960s.) I stress this side of things—the interest of the master in slave family stability and the effort of the slave to protect his stake in a home, however impoverished—because it is now fashionable to believe that black people came out of slavery with little or no sense of family life. But if so, then we need to know why, during early Reconstruction, so many thousands wandered over the South looking for their spouse or children. We do not know just how many slaves lived as a family or were willing and able to maintain a stable family life during slavery. But the number was certainly great, whatever the percentage, and as a result, the social norm that black people carried from slavery to freedom was that of the nuclear family. If it is true that the black family has disintegrated in the ghettos—and we have yet to see conclusive evidence—then the source will have to be found in the conditions of economic and social oppression imposed upon blacks during recent decades. The slave experience, for all its tragic disruptions, pointed toward a stable postslavery family life, and recent scholarship demonstrates conclusively that the Reconstruction and post-Reconstruction black experience carried forward the acceptance of the nuclear family norm.[3]

Let us consider the role of the male and the legend of the matriarchy. Almost all writers on slavery describe the slave man as "a guest in the house" who could have no role beyond the purely sexual. The slave narratives and the diaries and letters of white plantation owners tell us something else. His position was undeniably precarious and frustrating. If his wife was to be whipped, he had to stand by and watch; he could not fully control his own children; he was not a breadwinner in the usual sense; and, in a word, there were severe restrictions imposed upon the manifestations of what we somewhat erroneously call manliness. But, both masters and ex-slaves tell us about some plantations on which certain women were not easily or often punished because it was readily understood that, to punish the woman, it would be necessary to kill her man first. These cases were the exception, but they tell us at the start that the man felt a duty to protect his woman. If circumstances conspired to prevent his fulfilling that duty, those circumstances often included his woman's not expecting it and, indeed, consoling him about the futility of such a gesture. We cannot know what was said between a man and a woman when they lay down together at night after such outrages, but there are enough hints in the slave narratives to suggest that both knew what a man could do, as well as what he "should" do, especially when there were children to consider. Many scholars suggest that black women treated their men with contempt for not doing what circumstances made impossible. This is a deduction from tenuous assumptions; it is not a demonstrated fact.

Beyond that, the man of the house did do various things. He trapped and hunted animals to supplement the diet in the quarters, and in this small but important and symbolic way he was a breadwinner. He organized the garden plot and presided over the division of labor with his wife. He disciplined his children—or divided that function with his wife as people in other circumstances do—and generally was the source of authority in the cabin. This relationship within the family was not always idyllic. In many instances, his authority over both wife and children was imposed by force. Masters forbade men to hit their wives and children and whipped them for it; but they did it anyway and often. And there is not much evidence that women readily ran to the master to ask that her husband be whipped for striking her. The evidence on these matters is fragmentary, but it suggests that the men asserted their authority as best they could; the women expected to have to defer to their husbands in certain matters; and that both tried hard to keep the master out of their lives. The conditions were unfavorable, and perhaps many men did succumb and in one way or another became emasculated. But we might also reflect on the ways in which black men and women conspired to maintain their own sense of dignity and their own autonomy by settling things among themselves and thereby asserting their own personalities.

Black women have often been praised—and justly so—for their strength and determination in holding their families together during slavery, when the man was supposedly put aside or rendered irrelevant. It is time, I think, to praise them for another thing they seem to have been able to do in large numbers: to support a man they loved in ways deep enough and varied enough to help him resist the mighty forces for dehumanization and emasculation. Without the support of their women, not many black men could have survived; but with it—and there is plenty of testimony that they often had it—many could and did.

If our failure to see the plantation from the vantage point of the slave quarters has led us to substitute abstractions for research on the slave family, so has it saddled us with unsubstantiated and erroneous ideas on house slaves. According to the legend, house slaves were the Uncle Toms of the system—a privileged caste apart, contemptuous of the field hands, jealous of their place in the affection or at least eye of the white master and mistress, and generally speaking, finks, sellouts, and white man's niggers. Like most stereotypes, this one has its kernel of truth. There were, indeed, many house slaves who fit the description. But we might begin by considering a small fact. Half the slaves in the rural South lived on farms of twenty or fewer slaves; another twenty-five per cent lived on plantations with twenty to fifty slaves. Only twenty-five per cent, in other words, lived on plantations of fifty or more, and of those, the overwhelming majority lived on units of less than one hundred—that is, on units of less than twenty slave families. In short, the typical house slave serviced either a small farm or, at best, a moderate plantation. Only a few lived and worked on plantations large enough to permit the formation of a separate group of house slaves—of enough house slaves to form a caste unto themselves.

Our idea of the fancy-dressed, uppity, self-inflated house slave who despised the field blacks and identified with the whites is a product of the relatively small group who lived in the towns and cities like Charleston, New Orleans, and Richmond. These townhouse slaves and a tiny group of privileged house slaves on huge plantations could and sometimes did form a separate caste with the attributes described in the literature. Certainly, the great planters and their families, who left most of the white-family records that have been relied on as the major source, would most likely have remembered precisely these slaves. Even these blacks deserve a more careful look than they have received, for they were much more complicated people than we have been led to believe. But, the important point is that the typical house slave was far removed from this condition. He, or more likely she, worked with perhaps one to three or four others on an estate too small to permit any such caste formation.

If the typical house slave was an Uncle Tom and a spoiled child of the whites, then we need to be told just why so many of them turn up in the records of runaways. There is abundant evidence from the war years. We hear much about the faithful retainers who held the Yankees off from the Big House, or protected young missus, or hid the family silver. Such types existed and were not at all rare. But they do not appear to have been nearly so numerous as those house slaves who joined the field slaves in fleeing to the Yankee lines when the opportunity arose. The best source on this point is the planters themselves, who were shocked at the defection of their favorite slaves. They could readily understand the defection of the field hands, whom they considered stupid and easily led, but they were unable to account for the flight, sometimes with expressions of regret and sometimes with expressions of anger and hatred, of their house slaves. They had always thought they knew these blacks, loved them, were loved by them, and they considered them part of the family. One day they learned that they had been deceiving themselves and living intimately with people they did not know at all. The house slaves, when the opportunity presented itself, responded with the same range of behavior as did the field slaves. They proved themselves just as often rebellious and independent as they did docile and loyal.

This display of independence really was nothing new. If it is true that house slaves were often regarded as traitors to the black cause during slave rebellions, it is also true that their appearance in those rebellions was not as rare as we are led to believe. A black rebel leader told Denmark Vesey and his followers not to trust the house slaves because they were too tied to the whites, but we ought also note that some of the toughest and most devoted of those leaders in Charleston in 1822 were themselves house slaves. In particular, the great scandal of the event in Charleston was the role played by the most trusted slaves, of the governor of South Carolina. Certainly, the role of the house slave was always ambiguous and often treacherous. But if many house slaves betrayed their fellows, many others collected information in the Big House and passed it on to the quarters. We know how well-informed the field slaves were about movements of Yankee troops during the war; we know that these field slaves fled to the Yankee lines with uncanny accuracy in timing and direction. Probably no group was more influential in providing the necessary information than those very house slaves who are so often denigrated.

The decision of slaves, whether house slaves or not, to protect whites during slave insurrections or other catastrophes, hardly proves them to have been Toms. The master-slave relationship, especially when it occurred in the intimacies of the Big House, was always profoundly ambivalent. Many of the same slaves who protected their masters and mistresses from harm and thereby asserted their own humanity were anything but docile creatures of the whites.

Since most house slaves worked on estates too small for a separate existence, their social life was normally down in the quarters and not apart or with the whites. The sexes were rarely evenly matched in the house, where women predominated, and even when they were, the group was too small for natural pairing off. A large number of house slaves married field hands or, more likely, the more skilled artisans or workers. Under such circumstances, the line between house slaves and field hands was not sharp for most slaves. Except on the really large units, house slaves were expected to help out in the fields during picking season and during emergencies. The average house slave got periodic tastes of field work and had little opportunity to cultivate airs.

There are two general features to the question of house slaves that deserve comment: first, there is the ambiguity of their situation and its resultant ambivalence toward whites; the other is the significance of the house slave in the formation of a distinctly Afro-American culture. The one point I should insist upon in any analysis of the house slave is ambivalence. People, black and white, slave and master, thrown together in the intimacy of the Big House, had to emerge loving and hating each other. Life together meant sharing each other's pains and problems, confiding secrets, having company when no one else would do, being forced to help one another in a multitude of ways. It also meant jointly experiencing, but in tragically opposite ways, the full force of lordship and bondage: that is, the full force of petty tyranny imposed by one woman on another; of expecting someone to be at your beck and call regardless of her own feelings and wishes; of being able to take out one's frustrations and disappointments on an innocent bystander, who would no doubt be guilty enough of something since servants are always falling short of the expectations.

To illustrate the complexity of black slave behavior in the Big House, let us take a single illustration. It is typical in the one sense that it catches the condition of ambiguity and of entwined, yet hostile, lives. Beyond that, it is of course unique, as is all individual experiences. Eliza L. Magruder was the niece of a deceased planter and politician from the Natchez, Mississippi, region and went to live with her aunt Olivia, who managed the old plantation herself. Miss Eliza kept a diary for the years 1846 and 1847 and then again for 1854 and 1857.[4] Possibly, she kept a diary for the intermittent years which has been lost. In any case, she has a number of references to a slave girl, Annica, and a few to another, Lavinia. We have here four women, two white and two black, two mistresses and two servants, thrown together in a single house and forced on each other's company all year long, year after year.

On April 17, 1846, Miss Eliza wrote in her diary more or less in passing, "Aunt Olivia whipped Annica for obstinacy." This unladylike chastisement had followed incidents in which Annica had been "impudent." About a month later, on September 11, Annica took another whipping—for "obstinacy." Miss Eliza appears to have been a bit squeamish, for her tone, if we read it correctly, suggests that she was not accustomed to witnessing such unpleasantness. On January 24, 1847, she confided to her diary, "I feel badly. Got very angry and whipped Lavinia. O! for government over my temper." But the world progresses, and so did Miss Eliza's fortitude in the face of other people's adversity. When her diary resumed in 1854, she had changed slightly: the squeamishness had diminished. Annica had not changed: she had remained her old, saucy self. October 26, 1854: "Boxed Annica's ears for impertinence."

Punctuated by this war of wills, daily life went on. Annica's mother lived in Jackson, Mississippi, and mother and daughter kept in touch. Since Annica could neither read nor write, Miss Eliza served as her helpmate and confidant.

December 5, 1854: "I wrote for Annica to her mother." Mamma wrote back in due time, no doubt to Annica's satisfaction, but also to her discomfiture. As Miss Eliza observed on January 25, 1855, "Annica got a letter from her mammy which detected her in a lie. O! that negroes generally were more truthful." So, we ought not to be surprised that Miss Eliza could not write without a trace of the old squeamishness on July 1, 1855, "I whipt Annica."

The impertinent Annica remained undaunted. November 29, 1855: "Aunt Olivia gave Annica a good scolding and made her ask my pardon and will punish her otherwise." Perhaps we should conclude that Annica's atrocious behavior had earned the undying enmity of the austere white ladies, but some doubts may be permitted. On July 24, 1856, several of their neighbors set out on a trip to Jackson, Mississippi, where, it will be recalled, Annica's mother lived. Aunt Olivia, with Miss Eliza's concurrence, sent Annica along for a two-week holiday and provided ten dollars for her expenses. On August 3, Annica returned home in time for breakfast. In the interim Miss Eliza had Lavinia as an object of wrath, for Lavinia had "very much provoked" her by lying and by being impertinent. "Aunt Olivia boxed her ears for it." Lavinia's day of glory did not last; it was not long before Annica reclaimed full possession of the title of the most impudent nigger in the Big House. On September 4, 1856, "Annica was very impertinent, and I boxed her ears." Three days later, wrote Miss Eliza, "I kept Annica in in the afternoon for impudence." The next day (September 8) Miss Eliza told Aunt Olivia about Annica's misconduct. "She reproved her for it and will I suppose punish her in some way." Life traveled on into November, when on the tenth day of the month, "Aunt Olivia whipt Annica for impertinence."

At this point, after a decade of impudence, impertinence, obstinacy, whipping, and ear-boxing, one might expect that Annica would have been dispatched to the cotton fields by women who could not abide her. But she remained in the Big

House. And what shall we make of such incidents as that which occurred on the night of December 29, 1856, when poor Annica was ill and in pain? It is not so much that Miss Eliza sat up with her, doing what she could; it is rather that she seemed both concerned and conscious of performing a simple duty. On the assumption that the illness left Annica weak for a while, Miss Eliza of course still had Lavinia. January 30, 1857: "I boxed Lavinia's ears for coming up late when I told her not."

On April 23, 1857, Annica greatly pleased Miss Eliza by making her a white bonnet. But by April 26, Annica was once again making trouble: "Aunt Olivia punished Annica by keeping her in her room all afternoon." And the next day: "Aunt Olivia had had Annica locked up in the garret all day. I pray it may humble her and make further punishment unnecessary."

On August 18, 1857, "Aunt Olivia held a court of enquiry, but didn't find out who ripped my pattern." There is no proof that Annica did it; still one wonders. Two weeks later in Miss Eliza's Sunday school, "Annica was strongly tempted to misbehave. I brought her in however." The entries end there.

Let us suppose the ladies had carried their household into the war years: What then? It would take little imagination to see Annica's face and to hear her tone as she marched into the kitchen to announce her departure for the federal lines. It would not even take much imagination to see her burning the house down. Yet, she had never been violent, and we should not be too quick to assume that she would easily have left the only home she had known as an adult and the women who wrote letters to her mamma, exchanged confidences, and stayed up with her on feverish nights. The only thing we can be sure of is that she remained impudent to the day she died.

What I think this anecdote demonstrates above all is the ambivalence inherent in the Big House relationship and the stubborn struggle for individuality that house slaves, whip or no whip, were capable of. Yet it may also hint at another side and thereby help explain why so many black militants, like so many historians before them, are quick to condemn the whole house-slave legacy as one to be exorcized. The house slaves were, indeed, close to the whites, and of all the black groups they exhibited the most direct adherence to certain white cultural standards. In their religious practices, their dress, their manners, and their prejudices they were undoubtedly the black group most influenced by Euro-American culture. But this kind of cultural accommodation was by no means the same thing as docility or Uncle Tomism. Even a relatively assimilated house slave could and normally did strike back, assert independence, and resist arbitrariness and oppression. We are today accustomed to thinking of black nationalists as "militants" and civil rights integrationists as "moderates," "conservatives," or something worse. Yet, Dr. Martin Luther King, Jr., and his followers were and are militant integrationists, prepared to give up their lives for their people; on the other hand, there are plenty of black nationalists who are anything but militant. The tension between integration and separatism has always rent the black community, but now it has led is to confuse questions of militancy with those of nationalism. In fact, the combinations vary; there is no straight identification of either integrationists or separatists with either militancy or accommodation. Field hands or house slaves could be either docile, "accommodating," or rebellious, and in all probablity most were all at once.

If today the house slaves have a bad press, it is largely because of their cultural assimilationism, from which it is erroneously deduced that they were docile. The first point may be valid; the second is not. LeRoi Jones, for example, in his brilliant book, *Blues People,* argues convincingly that field slaves had forged the rudiments of a distinct Afro-American culture whereas the house slaves largely took over the culture of the whites. He writes primarily about black music, but he might easily extend his analysis to language and other fields. There are clearly two ways of looking at this side of the house-slave experience. On the one hand, the house slaves reinforced white culture in the slave quarters; they were one of the Americanizing elements in the black community. On the other hand, they wittingly or unwittingly served as agents of white repression of an indigenous Afro-American national culture. Of course, both these statements are really the same; it is merely that they differ in their implicit value judgments. But we ought to remember that this role did not reduce the house slave to Uncle Tomism. Rather, it was played out by house slaves who were in their own way often quite rebellious and independent in their behavior. And therefore, even these slaves, notwithstanding their assimilationist outlook and action, also contributed in no small degree to the tradition of survival and resistance to oppression that today inspires the black liberation movement.

If today we are inclined to accept uncritically the contemptuous attitude that some critics have toward the house slave, we might ponder the reflections of the great black pianist, Cecil Taylor. Taylor was speaking in the mid–1960s —a century after slavery—but he was speaking of his own father in a way that I think applies to what might be said of house slaves. Taylor was talking to A. B. Spellman, as reported in Spellman's book, *Four Lives in the Bebop Business:*

> Music to me was in a way holding on to Negro culture, because there wasn't much of it around. My father has a great store of knowledge about black folklore. He could talk about how it was with the slaves in the 1860s, about the field shouts and hollers, about myths of black people . . . . He worked out in Long Island for a State Senator. He was a house servant and a chef at the Senator's sanatorium for wealthy mental wrecks. And actually it was my father more than the Senator himself who raised the Senator's children . . . .
>
> And I really used to get dragged at my father for taking such shit off these people. I didn't dig his being a house

> servant. I really didn't understand my old man; well, you're my generation and you know the difference between us and our fathers. Like, they had to be strong men to take what they took. But of course we didn't see it that way. So that I feel now that I really didn't understand my father, who was a really lovely cat. He used to tell me to stay cool, not to get excited. He had a way of letting other people display their emotions while keeping control of his own. People used to say to me, 'Cecil, you'll never be the gentleman you father was.' That's true. My father was quite a gentleman . . . . I wish that I had taken down more about all that he knew about black folklore, because that's lost too; he died in 1961.[5]

We may end with another misunderstood group of slaves—the drivers. These black slave foremen were chosen by the master to work under his direction or that of an overseer and to keep the hands moving. They would rouse the field slaves in the morning and check their cabins at night; would take responsibility for their performance; and often, would be the ones to lay the whip across their backs. In the literature the drivers appear as ogres, monsters, betrayers, and sadists. Sometimes they were. Yet, Mrs. Willie Lee Rose, in her book, *Rehearsal for Reconstruction,* notes that it was the drivers in the Sea Islands who kept the plantations together after the masters had fled the approach of the Yankees, who kept up discipline, and who led the blacks during those difficult days. Now, it is obvious that if the drivers were what they have been reported as having been, they would have had their throats cut as soon as their white protectors had left. In my own research for the war years I have found repeatedly, almost monotonously, that when the slaves fled the plantations or else took over plantations deserted by the whites, the drivers emerged as the leaders. Moreover, the runaway records from the North and from Canada reveal that a number of drivers were among those who successfully escaped the South.

One clue to the actual state of affairs may be found in the

agricultural journals for which many planters and overseers wrote about plantation matters. Overseers often complained bitterly that masters trusted their drivers more than they trusted them. They charged that quite often overseers would be fired at the driver's instigation and that, in general, masters were too close to their drivers and too hostile and suspicious toward their white overseers. The planters did not deny the charges; rather, they admitted them and defended themselves by arguing that the drivers were slaves who had earned their trust and that they had to have some kind of check on their overseers. Overseers were changed every two or three years on most plantations whereas drivers remained in their jobs endlessly. The normal state of affairs was for any given driver to remain in his position while a parade of overseers came and went.

It had to be so. The slaves had to be controlled if production was to be on schedule, but only romantics could think that a whip alone could effect that result. The actual amount of work done and the quality of life on the plantation was the result of a compromise between masters and slaves. It was a grossly unfair and one-sided compromise, with the master holding a big edge, but the slaves did not simply lie down and take whatever came. They had their own ways of foot-dragging, dissembling, delaying, and sabotaging. The role of the driver was to minimize the friction by mediating between the Big House and the quarters. On the one hand he was the master's man: he obeyed orders, inflicted punishments, and stood for authority and discipline. On the other hand, he could and did tell the master that the overseer was too harsh, too irregular; that he was incapable of holding the respect of the hands; that he was a bungler. The slaves generally knew just how much they had to put up with under a barbarous labor system but they also knew what even that system regarded as going too far. The driver was their voice in the Big House as well as the master's voice in the quarters.

Former slaves tell us of drivers who were sadistic monsters, but they also tell us of drivers who did everything possible to soften punishments and to protect the slaves as best they could. It was an impossible situation, but there is little evidence that drivers were generally hated by the field hands. The selection of a driver was a difficult matter for a master. First, the driver had to be a strong man, capable of bullying rather than being bullied. Second, he had to be uncommonly intelligent and capable of understanding a good deal about plantation management. A driver had to command respect in the quarters. It would be possible to get along for a while with a brutal driver who could rule by fear, but generally, planters understood that respect and acquiescence were as important as fear, and that a driver had to do more than make others afraid of him. It was then necessary to pick a man who had leadership qualities in the eyes of the slaves.

The drivers commanded respect in various ways. Sometimes they became preachers among the slaves and got added prestige that way. Sometimes, possibly quite often, they acted as judge and jury in the quarters. Disputes among slaves arose often, generally about women and family matters. If there were fights or bitter quarrels, and if they were called to the attention of the overseer or the master, the end would be a whipping for one or more participants. Under such circumstances, the driver was the natural choice of the slaves themselves to arbitrate knotty problems. With such roles in and out of the quarters, it is no wonder that so many drivers remained leaders during and after the war when the blacks had the choice of discarding them and following others.

Every plantation had two kinds of so-called "bad niggers." The first kind were those so designated by the masters because they were recalcitrant. The second kind were those so designated by the slaves themselves. These were slaves who may or may not have troubled the master directly but who were a problem to their fellow slaves because they stole, or bullied, or abused other men's women. The drivers were in a position to know what was happening in the quarters and to intervene to protect weaker or more timid slaves against these bullies. In short, the drivers' position was highly ambiguous and on balance was probably more often than not positive from the slave point of view. Whatever the intentions of the master, even in the selection of his own foremen—his own men, as it were—the slaves generally were not passive, not objects, but active agents who helped shape events, even if within narrow limits and with great difficulty.

We know that there were not many slave revolts in the South, and that those that did occur were small and local affairs. There were good reasons for the low incidence of rebellion: In general, the balance of forces was such that revolt was suicide. Under such conditions, black slaves struggled to live and to make some kind of life for themselves. If their actions were less bombastic and heroic than romantic historians would like us to believe, they were nonetheless impressive in their assertion of resourcefulness, dignity, and a strong sense of self and community. Had they not been, the fate of black America after emancipation would have been even grimmer than it was. For the most part the best that the slaves could do was live, not merely physically but with as much inner autonomy as was humanly possible.

Every man has his own judgment of heroism, but we might reflect on the kind of heroism alluded to by Cecil Taylor in his moving tribute to his father. There are moments in the history of every people—and sometimes these historical moments are enturies—in which they cannot do more than succeed in keeping themselves together and maintaining themselves as human beings with a sense of individual dignity and collective identity. Slavery was such a moment for black people in America, and their performance during it bequeathed a legacy that combined many negative elements to be exorcized[6] and repudiated with decisive elements of community self-discipline. If one were to tax even the privileged house slaves or drivers with the question, "Where were you when your people were groaning under the lash," they could, if they chose, answer with a paraphrase of the Abbé Sieyès, but proudly and without his cynicism, "We were with our people, and together we survived."

NOTES

1. See, e.g., C. L. R. James, "The Atlantic Slave Trade and Slavery: Some Interpretations of Their Significance in the Development of the United States and the Western World," *Amistad*, #1 (Vintage Books, 1970). Du Bois's writings are full of important ideas and hypotheses. See especially *Black Reconstruction in America* and *Souls of Black Folk*.

2. Vincent Harding, "Religion and Resistance Among Ante-Bellum Negroes, 1800–1860," August Meier and Elliott Rudwick, eds., *The Making of Black America* 1 (New York, 1969), 179–197.

3. Herbert Gutman has presented several papers to scholarly meetings and is close to completing a major book on the historical development of the black family from slavery to World War I. I am indebted to him for allowing me to see the manuscript in progress and for discussing the data with me.

4. Ms. diary in Louisiana State University library, Baton Rouge, La.

5. A. B. Spellman, *Four Lives in the Bebop Business* (New York, 1966), pp. 49–50.

6. I have discussed some of these negative features in "The Legacy of Slavery and the Roots of Black Nationalism," *Studies on the Left*, 6 (Nov.–Dec., 1966), 3–26. I stand by much of what I wrote there, but the essay is doubtless greatly weakened by a failure to appreciate black slave culture and its political implications. As a result, the political story I tried to tell is dangerously distorted. Still, that legacy of slavishness remains an important part of the story, and I think I identified some of its features correctly. I am indebted to many colleagues and friends for their criticism, without which I could not have arrived at the reconsiderations on which the present essay is based; in particular, the criticism of George Rawick has been indispensable.

Chapter 6

THE LEGACY OF SLAVERY AND THE ROOTS OF BLACK NATIONALISM (Revised)

Originally read to the Socialist Scholars Conference in New York City, September, 1966, this paper was subsequently published in Studies on the Left, 6, no. 6 (1966), *together with critiques by Herbert Aptheker, Frank Kofsky, and C. Vann Woodward, and a rejoinder by the author. Later, it was criticized privately and in print by a number of friends and colleagues, including George Rawick, Herbert Gutman, Sterling Stuckey, and August Meier. Much of the criticism was on the mark and forced me to make considerable revisions, as anyone who contrasts the original version with the essay "American Slaves and Their History" will readily see. Consequently, I found myself in something of a quandary as this volume was being prepared: Should I simply omit this one, try to correct errors by means of an introduction and postscript, or revise it altogether and thereby break my own rule and incur the displeasure of the several colleagues who have reprinted it in various anthologies of their own? I tried the second course first and found it wanting: the revision suggested in the introduction and postscript was simply too sweeping. I thought*

This essay was originally published in *Studies on the Left,* 6, Nov.–Dec. 1966. Reprinted by permission.

of omitting it altogether but could not do so because it embraces too much of my thinking on the central questions; I would be just as uneasy allowing the later essay to stand alone as I would be allowing the original version of this one to appear unaltered. My hope is that the two essays will be read together—as two ways of looking at a single reality. Taken together, even with drastic revisions in this essay, they present some apparent contradictions, for they proceed on different levels of analysis. Matters obviously cannot be left there; an effort must be made to reconcile or rather transcend these levels. To do so will require a big book, with much empirical data. Meanwhile, these explorations are offered in the hope that they contribute something toward that synthesis of the slave experience which will have to be the product of many hands.

AMERICAN RADICALS have long been imprisoned by the pernicious notion that the masses are necessarily both good and revolutionary, and by the even more pernicious notion that if they are not, they should be. The principal responsibility of radical historians, therefore, has too often been to provide the masses with historical heroes, to make them aware of their glorious tradition of resistance to oppression, and to portray them as having been implacably hostile to the social order in which they have been held. This viewpoint now dominates the black liberation movement, which for all its rhetoric about "thinking black," has merely followed a romantic line long ago laid out by radical and liberal white historians. It has become virtually sacrilege, if not blatant white racism, to suggest that slavery was a social system within which whites and blacks lived in harmony as well as antagonism, that there is little evidence of massive, organized opposition to the regime, that the blacks did not establish a revolutionary tradition of much significance, and that our main problem is to discover the reasons for the widespread accommodation and, perhaps more important, the long-term effects both of the accommodation and of that resistance which did occur.

In 1831 Nat Turner led a slave revolt on which has hung most of the legend of armed resistance to slavery. Of the 250 or so revolts chronicled and analyzed in Herbert Aptheker's *American Negro Slave Revolts,*[1] Turner's has pride of place and was described by Aptheker as a "cataclysm." Yet, when we look closely, this revolt, like the total history of such revolts, recedes in magnitude and actual intensity. As many of Aptheker's critics have pointed out, most of the 250 revolts probably never happened, being the imagination of hysterical, self-serving whites, minor plots that never matured, or mere local disturbances of a questionable nature. Of the four major revolts, two were crushed before the damage was done, although both (Gabriel Prosser's in 1800 and Denmark Vesey's in 1822) badly frightened the white South. During the nineteenth century only the big rising in Louisiana in 1811, about which we know almost nothing, and Turner's in 1831 came to fruition and reached impressive proportions. Even so painstaking and thorough a scholar as Aptheker has been unable to discover firm evidence of a major revolt between 1831 and 1865.

As for Turner's, less than one hundred slaves joined. A revolt of this size would rate little more than a page or two in a comprehensive study of slave revolts in Brazil and the Caribbean. To cite only two outstanding examples from Brazil, runaway slaves in the northeast of Brazil organized their own colony, Palmares, and waged an almost-century-long struggle for autonomy against both the Dutch and Portuguese. The history of Palmares stretches across the seventeenth century and culminates in the defeat of a regime that embraced twenty thousand black people.[2] During the first four decades of the nineteenth century there was a series of violent and extensive risings in Bahia, which culminated in the dramatic, Muslim-led, and almost successful attempt of the blacks to take the city in 1835.[3] We need not review the story of Haiti,[4] and the record of revolt in Jamaica, Cuba, the Guianas, and other slave countries is also impressive and unmatched in the United States. Even if, as Aptheker suggests, news of smaller risings was suppressed, the effect would have been to prevent the accumulation of a tradition to encourage and sustain revolt-prone slaves. On the balance, we find the absence or extreme weakness of such a tradition in the United States.

There were many reasons for this extreme weakness, a few of which should be noted briefly. The slave trade ended in 1808, although illegal importations continued to trickle in; in contrast, the trade to Cuba and Brazil remained open until the middle of the nineteenth century, and the trade to the Anglo-French Caribbean closed only a few decades before the fall of the slave regimes. The presence of a large number of newly imported Africans can generally be correlated with the incidence of revolt.[5] In the United States the overwhelming majority of the slaves during the ante-bellum period had been born and raised on Southern plantations. Their ranks received little reinforcement from newly enslaved and aggressive Africans.

A review of the history of Brazil and the Caribbean suggests that an important ingredient in the development of revolts out of local disturbances was the division of the whites into warring factions and the general weakness of the state apparatus. Together with these conditions went the general influence of geography in relation to state power. Where suitable terrain was combined with a weak state, runaway slaves could and did found maroon colonies, which directly fomented revolts and kept alive a tradition of armed resistance. With minor qualifications, these conditions did not exist in the United States.

A substantial revolt presupposed the formation of ideology and leadership. In Brazil and the Caribbean two circumstances combined to encourage both: the cultivation of sugar led to the establishment of plantations averaging more than 150 slaves, and the size of the white population was small. As a result, the blacks could keep alive much of their African culture or could develop a syncretized Afro-Brazilian or Afro-Cuban culture, which militated against the loss of identity and which, under proper conditions, could nurture resistance movements. Apart from Islam, non-Christian religious cults, generally of a syncretized type, played a great role in hemispheric slave revolts. In the United States an imposed Protestant Christianity was used to keep the slaves docile. The slaves, for their part, shaped that Christianity to their own needs and often turned it into a weapon of resistance. But there were two limitations. First, Southern slaves shared their religion with their masters; no matter how distinct their own Christianity, it was a religion that bound them to their masters on some important levels of thought and feeling. It could not, then, create the sharp distinction that separated the religion of the *vaudoun* priests of Saint-Domingue from the Catholic priests of the master class. Slave revolt in the United States could not so easily emerge as a holy war, as it did so often elsewhere in the hemisphere. Second, the religious efforts of the slaves could provide them with tools for survival and even an important degree of cultural autonomy, but in the context of Southern military and political relations it could rarely serve as a rallying point for total or armed resistance. If religion was one of the ingredients in the genesis of slave revolts, the complex of all those ingredients set limits to the subversive force of the religion itself.

Half the slaves in the United States lived on units of twenty or less; most of the others lived on plantations of not much more than fifty. Although blacks heavily outnumbered whites in large areas of the South—generally the areas of the most serious slave revolts—the blacks were, in general, floating in a white sea. The white planters were residents, not absentees; the non-slaveholders were loyal, armed, and disciplined; the country immediately beyond the plantation areas was inhabited by armed whites completely hostile to the slaves. Despite an occasional exception in the Dismal Swamps or Florida, death not refuge lay beyond the plantation. For this reason, among others, blacks often had to look to their masters to protect them against the depredations and viciousness of the poorer whites.

The residency of the planters and their hegemony across the South gave American slavery its particular quality and especially set it off from Caribbean slavery. Between the Revolution and the War for Southern Independence the treatment of slaves, defined as day-to-day conditions of life (food, housing, rigor of work routine, leisure time, incidence and character of corporal punishment) improved steadily and perceptibly. Although manumission was made increasingly difficult and escape from the system was sealed off, the harsh slave codes were steadily tempered by community sentiment and the interpretations of the state supreme courts. During the late ante-bellum period, steady pressure built up to reform the slave codes in order to protect slave family life and to check the more glaring abuses of the slave's person. The purpose and effect of these halting attempts and of the actual amelioration in practice and at law were not to pave the way to freedom, but to consolidate the system from within and without. Like all liberal reformism, it aimed to strengthen the social system.

For the planters these trends formed part of a developing world view within which paternalism became the specific manifestation of class consciousness. Paternalism did not mean kindness or generosity or love, although it embraced some of each; essentially it meant a special notion of duty and responsibility toward one's charges. Arbitrary power, harshness toward disobedience, even sadism, constituted its other side. For immediate purposes paternalism and the trend of treatment are especially noteworthy in confronting the slave with a world in which resistance could be quickly, severely, and legitimately punished whereas obedience placed him in a position to benefit from the favor of a master who more often than not had a genuine interest in his welfare. The picture of the docile, infantilized Sambo, drawn and analyzed so brilliantly by

Stanley Elkins, is one-sided, but Elkins is not far from the mark when he argues that the Southern regime greatly encouraged acceptance of and dependence on despotic authority.[6] Elkins errs in thinking that the Sambo personality arose only in the United States, for it arose wherever slavery existed. He does not err in thinking that it was especially marked and extensive in the United States where recourse to armed resistance was minimal and the tradition of paternalism took such firm root.

To say that slaves generally accommodated is not to say that they were dehumanized or failed to protest their condition. Historians have been quick to claim rebelliousness every time a slave broke a plow or stole a hog, but at least some room might be left for lack of initiative, thoughtlessness, stupidity, and venality. Yet, we do know of enough instances of deliberate sabotage to permit us to speak of a strong undercurrent of dissatisfaction and hostility, the manifestations of which require analysis. And we need to remember, apart from these, or rather side by side with them, that the pattern of behavior we call accommodation (for want of a better word) itself represented a struggle for cultural autonomy and unity and as such had its own positive value for black people beyond the terrible and basic question of staying alive.

One of the more prominent and irritating habits of recalcitrant slaves was stealing. Plundering the hog pen and the smokehouse was an especially happy pastime. Radical and liberal historians have taken particular delight in picking up the slaves' own shrewd suggestion that they might steal from each other but could only "take" from the master. The slaves reasoned that since they were chattel they could not steal a hog from the master because by eating it they merely transformed his property from one form to another. The trouble with being too quick to take delight in these charming stories of the Good Soldier Sambo is that they had their ominous side. Too often the masters enjoyed being outwitted in the same way that a tyrannical father sometimes enjoys being outwitted by a child. Every contortion necessary to do the job implied for the slave his own inferiority—certainly as understood by the whites and sometimes as perceived by the slaves themselves. Pilfering, lying, dissembling—these and other ways of warding off blows, settling scores, getting something extra to eat—helped keep the slaves sane and resilient, but they also provided a poor preparation for life in freedom. It is one thing to admire the slaves' resourcefulness, cunning, and toughness; it is another to pretend that a high, long-term price was not being paid in the process.

Arson and the mishandling of tools stand out as more positively rebellious acts. As expressions of frustration and resentment they might have, in a more explosively revolutionary context, constituted important political actions. As it was, they usually amounted to individual protests that often exposed all the slaves to terror and retaliation. It is not surprising that the slaves themselves often helped to put down such behavior and even cooperated to punish offenders. When they did so, they may simply have been playing the Tom, but in many cases they may have been protecting themselves collectively against having to take responsibility for individual actions that could in no way strengthen their position. If slaves generally sympathized with the outburst of a particular slave who could no longer stand his condition, they also understood how dangerous his behavior could be to the group and how futile it was. With luck a few slaves might do enough damage to ruin a planter, in which case he would be forced to sell out and probably to separate families and friends. Advocates of the philosophy of burn-baby-burn, whether on a Mississippi plantation in the 1850s or in a Northern ghetto in the 1970s, must surely know that, of necessity, it is the blacks who usually get burned most severely. On occasion a slave took direct action against a particularly unpleasant master or, more often, overseer, and killed him. For that manly act he would, if lucky, be hanged.

As we review these actions, which by no means exhaust

the range, we find the formation of a tradition of recalcitrance but not revolution; individual protest but not collective political action; awareness of oppression but not cumulative ideological growth. Thus, whereas many, and possibly even most, slaves came out of slavery with a psychology of dependence conditioned by paternalism, the most active spirits came out having learned little more than that they could get away with individual acts of undirected, misdirected, or naively directed violence (when they could get away with them at all). On other important levels of existence, they hammered out a rich culture in the slave quarters and guaranteed their survival as a community of individuals capable of resisting the worst of the pressures for infantilization and dehumanization. Important as this achievement was and remains, in combination with their more specifically political behavior it evoked its own high price. What was missing was that sense of group political consciousness and collective responsibility in political effort which form the essence of a revolutionary tradition. The slaves learned well how to defend themselves by collective effort; they had little chance to learn how to use that collective effort to counterattack.

The formation of class leadership presents another side of this development. Legend has it that house slaves and drivers, by virtue of their special positions, arrayed themselves on the side of the master against the field hands, who as the most oppressed were of course the most revolutionary and pure. Examination of plantation documents casts grave doubts on this legend. The range of behavior was wide, but there were many instances of identification and sympathy. The drivers, or slave foremen, present an even clearer case. In general, they compromised as best they could between the master to whom they had pledged loyalty and to whom they were indebted for special favors, and the slaves who constituted their everyday fellows. Often the driver stood as a protector or interpreter between slave and master or overseer. Drivers and house slaves often, although certainly not always, comprised a leading stratum in the eyes of the blacks as well as in the eyes of the whites.

In the Caribbean these privileged slaves led revolts; in the United States they served as agents of accommodation. Toussaint L'Ouverture was only the most prominent of insurrectionary leaders who had been trained to leadership within the system. The problem in the United States was not that the system did not create such privileged strata, nor that these strata were more docile or less courageous than those in the Caribbean. The problem was that the total environment reduced the possibilities for successful insurrection virtually to zero and therefore made accommodationists out of the most high-spirited slave leaders. When the mass exodus from the plantations took place during the War for Southern Independence, drivers and house slaves often led their people to the Union lines. Not docility but lack of a tradition of armed resistance conditioned their leadership.

Potential recruitment of insurrectionary leaders was hampered by many other circumstances, of which two are especially noteworthy. A group of potential leaders recruited from all strata were those who had sufficient strength, daring and resourcefulness to flee. The runaways are black folk heroes, with good reason, but they also drained the best elements out of the slave class. In much of Brazil and the Caribbean, runaways had nowhere to go except into the back country to form maroon colonies, the existence of which encouraged slave disorder and resistance. Then, too, the free blacks and mulattoes in the United States had little opportunity for self-development and rarely could or would provide leadership to slaves. Elsewhere in the hemisphere, where whites were relatively few, these free blacks and mulattoes were needed to fill a wide variety of social and economic functions. Often they prospered as a middle class. In some cases, feelings of racial solidarity or, as in Haiti, the racist stupidity of the whites, led them into partial indentification with the cause of black freedom. Thus, with the exception of a rare Nat Turner, black leadership fell to those whose position within the plantation itself encouraged accommodation and negated the possibilities of effective political organization.

The War for Southern Independence brought these tendencies to a head. The staggering truth is that not one full-scale slave revolt broke out during a war in which local white police power had been drastically reduced. In only a few isolated cases did slaves drive off their masters and divide the land among themselves. Many, perhaps most, struck for freedom by fleeing to Union lines at the first opportunity. The attitude of the slaves toward the Federals varied, but the great majority welcomed them with an adulation, trust and dependence that suggests the full force of the old paternalism.[7] Many blacks, free and slaves, Northern and Southern, entered the Union army, where despite humiliating discrimination they gave a creditable account of themselves in action.

For all that, the record of the slaves and ex-slaves during the war constituted a disaster. Having relied previously on the protection and guidance of their masters, they now threw themselves on the mercies of the Union army. As might be expected, untold thousands died in and out of virtual concentration camps, countless women were raped by Union troops, black soldiers generally found themselves used as menials and had to suffer insult and discrimination. Many decent and selfless white and black abolitionists accompanied the Union army south and earnestly worked to educate and organize the freedmen; they deserve all the praise and attention historians are now heaping on them. The fact remains that no black movement and only a weak black leadership emerged from the war.

As the war years passed into the period of Reconstruction, these patterns were reinforced. The blacks could and did fight for their rights, but rarely under their own leadership. When they offered armed resistance under competent leadership they did well enough, but mostly they relied on the leadership of white politicians, or on the protection of Federal troops, or on the advice of their own inexperienced leaders who in turn relied on whites. As Vernon Lane Wharton has observed, "The lesson learned was that the Negroes, largely unarmed, economically dependent, and timid and unresourceful after generations of servitude, would offer no effective resistance to violence."[8] When Whitelaw Reid asked black school children what they would do if someone tried to re-enslave them, most responded that the troops would not permit it. No wonder Northern public opinion asked contemptuously in 1875 why a black majority in Mississippi constantly had to call for outside help.

The blacks sealed their own fate by relying on the protection of others, although they hardly had much choice. The Republican party, the Union army and the Freedmen's Bureau all took on the role of protectors, but, if anything, the new paternalism proved much more flimsy and more insincere than the old. The best illustration may be found in the history of the Republican-sponsored, largely black militias. Ex-slaves responded to the calls of Republican governors and filled the ranks of state militias, which were put to effective use in guaranteeing Republican electoral victories. In several instances, especially toward the end of Reconstruction, militia units opposed each other on behalf of rival Republican factions. In the most appalling of these instances, the so-called Brooks-Baxter War in Arkansas in 1874, the Republican machine so discredited itself that the Democrats soon rode back to power. As Otis A. Singletary has sardonically observed, "The Negroes had been called to arms to fight in behalf of two white claimants for the governorship, as a consequence of which the Negro was eliminated as a political factor in Arkansas."[9] In Mississippi the radical governor, Adelbert Ames, called the blacks to arms in 1875 to counter Democratic violence and then lost his nerve and disarmed them in return for a worthless pledge from the opposition. Significantly the black politicians in his party almost unanimously opposed using the black troops in a showdown. The militia movement failed because it faced greater force, but no less because its leaders were never willing to see it steeled in battle, especially in defense of specifically black interests.

In other respects the Reconstruction experience followed parallel lines. In the famous Sea Island experiment the blacks placed their trust in white generals, some of whom meant well and tried hard but could not prevail in the face of Washington's duplicity. When the old plantation owners returned with Federal support, the blacks protested but ultimately accepted defeat without recourse to arms. Here, as with the militias, the masses seem to have been well ahead of their leaders. Demands for resistance were heard, antiwhite feeling was manifest and the desire for land grew apace, but the leadership proved timid or mortgaged, and action independent of whites was deemed impractical. Black congressmen and state legislators rarely fought for basic black interests and even opposed disfranchisement of ex-Confederate whites. With no powerful separate organizations and paramilitary units, without experience in leading their masses, they temporized and collapsed. Their fault did not lie in having coalesced with Northern whites, but in having coalesced from a position of weakness, without independent demands, organization and force. The masses moved sharply to the left and expressed an intense desire for land, but the old pattern persisted; they could not cut loose from accommodating leaders and from dependence on the ultimate authority of the whites. They did not so much demand, much less fight for, land, as they hoped it would be given them.

The black leaders saw the duplicity of their white Republican allies, but had nowhere to go. Many had been Northerners or privileged Southern mulattoes; their links with the masses had never been firm. When election time arrived they swallowed their doubts and frustrations and, with the best of intentions, lied to their people. Without adequate traditions and without confidence in their masses they made the best deals they could. This lying carried on an old habit.

Every slave, at some time or other, would outwit the white folks by pretending to be stupid or docile; unfortunately too often he simultaneously outwitted himself. When carried into slave leadership, it was generally impossible to outwit the whites without also outwitting the blacks. During the war, for example, the respected black pastor of the Baptist church in Virginia offered a prayer for the victory of the Confederate army. Subsequently, he was berated by his deacons for betraying the cause of the slaves, but he pacified them by saying, "Don't worry children; the Lord knew what I was talking about."[10] Undoubtedly, the Lord did, but the good pastor apparently never wondered whether or not his flock did also. If they did, the deacons would have no reason to be upset in the first place.

Some of the Reconstruction leaders simply sold out. As a distinguished South Carolina planter noted, they promised their people land and mules at every election but delivered only offices and jobs for themselves and their friends.[11] (Any resemblance to the War on Poverty is not of my making.)

Slavery and its aftermath left the blacks in a state of acute economic and cultural backwardness. They also left a tradition of accommodation to paternalistic authority on the one hand, and a tradition of nihilistic violence on the other. Not docility or infantilization, but innocence of organized effort and political consciousness plagued the black masses and kept plaguing them well into the twentieth century. As a direct result of these effects and of the virtually unchallenged hegemony of the slaveholders, the blacks had little opportunity to develop a sense of their own worth and had every opportunity to learn to despise themselves. The inability of the men during and after slavery to support their families adequately, and especially to protect their women from rape or abuse without forfeiting their own lives, reproduced those psychological deformities against which they had long had to struggle.

The remarkable ascendancy of Booker T. Washington

after the post-Reconstruction reaction must be understood against this background. We need especially to account for his enormous influence over the black nationalists who came after him. Washington tried to meet the legacy of slavery on its own terms. He knew that slavery had ill-prepared his people for political leadership; he therefore retreated from political demands. He knew that slavery had rendered manual labor degrading; he therefore preached the gospel of hard work. He knew that slavery had circumscribed the family and weakened elementary moral standards; he therefore preached the whole gamut of middle-class virtues and manners. He knew his people had never been able to stand on their own feet and face the whites as equals; he therefore preached self-reliance and self-help. Unhappily, apart from other ideological sins, he saw no way to establish self-reliance and self-respect except under the financial and social hegemony of the white upper classes. Somehow he meant to destroy the effects of paternalism in the long run by strengthening paternalism in the short run. It would be easy to say that he failed because of this tactic, but there is no way to be sure that the tactic was wrong in principle. He failed for other reasons, one of which was his reliance on the paternalistic, conservative classes at a time when they were rapidly losing power in the South to racist agrarian demagogues.

Washington's rivals did not, in this respect, do much better. The leaders of the NAACP repeatedly returned to a fundamental reliance on white leadership and money. Even Du Bois, in his classic critique of Washington, argued:

> While it is a great truth to say that the Negro must strive and strive mightily to help himself, it is equally true that unless his striving be not simply seconded, but rather aroused and encouraged by the initiative of the richer and wiser environing group, he cannot hope for great success.[12]

The differences between these militants and Washington's conservatives concerned emphases, tactics and public stance much more than ideological fundamentals. The differences were important, but their modest extent was no less so. The juxtaposition of the two tendencies reveals how little could be done even by the most militant without white encouragement and support. The wonder is that black Americans survived the ghastly years between 1890 and 1920 at all. Survival—and more impressive, growing resistance to oppression—came at the price of continuing many phases of a paternalistic tradition that had already sapped the strength of the masses.

The conflict between Washington and Du Bois recalled many earlier battles between two tendencies that are still with us. The first has accepted segregation at least temporarily, has stressed the economic development of the black community, and has advocated self-help. This tendency generally prevailed during periods of retrogression in race relations until the upsurge of nationalism in our own day. Washington was its prophet; black nationalism has been its outcome. The second has demanded integration, has stressed political action and has demanded that whites recognize their primary responsibility. Frederick Douglass was its prophet; the civil rights movement has been its outcome. Yet, the lines have generally been blurred. Du Bois often sounded like a nationalist, and Washington probably would have thought Malcolm X a madman.[13] This blurring reflects the dilemma of the black community as a whole and of its bourgeoisie in particular: How do you integrate into a nation that does not want you? How do you separate from a nation that finds you too profitable to release?

To probe the relationship between this past and the recent upsurge of the black masses requires more speculation and tentative judgment than one would like, but they cannot be avoided. Let us, at the risk of being schematic and one-sided, select several features of the developments of the last few decades and especially of the recent crisis for such analysis. In doing so let us bear in mind that the majority of blacks today live outside the South; that they are primarily urban, not rural, in all parts of the country; that whole cities are on the way to becoming black enclaves; that the problem increasingly centers on the urban North and West.[14] Let us bear in mind also that the only large-scale, organized black mass movements until recently have been nationalist. Garvey commanded an organization of hundreds of thousands; the Muslims have tens of thousands and influence many more. No integrationist organization has ever acquired such numerical strength; none has ever struck such deep roots in the black ghettos.

Garvey's movement emphasized blackness as a thing of beauty, and struggled to convince the black masses to repudiate white leadership and paternalism. The pompous titles, offices, uniforms and parades did and do evoke ridicule, but their importance lay, as Edmund David Cronon says, "in restoring the all but shattered Negro self-confidence." There was enormous ideological significance in Garvey's delightful description of a light-skinned mulatto opponent as "a white man passing for Negro."[15]

A decisive break with the white man's church, if not wholly with his religion, has formed a major part of black nationalist thinking. In view of the central role of anti-Christian ideology in the slave risings of Brazil and the Caribbean, and the generally accommodationist character of American Christianity, this has been a rational response to a difficult problem. Garvey tried to organize his own African Orthodox church. The Islamic tendency, including that of Elijah Muhammed's Nation of Islam, has followed the maxim of Noble Drew Ali's earlier black-nationalist Islamic movement: "Before you can have a God, you must have a nationality." Garvey's Black Jesus and Muhammed's Allah have had many attributes of a tribal deity. Of special importance in Muhammed's teaching is his decidedly un-Islamic denial of an afterlife. In this way Black Muslim eschatology embodies a sharp reaction against accommodationist ideology. The tendency to turn away from the white man's religion has taken many forms, including conversion to Catholicism ostensibly because of its lack of a color line. In Catholic Brazil, on the other hand, an equivalent reason is given by blacks who embrace Protestantism.[16]

Black Protestants in the United States have largely attended self-segregated churches since Reconstruction. With the collapse of Reconstruction these churches, especially in the South, played an increasingly accommodationist role, but they also served as community centers, protective agencies, marriage counseling committees and leadership training schools. As objective conditions changed, so did many ministers, especially the younger ones. One of the great ironies of the current struggle for integration has been the leading role played by ministers whose training and following have been made possible by segregated organizations. The experience of the Protestant churches and their anti-Christian rivals brings us back to slavery's legacy of accommodationist, but by no means necessarily treasonable, leadership, of an absence of collective political effort, of paternalistically induced dependence and of the constant threat of emasculation. Theoretically, a militant mass leadership could have arisen from sources other than enforced segregation; historically there seems to have been no other way.[17]

The first difficulty with the integrationist movement arises not from its ultimate commitment, which may or may not be desirable, but from the determined opposition of the whites, whose hostility to close association with blacks recedes slowly if at all. Integration may mean only desegregation, and outstanding black intellectuals insist that that is all they want it to mean; it need not mean assimilation. In fact, however, the line is difficult to hold, and segregationists probably do not err in regarding one as the prelude to the other. In any case, de facto segregation in education and housing is growing worse, and many of the professed goals of the civil rights movement look further away than ever. Communities like Harlem face substantially the same social problems today as they did forty years ago.[18] We need not dwell on the worsening problem of black unemployment and its implications.

Even where progress, however defined, occurs, the frustration of the black masses deepens. The prosperity of recent decades has widened the gap between blacks and whites, even of the same class. The rise of the African peoples has inspired blacks here, but has also threatened to open a gap in political power and dignity between Africans and Afro-Americans.[19]

The resistance of whites and the inflexibility of the social system constitute only half the problem. A. James Gregor, in an article published in *Science & Society* in 1963,[20] analyzes an impressive body of sociological and psychological literature to demonstrate that integration under the disorderly conditions of American capitalist life more often than not undermines the development and dignity of the participating blacks. He shows that the problems of the black masses, in contradistinction to those of the bourgeoisie, become intensified by an integration which, in the nature of things, must pass them by. As Gregor demonstrates, black nationalism has been the political reply of these masses and especially of the working class. Similarly, in his honest and thoughtful book, *Crisis in Black and White,* Charles E. Silberman analyzes cases such as that in New Rochelle, in which poor black and rich white children had the wonderful experience of integrating in school. Why should anyone be surprised that the experiment proved a catastrophe for the black children, who promptly lost whatever ambition they might have had?[21]

When liberals and academics speak of a "crisis of identity," they may sometimes merely wish to divert attention from the prior fact of oppression, but, by whatever name, that crisis exists. Slavery and its aftermath severely damaged the black masses; they remain today profoundly shaken. It does us no good to observe, with Kardiner and Ovesey, that a psychology of oppression can disappear only when the oppression has disappeared.[22] It does us no good to admit that the sickness of white racism is more dangerous than the sickness it has engendered. We face an aroused, militant black community that has no intention of waiting for others to heal themselves. Those who believe that this disorder, suggestively but dangerously miscalled emasculation, is the figment of the liberal imagination ought to read the words of any militant leader from David Walker to W. E. B. Du Bois, from Frederick Douglass to Martin Luther King, from Robert F. Williams to Malcolm X. The cry has been to assert manhood and renounce servility. Black intellectuals today—Killens, Baldwin, Ellison—make the point in one way or another. Let me quote only one, Ossie Davis, on the death of Malcolm X:

> Negroes knew that Malcolm—whatever else he was or was not—*Malcolm was a man!*
> White folks do not need anybody to remind them that they are men. We do! This was his one incontrovertible benefit to his people. Protocol and common sense require that Negroes stand back and let the white man speak up for us, defend us, and lead us from behind the scene in our fight. This is the essence of Negro politics. But Malcolm said to hell with that! Get up off your knees and fight your own battles. That's the way to win back your self-respect. That's the way to make the white man respect you. And if he won't let you live like a man, he certainly can't keep you from dying like one.[23]

Is it any wonder, then, that Dr. King could write, almost as a matter of course, that the blacks in Birmingham during the summer of 1963 shook off three hundred years of psychological slavery and found out their own worth?[24] It is no less instructive that his aide, the Reverend Wyatt T. Walker, denounced as "hoodlums" and "winos" those who responded to the attempt on King's life by attacking the white racists. King himself put it bluntly when he pleaded that the black militant be allowed to march and sit-in. "If his repressed emotions do not come out in these nonviolent ways, they will come out in ominous expressions of violence."[25]

King and his followers apparently have believed that concerted action for integration can cure the ills engendered by slavery and subsequent oppression and break down discrimination at the same time. In one sense he was right. His greatest achievement was to bring order and collective political effort to a people who had learned little of the necessity for either. But King's followers must deliver victory or face grave consequences. As we have seen, not all slaves and freedmen yielded meekly to the oppressor. Many fought, sometimes with great ferocity, but they generally fought by lashing out individually rather than by organized revolutionary effort. It would be the crowning irony if the civil rights movement has taught just enough of the lesson of collective political effort to guarantee greater and more widespread nihilism in the wake of its inability to realize its program.

More and more young black radicals are currently pouring over Frantz Fanon's psychopathic panegyric to violence. Fanon argues that violence frees the oppressor from his inferiority complex and restores his self-respect.[26] Perhaps; but it is also the worst way to do either. Black Americans, like colonials, have always resorted to violence without accomplishing those goals. A slave who killed his overseer did not establish his manhood thereby—any wild animal can kill—he merely denied his docility. Violence can serve Fanon's purpose only when it is collective; but then, it is precisely the collective effort, not the violence, that does the healing.[27]

The legend of black docility threatens to betray those who perpetuate it. They are ill-prepared for the yielding of one part of the slave tradition—accommodation and servility—to another part—antisocial and nihilistic action. The failure of integration and the lawlessness to which the blacks have for so long been subjected combine to produce that result. James Baldwin, and especially Malcolm X in his remarks on the prestige of the ghetto hustler, have each warned of this danger.[28] Bayard Rustin has made a similar point with gentle irony:

> From the point of view of motivation, some of the healthiest Negro youngsters I know are juvenile delinquents: vigorously pursuing the American Dream of material acquisition and status, yet finding the conventional means of attaining it blocked off, they do not yield to defeatism but resort to illegal (and sometimes ingenious) methods. They are not alien to American culture.[29]

Those historians who so uncritically admire the stealing of hogs and smashing of plows by slaves might consider its modern equivalent. In the words of Silberman:

> There are other means of protest, of course: misbehaving in school, or dropping out of school altogether; not showing up for work on time, or not showing up at all (and lying about the reason); breaking school windows or ripping telephone receivers out of outdoor phone booths; or the oldest form of protest of all, apathy—a flat refusal to cooperate with the oppressor or to accept his moral code.[30]

Black nationalism, in its various manifestations, constitutes a necessary response on the part of the black masses. The Muslims, for example, have understood the inner needs of the working-class blacks who have filled their ranks and have understood the futility—for these people at least—of integrationist hopes. Their insistence on the forcible assertion of a dignified, disciplined, collectively responsible black community represents a rational response to a harsh reality.[31] We need waste little time on what is unrealistic, romantic or even reactionary in the Nation of Islam or other nationalist groups; they are easy to see. Ralph Bunche, in his radical days, Gunnar Myrdal, and many others have for years pointed out that the idea of a separate black economy is a will-o'-the-wisp and that the idea of a separate territory is less than that. Yet I am not sure how to answer Marc Schleifer, who in 1963 asked whether these goals were less realistic than those of equality under capitalism or a socialist revolution in in the foreseeable future.[32] I am not sure, either, that Malcom X, Harold W. Cruse, and others have not been wiser than their Marxist critics in demanding black ownership of everything in Harlem.[33] Such ownership will do little toward the creation of a black economy, but many of its advocates are easily bright enough to know as much. The point is that it may, as Malcolm X suggested, play a decisive role in the establishment of community stability and self-respect.

The black struggle for equality in America has always had two tendencies—integrationist and separatist—and it is likely to retain both. Since a separate economy and national territory are not serious possibilities, the struggle for economic integration will undoubtedly be pressed forward. For this reason alone some degree of unity between the civil rights and nationalist tendencies may be expected. The black bourgeoisie and its allied stratum of skilled and government clerical workers will certainly continue its fight for integration, but the interest of the black workers in this fight is, at bottom, even greater. At the same time, clearly there will be serious defeats, as well as some victories, and the slogan "Freedom Now!" is now turning to ashes.

The cumulative problems of past and present nonetheless demand urgent action. The assertion of black hegemony in specific cities and districts—nationalism if you will—offers the only politically realistic hope of transcending the slave heritage. First, it seems the only way for black communities to police themselves, to curb antisocial elements and to enforce adequate health and housing standards, and yet break with paternalism and instill pride and a sense of worth. Second, it seems the best way to build a position of strength from which to fight for a proper share of jobs and federal funds as a matter of right not privilege. Black nationalism may yet prove to be the only force capable of building upon the genuine achievements of Afro-American culture, as well as of restraining the impulse to violence, of disciplining black rebelliousness and of absorbing the nihilistic tradition into a socially constructive movement. If this seems like a conservative rendering of an ostensibly revolutionary movement, I can only answer that there are no ingredients for a successful, independent black revolution, and that black nationalism can ultimately go only a few steps further toward the left than the white masses. The rise of specifically black cities, countries and districts with high-quality black schools, well-paid teachers, as well as political leaders, churches and community centers, could and should uproot the negative features of the slave tradition once and for all, could and should act as a powerful lever for structural reform of the American economy and society.

I do not offer these remarks as a program for a black movement, for the time is past when white men can offer programs to black militants. They are, happily, no longer listening. But I do submit that they are relevant to the formation of a program for ourselves—for the American Left. If this analysis has merit, the demands of the black community will increasingly swing away from the traditional appeal to federal power and toward the assertion of local and regional autonomy. Even now Bayard Rustin and others warn that federal troops can only preserve the status quo. I should observe, further, that the appeals to Washington reflect the convergence of two powerful and debilitating traditions: slave-engendered paternalistic dependence and the growing state paternalism of white America. Let us admit that the naive fascination of leftists for centralized power has, since the 1930s, greatly strengthened this tendency. With such labels as "progressive" and even "socialist," corporate liberalism has been building what William Appleman Williams has aptly called a nonterroristic totalitarian society. Yet American socialism has never even posed a theoretical alternative. When Professor Williams called for a program of regional and local reassertion and opposition to centralization, he was dismissed by most radicals as a utopian of doubtful mental competence. We may now rephrase his question: How do we propose to support an increasingly nationalistic black radicalism, with its demands for local hegemony, unless we have an ideology and program of opposition to the centralization of state power?

The possible courses for the black liberation movement include a total defeat in an orgy of violence (we ought to remember that there is nothing inevitable in its or our victory), a compromise with imperialism in return for some degree of local rule or the integration of its bourgeois strata, and the establishment of black power on the basis of a developing opposition to American capitalism. Since its future depends to a great extent on the progress of its integrationist struggle for a place in the economy, the black community must for a while remain well to the left of the current liberal consensus by its demands for public works and structural reform. But reform could occur under the auspices of an expansion rather than a contraction of state centralization, and the most militant of the black leaders may have to settle for jobs and local political control in return for allegiance to a consolidating national and international empire. The final result will be decided by the struggle within white America, with the blacks playing the role of an increasingly independent ally for one or another tendency. Notwithstanding some offensive and pretentious rhetoric, the advocates of black power have judged their position correctly. They are determined to win control of the ghettoes, and we would be foolish not to bet on them. The use to which they put that power, however, depends neither on our good wishes nor on their good intentions, but on what they are offered as a *quid pro quo*. For American socialism the black revolt opens an opportunity for relevance that has been missing for decades. What we do with that opportunity is our problem, not theirs.

Written in July, 1966; revised, August, 1970

Postscript: On the relationship between Dr. Du Bois and Mr. Washington, Dr. Conor Cruise O'Brien, having heard the original version of this paper as delivered to the SSC, kindly wrote me about a conversation he had with Dr. Du Bois in Ghana. The letter follows, with Dr. O'Brien's permission:

> During the last year of his life in Ghana, W. E. B. Du Bois had dinner with me at Legon. Normally, in his extreme old age, he did not say very much, but his mind was perfectly clear; if something came up which he felt to be of importance, he would put his oar in, memorably. On this occasion someone mentioned Booker T. Washington in a context that implied that he had been a stooge for the bosses. Du Bois strongly demurred. He said that he had in his youth spoken slightingly of Booker T. Washington and had been memorably reprimanded by his aunts, who told him that it ill became one who had been born free to speak disrespectfully of a man whose back bore the marks of the lash. He went on to say that in the circumstances of the South in Washington's day, he could not have done anything effective in any other way. He —Du Bois—with his Northern and relatively privileged background, had been able to take a different stance and had been obliged to enter into public controversy with Washington. He did not want that controversy to obscure the merits of what Washington had achieved. He spoke with evident strong feeling, and all of us who heard him were deeply impressed.

NOTES

1. Herbert Aptheker, *American Negro Slave Revolts* (New York, 1943, 1963).
2. Edison Carneiro, *O Quilombo dos Palmares, 1630–1695* (São Paulo, 1947).
3. Cf., Abbé Ignace Etienne, "La Secte musulmane des Malès du Brésil et leur révolte en 1835," *Anthropos,* 4 (1909), 99–105; 405–415.
4. Cf., esp. C. L. R. James, *The Black Jacobins: Toussaint L'Ouver-*

ture and the San Domingo Revolution, 2nd ed. rev. (New York, 1963), which deserves to rank as a classic of Marxian historiography but has been largely ignored, perhaps because of the author's Trotskyist politics.

5. For example, Palmares was established by Angolans. See "Carta do Governador Fernao de Souza Coutinho . . ." in Ernesto Ennes, *As Guerras nos Palmares* (São Paulo, 1938), pp. 133-138, Nina Rodrigues, *Os Africanos no Brasil,* 3rd ed. (São Paulo, 1945), chap. 3.

6. Stanley M. Elkins, *Slavery: A Problem in American Institutional and Intellectual Life* (Chicago, 1959), esp. chap. 3.

7. Bell Irvin Wiley, *Southern Negroes, 1861–1865* (New Haven, 1965; first pub., 1938), esp. pp. 14–15.

8. Vernon Lane Wharton, *The Negro in Mississippi, 1865–1900* (New York, 1965; first pub. 1947), p. 190.

9. Otis A. Singletary, *Negro Militia and Reconstruction* (Austin, 1952), p. 65.

10. Wiley, *Southern Negroes,* p. 107.

11. Charles Manigault, "Souvenirs of Our Ancestors & of My Immediate Family," ca. 1873. Ms. in the Manigault Papers, University of North Carolina.

12. W. E. Burghardt Du Bois, *The Souls of Black Folk* (New York, 1964; first pub. 1903), p. 53.

13. For the period 1890–1915 see August Meier's careful and illuminating *Negro Thought in America: Racial Ideologies in the Age of Booker T. Washington* (New York, 1964).

14. For a perceptive discussion of these trends see Charles E. Silberman, *Crisis in Black and White* (New York, 1964), esp. pp. 7, 29–31.

15. Edmund David Cronon, *Black Moses: The Story of Marcus Garvey and the Universal Negro Improvement Association* (Madison, 1955, 1964), p. 174. It was never Garvey's intention to send all blacks back to Africa; he wanted a strong African nation to serve as a protector to blacks everywhere. See esp. the interview with Garvey in James Weinstein, ed., "Black Nationalism: The Early Debate," *Studies on the Left,* 4, no. 3 (1964), 50–58.

The idea of black nationality in America stretches back to the beginnings of the nineteenth century, if not earlier. See esp. Herbert Aptheker, "Consciousness of Negro Nationality to 1900," *Toward Negro Freedom* (New York, 1956), pp. 104–111; also, Benjamin Quarles, *The Negro in the Making of America* (New York, 1964), p. 157.

16. Roger Bastide, and Florestan Fernandes, *Brancos e negros em São Paulo,* 2nd ed. (São Paulo, 1959), p. 254.

17. This recent experience, especially of SCLC, reveals the legacy of the past in other ways as well. Louis E. Lomax has criticized Dr. King for organizational laxness and has related the problems of the SCLC to the structure of the Baptist Church, "The Negro Baptist Church is a nonorganization. Not only is each congregation a sovereign

body, dictated to by no one, but it would appear that the members who come together and form a Baptist Church are held together only by their mutual disdain for detailed organization and discipline." *The Negro Revolt* (New York, 1962), p. 86. As a result, according to Lomax, the SCLC is a loose, scattered organization that mobilizes itself only with great difficulty. Lomax makes good points but fails to note the extent to which this weakness flows from the entire history of black America and especially the black South. With justice, one could argue that the remarkable strength of SCLC in the face of this amorphousness is a singular tribute to Dr. King's political genius. He has mobilized masses who are ill prepared for the kind of puritanical discipline preached by Elijah Muhammed.

18. Gilbert Osofsky, *Harlem: The Making of a Ghetto* (New York, 1966), p. 179.

19. See the perceptive remarks on these two kinds of gaps in Oscar Handlin, *Fire-Bell in the Night: The Crisis in Civil Rights* (Boston, 1964), pp. 21–22, 53; C. Eric Lincoln, *The Black Muslims in America* (Boston, 1961), p. 45; and James Baldwin, *The Fire Next Time* (New York, 1964), pp. 105–106.

20. A. James Gregor, "Black Nationalism: A Preliminary Analysis of Negro Radicalism," *Science & Society,* 27 (Fall 1963), 415–432.

21. Silberman, *Crisis in Black and White,* p. 298. Even under more favorable conditions, as John Oliver Killens has noted, black children in the South often have a feeling of belonging that is undermined when they move north. *Black Man's Burden* (New York, 1965), pp. 84–85.

22. Abram Kardiner, and Lionel Ovesey, *The Mark of Oppression: Explorations in the Personality of the American Negro* (New York, 1951, 1962), p. 387.

23. Ossie Davis, "On Malcolm X," in *The Autobiography of Malcolm X* (New York, 1965), p. 453.

24. Martin Luther King, Jr., *Why We Can't Wait* (New York, 1964), p. 111.

25. Silberman, *Crisis in Black and White,* pp. 122, 199.

26. Frantz Fanon, *The Wretched of the Earth* (New York, 1965). But see also two good critiques in *Studies on the Left,* 6, no. 3 (May–June, 1966): Samuel Rohdie, "Liberation and Violence in Algeria," 83–89, and esp. A. Norman Klein, "On Revolutionary Violence," 62–82.

27. The warning of Killens on this matter is worth quoting:

> The advocates of absolute nonviolence have reckoned without the psychological needs of Black America. Let me state it plainly: There is in many Negroes a deep need to practice violence against their white tormentors. *Black Man's Burden,* p. 113.

The Muslims understand this very well, as does Dr. King; they try to substitute internal discipline and collective effort for the violence itself.

28. Baldwin, *The Fire Next Time,* pp. 35–37; *The Autobiography of Malcolm X,* pp. 315–316.

29. Bayard Rustin, "From Protest to Politics: The Future of the Civil Rights Movement," in F. L. Broderick and A. Meier, eds., *Negro Protest Thought in the Twentieth Century* (Indianapolis, 1965), p. 410.

30. Silberman, *Crisis in Black and White,* pp. 47–48.

31. The best study of the Muslims is E. U. Essien-Udom, *Black Nationalism: A Search for Identity in America* (New York, 1964). Elijah Muhammed has demonstrated remarkable awareness of the persistence of the slave tradition, even in its most elusive forms. His denunciation of black conspicuous consumption, for example, correctly views it as essentially a reflection of the mores of the slaveholders and counterpurposes to it standards that recall those of revolutionary petty bourgeois puritanism.

32. Marc Schleifer, "Socialism and the Negro Movement," *Monthly Review,* 15 (Sept. 1963), 225–228.

33. For a suggestive theoretical defense of such a demand see Harold W. Cruse, "Revolutionary Nationalism and the Afro-American," *Studies on the Left,* 2, no. 3 (1962), 12–25; and his subsequent communication in 3, no. 1 (1962), esp. p. 70. See also *The Autobiography of Malcolm X,* p. 318.

Chapter 7

THE TREATMENT OF SLAVES IN DIFFERENT COUNTRIES Problems in the Applications of the Comparative Method

AFTER A LONG and often discouraging struggle, the comparative method is finally beginning to triumph over parochialism in the study of Afro-American slavery. As it is extended, almost every question relevant to Southern slavery will take on a new and richer meaning, but only if considerable rigor is brought to our analyses. To demonstrate the possibilities and pitfalls, let us consider the seemingly narrow and simple problem of the treatment of slaves in the several New World plantation systems.

When scholars discuss the treatment of slaves, they ought to make clear the meaning of the word "treatment," but they rarely do. As a result, there has been much waste of time, effort, and good temper. In such circumstances comparative analysis tends to obscure rather than illuminate. We ought to distinguish carefully the different meanings of the word, for there are at least three. Once proper distinctions have been made, many quarrels disappear. Ulrich Phillips was right in thinking that Southern slaves were better treated than others, and Gilberto Freyre was right in thinking that Brazilian

This essay was originally published in Laura Foner and Eugene D. Genovese, Editors, *Slavery in the New World: A Reader in Comparative History* © 1969. Reprinted by permission of Prentice-Hall, Inc., Englewood Cliffs, New Jersey.

slaves were: They were talking about quite different things. No wonder so fine a scholar as C. R. Boxer has scoffed at the claims. Without close definition all such statements reduce themselves to romantic speculations.

The three basic meanings of "treatment" are:

1. *Day-to-day living conditions:* Under this rubric fall such essentially measurable items as quantity and quality of food, clothing, housing, length of the working day, and the general conditions of labor.
2. *Conditions of life:* This category includes family security, opportunities for an independent social and religious life, and those cultural developments which, as Elkins has shown, can have a profound effect on the personality of the slave.
3. *Access to freedom and citizenship:* This is the meaning for "treatment" that is implied in the work of Frank Tannenbaum and those who follow him closely. It ought to be immediately clear that there is no organic connection between this and the first category and only an indirect connection between this and the second.

When Ulrich Bonnell Phillips insisted that Southern slaves were the best treated, he meant in terms of the first category. Those who have argued in favor of the proposition that Brazilian slaves were the best treated have meant in terms of the third category and sometimes the second; occasionally, as in Freyre's case, they have also argued in terms of the first, but in doing so, they have certainly talked nonsense.

Tannenbaum, in his seminal essay, *Slave and Citizen,* accepts Freyre's assertion that Brazilian slaves were better treated than others, but his celebrated thesis requires only that they had greater access to freedom and citizenship. There was in fact no necessary relationship between good treatment in Tannenbaum's sense—which describes primarily the treatment of the black slave as a black man—and good treatment in the sense of day-to-day conditions of life. When Davis writes that the ease and frequency of manumission provides the "crucial standard in measuring the relative harshness of slave systems," he creates unnecessary difficulties and is in danger of confusing the extent to which a slave society is closed with the extent to which it deals severely with its slaves on a day-to-day basis. Often, as Davis himself notes, a slave system is harsh in one sense, but mild in another.[1] Davis's ambiguity is usually nothing more than a certain carelessness —the more striking since his book is a model of careful work—in the use of the appropriate terms. It nonetheless contributes to his unfortunate insistence that we cannot make a judgment on the relative severity of the slave systems. We can, but only if we compare specific kinds of treatment and their consequences, instead of trying to use a single standard of judgment.

The relationship among these different meanings may be observed in such matters as miscegenation and manumission. In some ways miscegenation and the doctrine that "money whitens the skin," which is often taken as indicative of good treatment, damaged the standard of living of those who remained field slaves. Brazilian planters took the precaution of locking up their allegedly well-treated slaves, including house slaves, every night. (What Southern slaveholder had to do that?) In order to do so, the Brazilians had to build tight, often windowless, escape-proof cabins. Thus, Brazilian slave quarters were generally inferior to those in the United States. These precautions were made necessary by the enormous free colored population in Brazil, where racial bars were minimized and where even blacks were often presumed to be free men. The resultant ease with which runaway slaves could pass for free men made greater police control of the plantations necessary. Similarly, with respect to the practice of manumission, it was much easier for Brazilian than for American masters to liberate their slaves and thereby escape their patriarchal responsibilities. There is evidence that at least some of Brazil's vaunted voluntary manumissions were of this kind.

If we consider such matters as slave food supplies, we may see at a glance how good treatment in one sense implies bad treatment in another. In the United States masters generally provided slaves with food; individual garden plots were supplementary and inessential. In the British West indies and elsewhere slaves had to raise their own food on special provision grounds. As a result, the slaves in the United States received the better treatment in two ways: their food supply was steady and generally adequate at least in bulk; and their free time was their own. In the West Indies slaves had to choose between a good deal of extra work after field hours and on weekends and seeing their families go without sufficient nourishment. Yet, these same circumstances represented better treatment for the West Indian slaves—more favorable conditions of life—in the second of our senses of the word. Although not supported at law, the system of provision grounds became so well established in custom that the slaves developed a strong sense of private property, which was almost always respected by the masters. The system required that slaves be allowed to travel into town on "Market Sundays" to sell their produce and buy items they could not grow on their particular land. West Indian slaves thereby developed a much freer social life and much stronger sense of independence.

Similarly, with respect to clothing and the condition of the quarters, Southern masters appear to have taken far greater pains than West Indians to guarantee adequate supplies and to police for cleanliness and order. In so doing they could pride themselves on providing the better treatment in the first, purely material, sense and yet unwittingly plead guilty to the greater throttling of their people's independence and personality development.

By separating the different categories of treatment we can begin to measure those features which lend themselves to measurement, as well as to assess more easily those which require qualitative judgment. Having done that much we can study the different kinds of treatment to see to what extent they were mutually encouraging, directly contradictory, or merely compatible. In general, for example, it is a striking fact that the marked improvement in the day-to-day conditions of American slave life during the nineteenth century proceeded hand-in-hand with the rapid disappearance of the possibilities for escaping the system.

A comparative analysis of treatment, in any of its meanings, must take place on at least two different levels simultaneously. First, conditions must be measured or assessed at a given historical moment. Race relations or working conditions must be evaluated for Cuba, Brazil, Jamaica, Saint-Domingue, and Virginia for a certain year or decade, for each slave system reflected the exigencies of the world market at any given moment in time. Second—more difficult but probably more important—conditions must be measured or assessed according to corresponding points of historical development. The second half of the seventeenth century in Barbados, for example, must be compared and contrasted with the second half of the eighteenth century in Saint-Domingue or the middle of the nineteenth century in Cuba. One sugar boom has to be measured in economic and social effects against another. These two sets of investigations, undertaken with care in their particulars and a reasonable degree of historical imagination in their combination, should lay bare the details of life in time and place with due attention to the state of the world market and the technological level of each section of the slave economy.

The work of Gilberto Freyre provides a good opportunity for a review of the methodological problems inherent in comparative analysis in general and a comparative analysis of the treatment of slaves in particular. The notion that Brazilian slaves received better treatment than others stems principally from his work, in which it has been a running thread for more than forty years. In his youthful paper on "Social Life in Brazil in the Middle of the Nineteenth Century," he asserted simply that slaves were well fed, well housed, well clothed, and generally well treated.[2] He attributed the belief that they were victims of cruelty to British-inspired antislavery crusaders and to the propagandistic zeal of Brazilian abolitionists. Gross exaggerations, he argued, reinforced guilt feelings to convince Brazilian public opinion that this distortion was the historical reality whereas that reality was in fact another matter: "The Brazilian slave lived like a cherub if we contrast his lot with that of the English and other European factory workers in the middle of the last century." Cruelty did exist, of course, but it was exceptional. Freyre added to these judgments a perceptive and essential observation: He noted that the cruelty of masters to slaves must be evaluated in the light of the cruelty of fathers to children, which in patriarchal Brazil was common. In the patriarchal setting of a quasi-feudal colony, the word and whim of the father was absolute law. Children were punished severely and even killed for disobedience. The evidence of cruelty to slaves to some degree indicates the extension of the brutal side of family relations to the wider social family. In this way Freyre inadvertently showed how cruel treatment in one sense could imply good treatment in another.

Freyre extended these judgments back into the sixteenth and seventeenth centuries in his most famous work, *The Masters and the Slaves,*[3] but he said too much in defense of his thesis. When, for example, he noted that slaves could and did become artists, entertainers, dentists, barbers, teachers, and so forth—that they were well treated in several senses of the word—he failed to note that the very possibility of escape from the rigors of gang labor necessarily made the lot of the overwhelming majority the more unbearable. Fluidity of caste, under certain conditions, might have rendered the Brazilian slaves, as a class, more rebellious, dissatisfied, and alienated from the plantation community than were the slaves of the Old South.

Freyre's argument wavers when considered over time. On

the one hand, he insists that Luso-Brazilian patriarchalism, with its medieval and Moorish ideas of family and society, guaranteed the slaves protection during the sixteenth and seventeenth centuries whereas the inroads of urbanization, industrialization, and increased production for the world market undermined patriarchalism during the second half of the eighteenth and especially during the nineteenth century. On the other hand, he insists on maintaining his thesis for the mid-nineteenth century as well. Specifically, he is forced—in *The Mansions and the Shanties* and retrospectively in *Ordem e Progresso*[4]—to proclaim the patriarchalism of the mine-owners of Minas Gerais and of the parvenu coffee planters of São Paulo and Rio de Janeiro. Yet, in order to accent the patriarchalism of the sugar planters of the northeast of the country, he repeatedly contrasts them with the cruder, more avaricious men of southern Brazil. Since the center of slaveholding shifted away from the northeast during the nineteenth century, the admission gravely compromises his thesis.

In *The Portuguese and the Tropics,* Freyre replies to Lewis Hanke's criticism by asserting that his own thesis has not been effectively challenged by contrary evidence.[5] As a matter of fact, it has been challenged by many writers. Ironically, Freyre dedicates this book to C. R. Boxer, whose own work, particularly *Salvador de Sá and the Struggle for Brazil and Angola* and *The Golden Age of Brazil,* demolishes much of Freyre's argument. One looks in vain in Freyre for evidence, but more important, one looks in vain for definite criteria by which treatment may be judged good or bad, kind or cruel. Freyre's evidence amounts mostly to generalizations about Portuguese and Brazilian national character, which are objectionable not because they are not measurable—for Freyre's poetic insights give his sociology a depth that only the most superficial positivists could ignore; they are objectionable because he has not applied to them available tests of objective analysis. If, for example, he is right in asserting in his essay, *O Mundo que o Português criou,* that the Portuguese colonizer carried with him a special kind of Christian sympathy for allegedly inferior races, then this sympathy ought to show up in specific circumstances of master-slave relations.[6]

As we review Freyre's argument, numerous methodological problems emerge, and we may therefore use it to begin to establish criteria for comparative analysis. By good treatment he usually means day-to-day treatment—food, shelter, work routine, leisure, and the like—but often he defends his thesis with reference to treatment in the other two senses. In an absolute sense these can be measured reasonably well. But how useful would comparisons of absolute levels be? For example, suppose we could establish that slaves in the United States received more and better food, had bigger and more comfortable cabins, and were better clothed than those in Brazil. We should then have proven one of Freyre's contentions wrong, but not necessarily another and more significant one. For, if at the same time we found that the material gap between masters and slaves was greater in the United States than in Brazil, then his thesis of a more developed patriarchalism in Brazil might obtain. Since American slavery existed within a more advanced technological and economic national framework than did the Brazilian, the American slaves could have been the more comfortable and yet the more exploited simply because they produced a greater surplus. Kenneth M. Stampp errs in his discussion of this problem and in his criticism of the work of Ulrich B. Phillips. Stampp writes, "If . . . the quantity of labor were compared with the compensation the inevitable conclusion would be that most slaves were overworked."[7] And more to the point:

> The slave's labor was controlled labor: his bargaining power was, by design, severely circumscribed. His labor was cheap labor: his compensation was, also by design, kept at a minimum. The free worker was, inevitably, more independent,

> more often successful in his efforts to increase his material comforts; and as a rule his labor was therefore more expensive.[8]

And again:

> The southern master's capitalization of his labor force has caused more confusion than anything else about the comparative cost of free and slave labor. This capital investment was not an added expense; it was merely the payment in a lump sum of a portion of what the employer of free labor pays over a period of years. The price of a slave, together with maintenance, was the cost of a lifetime claim to his labor; it was part of the wage an employer could have paid for a free laborer.[9]

Since this viewpoint has been criticized elsewhere,[10] we may limit ourselves to a brief reply. The cost of purchase, which Phillips incisively analyzed as contribution toward the "overcapitalization of labor," roughly corresponds to the capitalists' investment in plant and equipment whereas the cost of maintenance precisely corresponds to the wage bill. To measure the extent to which labor's product was being appropriated by capital—Marx's "rate of exploitation"[11]—we need to divide the surplus (the total product less the wage bill) by the wage bill or investment in living labor (Marx's "variable capital"). It will be easily perceived that the entire relationship cannot be fruitfully examined without consideration of the productivity of labor and, specifically, that the low costs of maintenance may and often do produce dear, not cheap, labor. The less comfortable Brazilian slaves might have been, in this sense, less exploited and perhaps as a result, less alienated in a sociological and psychological sense, from their masters. Freyre's claim of greater patriarchalism might not fall with the appearances of negative evidence on living standards.

Several questions bear on the establishment of standards

of judgment: Were the slaves of the Southern United States materially better off than those of Barbados, Cuba, or Brazil? Was the material gap between the classes greater or less than in other countries? What was the relationship between the standards of treatment and the technological possibilities inherent in the national and international economy at particular moments? Did slaves fare much worse than the depressed peasants of Eastern Europe, or the more advanced peasants of Western Europe, or the factory workers of England and New England?[12] These are quite different questions, requiring detailed research, but they only begin the discussion.

Let us consider the bearing of economic conditions, narrowly considered, on these questions. Boxer notes the appalling accident rate on the Brazilian sugar *engenhos*. If that rate was—as seems evident—significantly higher than the rate in Louisiana, then the slaves were less safe and worse treated in Brazil. But Louisiana developed its sugar industry later and under radically different conditions. First, the later development made it possible to introduce safer and more efficient machinery. Second, it occurred on virgin land, produced higher profits during the nineteenth century, and facilitated a more comfortable life for the laborers without special sacrifice on the part of the planters. Third, the location of the Louisiana sugar industry within a relatively advanced country offered masters and slaves alike more products and services at lower costs than were possible in Brazil. In short, in strictly economic terms, time and circumstance favored the American over the Brazilian slaves in the sugar districts. We might also note parenthetically that the national economic structure of the United States greatly facilitated the provision of food supplies for slaves whereas that of Brazil inhibited it.[13]

Or, let us consider another set of economic and demographic data: those bearing on the importation of African slaves. Examination of data on living conditions in French Saint-Domingue, the British Caribbean, Cuba, Brazil, and the Southern United States reveals a common pattern: so long as the slave trade remained open, slaves were greatly abused in all systems. Conversely, the shutting off of the slave trade and the sources of cheap labor generally stimulated increased attention to the health and comfort of the slaves. For Brazil and Cuba, the continuation of an active slave trade into the middle of the nineteenth century militated against kind treatment, however defined. Demographic analysis of Brazil demonstate that the death rate of slaves probably ran ahead of the birth rate during the nineteenth century. For Cuba and, indeed, for many of the sugar islands at one time or another, an open slave trade, when combined with the rapid expansion of the sugar market, greatly increased the tendency toward brutality and dehumanization. The evidence from the Caribbean, whether British, French, or Spanish, is clear and decisive.[14]

These data raise another problem, which existed in Brazil as well as in the Caribbean. Almost invariably, male slaves greatly outnumbered female slaves. Stein has shown that this imbalance was especially serious on the coffee *fazendas* of southern Brazil. To take several local illustrations: in São Paulo in 1797, white females outnumbered males 47,053 to 42,270, but black males outnumbered females 20,699 to 17,971; as late as 1872 in Rio Grande do Sul, male slaves outnumbered female 35,686 to 32,705.[15] We might then ask how the resultant sexual deprivation of the male slaves ought to be weighed in the pros and cons of good treatment. It is difficult to assess the effects of promiscuity and loosely structured mating patterns on the slaves, but Orlando Patterson's book, *The Sociology of Slavery,*[16] which analyzes in depth similar patterns in Jamaica, suggests grave short- and long-run consequences. In any case, what are we to make, in the face of these data, of those hymns to slave family life in the Hispanic countries?

We are led again, even by our economic data, to the social plane. Tannenbaum also argues that Brazilian slaves were better treated than American, but unlike Freyre he restricts himself to two sets of related questions: those relating to the possibilities of escape from slave status altogether, and those relating to the possibilities for absorbing the freedmen into the national culture. Freyre himself did pioneering work on these questions, and had he, like Tannenbaum, left matters there, he would have remained on strong ground.[17] The image of Brazil as a "racial democracy" is being subjected to hard blows by a growing number of scholars who are making intensive sociological investigations. There is no longer any doubt that Brazil, too, has had a color problem since slavery times and that Negroes still suffer from considerable discrimination and prejudice. Yet, there is also no doubt that these problems exist on a different level from those in the United States, that Brazil has avoided the extreme forms of racism characterizing the American experience, and that the older view popularized by Freyre needs to be qualified, not discarded.[18] David Brion Davis, for example, skillfully juxtaposes an admission that Hispanic peoples have been more tolerant and therefore more able to assimilate colored peoples, with the plausible assertion that slave systems have generally come to rest on one or another kind of discrimination.[19]

Care in definition of terms and precision in comparison of the strictly comparable should take us a long way toward the solution of many problems, the ramifications of which far transcend the study of slavery. Once we have brought order to the subject of slave treatment—once we have made separate estimates of its several meanings—we can begin to evaluate in more than an abstract way the quality and significance of paternalism and patriarchalism in the several slaveholding classes. Such an evaluation should provide an essential ingredient for the construction of a history of the intersection of bourgeois and prebourgeois social formations in the modern world. A proper comparative study of treatment will simultaneously lead us into another question that extends by implication into every historical period and that has particular importance for our own: In what ways do the particular circumstances of the lower classes and their treatment (in each particular sense) by the individuals and classes in power condition their consciousness and perception of reality? condition the extent and form of their acquiescence in oppression, and the extent and form of their will to revolution?

NOTES

1. David Brion Davis, *The Problem of Slavery in Western Culture* (Ithaca, 1966), p. 54.

2. Gilberto Freyre, Social Life in Brazil in the Middle of the Nineteenth Century," *Hispanic American Historical Review,* 5 (November, 1922), 597–628.

3. Gilberto Freyre, *The Masters and the Slaves: A Study in the Development of Brazilian Civilization,* 2nd English language ed. (New York, 1956).

4. Gilberto Freyre, *The Mansions and the Shanties: The Making of Modern Brazil* (New York, 1963), *Ordem e progresso: Processo de disintegraçâo das sociedades patriarcal e semipatriarcal no Brasil sob o regime de trabalho livre . . . ,* 2 vols. (Rio de Janeiro, 1962).

5. Gilberto Freyre, *The Portuguese and the Tropics* (Lisbon, 1961), p. 283.

6. Gilberto Freyre, *O Mundo que o português criou & Uma Cultura ameaçada: a Luso-Brasileira* (Lisbon, 1940).

7. Kenneth M. Stampp, *The Peculiar Institution* (New York, 1956), p. 75.

8. *Ibid.,* p. 282.

9. *Ibid.,* pp. 403–404.

10. Eugene D. Genovese, *The Political Economy of Slavery* (New York, 1965), esp. chaps. 1 and 2.

11. Karl Marx, *Capital,* 3 vols. (Moscow, 1961), 1: chap. 18.

12. Raimondo Luraghi has recently made an estimate:

"Questa era la schiavitù nel sud; e bilaneiadone tutti gli aspetti, non si può negare che la condizione degli sehiavi fosse indubbiamente nel suo complesso assai meno crudela che quella dei lavoratori liberi d'Europa quale ci è descritta per esempio da Friedrich Engels nelle *Condizioni della classe operai in Inghilterra,* o da Rodolgo Morandi nella sua *Storia delle grande industria italiana;* e certamente meno dura di quella che ancora per anni sarebbe esistita nella compagni italiane, tra i braccianti, quale la possiamo veder descritta nelle terribili pagine della *Inchiesta agraria Jacini." Storia della guerra civile americana*

(Torino, 1966). Luraghi adds that the average conditions—he means the material conditions of our first category—were "certainly better" than those of the East European and South Italian peasants and even perhaps of those of the economically advanced Po Valley.

13. This point has been made by Celso Furtado, *The Economic Growth of Brazil* (Berkeley, 1963), p. 128. The generalization, however, needs to be subjected to a more careful analysis than has yet been provided.

14. Cf., Furtado, *Economic Growth*, pp. 127–129; C. R. Boxer, *Portuguese Society in the Tropics: The Municipal Councils of Goa, Bahia, and Lunda, 1510–1800* (Madison, 1965), p. 130; Caio Prado Júnior, *Historia Econômica do Brasil*, 7th ed. (São Paulo, 1962), esp. chaps. 10–18. For a perceptive and suggestive discussion of the relationship between commercialization of agriculture and the deterioration of institutional arrangements designed to protect Caribbean slaves see the review-essay by Sidney W. Mintz of Elkins's *Slavery* in *American Anthropologist*, 63 (June 1961), 579–587, esp. 582. Herbert Klein, *Slavery in The Americas* (Chicago, 1967), which contrasts the experience of Virginia and Cuba, supports Elkins's view and insists on the continued vitality of Cuban institutions during the sugar boom. Yet, even if Klein is right, the appearance of a strong countertendency cannot be denied. An older, less defensible but still suggestive treatment may be found in Hubert H. S. Aimes, *A History of Slavery in Cuba* (New York, 1907), p. 266.

15. Roger Bastide and Florestan Fernandes, *Brancos e Negros em São Paulo,* 2nd ed. rev. (São Paulo, 1959), p. 16; Cardoso, *Capitalismo e Escravidão,* p. 78.

16. Orlando Patterson, *The Sociology of Slavery* (London, 1967).

17. These criticisms hardly add up to a general assessment. His great contributions, which alone make *The Masters and the Slaves* a masterpiece, have been his penetrating studies of the ways in which slavery resulted in the amalgamation of whites and Negroes, not only biologically but on every level of culture. It is therefore pointless to berate him for concentrating on house slaves and for judging the life of the field slaves by the standards of the Big House. His primary concern has been the interpenetration of diverse peoples, and it is merely a matter of qualification to argue that the majority of the slaves did not participate immediately and in a comfortable way. The essential point was the effect of racial interpenetration on the consciousness of whites and blacks; the full participation of both races was not decisive here. Frank Tannenbaum is therefore correct in demanding that American historians reassess Southern slavery along Freyre's lines of inquiry.

18. For critical appraisals of Brazilian race relations see especially, Bastide and Fernandes, *Brancos e Negros;* Fernando Henrique Cardoso and Octávio Ianni, *Côr e Mobilidade Social em Florianópolis,* (São Paulo, 1960); Roger Bastide, "The Development of Race Relations in

Brazil," chap. 1 of Guy Hunter, ed., *Industrialisation and Race Relations: A Symposium,* (London and New York, 1965); and Oracy Nogueira, "Skin Color and Social Class," in *Plantation Systems of the New World: Papers and Discussion Summaries of the Seminar Held in San Juan, Puerto Rico* (Washington, D.C., 1959), pp. 164–178.

19. Davis, *Problem of Slavery,* p. 53.

Chapter 8

BLACK CULTURE AND ST. GRONLESEX PATERNALISM

The following is a review of the special photographic exhibit, "Harlem on My Mind," which was presented at the Metropolitan Museum of Art, January 18–April 6, 1969. The exhibit incurred the wrath of white art critics, black artists, and the black community generally and became a major point of political and social controversy in New York City.

PERVERSE FASCINATION for the oppressed and beleaguered has always run strong among Americans, and the temptation to defend Mr. Hoving against the current critical onslaught is therefore hard to control. Besides, any man who could combine so many political and aesthetic atrocities in one effort surely deserves the thanks of a people in danger of being suffocated by ennui. Apparently upset by the tranquility that has descended on Fun City, especially in the realm of race relations, Mr. Hoving boldly set forth to shake things up and make us think. What else, after all, are the *bourgeois gentilshommes* of the WASP Establishment for?

This essay was originally published in *Artforum,* Feb. 1969, pp. 34–37.

There is not a great deal to be said about "Harlem on My Mind," which is at best a poor exhibit, but there may be some profit in reviewing a few of its horrors, if only because they lead us into questions that Americans cannot continue to ignore unless they have ceased to value their lives. I shall leave a full aesthetic evaluation to those with better credentials, but must confess to having been shocked. It was perfectly clear from the start that the show would prove a political disaster: Despite the expected pretenses, it was not the product of Harlem and was therefore certain to be received with justifiable hostility by a community that has had enough of carpetbaggers and well-intentioned meddlers. It was no less clear that serious distortions would arise from a cultural history of Harlem presented by outsiders, even if with local consultants, some of whom are people of unquestioned ability. Nevertheless, being a novice in matters affecting the art world, I naturally assumed that within the narrow limits of their understanding, Mr. Hoving and his staff would offer a technically impressive show. Hence, the shock. Black people may protest that the psychedelic lighting, the blatant sensationalism, and the imparted sense of perpetual turmoil hardly do justice to a proud and living community that has been far more stable and culturally vital than whites generally appreciate. They would doubtless be right, but even worse than these insults is an unforgiveable one: The insults are not even well delivered. You will, for example, find more interesting lighting at Arthur or even one of the less fashionable discotheques in New York. The one thing we have come to expect from Madison Avenue hucksterism is extraordinary technical proficiency within its own prescribed sphere; even this Mr. Hoving has denied us.

The show consists primarily of a photographic exhibition and recordings by outstanding community personalities. Mr. Hoving set out to do a show on Harlem for the Metropolitan Museum of Art but decided to ignore black painting and sculpture. The judgment implied in his astonishing decision has been lost on no one, least of all black artists. For a white Establishment institution to promote a show on black Harlem in 1969, amidst a veritable revolutionary wave of black nationalism and demands for local autonomy, self-determination, and self-expression was incredible enough. To put the show under the direction of a Jew whose credentials rest on his excellent work at a Jewish museum was at least ill advised, as was the decision to engage a black man from Milwaukee to assist him (on the assumption, I suppose, that Harlem is a state of mind, not a real place, and that therefore every black man has Harlem in his soul). The organizers tried to include the good and bad, the successes and the failures, the beauty and the squalor, the fun and the agony. They did try, but even so, the exhibit is given over to the kind of trivia that so fascinates tourists. Since they knew nothing about their subject, they inevitably ruined everything.

I shall pass over the criticisms of detail, which blacks have been filing at some length, but one or two matters should suffice to carry us beyond this abortion to such important matters as the claims of Afro-American art and the proper contribution of institutions like the Metropolitan Museum of Art in the fight against white racism. A large amount of space is given to Malcolm X, whose prestige in Harlem remains strong and probably grows stronger. There are pictures of Malcolm the Muslim minister and streetcorner speaker and of Malcolm the corpse, together with indifferent excerpts from his magnificent autobiography. The exhibit immediately involved political decisions: Should you emphasize the early or the late Malcom? Malcolm the uncompromising black nationalist or Malcolm the man who ended his life edging toward a new position? The exhibit settles these questions in a manner that will not be to everyone's taste, but the real problem lies elsewhere: Who is making the decision to interpret Malcolm? Since the show purports to be a cultural expression of Harlem only that community as a whole or, more realistically, one or more of the clearly identified groups recognized as legitimate by the people of Harlem have that right.

Similar problems plague the exhibit throughout. We see a little of Dr. Du Bois and much of Garvey—itself a striking political judgment—but are not told that Garvey called Du Bois "definitely a white man's Negro," or that Du Bois had a few unpleasant things to say about Garvey and his movement. What is left out everywhere is any suggestion of a community with contrary voices and bitter divisions, struggling painfully toward its present sense of identity and unity—that is, with a genuine inner political life. I stress politics only because the show does, but the failure of the show transcends such questions. To return to Malcolm X as an example: Where, one wonders, is the Malcolm X of whom so many black people, even those who opposed him ideologically, speak? Malcolm the husband, father, and family man, whose warmth and concern for the daily woes of black people provided a symbol and a place of refuge to so many men and women in trouble? How, if one is not intimately in touch, does one judge the relative importance of these aspects of a man's life and legacy?

One would like, at this point, to comment on Malcolm's speeches, as presented in the exhibit. It is not possible, for the loudspeaker in one room drowns out the one in the next. This effect was probably intended. We are no doubt supposed to hear everything at once and so get a proper sense of the turmoil and rage of an oppressed community, although the actual mechanisms of oppression and the oppressors themselves are hardly in evidence. The last room of the exhibit presents, for the most part, Harlem in riot and disorder. That turmoil, rage, riot, and disorder comprise part of the story no one would or should deny. But a few other things that are also present in Harlem are not in evidence in the exhibit—not the least of which is the determined effort of painters, writers, and musicians to build an Afro-American culture.

These complexities escaped Mr. Hoving, but it would be

a mistake to dwell too long on this level of criticism. If these weaknesses attract our interest, they do so because they lead to fundamental questions of black-white relations in general and of the struggle of the black artist in particular. Mr. Hoving has tried to defend his use of the Metropolitan Museum of Art for this kind of show by arguing that "one of the stated missions of the museum is to relate art to practical life, and practical living to art." All right. But the questions remain: Who should speak for Harlem? What is the role of a specific institution, such as a museum, in community affairs? And what about those strangely absent black painters? To these and other questions Mr. Hoving replies, in one of his more offensive press releases: "At no time in this country's history has there been a more urgent need for a creative confrontation between the white and black communities than today . . . . It's one thing to drop renewal into Harlem, but let's not renew the heart out of Harlem before we look at what is there." I shall not subject these words to close scrutiny, for their vulgarity and presumption will be so readily apparent even to most whites that we need not waste an instant wondering at the harsh reaction of so many blacks.

Mr. Hoving's folly has extended to include announcement of a special program of five panel discussions on Harlem. The topics are revealing: (1) Harlem in Perspective; (2) The Harlem Art Movement; (3) Harlem Politics, Past and Present; (4) Business and the Harlem Economy; and (5) Harlem Youth: What Now? In short, only one panel falls within the legitimate province of the museum. White critics are protesting against these perversions of the museum's function, but they ought to realize that their just complaint is much less important than another: How dare Mr. Hoving intrude himself into the affairs of a community of which he is not a part and of which he is demonstrably ignorant? Mr. Hoving has a responsibility toward the art world in general, toward those black artists who have been so shamelessly wronged for so long, and toward the white and black communities of New

York City, but that responsibility consists of strengthening the museum as a vehicle for the presentation and development of the arts, including Afro-American arts. It does not consist of his intrusion into matters beyond his competence and beyond the museum's proper institutional function.

The question of proper function leads us to a consideration of the position of black painting in American and Afro-American culture, which alone can provide the foundation for an assessment of the political significance of "Harlem on My Mind." The recent exchange in *The New York Times* between Mr. Hilton Kramer and Mr. Henri Ghent over the Whitney Museum's lily-white show on the 1930s and the black community's counter-show reveals, with that full display of misery which only brevity makes possible, that even the best of white America remains deaf to black voices. Mr. Kramer, an astute and serious critic, raises an important problem, which cannot easily be dismissed as white chauvinist apologetics. He notes that black artists have suffered a long and as yet uncatalogued assortment of outrages and thinks that whites should feel shame and indignation. Then he adds:

> But these feelings, though they have an important role to play in the redress of social grievances, are of little use in judging the quality of works of art. In matters of artistic standards there is no "justice" in the social sense. There are only the values which artists themselves have established through the practice of their art . . . . Mr. Ghent is inviting us to judge black artists by standards greatly inferior to those we bring to the appreciation of—the term is absurd but unavoidable—white artists.[1]

Mr. Kramer poses the question fairly but fails to grasp the main point that blacks have been making. Mr. Ghent, who has been thrust into acting as a spokesman for black artists, replies with interesting and useful observations on the position of the black painter, but he does not, in my opinion, join the issue satisfactorily. Apparently anxious to defend the contribution of black painters to American culture, he largely limits himself to the suggestion that the Whitney show was a blow to integration. He concludes:

> Mr. Kramer, in his article, is perpetuating a pervasive myth, one which could be explosively dangerous: the myth of the inferiority of black artists; in fact, the myth of the inferiority of blacks generally in areas of intellectual endeavor . . . .
>
> To continually perpetuate this lamentable situation is a very sad commentary on the country as a whole when you consider that we are *all* Americans anxious to make our most significant contribution in a truly positive way. However, the establishment *forces* black artists to set themselves apart (physically but not esthetically), thereby robbing America and the world of the opportunity to share in their creativity which is, and always has been, an integral part of their aspirations.[2]

So, it would seem that the tragedy of white America's indifference reduces to its having closed itself to those blacks who yearn to contribute to the common stream. Mr. Ghent's position, at least as expressed in this one exchange, does not adequately meet Mr. Kramer's objection, nor does it reflect adequately those essential claims of the black intelligentsia which Mr. Ghent could probably explore much better than I, were he to offer us a more leisurely presentation.

Let us return to Mr. Kramer's fair question. Do we, in fact, want a double standard by which blacks could be excused for technical mediocrity? The answer is certainly "No," and no self-respecting black painter would tolerate such a thing. The question is badly directed and can be judged to be fair only because the white art world has been so blinded by that very racist indifference which Mr. Kramer has himself tried to combat.

The argument of black painters today is very much like that advanced by black jazz musicians during the last several decades. Black musicians have had to fight a lonely and bitter uphill battle to convince whites that jazz is a serious art form and not an entertainment, but this battle, in which they have been joined by white jazzmen, has never been the only one for them. Their effort has also been aimed at demonstrating that black jazz and white jazz are not, and could not be, quite the same. This assertion has been treated, by those whose intellect and sensibility have been formed in a liberal bourgeois milieu, as some kind of obscurantist black racism. No doubt it has sometimes taken such forms, but essentially it is no more than an assertion of cultural difference. Jazz reflects the historically conditioned sensibilities of those playing it, and blacks, with their own traditions which extend back through such Afro-American forms as the slave songs, reach back to Africa itself. Blacks in America cannot avoid being Europeans too, just as to a lesser extent whites, especially Southern whites, cannot avoid being Africans too, however much they may howl at the thought; but the locus in each case has clearly been different. They share many things, and perhaps everything, but they combine them in entirely different ways to form distinct cultural configurations. The argument over culture versus subculture is rapidly losing its force, for blacks are now consciously molding a national Afro-American culture of their own.

The pianist, Cecil Taylor, sharply expressed the viewpoint held by many blacks:

> But when I heard Horace [Silver], now that was a thing that turned me around and finally fixed my idea of piano playing. Horace was playing with Getz. Getz was all over the sax, and Horace was right on him. Listening to Horace that night I dug that there were two attitudes in jazz, one white and one black. The white idea is valid in that the cats playing it play the way their environment leads them, which is the only way they can play. But Horace is the Negro idea because he was playing the real thing of Bud [Powell] with all the physicality of it, with the filth of it, and the movement in the

> attack. Yet Horace supposedly had no technique, which again brings us to the idea of what technique is.[3]

Taylor argues, in effect, that black music has its own environmental moorings and seeks to express a particular culture, and he is quick to see, as white critics do not seem able to, that a particular culture must find its own forms and must evaluate technique in a manner appropriate to those forms.

The evaluation of black painting in the 1930s must be approached from this vantage point, and it must be approached as a problem appropriate to a given time and place, not as an abstract question in aesthetic theory. The position of the black painters of the 1930s and their place in both American national and Afro-American culture raises a great many issues, which the white art world must begin to face with a degree of modesty and intellectual maturity it has not yet displayed. Not being an art critic, I shall leave specific judgments to those qualified, but the general problems require no special training to appreciate. Let us take three hypothetical black painters of the 1930s: one who was willing to give a white audience what it would pay for in "Negro subjects"; a second who sought acceptance in the American mainstream (however defined); and a third who consciously struggled for an Afro-American viewpoint in his art and who therefore had to struggle for new forms. The first could hardly have made much of a contribution to art—either American or Afro-American—but his works are probably most in evidence since he could find at least a small market among tasteless bourgeois.

The second might or might not have been a competent artist. Since, as was certainly his privilege, he chose to work in an essentially Euro-American tradition the American art world should at least be able to evaluate his work without difficulty. In view of the discrimination and indiffence to which he was subjected we ought not to be surprised that work of the highest quality was not forthcoming; it is a tribute to black Americans that they produced any work of real quality at all. But we are entitled to wonder: Since such men were ignored and despised how much of their work was ever bought and exhibited and how much has survived? Can we be sure that great works have not been sacrificed in each generation? It is probably too late to do anything about this record of white vandalism, but one question remains and cries out for an unbiased answer from whites and blacks alike. If it were to be established that the best black painters of the 1930s were second-rate, to what extent was their failure to achieve greatness due to that schizophrenia against which Afro-American artists are so vigorously fighting today? To what extent, for example, were even these "mainstream" artists trying to express a specific Afro-American sensibility, and to what extent was their failure to reach peak achievement the result of a socially directed attempt to ram their content into inappropriate forms? I cannot answer my own questions and doubt that experts as yet can, for to the best of my knowledge, even the most discerning of our art critics have insisted on viewing black painting through ethnocentric white eyes.

Our third hypothetical painter presents the most difficult problems and brings us to a consideration of the present crisis and to future prospects. If whites can recognize, as they increasingly do, that black jazz musicians have been consciously striving to express a distinct Afro-American national sensibility, then they ought to have no trouble in recognizing the same tendency among painters. The two art forms have had radically different histories in black America, and there is no doubt that black painting is far less developed than black music. Painters and sculptors have had a difficult time in preserving and developing an African tradition. Black slaves could and did sing and dance and did blend African, American, and specifically slave-quarter elements into their effort. The line from African music through the slave songs to modern black music is neither simple nor straight, but it is discernible.

The great African traditions in sculpture and the visual arts largely had to be left behind since, for obvious reasons, the slave plantation offered neither a shelter for artists nor a clientele. The slaves themselves might have kept the tradition alive in their work as skilled craftsmen and artisans, but even these possibilities were severely circumscribed in the United States. Other slaveholding countries such as Saint-Domingue (Haiti), Brazil, Cuba, and to a lesser extent Jamaica and the other British islands imported African slaves almost up to the time of emancipation, and the preservation of elements of African art and religion followed suit. African elements also benefited in these countries from such factors as the size of the plantations: whereas cotton plantations in the United States were small units, and tobacco farms even smaller, most of the slaves in the Caribbean and in Brazil lived on large sugar estates, which permitted considerably more freedom of movement in the quarters. The United States closed the African slave trade formally in 1808, but most states had already taken the step well before. The great period of slavery expansion came after that date; the westward march of the Cotton Kingdom did not begin in earnest until 1820 or so. The slave population of the United States during the nineteenth century was therefore a native-born population, with minimal and almost nonexistent reinforcements from Africa. Moreover, during this same period black craftsmen and artisans, both free and slave, were steadily driven from their trades by white racist pressure. In such a setting the preservation of an African tradition in the visual arts became almost impossible, although we may find—when the subject is explored fully without racist blinders—that more has survived than we can now appreciate.

What we especially need to know is the extent of the effort of blacks to develop an Afro-American point of view during the postslavery generation. It is quite possible that every generation during the last century has had its black artists who have had to begin anew each time because the work of the previous generation was not preserved. The black communities of the United States have been too poor, and until recently perhaps too psychologically defensive, to sustain their painters and sculptors, and the art patrons of the white world have had no interest in work they could not begin to understand. White America, at its best, has looked either for "Negro subjects" or for black painters who measure up to "standards" in work with other subjects; it has yet to realize that black painters properly insist on the right to paint any subject but to bring to it a sensibility and point of view of their own. To the question, "How do you know such a thing has any real artistic merit," it is only necessary to reply that white Americans will never know until they take a long and unbiased look. In any case, whatever white Americans do, black artists are certain to keep going with redoubled effort, and it would be ridiculous and self-defeating for whites to cut themselves off from a movement that is destined to gain in vigor and intensity. (But then, indulgence in the ridiculous and self-defeating has always been among the hallmarks of white racism in America.)

In the face of this long history of white crimes against black culture and the black intelligentsia, one would think that the white art world would be ready to meet its responsibility to investigate black painting, to contribute to the growth and security of black artists, and to recognize the principle of a difference in national culture and tradition. The responsibility of Mr. Hoving is especially clear. So, instead of doing what he is supposed to do as director of the nation's greatest museum, he shirks his duty and then tries to atone with an exhibit that has nothing to do with the proper function of the museum, tramples on the dignity of the Harlem community, and plunges into a political labyrinth, the depths of which have yet to be reviewed even by his most severe critics.

The show's politics transcends the readily apparent implications for American society in general and for the increasingly ominous white-black confrontation; it represents a thrust, probably mindless, by Mr. Hoving into the politics of Harlem itself. The black community understandably tries to put one face toward the white especially in matters of local control, but there can be no doubt that the blacks are rent by profound social and political differences. The inner turmoil in the black community is difficult for a white man to evaluate; it may even be difficult for any but the most sophisticated black participants, for the pace of change is breathtaking. Certain things are nonetheless clear, notably the sharpening struggle between radical nationalists and cultural nationalists. The traditional dichotomy between integrationist and separatist tendencies within black America extends far back into our history and dates from the very first black protests against discrimination and racism; this dichotomy still exists but in new forms. The "Black Power" slogan and incipient ideology, for all their confusion and contradictions, represent a serious attempt to combine the more realistic and politically feasible features of both. In any case, the demand for autonomy in the black communities is disappearing as a divisive issue; the divisions increasingly center on the specific content of the demand. The struggle for power in the black communities has therefore broken out even before autonomy has been won. The lines are blurred and shifting, but the "black capitalism" aspirations of the black bourgeoisie are predictably drawing heavy fire from the radicals. These differences may be papered over for public consumption, united fronts may be presented to the Man, and the deepening internal crisis may be obscured by the enthusiastic salutations of "brother" and "sister" and a common militant, nationalistic rhetoric; but the settlement of old scores appears to be merely a question of time.

If the Harlem community had in fact organized its own show, certain political as well as artistic tendencies would have gained while others lost. It makes a great deal of difference to various factions how, for example, one emphasizes and interprets the various phases of Malcolm X's career. Any such show would therefore provoke a fierce struggle in the inner political core of Harlem even while all tendencies were uniting to demonstrate a certain degree of unity in confrontation with whites. An analysis of these contradictions and trends, even were one appropriate here, would be beside the point, for, whatever the preferences of whites, blacks will settle these questions among themselves.

Enter Mr. Hoving. Since I am both naive and suspicious by nature, I assumed that Mr. Hoving possessed the last word in sophistication in these matters and that he intended a deliberate intrusion into Harlem's politics. His political ambitions, which no one would begrudge him, have been a matter of gossip in New York City, and we would have been justified in assuming that he meant to strengthen his position with the politically powerful, ideologically conservative cultural-nationalists. Mr. Hoving, on the face of it, was attempting to woo the middle-class advocates of black capitalism, who are, incidentally, the most vigorous practitioners of antiwhite rhetoric in the black community. All this makes good Establishment sense, and Mr. Hoving, a man from the very marrow of the WASP Establishment, seemed to have been intent on providing a lesson in how to do it with grace and elegance.

But if any of my fears were justified, then how is it possible that he should have excluded the essential personalities, offended almost everyone, and elicited a general outcry from people who normally split on these issues? These were truly remarkable achievements. Mr. Hoving's level of political astuteness is obviously somewhat below that of his aesthetic sense, which is itself not above criticism; apparently, the poor soul never even had a clue. Now, there is no disgrace for an American in being a political manipulator who minds other people's business, tries to adjust their political alignments, meddles in their social life, and sets himself up as the arbiter of their taste. Americans have long good-naturedly regarded such impertinence as a part of our national life—as something that falls into the category of "Why not, if you can get away with it." Unfortunately for Mr. Hoving, these same Americans, both black and white, are not nearly so tolerant of incompetence. Had Mr. Hoving limited himself to behaving like an impudent and insensitive bourgeois, he might have escaped with a restrained and passing rebuke; once he revealed himself as a damned fool, the worst became inevitable.

What has happened at the Metropolitan Museum of Art is neither more nor less than what appears to have happened: a decent, well-meaning, politically influential and ambitious, socially responsive man of affairs, honestly concerned with the deterioration of race relations, has done his thing. Unhappily, the world, especially the black world, has no further use for his thing. His gaffe comes at a moment at which the black community in general and Harlem in particular are finding their own ways to dramatize the power and legitimacy of their culture, and it represents one of those ghastly miscalculations which one only wishes would just go away.

At bottom, Mr. Hoving's effort reduces to Saint Gronlesex paternalism. There is no point, therefore, in crediting his good intentions. All paternalism rests on good intentions, and the paternalism of New York's *grande bourgeoisie* is neither better nor more well intended than that of the ill-fated Southern slaveholders. In some ways it is much less palatable. The slaveholders, after all, had the wisdom and decency to own their niggers outright before they presumed to run their lives.

NOTES

1. *The New York Times,* November 24, 1968.
2. *The New York Times,* December 8, 1968 (original emphasis).
3. Quoted in A. B. Spellman, *Four Lives in the Bebop Business* (New York, 1967), p. 62.

Chapter 9

BLACK NATIONALISM AND AMERICAN SOCIALISM

A Comment on Harold Cruse's "Crisis of the Negro Intellectual"

EVERY YEAR NOW we are offered many more books on black America and the racial crisis than anyone could possibly find time to read. Fortunately, with periodic exceptions, no one loses much if the books go unread. Harold Cruse's *Crisis of the Negro Intellectual* (New York, 1967) is more than one of those periodic exceptions; in focus and depth it transcends anything written in our generation. Whatever the ultimate assessment of its general and particular theses, its lasting achievement lies in its having dramatically raised the level of discussion at every important point and in having overthrown decades of ideological drivel in the process. Since Cruse intended his book to be an ideological manifesto as well as a sober work of history and sociology and since he denied himself little in polemical thrusts, it would be possible to praise or damn him on an almost unlimited number of questions. To do so, however, would be both impertinent and fruitless for a predominantly white socialist conference. Accordingly, I shall confine my remarks to several more general problems

This paper was read to the Socialist Scholars Conference, Sept. 1968.

of importance for the future relations of the American Left and the black liberation movement—specifically, to the problems of black nationalism, the role of the intelligentsia, and the relevance of Marxism.

Cruse begins with a theoretical formulation according to which the primary social dynamic in American society is an ethnic struggle. He makes this formulation central to his argument but does not convince us either of its centrality or its correctness. He sharply attacks Herbert Apatheker for asserting that racism and the Negro Question are manifestations of class struggle, for in his own view they are manifestations of a persistent ethnic struggle. Neither Aptheker's vulgar Marxism nor Cruse's hasty inversion exhaust the possibilities. The evidence being compiled by historians increasingly suggests that white racism predated class exploitation—that a previous ethnocentricity and prejudice against things black facilitated slavery, which in turn transformed prejudice into an elaborate racist mythology. When Cruse makes racism a special case of a more general ethnic struggle, he commits an error almost as grave as Aptheker's mechanical formulation according to which slavery created racism and bourgeois exploitation developed it. Wherever slavery existed, racism existed also, but its intensity and significance varied enormously from one culture to another. The American form grew out of a long and special Protestant, bourgeois, Anglo-Saxon cultural tradition and is among the most tenacious and vicious in the world. At the same time, white racism, as a fully developed ideology, in contradistinction to a loose body of prejudice, arose with the imperialist expansion of the leading capitalist countries during the second half of the nineteenth century. I should not dwell on what might seem a pedantic criticism were it not that Cruse's formulation implies a dangerous underestimation of the uniqueness and the depth of American racism, and were it not that it rests on a highly dubious reading of the present political and social situation.

Cruse interprets American society and politics in ethnic

terms and sees WASPS, Slavs, Italians, Irish, Jews, and other groups as facing each other in unassimilated cooperation or hostility. In his view, American politics is an ethnic politics, and no group really aspires to national assimilation. The first part of his argument comes at least one generation too late, and the second cries out for a documentation he does not provide. We may grant that the various national groups had to preserve community identity and play ethnic politics to win acceptance, but since the end of open immigration and the victory of the big-city machines, a reverse tendency has set in. The major immigrant groups give every indication of aspiring to assimilation and of progressing toward it with each new generation, and the WASPs, with the exception of the socially prominent but economically and politically declining families, have been beating a steady and relatively graceful retreat. The strong and even violent resistance of the ethnic groups to the integration of the Negro must therefore be understood not as a special case of ethnic exclusiveness, but as a particular combination of white racism and an impulse to defend newly acquired property. As such, it presents a class question with a deep racial dimension and not at all a new version of an old ethnic problem.

Cruse may therefore be too late in calling for a new United States Constitution to account for ethnic diversity. His insistence on a campaign for constitutional revision makes good sense, but only in somewhat different terms—to satisfy the need for greater local participation and control, which the black communities alone must translate into ethnic self-determination. In these terms white America might be expected to support black demands within a broader program, but it is hardly likely to rally to a demand for a general ethnic autonomy it neither needs nor wants. Cruse stresses the pernicious role of Zionist ideology within the black intelligentsia, the Left, and American culture generally, but ironically, he does not consider that his own analysis could be understood as an expression of that ideology. If there is one ethnic group in America that fits his description of all ethnic groups, it is the Jews. To extrapolate from Zionist chauvinism to the whole range of American ethnic behavior is, however, to pursue a politically perilous course.

The demand for some variation of national self-determination for black communities must stand as a particular demand, which arises out of the particular oppression suffered by black people in the United States. Cruse offers an ideology and a program for such a nationalism and, in so doing, has sought to bypass the question of socialism. Whatever blacks have gained, he argues with evident truth, they have gained within the structure of American capitalism and are not likely to depart from that structure without contrary experience. He also warns against absorption by the Welfare-Warfare State and proposes an independent black position from which this absorption could be resisted. Cruse goes into great detail to expose the opportunism and treachery of certain leftwing political movements, but he is silent on the long and painful history of such opportunism and treachery within every known nationalist movement of modern times. This silence is the more regrettable in view of the experience of postwar Asia and Africa. Cruse himself notes the alarming progress of neocolonialism and of comprador-bourgeois ascendancy, but he does not consider the implications for black America with anything like his customary care and thoroughness.

As a result, Cruse neglects the decisive class dimension of the national struggle even while he warns of growing class divisions and divergent class interests within the black community. Among the great strengths of this book are its insistence on the centrality of the cultural front and its impressive use of dialectical method. Yet, at this crucial juncture, Cruse slips into a mechanism that momentarily negates these strengths. We ought to be put on guard by the recent debacle in countries like Algeria, with its disillusioning refutation of the claims and hopes of men like Frantz Fanon—claims and hopes which seem to me to come very close to those of Cruse.

It is not enough for Cruse to speak about the cultural struggle in its national aspect, nor about the necessity for a black political party, which merely transfers the same question to a definite political terrain; the struggle to define the social content and ideology of an autonomous black community must proceed simultaneously with the struggle to bring that autonomy into being. Cruse seems to think that without the social content and ideology to which he subscribes, no autonomous black community could emerge at all. The experience with neocolonialism suggests, on the contrary, that national capitalism and international imperialism have much more room to maneuver and that, even now, a new generation of black opportunists and reactionary rightwing nationalists is biding its time.

For this reason alone Cruse cannot be allowed to escape censure for writing: "All white socialist and leftist trends should be banned from the ghettos, using any means possible to enforce their exclusion." The adjective "white" is an evasion, for if the object is to defend black autonomy, then the same words ought to be directed, with much greater force, to the poverty program, to Nixon's black capitalism, and to the Democratic and Republican parties. Cruse makes clear his commitment to democracy and his opposition to totalitarianism, but his words at this point can only play into the hands of the Right. I have no wish to defend any existing white leftwing organization against Cruse's criticisms, but I do suggest that black socialists must be free to work and speak or black nationalism will end far removed from where Cruse wants it to. Because black socialists in the past have used internationalist slogans to cover their subservience to outside opportunists does not mean that those of the present or future are likely to repeat the mistakes of those against whom they are themselves arrayed. And Cruse offers no evidence that the record of the Left, bad as it may be, is one whit worse than the record of any other political tendency. Cruse might ponder his words of praise for the Zionist Irgun. He admires its "extremism," its willingness to resort to terror, its determination to put the goal of national liberation ahead of everything else. But he does not mention the outcome. Although he denounces Israel's imperialism and attacks its virulent chauvinism, he neglects to mention that the Herut—the direct heir of the Irgun—represents the most reactionary, imperialist, and racist elements in Israeli life. Does he think that the Herut could be judged apart from its Irgun origins? The greatest failure in Cruse's admirable book is the omission of any attempt to analyze this side of nationalism, so as to provide for an ideological struggle against such an outcome. Cruse expresses concern about the rise of a nihilist and terrorist wing of black nationalism, but without an internal black radical movement we can see little to check the ascendency of this wing or, rather, the ascendency of those, black and white, who have the experience and wherewithal to use it.

This question of internal struggle casts its shadow across the best and most suggestive sections of the book. Cruse asserts that a black enclave economy is possible and necessary, but he does not provide an adequate economic analysis to support his judgment. Notwithstanding some ambiguity, his suggestions for a cooperative approach to the reorganization of economic life in the ghettos offer a creative solution to some vexing problems. Undoubtedly, his economic program has something to offer on the directly economic plane and even more on the psychological and sociological plane. Certain problems, nevertheless, remain. Cruse's implication that enough industry could be located in autonomous black enclaves to sustain a black economy has little to recommend it. Nothing in his book leads us away from the probability that a large proportion of the black population would have to be employed outside the enclaves. In any case, he cannot seriously be suggesting autarky, and therefore those ostensibly autonomous enclave economies would continue to operate as an element within the larger structure of American capitalism. From either point of view, there would be a great and persistent danger of internal neocolonialism, even if the industry and trade of the ghetto were black controlled. The guarantee against neocolonialism could not be provided by a black political party per se, for it might easily go down the road of the ruling parties of Liberia, Gabon, or the Ivory Coast. The guarantee could only be provided by a radical black political party with powerful white allies. Cruse hints at such requirements but nowhere discusses them adequately or stresses their importance.

It is one thing for Cruse to eschew dogmatic socialist formulas and to call for new institutional structures within the present system; it is quite another for him to try to bypass the question of class power within and without the black community. Only once in his long book does he speak of the worldwide setting of this problem—when he says that the black movement is in a crisis within a larger American crisis and an even larger world-wide crisis of war, poverty, and national survival. Yet, Cruse says not a word about the nature of that international crisis and its relationship to the black struggle. He calls for a black political party and clearly states the need for an alliance between that party and white political groups, but he does not say on what basis such an alliance ought to be projected. What position should his black party take on foreign policy in general or on Vietnam in particular? How much does it matter from his point of view? We are left in the dark, but these are essential questions. A black party would not automatically be anti-imperialist; it might well make a deal for local privileges in return for its support of a world-wide imperialist offensive. Without a clear line from the beginning—without a definite commitment to national and international responsibilities—such a party could easily be the vehicle for co-opting black America into support even for a racist foreign policy. We have ample precedent to warn us. I do not have to tell Cruse that such an outcome would be a disaster for his people, for the United States, and for the world.

Cruse calls for major constitutional revision and general structural reform. Although he casts his discussion in ethnic terms—and thereby weakens it—his basic demands are increased local autonomy, economic and administrative decentralization, and the liberation of the mass media and cultural apparatus from the control of the ruling class. He argues, quite soundly, that these are needed by the whole country but especially by the blacks. He proceeds to assign the black liberation movement a place in the vanguard of the movement for the reshaping of American life. We need not credit the assignment, although no one would deny that the blacks are providing an essential part of the thrust. It ought to be clear that white America must be restructured if black America is to be free; it is by no means clear that black America can play the leading role in this work. Nevertheless, Cruse's excellent programmatic suggestions and his cogent discussion of the position of American capitalism come at an opportune moment. They parallel the neo-Marxian approaches of Andre Gorz and Lelio Basso—to mention only the two writers whose work has been current in this country. For all his professed hostility to Marxism, Cruse comes close to the point at which a growing number of Marxists are converging. For these Marxists, the problem has been to avoid the twin errors of social democratic opportunism, as manifested most conspicuously in the American Socialist and Communist parties, and ostensibly Maoist sectarianism, as manifested most conspicuously in the Progressive Labor Party and the direct-action appeals of certain well-known Quaker radicals. Marxists know, as Cruse knows, that we live in an age of enormous economic surpluses suitable for bribery and corruption and of nuclear weapons for keeping spirits sober, and that, therefore, strategies of direct confrontation with the state in the style of 1917 will not do in the advanced countries. They also know, as Cruse knows, that social-democratic reformism leads only to disgraceful and self-defeating absorption. Accordingly, they are fighting for a new socialist strategy, designed to create unassimilable enclaves within the existing order and to transform this existing order by the expansion of an indigestible and profoundly antagonistic base. The nationalist demands of black America, given such sharp theoretical formulation in this book, represent an essential element in this projected struggle for structural reform. Cruse speaks of a cooperative economy in the black communities; I am sure that he knows very well that the ultimate significance of such a development would depend on how it links up with developments outside the enclaves. If it is to be rescued from bourgeois suffocation and degeneracy, it will have to be paralleled by similar developments on a broad national front. In this sense, it remains true that black America can neither expect liberation as a gift from others nor liberate itself outside a wider national reconstruction.

The prospects for structural reform are inseparable from the mobilization of the intelligentsia in a war for hegemony on the cultural front. Without depreciating his many other contributions, we may safely say that at no other point does Cruse have so much to offer us. No other American writer has seen the cultural issue so clearly as a political issue, nor so ably linked the general and theoretical issues to the most ordinary practical ones. (And precisely because of his clarity, we must repeat that his failure to stress the class ideological struggle simultaneously with the national can evoke only criticism and foreboding.) Cruse sees the main task as one of winning minds and reshaping souls, both as ends and as strategies. His analysis exposes the superficial anti-intellectualism and irrationality of certain sections of the Left and shows that without a hard cultural battle, the political battle will be lost and all gains absorbed by a capitalist regime of unprecedented strength. It is, therefore, the more ironical that he should combine his brilliant theoretical advance with a misplaced assault on Marxism.

Cruse delivers a bitter attack on what he calls communist Marxism and thereby shows an uneasy conscience, for he seems to realize that all he is attacking is the superficial and opportunistic Marxism of the Communist party and some other sects. This vulgar Marxism grew up in a definite historical epoch as the product of particular social forces. By making a broadside attack on Marxism, however, Cruse attempts, wittingly or no, to destroy Marxism as an intellectual tendency within the black community. One may sympathize with his caustic remarks on the Communist party's pretensions to cultural leadership: "All the Michael Golds accomplished was to inject a foreign cultural and political ideology into a basically American cultural phenomenon and engender confusion upon confusion." The trouble with this thrust is that the issue is not one of a foreign ideology but of a perversion of Marxism and its translation into a self-serving totalitarianism. It is worth noting that Cruse's harsh attack on Gold is no harsher than that of the great communist writer, Sean O'Casey. What Cruse obscures is the continuing and sharpening struggle within the Marxist movements against the very tendencies he deplores. Only once does he seem to recognize this—when he notes that C. Wright Mills, whom he admires, sought not to destroy or even bypass Marxism but to provide it with a new opportunity for relevance and self-regeneration.

The greatest irony in Cruse's one-sided attack on Marxism lies in its congruence with the attack of neo-Marxists all over the world on the Old Guard. Cruse identifies Marxism with a particular attitude toward the industrial proletariat and its allegedly decisive revolutionary role, but Marxists everywhere are re-evaluating and redefining both. The Chinese revolution, with its peasant base, the Cuban revolution, and the rising influence of Gramsci in European socialist and communist circles are combining to undermine the dogmatism that Cruse attacks. He rebukes Marxism for underestimating the intelligentsia, for failing to see its growing centrality, and for ignoring the cultural struggle, but all these points formed part of Gramsci's critique of dogmatic Marxism in the 1920s and 1930s. True, Gramsci's work is only beginning to be studied outside Italy, but it is enough that the dogmatism and vulgarity Cruse abhors is steadily being driven out of Marxist thought by Marxists themselves. Cruse's brilliant analysis of the importance of the cultural front constitutes part of a wider analysis being offered by Marxists all over Europe. I do not stress this point to reduce Cruse's achievement nor to defend any particular ideology or political tendency, but to protest against a line of attack that, if followed through especially by those less cultured and sophisticated than he, can only lead to a catastrophic split at the very moment when conditions are more favorable than ever before for mutual respect, cooperation, and effective unity.

When Cruse tells us that American society must be overhauled from within, that the mass media and general technological advances have drastically altered the nature and relationship of class forces, and that the intelligentsia is emerging as a decisive stratum, he tells us things serious Marxists are ready to accept on principle and to discuss in depth. When he tells us that control of the means of communication provides a major political battleground, he will get no argument from us. When he tells us that only the black intelligentsia is ready and able to fight this battle and that it alone can stir the white intelligentsia to action, then we must tell him that we do not believe a word of it. I shall not press the issue here, except as a warning to the white Left. Cruse's challenge is fair enough but not without ominous implications. We must not surrender this ground, no matter how weak our present position. Cruse's expression of faith in the power of his people is his business. We dare not accept it for ourselves. Either the Left reorganizes and opens a fight for cultural hegemony or the political battle will be lost. And no amount of good will, either on the part of Harold Cruse or ourselves, will alter two essentials: without a power base of our own we have nothing to bring to an alliance with the blacks and therefore there will be no alliance; and if there is no alliance, the blacks will protect themselves as best they can but are not likely to avoid absorption into an imperialist framework. The emergence of a radical black nationalism, such as Cruse outlines, would be a major event with unlimited possibilities in the struggle for a new America. But possibilities are not actualities, and we must put an end to the nauseating and degrading tendency of the white Left to live vicariously through the black revolt, to surrender its own prerogatives, and therefore to abdicate its responsibilities. For us, everything depends on our ability to build our own party and movement. No flights of fancy over black militancy will save us; we shall have to save ourselves.

Chapter 10

WILLIAM STYRON BEFORE THE PEOPLE'S COURT

THE PRAISE GIVEN to William Styron's current prize-winning, best-selling novel, *The Confessions of Nat Turner,* has been followed by strong dissent and hostility from many members of the black intelligentsia. Black writers have denounced the novel in essays and public statements; black actors have threatened to boycott the film version. *William Styron's Nat Turner: Ten Black Writers Respond*[1] presents the essential points of the attack. It is a book that demands attention not so much because of the questions it raises about Styron's novel as for what it reveals about the thinking of intellectuals in the Black Power movement.

That the novel lends itself to historical or other criticism is true but irrelevant to this collection. What is at issue here is the ferocity and hysteria of the attack, which claims Styron to be a racist, a liar, an apologist for slavery, and a man who displays "moral cowardice" and "moral senility." A few of the writers dissociate themselves from these slanders and argue that his book is "objectively" racist and ahistorical—an argu-

This essay was originally published in *New York Review of Books,* Sept. 12, 1968, pp. 34–38.

ment that at least makes discussion possible—but the editor, John Henrik Clarke, editor of *Freedomways* magazine and a member of the staff of HARYOU, is right in claiming that the authors as a group insist on the "deliberate" quality of Styron's alleged crimes. The writers insist on most points as a group, and the essays themselves repeat one another; thus most of the criticism may properly be discussed as a collective effort.

Except for occasional entertainment, we need deal only with the essays of two writers, Mike Thelwell, who teaches English at the University of Massachusetts, and Vincent Harding, who directs the Institute of the Black World in Atlanta, Georgia. Virtually all the serious points made in the book may be found, skillfully presented, in Thelwell's essay, but for some suggestive material on slave religion we must turn to Harding's. Of the rest, the less said the better.

Clarke's introduction begins with a quote from Herbert Aptheker: "History's potency is mighty. The oppressed need it for identity and inspiration; oppressors for justification, rationalization, and legitimacy." This nonsense sets the tone for the book. I should respectfully suggest that although the oppressed may need history for identity and inspiration, they need it above all for the truth of what the world has made of them and of what they have helped make of the world. This knowledge alone can produce that sense of identity which ought to be sufficient for inspiration; and those who look to history to provide glorious moments and heroes invariably are betrayed into making catastrophic errors in political judgment. Specifically, revolutionaries do not need Nat Turner as a saint; they do need the historical truth of the Nat Turner revolt—its strength and its weakness.

One might have thought that black and white Americans who are committed to racial equality would be pleased that William Styron, a white Southerner, has rescued the great rebel slave leader, Nat Turner, from obscurity. Instead, the claim is made throughout these essays that black America has always known of and admired the historical Nat Turner. This is pretense. When Vincent Harding, for example, writes of a Nat Turner who exists "in the living traditions of black America," he is deceiving himself and, inadvertently, the rest of us. Certain great slave revolts in Brazil and the Caribbean have been celebrated in tales and in songs and have contributed to subsequent uprisings; but we have yet to be shown evidence that slaves and postslavery blacks kept alive a politically relevant legend of Nat Turner or of any other Southern slave leader. If Nat Turner is now a name widely known to black and white America, and if the existence of armed resistance to slavery is now generally appreciated, William Styron deserves as much credit as any other writer.

The burden of the attack on Styron's book is the charge of historical falsification. These writers claim that he transforms Turner, the revolutionary general, into a man of indecision and even cowardice; presents slavery as a benign system and reduces the causes of the revolt to trivial personal complaints; denies the influence on Turner of the slave quarters, and makes his virtues the result of his having been a pampered "house nigger"; fails to understand the hold that Turner had on his people as a preacher; and—greatest offense of all—ignores evidence that Turner had a black wife and assigns a central role to his relationship with a lily-white Southern belle. For the most part the criticisms are historical and ideological, and only rarely aesthetic. Some critics praise Styron's writing and see it as enhancing the ideological threat; others deride it, more or less in passing. Thelwell's sarcastic discussion of Styron's handling of Turner's preaching style is a brilliant set piece on black language and deserves to be read quite apart from either Styron or Nat Turner. The social content, not the artistic performance, is, however, the issue and therefore will be my concern here.

The novel is historically sound. Styron takes liberties with fact, as every novelist does, but he does not do violence to the historical record. The same cannot be said for his critics.

Thelwell criticizes Styron for denying that Virginia masters deliberately bred slaves, and refers to the incontrovertible evidence of huge slave sales to the lower South. Certainly every historian knows of those sales, and so does Styron. But had Thelwell read the historical literature carefully, he would have found there a distinction between a system of deliberate breeding and the process of transferring surplus populations. Styron understands the distinction, which is of great importance to the moral question of slavery, but Thelwell misses it completely. There is no disagreement on this matter among historians, black and white, radical, liberal, or conservative.

William Styron's Nat Turner: Ten Black Writers Respond contains a useful appendix with the original confessions of Nat Turner as told to T. R. Gray. For clarity, since Styron's novel has the same title as that Gray gave to the original, I shall refer to the latter as Turner's *Testimony.* Lerone Bennett, the editor of *Ebony* Magazine, tells us that the historical data reveal the real Nat Turner as commanding, virile, and courageous whereas Styron makes him impotent and cowardly. The historical data reveal no such thing; in fact, they do not reveal much at all about Nat Turner's qualities. In his *Testimony,* Turner naturally makes himself appear as if he always knew what he was doing, but his words merely suggest a human being who had respect for himself and no wish to bare his innermost thoughts to the enemy. The historical Turner had resourcefulness and courage, as his conduct shows, but surely nothing in the novel suggests anything else. Styron gives him a human complexity, attributing to Turner doubts and self-doubts, and thereby makes his action the outcome of intelligent and sensitive consideration.

To this extent Styron may well exaggerate Turner's virtues, for it is possible to read the *Testimony* as the reflections of one of those religious fanatics whose single-minded madness carried him to the leadership of a popular cause. Instead, Styron sees enough in the *Testimony* and in the events of the time to suggest that Turner may well have had a more impressive character, including a humanity and sensitivity that could sharpen his resolve to liberate his people and, at the same time, fill him with doubt and foreboding about the means. When Styron sees Turner as racked by self-doubts and unable to kill anyone except Margaret Whitehead, he does not convict him of cowardice. When it could no longer be avoided, he killed. The inner conflict and pain can be interpreted as cowardice and irresolution by those who wish to do so, but this interpretation seems to me more revealing of its authors than of either Styron or the historical Turner.

The historical record is clear enough: Turner hit a defenseless man on the head with a hatchet and could not kill him; he hit a woman on the head with a sword and could not kill her. He explains: it was dark, the hatchet glanced, the sword was dull and light. But neither darkness nor inferior weapons kept his associates from doing better. Surely a serious novelist might be moved to meditate on the reasons. That Turner did kill only Margaret Whitehead—and then only with considerable difficulty—raises questions about human character that are appropriate to a serious novel. Yet the description of the ambivalent relationship between Turner and Margaret, which is of course fictional, has infuriated Styron's critics perhaps more than anything else in his novel.

What of "General Nat," about whom we hear so much? According to the *Testimony,* Turner met with his associates the night before the insurrection to devise a plan. Although he had brooded over his revolutionary calling for a long time, he had as yet no plan at all. Nat Turner led a slave revolt under extremely difficult conditions and deserves an honored place in our history, but there is a limit to what may be claimed for a general who on the day before he marches does not know where he is marching to. In fact, Turner had no place to go. These facts do not make Turner a fool or a madman or less than a hero; they do suggest the desperate circumstances in which he and other Southern slave rebels had to operate. If Styron's presentation of a white-influenced, doubt-ridden Turner insults the hero, what shall we do with the historical figure of the greatest of black revolutionaries, Toussaint L'Ouverture, who enjoyed a privileged position in slavery; who played it safe while his fellow slaves sent the fertile North Plain of Saint-Domingue up in flames; who, when in command, offered to deliver masses of blacks back into slavery in return for amnesty and freedom for his own officers; and who took care to lead his master's family to safety before doing anything at all? Toussaint stands as one of the greatest revolutionary leaders in world history, but not being a statue, he had all the frailties and contradictions common even to the greatest of men.

Styron draws especially heavy fire for showing loyal slaves helping to shoot down the insurgent blacks. Relying on the authority of Aptheker, the black writers tell us that it did not happen and could never have happened. This is nonsense. Many planters claimed that it did happen, but we may dismiss their testimony for a moment. During the War for Southern Independence some loyal slaves defend their masters' families with guns in hand, but we may put that fact aside also. When we turn from the United States, which had only small and scattered slave revolts, to Brazil and the Caribbean, where large black slave revolts were frequent, we find all the evidence we need. Armed, loyal slaves often fought against insurgents, as every historian of those regions knows. It is pardonable for Styron to take liberties with the particular history of the Nat Turner revolt, so long as he does no violence to the history of the slave revolts generally. Here, as in his handling of the rape episode, he has proved himself a better student of history than his critics.

Styron apparently knows, as his critics do not, that a ruling class incapable of applying the rule of divide and conquer could not last a year. Turner's *Testimony* itself tells of loyal slaves who protected their masters. Of special relevance is Turner's own account of his last days in hiding, wherein he tells us of being discovered by two Negroes to whom he revealed his identity; he adds that they immediately fled and that he knew they would betray him.

Styron's critics miss his irony. In the novel, Gray reveals to Turner the slaveholder's conventional wisdom on slave loyalty when he announces, with all the sensitivity and genius for miscalculation characteristic of ruling classes, that this is why "nigger slavery will last a thousand years." Styron invokes here the image of the Thousand-Year Reich, which lasted twelve years; by linking the two systems he is ironically demonstrating the stupidity of those who think that divisions among the lower classes may forever be counted upon to maintain systems of oppression. For this he is accused of being a "white Southern racist." It is not surprising that the White Citizens Councils cannot recognize Styron as one of their own, and have denounced him as a traitor to his race and class; but it is surprising that Styron's black critics have insisted on reading the incident with eyes of a T.R. Gray.

In the novel, Turner winces when Gray tells him that his revolt has been crushed with black help; and throughout Styron's book, Turner expresses contempt, even hatred, for his fellow blacks. The critics of Styron's book insist that love, not hatred, must have driven Turner forward. Such love for his people is also in the novel. Had he not loved them, he would not have protested so much against their weakness in the face of oppression; he could not even have perceived them as victims of oppression. No revolutionary could be free of such feelings of hatred, which is essentially a hatred for the oppression rather than for the oppressed.

John Oliver Killens cites David Walker's magnificent call for slave insurrection (1829), *The Appeal to the Colored Citizens of the World*. But Walker never feared to mix his professions of love for his people with the harshest condemnation:

> Why is it that those few, weak, good for nothing whites are able to keep so many able men, one of whom can put to flight

> a dozen whites, in wretchedness and misery? It shows at once what the blacks are, we are ignorant, abject, servile and mean —and the whites know it, they know that we are too servile to assert our rights as men—or they would not fool with us as they do . . . . Why do they not bring the inhabitants of Asia to be body servants to them? They know they would get their bodies rent and torn asunder from head to foot.[2]

This, the language of a genuine revolutionary, is what Styron gives Nat Turner; both display the humanity of men capable of doubt and anguish.

The critics claim that Styron's Turner and his followers revolted for trivial personal reasons, and that Styron pictures slavery as a benign and reasonably humane system. None of this is true. By giving Turner a kind master, Styron shows, as Mrs. Stowe did long ago, that the kindest masters could not offset the inhumanity and injustice of the system. Styron's Turner chooses insurrection because a series of betrayals, which his old master could not help, awakens him to the injustice of his general, not specific, condition. Will, the slave, makes the same choice because the exceptional brutality to which he is subjected produces the same effect. Hark, one of the most attractive and interesting of the rebels, has to be urged by Turner to transform his own personal misery into political consciousness.

All this is simple and sound both as history and as psychology. One of the essential qualities of a great revolutionary leader (or, for that matter, of a great counterrevolutionary demagogue like Hitler) is the ability to raise the consciousness of his people from the personal to the social. People, especially simple people, normally experience an oppressive social system in a thousand seemingly meaningless and disconnected ways: It is the leader's task to make them see their oppression as flowing from a common social source and to help them to identify the oppressor. The "personal" suffering Styron describes flows from the slave condition; he is correct to dwell on this as the basis for revolutionary consciousness and to make Turner's religious preaching the vehicle for the transformation. Styron does not, as some charge, make Turner's feeling for Margaret Whitehead the spring of his action. Nothing in the novel suggests anything so absurd.

The critics accuse Styron of presenting Turner as a pampered house nigger and denying the influence on him of the slave quarters. Styron's Turner allegedly does not adequately reflect the influence of his own mother and father and the friendship of his fellow slaves; the positive influences on his life seem to have been white. Historians, black and white, have done little work on house slaves, drivers, preachers, and especially field slaves, so that if Styron underestimates the influence of the slave quarters on the personality and character of its inhabitants, so does virtually everyone else who has written on the subject. Nat Turner, in his *Testimony,* does say a few words about a grandmother, about his parents who taught him to read, and about some relations with other slaves. Because Turner is taught to read by the white family in the novel, Styron is accused of falsifying history, of denying a vital culture among the blacks, and of seeing slave life from the view of the Big House.

How much can we make of Turner's having been taught to read by his parents? Who, after all, probably taught them? Turner himself says that he used white children's books. Styron did not invent white paternalism. That attitude was part of the history of slavery and, as Styron shows in many ways, in no way could compensate for the injustice of the system.

Thelwell condemns Styron because Turner aspires to white culture, speaks a white language, and thinks and dreams like a white man, although Frantz Fanon, whose work Thelwell must know, provides adequate theoretical justification for this side of the experiences of the oppressed. Thelwell cites sections of the *Testimony* which suggest Turner's early alienation from the system and a distinctly religious and political opposition to it. It is hard to believe that so sophisticated a man as Thelwell should take Turner's claim to lifelong dedication at face value. Every revolutionary can give the social reasons for his conduct, but we must still explain how the same circumstances make one man a revolutionary and his brother the opposite. It is impossible to expect the *Testimony* to yield more than unconscious hints. Out of these, Styron created a believable Nat Turner although by no means the only possible one. But then, nothing prevents (or has ever prevented) black intellectuals, who claim to have the living traditions of black America at their disposal, from creating their own version.

Turner's aspiration to white culture is not the same as hatred for things black. Slaves of any race normally reach out for the culture of the class above them, even as they create a viable world of their own. So do colonials, as Fanon shows. So do industrial workers, for all their freedom and leisure, unless they are organized in a struggle to develop a larger view. Again, consider the example of Toussaint and the other black leaders who were, at one bad moment, prepared to betray their army back into slavery. Their excuse was that the newly imported African Coast Niggers "cannot even speak two words of French"!

Styron's black critics, especially Harding and Thelwell, insist that there was a special kind of subterranean life in the slave quarters which might have proven far more powerful than we now appreciate. Since we know so little and can say so little, the anger and hostility toward Styron, who has created something out of what we do know, is hard to justify. One is tempted to say, if you say that black folk life can be unearthed and made relevant, then do it; if white historians —for whatever reasons—have been blind to whole areas of black sensibility, culture, and tradition, then show us. We can learn much from your work, but nothing from your fury.

The most important and damaging criticism by Thelwell and Harding concerns religion. They argue that Styron pays insufficient attention to Turner's role as a preacher and misses the central role of black religion. It is true that all black slave revolts in the Americas had a religious side, which provided ideological and often organizational cohesion. But Styron's critics claim more than an artistic failure to convey the full power of Turner's preaching. According to Harding, Styron shows Turner as a man abandoned by God until he repents, not for the dead white children but for the young white women who opened him to love. Such a God ostensibly belongs neither to the black man nor to the white, but only to the private world of William Styron. Harding is entitled to his reading, but I fail to see much in it. The young woman in question was the one person Turner did kill—in the novel and in fact—and guilt tends to be an intensely personal matter. In saying that he would have spared her, Styron's Turner acknowledges the love that accompanied his hatred; he repents not for having led his slaves in revolt—he affirms his cause decisively—but for having allowed the justice of his cause to generate personal hatred. He thereby reaffirms his Christianity and his humanity: he sees his own tragedy in his inability to wage uncompromising class war without personalizing the hatred it engenders.

Of all the criticisms, the most violent are directed at Turner's relationship with Margaret Whitehead. The objections are primarily these: that the historical Nat Turner had a black wife whom Styron ignores; that Styron-Turner's romance with Margaret goes hand in hand with Styron's portrayal of Will as a lunatic hell-bent on raping white women; that Styron gives Turner homosexual and asexual tendencies and thereby denies his manhood; and that the interracial love affair arises from a white man's fantasy life, has racist overtones, and has nothing to do with Nat Turner and the slave experience.

The evidence for Turner's alleged black wife is slim and not beyond challenge. The black critics make much of Turner's references to his grandmother and his parents in the *Testi-*

mony. How incredible, then, that he failed to mention his wife. Perhaps she existed, perhaps not; perhaps she had some importance in his life, perhaps not. We do not know. Given the slim thread of evidence—or gossip—Styron has not falsified history by ignoring her. The discussion, therefore, must focus on whom and what he put in her place.

A similar attack is aimed at the characterization of Will as a man obsessed with the idea of rape. We know little or nothing of the historical Will. One historical account, without evidence to support it, presents a different man from that in the *Testimony.* Styron had nothing to work from, and was free to invent him as bloodthirsty, nihilistic, consumed by hate—a type who has appeared in the noblest of uprisings and revolutions throughout history. It is ridiculous to infer an insult to black people from this characterization. We are told that, in fact, there was not a single episode of rape during the revolt and that the issue is, therefore, viciously injected. No rape did occur, but so far as I can recall, no one except Herbert Aptheker bothered to note the absence until Styron himself commented on it in an essay published several years ago. In any case, there are no instances of rape in Styron's book. If Styron's Will is hungry for white women, his Nat Turner is a man who will stand for none of it and who is strong enough to prevail.

What, then, is the complaint? The rape question is supposed to be Styron's invention and the creation of his racist mind. But Styron knows, as his black critics ought to know, that evidence of rape appears frequently in the histories of the slave revolts. It would be astounding if it did not. Evidence from the United States is cloudy, but we can also turn to Saint-Domingue's great revolution. The radical and black (by United States classification) historian of the revolution, C. L. R. James, in his superb book, *Black Jacobins,* refers without fuss to the raping of white women and says all that needs to be said: those whose women had for so long been objects of white violence settled old scores. To deny these common occurrences during social struggle is to betray a curiously rosy view of the effects of oppression.

Styron's Turner has a homosexual experience and afterwards remains continent; accordingly, we are told that Styron has deprived him of his manhood. Twenty years ago the *Kinsey Report* reported that the majority of white males had homosexual experiences during pre- and early adolescence. By assuming that black men follow similar lines of development, Styron merely gives Nat Turner something of a normal early life. Perhaps black men do not share with decadent whites these delightful early encounters. *Che peccato!*

The second matter is more serious. Why does Turner abstain from sexual relations? The answer seems to me clear throughout the novel. Styron has, in this way, dramatized Turner's single-mindedness, his devotion, even to the point of monomania, to his revolutionary calling. This characteristic, in its general if not necessarily specific form, may be found in many great revolutionaries. As a literary device it may or may not be successful; it is clearly meant not to denigrate, but to link Turner with a great historical tradition of revolutionary heroes. And those who think that sexual abstinence deprives a man of his manhood have a few questions to answer themselves.

Finally, we come to Margaret Whitehead, whose place in the novel has drawn the heaviest fire. The charges are by now familiar: Styron insults black men by suggesting that they hanker after white chicks; he insults black women by denying them the charms to lure their men away from these white chicks; and he is immersed in a white-racist sexual fantasy. To begin with, we may recall what his detractors never mention: Margaret Whitehead displays a feeling for Turner parallel to his feeling for her. She unconsciously tries to seduce him several times; Turner is, after all, the only sympathetic, different, and unobtainable man in her life. Perhaps the complaint should be reversed: Styron insults white women and attributes to them an irresistible fascination for that celebrated black penis. This is, in fact, exactly what white racists, especially in the South, are saying.

The attack on Styron's handling of the sexual aspect of race relations comes at a strange time, for in recent years various black writers have been exploring the issue in a similar way—e.g., Fanon's *Black Skin, White Masks,* Earl E. Thorpe's *Eros and Freedom in Southern Life and Thought,* and especially Calvin C. Hernton's indispensable *Sex and Racism in America.* With creditable research, professional integrity, and considerable good humor, Hernton argues that the racial problem in America does have a sexual aspect and that the sooner we face its implications, the better. American life throws whites and blacks together under circumstances in which they constantly affect one another and yet they remain apart. As one result, the sexual fantasies common to both sexes and races tend to be translated into racial terms. For example, whites often regard blacks as sexually uninhibited and more desirable, and blacks regard whites in exactly the same way. If the racial translation of sexual fantasy proves so strong in modern America, what must it have been like in the slave South?

By focusing on this side of the black-white confrontation, Styron does expose one of the most tragic features of the slave regime. On the one hand, slavery threw whites and blacks together intimately in relations often harsh and brutal, sometimes affectionate and loving, sometimes all at once. On the other hand, it forbade fruition to those feelings of love which its intimacy engendered. The tension was at once a matter of race and class. In Styron's novel, Margaret and Turner are drawn together because they glimpse a special sensitivity in each other. Each is drawn to the other by the attraction of the forbidden; but each is so remote from the other that neither can even know what he or she is feeling. The novel describes a social system that brought people together in intimate relationships, negated that intimacy, relentlessly suppressed any awareness of the feelings created, and necessarily turned love into hatred and fear. Here Styron sees how slavery crushed the feelings of those who faced each other from different sides of the line.

Styron's Turner is impressed by the fine white ladies, with their polish and elegance, and it would have been perfectly natural for Turner to focus his feelings on a lovely girl who seemed to embody everything in life that was desirable and unattainable. One wonders if Styron was thinking of the great Toussaint L'Ouverture, who, as our black critics surely know, steadily plowed his way through those aristocratic French ladies of Le Cap who sought his favors. If Styron's critics find some racial insult here, then they fail to see that the issue transcends race and is a question of class and status as well. The Margaret Whiteheads of the WASP bourgeoisie have long fluttered before working-class boys of other ethnic groups quite as much as they must have fluttered before black slaves.

The power of Styron's performance lies in his having carried his confrontation further. In establishing genuine love he also establishes genuine understanding, for to some extent Turner does come to see Margaret as a particular human being, rather than as a social type. That, I should suggest to Harding, is the reason he must repent of her murder before he can reestablish a relationship with his God. In repenting, he does not repudiate his revolt; he repudiates the hatred which led him to deny the love he felt for a human being who was as trapped as he. This may or may not be convincing artistically, but the charge that this part of the novel stamps Styron as a racist is outrageous. If anything, it may stamp him as an integrationist—which for some may well be his ultimate crime. Certainly, it stamps him as a man who has the courage to confront the depths of America's racial tragedy.

Of other complaints, great and small, little need be said, for they are, at best, more of the same and generally a good deal worse. I will only mention the complaint of Dr. Alvin

F. Poussaint, a psychiatrist. After telling us that Styron, as a white Southerner, must be the victim of racist ideology, Poussaint notes that Styron calls Turner "Nat" and then asks if this is an attempt by a white Southerner to keep Turner in his place. Perhaps. But what shall we say of Vincent Harding, the title of whose essay is "You've Taken My Nat and Gone"? Or of Aptheker, who also calls Turner "Nat" and who is cited throughout this book as a solid authority? And what of Genovese—I hold my breath!—who calls Turner "Turner," for surely Poussaint knows that Turner was the name of the master's family.

William Styron's Nat Turner: Ten Black Writers Respond shows the extent to which the American intelligentsia is splitting along racial, rather than ideological, lines. As such, the book needs to be taken with alarmed seriousness, no matter how absurd most of the contributions are. It is enough that Vincent Harding and Mike Thelwell appear here with no less passion than the others, although with considerably more grace and intellectual power. Certainly, we need not probe the motives of these ten writers as they try to probe Styron's. But it is clear that the black intelligentsia faces a serious crisis. Its political affinities lie with the Black Power movement, which increasingly demands conformity, myth-making, and historical fabrication. No one need believe that any of these writers would resort to deliberate falsification—which they so readily accuse Styron of—but the intellectual history of popular and revolutionary movements has overflowed with just such crises, in which dedicated, politically committed intellectuals have talked themselves into believing many things they have later had to gag on. The black intellectuals seem to be going through what Marxist intellectuals went through in the 1930s and 1940s. Let us hope that they come out a good deal better.

One thing remains certain: If they follow the line laid down by Aptheker with which they open the book, and if they proceed in a hysterical way, to demand new myths in order to serve current ends, they will find the same moral, political, and intellectual debacle at the end as did most of the Marxists of those days. Their political movement, being a genuine popular force, can only be served by the truth. The history of every people exhibits glory and shame, heroism and cowardice, wisdom and foolishness, certainty and doubt, and more often than not these antagonistic qualities appear at the same moment and in the same men. The revolutionary task of intellectuals is, accordingly, not to invent myths, but to teach each people its own particular contradictory truth. This historian has never been sure which lessons can be drawn from the past to serve the future. Except perhaps one: Until a people can and will face its own past, it has no future.

Postscript

The reaction to Styron's fictional treatment of the relationship between Turner and Margaret Whitehead has easily been the most obscene part of the discussion. For what it is worth, I think it appropriate to glance at one or two black treatments of the sexual dimension of the racial confrontation. Vincent Harding's essay, "Black Radicalism: The Road from Montgomery," Alfred F. Young, ed., *Dissent: Explorations in the History of American Radicalism* (DeKalb, Illinois, 1968), contains some thoughts and a quotation surprisingly missing from the polemics against Styron:

> How significant was the constant discussion of black revolution? One of its foremost exponents, Ron Karenga, said: "We are the last revolutionaries in America. If we fail to leave a legacy of revolution for our children we have failed our mission and should be dismissed as unimportant." Although Karenga, like others, believes the cultural revolution of black consciousness is most important at the present time, he has vividly pictured the next stage:

When word is given we'll see how tough you are. When it's "burn," let's see how much you burn. When it's "kill," let's see how much you kill. When it's "blow up," let's see how much you blow up. And when it's "take that white girl's head too," we'll really see how tough you are.

June, 1970

NOTES

1. John Henrik Clarke, Lerone Bennett, Jr., Alvin F. Poussaint, Vincent Harding, John Oliver Killens, John A. Williams, Ernest Kaiser, Loyle Hairston, Charles V. Hamilton, and Mike Thelwell (Boston, 1968).

2. Herbert Aptheker, ed., *"One Continual Cry": David Walker's Appeal to the Colored Citizens of the World (1829–1830)* (New York, 1965), p. 129.

Chapter 11

BLACK STUDIES: TROUBLE AHEAD

NO PROBLEM SO AGITATES the campuses today as that posed by the growing pressure for black studies programs and departments. The agitation presents special dangers since it can be, and sometimes is, opportunistically manipulated by the nihilist factions of the radical white student movement. For the most part, black students have shown considerable restraint in dealing with dubious white allies and have given strong indication of being much more interested in reforming the universities than in burning them down. The black student movement, like some parts of the white radical student movement and very much unlike others, represents an authentic effort by young people to take a leading role in the liberation of an oppressed people and, as such, exhibits impressive seriousness and developing sophistication. The political forms that the agitation takes and the deep frustrations from which it stems nonetheless open the way to reckless elements among

This essay was originally published in *The Atlantic Monthly*, June 1969, pp. 37–41.

black, as well as white, student militants.

The universities must now choose among three courses: a principled but flexible response to legitimate black demands; a dogmatic, repressive adherence to traditional, liberal, and essentially racist policies; and a cowardly surrender to all black demands, no matter how destructive to the university as an institution of higher learning or to American and Afro-American society in general. This last option, which has been taken in a notable number of places, ironically reflects as much racism in its assumptions and implications as the second, and it takes little skill in prophecy to realize that its conclusion will be a bloodbath in which blacks are once again the chief victims. Yet, the debate over black studies proceeds without attention to the major features of the alternatives; it proceeds, in fact, in a manner that suggests the very paternalistic white racism against which so many blacks are today protesting.

The demand for black studies and for special black studies departments needs no elaborate explanation or defense. It rests on an awareness of the unique and dual nature of the black experience in the United States. Unlike European immigrants, blacks came here involuntarily, were enslaved and excluded from access to the mainstream of American life, and as a result have had a special history with a profoundly national-cultural dimension. Unlike, say, Italo-Americans, Afro-Americans have within their history the elements of a distinct nationality at the same time that they have participated in and contributed immensely to a common American nationality. Despite the efforts of many black and some white scholars, this paradoxical experience has yet to be explored with the respect and intellectual rigor it deserves.

This essential justification for black studies, incidentally, raises serious questions about the demands by white radicals for "ethnic studies" and for special attention to people from the "third world," especially since the term "third world" is, from a Marxist and revolutionary point of view, a reactionary swindle. These demands, when sincere, have their origin in a proper concern for the fate of Mexican-Americans, Puerto Ricans, Asians, and other ethnic groups in a white-racist culture, but the study of the attendant problems, does not, at least on the face of it, require anything like an approach similar to that of black studies. For the most part, the discrimination against these groups is largely a class and normal (for America) ethnic question, requiring sober analysis of class structure in America; for the rest, much of the racism directed against these minorities can be traced directly to the by-products of the enslavement of blacks by whites and the ideology derived therefrom. In any case, the issues are clearly different, for the black question is simultaneously one of class and nationality (not merely minority ethnic status), and it is therefore a disservice to the cause of black liberation to construct a politically opportunist equation that can only blur the unique and central quality of the black experience in the United States.

The duality of the black experience haunts the present debate and leads us immediately into a consideration of the ideological and political features of the black studies programs. It is, at best, irrelevant to argue, as DeVere E. Pentony does in the April, 1969, issue of the *Atlantic,* that all professors of history and social science bring a particular ideology and politics to their classroom and that a black ideological bias is no worse than any other. There is no such thing as a black ideology or a black point of view. Rather there are various black-nationalist biases, from leftwing versions such as that of the Panthers to rightwing versions such as that of Ron Karenga and other "cultural nationalists." There are also authentic sections of the black community that retain conservative, liberal, or radical integrationist and antinationalist positions. Both integrationist and separatist tendencies can be militant or moderate, radical or conservative (in the sense generally applied to white politics in relation to social questions). The separatists are riding high today, and the integrationists are beating a retreat; but this has happened before and may be reversed tomorrow.

All these elements have a right to participate in the exploration of black historical and cultural themes. In one sense, the whole point of black studies programs in a liberal arts college or university ought to be to provide for the widest and most vigorous exchange among all these groups in an atmosphere of free discussion and mutual toleration. The demand for an exclusively black faculty and especially the reactionary demand for student control of autonomous departments must be understood as demands for the introduction of specific ideological and political criteria into the selection of faculty and the composition of programs. Far from being proposals to relate these programs to the black community, they are in fact factionally based proposals to relate them to one or another political tendency within the black community and to exclude others. The bloody, but by no means isolated, feud between black student factions on the UCLA campus ought to make that clear.

One of the new hallmarks of white racism is the notion of one black voice, one black experience, one black political community, one black ideology—of a black community without an authentic inner political life wracked by dissension and ideological struggle. In plain truth, what appears on the campuses as "what the blacks want" is almost invariably what the dominant faction in a particular black caucus wants. Like all people who fight for liberation, blacks are learning the value of organizational discipline and subordination to a firm and united line of action. Sometimes, the formulation of particular demands and actions has much less to do with their intrinsic merits or with the institution under fire than with the momentary balance in the struggle for power within the caucus itself. This discipline presents nothing unprincipled or sinister, but it does present difficult and painful problems, which must be evaluated independently by those charged with institutional and political responsibility in the white community.

The pseudo-revolutionary middle-class totalitarians who constitute one temporarily powerful wing of the leftwing student movement understand this dimension, even if few others seem to. Accordingly, they support demands for student control as an entering wedge for a general political purge of faculties—a purge they naïvely hope to dominate. These suburban putschists are most unlikely to succeed in their stated objectives of purging "reactionaries," for they are isolated, incoherent, and without adequate power. But they may very well help to re-establish the principle of the campus purge and thereby provide a moral and legal basis for a new wave of McCarthyism. The disgraceful treatment of Professors Staughton Lynd and Jesse Lemisch, among many who have been recently purged from universities by both liberal and rightwing pressure, has already set a tone of renewed repression, which some fanatical and unreasoning leftwing militants are unwittingly reinforcing. If black studies departments are permitted to become political bases and cadre-training schools for one or another political movement, the door will be open for the conversion of other departments to similar roles; that door is already being forced in some places.

Those blacks who speak in harsh nationalist accents in favor of all-black faculties, departmental autonomy, and student power open themselves to grave suspicions of bad faith. The most obvious objection, raised sharply by several outstanding black educators in the South, concerns the systematic raiding of black colleges by financially stronger white ones. The shortage of competent black specialists in black history, social science, and black culture is a matter of general knowledge and concern. Hence, the successful application of the all-black principle in most universities would spell the end of hopes to build one or more distinguished black universities to serve as a center for the training of a national Afro-American intelligentsia. One need not be partial to black nationalism in any of its varieties to respect the right of black people to self-determination, for this right flows directly from the duality of their unique experience in the United States. Even those who dislike or distrust black nationalism as such should be able to view the development of such centers of higher education as positive and healthy. If there is no place in the general American university for ideological homogeneity and conformity, there is a place in American society for universities based on adherence to a specific ideology, as the Catholic universities, for example, have demonstrated.

Responsible black scholars have been working hard for an end to raiding and to the scattering of the small number of black professors across the country. Among other obstacles, they face the effort of ostensibly nationalist black students who seek to justify their decision to attend predominantly white institutions, often of high prestige, by fighting for a larger black teaching staff. The outcome of these demands is the obscurantist nonsense that black studies can and should be taught by people without intellectual credentials since these credentials are "white" anyway. It is true that many black men are capable of teaching important college-level courses even though they do not have formal credentials. For example, the Afro-American tradition in music, embracing slave songs, spirituals, blues, jazz, and other forms, could probably be taught best by a considerable number of articulate and cultured, if sometimes self-taught, black musicians and free-lance critics who are largely unknown to the white community. But few good universities have ever refused to waive formalities in any field when genuine intellectual credentials of a nonacademic order could be provided. What has to be resisted firmly is the insanity that claims, as in one recent instance, that experience as a SNCC field organizer should be considered more important than a Ph.D. in the hiring of a professor of Afro-American history. This assertion represents a general contempt for all learning and a particular contempt for black studies as a field of study requiring disciplined, serious intellectual effort—an attitude that reflects the influence of white racism, even when brought forth by a black man.

The demand for all-black faculties rests on the insistence that only blacks can understand the black experience. This cant is nothing new: it forms the latest version of the battle cry of every reactionary nationalism and has clear antecedents, for example, in the nineteenth century German Romantic movement. To be perfectly blunt, it now constitutes an ideologically fascist position and must be understood as such. The general reply to it—if one is necessary—is simply that the history of every people can only be written from within and without. But there is a specific reply too. However much the black presence has produced a unique and distinctly national Afro-American experience, it has also formed part of a broader, integrated national culture. It would be absurd to try to understand the history of, say, the South without carefully studying black history. Any Southern historian worth his salt must also be a historian of black America—and vice versa—and if so, it would be criminal to deny him an opportunity to teach his proper subject. Certainly, these remarks do not add up to an objection to a preference for black departmental directors and a numerical predominance of blacks on the faculty, if possible, for every people must write its own history and play the main role in the formation of its own intelligentsia and national culture. These measures would be justified simply on grounds of the need to establish relations of confidence with black students, for they involve no sacrifice of principle and do not compromise the integrity of the university. But preference and emphasis are one thing; monopoly and ideological exclusion are quite another.

We might mention here the problem of the alleged "psychological need" of black people to do this or that or to be this or that in order to reclaim their manhood, re-establish their ostensibly lost dignity, and God knows what else. There is a place for these questions in certain kinds of intellectual discussions and in certain political forums, but there is no place for these questions in the formation of university policy. In such a context they represent a benevolent paternalism that is neither more nor less than racist. Whites in general and university professors and administrators in particular are not required to show "sympathy," "compassion," understanding," and other manifestations of liberal guilt feelings; they are required to take black demands seriously—to take them straight, on their merits. That is, they are required to treat political demands politically and to meet their responsibility to fight white racism while also meeting their responsibility to defend the integrity and dignity of the university community as a whole.

Only if the universities have a clear attitude toward themselves will they be able to fulfill their duty to the black community. Our universities, if they are to survive—and their survival is problematical—must redefine themselves as institutions of higher learning and firmly reject the role of cadre-training schools for government, business, or community organizations of any kind. Blame for the present crisis ought to be placed on those who, especially after World War II, opened the universities to the military, to big-business recruitment, to the "fight against communism," to the CIA, and to numerous other rightist pressures. If Dow Chemical or ROTC belongs on a college campus, so does the Communist party, the Black Panthers, the John Birch Society, the Campfire Girls, or the Mafia for that matter. Students have a clear political right to organize on campuses as Democrats, Republicans, Communists, Panthers, or whatever, provided their activities are appropriate to campus life, but the universities have no business making special institutional arrangements with this or that faction off campus and then putting down other factions as illicit. And government and business represent political intrusions quite as much as do political parties. The same is true for the anachronistic practice of having American universities controlled by boards of trustees instead of by their faculties in consultation with the students. In short, the black studies question, like the black revolt as a whole, has raised all the fundamental problems of class power in American life, and the solutions will have to run deep into the structure of the institutions themselves.

What the universities owe to black America is what they owe to white America: an atmosphere of freedom and dissent for the pursuit of higher learning. Black people have largely been excluded in the past, for the atmosphere has been racist, the history and culture of black people have been ignored or caricatured, and access to the universities themselves has been severely circumscribed. Black studies programs, shaped in a manner consistent with such traditional university values as ideological freedom and diversity, can help to correct this injustice. So can scholarships and financial assistance to black students and special facilities for those blacks who wish to live and work with some degree of ethnic homogeneity. But no university is required to surrender its basic standards of competence in the selection of faculty or the admission of students. If not enough black students are equipped to enter college today, it is because of atrocious conditions in lower education. The universities can take a few steps to correct this injustice, but the real fight must take place elsewhere in society and must be aimed at providing black communities with the financial resources, indepedence, and autonomy necessary to educate their people properly from the earliest appropriate ages. There are limits to what a particular institution like a university can do, and it dare not try to solve problems that can be solved only by the political institutions of society as a whole. And above all, no university need surrender its historical role and essential content in order to right the wrongs of the whole political and social system; it need only reform itself to contribute to a solution of the broader problems in a manner consistent with its character as a place of higher learning with limited functions, possibilities, and responsibilities.

Black studies programs have at least two legitimate tasks.

First, they can, by their very nature, provide a setting within which black people can forge an intelligentsia equipped to provide leadership on various levels of political and cultural action. Black studies programs themselves can do only part of this job. For that reason many able and sophisticated sections of the Black Student Alliance organizations wisely call on their brothers and sisters to participate in these programs but also to specialize in medicine, engineering, sociology, economic analysis, or in fact any scientific or humanistic field. They know that only the emergence of a fully developed intelligentsia, with training in every field of knowledge, can ultimately meet the deepest needs of the black community. In this respect, notwithstanding strong elements of nihilism in their own organizations, their seriousness, maturity, discipline, and realism stand in striking contrast to the childish anti-intellectualism of those bourgeois whites who currently claim to speak for the radical student movement and who impose upon it their own version of generational revolt.

Second, black studies can help immeasurably to combat the racism of white students. The exclusion of whites from the faculty and student body of the black studies programs would therefore defeat half the purpose of the programs themselves. Undoubtedly, there are problems. To the extent that black students view these courses as places of refuge where they can rap with their brothers, they are certain to resent the white presence, not to mention a possible white numerical predominance among the student body. Black students who want an exclusively black setting are entitled to it —in a black university. They are not entitled to tear any institution apart to suit their present mood. The universities owe black people a chance to get a liberal or technical education, but that debt can only be paid in a way consistent with the proper role of the university in society. Beyond that, no university may safely go. If it tries, the result can only be the end of any worthwhile higher education. The inability of so many radical whites to grasp this obvious point is especially galling. It ought to be obvious that the elite schools will protect themselves from this kind of degradation, even if they continue to accept the degradation that accompanies complicity with the war machine and with big business. It is the others—the ones serving the working-class and lower-middle-class youth—that will perish or be transformed into extensions of low-grade high schools. Universities must resist the onslaught now being made against them by superficially radical bourgeois students who have exploited the struggles over black studies programs to advance their own tactical objectives. Fortunately, these elements do not speak for the radical student movement as a whole but represent only a tendency within it; the internal diversity of organizations like SDS, for example, always exceeded the level revealed in the press.

No matter how painful some of the battles are or will become, the advent of black studies programs represents a momentous step toward the establishment of relations of equality between white and black intellectuals. But, if these programs are to realize their potential in support of black liberation and and in fostering genuinely free and critical scholarship, our universities must resolve honestly the questions of limits and legitimacy. Those who blindly ignore or cynically manipulate these questions, and the reforms they imply, corrupt the meaning of black studies and risk the destruction of institutions necessary to the preservation of freedom in American life.

Postscript

This article has come under strange attack. Dr. Nathan Hare, for example, has interpreted it as an attack on black studies programs; others, who at least bothered to read it, have interpreted it as an expression of support for conservative attempts to narrow such programs. In fact, it was intended as a warning that most of the campus liberals who were falling all over themselves to placate the least sensible and constructive black students were unprincipled scoundrels whose fancy rhetoric disguised an overriding commitment to peace and quiet at any price. I tried to say that as soon as they realized their error in thinking that doles, third-rate educational programs, and fireworks would buy peace—as soon as they learned that black students wanted a serious education, even if youth and inexperience led them to some mistakes in judgment—then these same liberals would send for troops to restore the peace and quiet that alone interest them. In asking that the more irrational and politically dangerous black demands be resolutely opposed, I thought I was taking a stand in support of black studies and in defense of the universities at the same time. Exactly one bloody year later, I still think so.

June, 1970

Chapter 12

THE INFLUENCE OF THE BLACK POWER MOVEMENT ON HISTORICAL SCHOLARSHIP

Reflections of a White Historian

THE PAINFUL and dangerous political crisis through which our nation and the world are now passing has had, among many ramifications, a pronounced effect on the humanities. Not for many centuries has the very value—the "usefulness" or "relevance," to use the absurd language of our fashionable youth—of the humanities been subjected to so much malicious and barbarous questioning. Few concerned scholars doubt that a relationship exists between the world-wide crisis in politics (and therefore in morals) and the decline in respect for humane learning, although the specific link occasions intense disagreement. Nor is it any longer possible to hide the unwitting complicity of so many humanists in their own degradation; the increasing acquiescence of the American intelligentsia in a vulgar instrumentalist attitude toward natural and social science has reached scandalous proportions, and few humanists any longer speak out strongly for scientific education informed by those historically developed values which only the humanities can lay bare and discipline.

This essay was originally published in *Daedalus*, 1, Spring, 1970, pp. 473–494. Reprinted by permission of *Daedalus*, Journal of the American Academy of Arts and Sciences.

If this condition forces humanists to reassess their own work and to reaffirm its value while appreciating its limits, then the disastrous decline can be arrested and the dangers, transformed into possibilities. I do not wish to enter here into a discussion of the roots of the crisis or of the proper place of the humanities; a separate essay would be needed to say anything of value on the former problem, and I could not hope to improve on Eric Weil's formulation of the latter. Rather, I should like to address this paper to only one of the constituent problems—the short- and long-term influences of political currents in a democratic society on historical scholarship. The recent upsurge of political awareness and participation has had an undeniable impact on historians, and no small number show increasing nervousness about the implications. The dangers are familiar: too many are unwilling or unable to resist the temptation to write politically serviceable ideological tracts, whereas too many others flee in panic toward a nonexistent ivory tower from which to view with despair and alarm the end of scholarly integrity. Yet, as a consideration of the impact of the black revolt on historical scholarship will show, neither course is justified. If the political threat to scholarly integrity is real, so are the possibilities for intellectual advance that the very same political thrust offers. A historical profession that knows what it is about and preserves a decent confidence in its own integrity and capacity for collective self-criticism has much to gain and little to risk by confronting political challenges on grounds of its own choosing.

The full impact of the black revolt of the late 1960s on American scholarship in general and Afro-American history in particular has yet to be felt. In part, this delay is the usual one, for even politically volatile scholars, if they are not demagogues or propagandists, need time to assess political trends and to do the work necessary to support their points of view. For this reason much of the secondary work of the 1960s still reflects the sensibilities and concerns of the civil rights movement of 1954–1964, which after only a few years already seems like some distant Golden Age. A quarter-century struggle to drive racist mystification out of history and social science culminated during those years. In American history this new sensibility encouraged advances in the treatment of such subjects as slavery and Reconstruction, but did not go much beyond the negative work of purging ideological nonsense and of restoring intellectual order. The breathtaking events of the late 1960s, on the other hand, foreshadow a decisive turn in the understanding of our national experience and of the black experience, while paradoxically they threaten the integrity of each discipline they affect. The dangers, which we shall review briefly, are real; the opportunities, fortunately, are far greater, and with them, the probabilities.

The direct impact of politics or, rather, of the immediate ideological mood upon historical scholarship has not been nearly so great as is often asserted. The "new history" that emerged from the Progressive Era provides no exception, for its strong and lasting qualities reflected not so much the immediate political concerns as an underlying shift in the economic and cultural life of the nation. Recognition of big business as a central fact of life; a growing acceptance of an imperial role for the United States in world affairs; a developing commitment to government action for social welfare; the shift of population cityward and its attendant problems; the end of general immigration—these and other major developments represented a fundamental change in the patterns of national life and the locus of ideological and moral concerns. Undoubtedly, more direct and limited political events influenced particular historians and histories, but we may doubt that they did so in a way to produce much of lasting value.

The vulgar Marxism of the 1930s and the abortive New Conservatism of the 1950s are more to the point. Little of lasting intellectual value came out of the leftist tumult of the 1930s, notwithstanding countless manifestos, confident proclamations of a new and more scientific history, and heavy disdain for all past "bourgeois" efforts. The reasons for the debacle are not to be sought in the so-called irrelevance of Marxism. This favorite charge of smug ideologues hardly deserves to be taken seriously. If Marxism has any value as a way of interpreting history, then it necessarily has something to say about the American experience. If not, then the problem is not its irrelevance to America, but its uselessness. No one with even an elementary understanding of Marxism could possibly fall into the trap of expecting this or any other country to display "Marxism categories" or to conform to some preconceived pattern of development. Marxism in the 1930s degenerated almost immediately into a politically serviceable doctrine designed to bolster one or another set of party strategies, but this prostitution could not have taken place with such ease had a Marxian tradition in American thought existed. Marxist parties in England can say or do as they please and can always produce hacks to write history accordingly. The Marxian interpretations of Hill, Bernal, Thompson, Hobsbawn, Mason, Hilton, and many others go their own way and do so, one suspects, because of the well-entrenched tradition of socialist thought on which to build. The Left in America, sharing, as it always has, in the prevailing and all-too-American contempt for intellectual tradition, has had little to measure each new dogmatic assertion against.

Similarly, the failure of the New Conservative history in the 1950s, after a brilliant start and an almost clean sweep of the field, suggests that, as a movement, it had no firm roots.[1] Like the vulgar Marxism of the 1930s, it grew up largely as a political and ideological reaction to immediate events. Consider, for example, how many of its leading figures remained liberals in their politics or were to become so again a few years later; how many shifted their politics only slightly while bending their intellectual efforts to conform with the times. Their work in the 1950s reflected a mood and a need to come to terms with momentous but momentary national and international crises; with few exceptions it did not arise from a deep and genuine conservative tradition or a disciplined and self-conscious attempt to inaugurate one.

Those who fear the negative impact on American scholarship of the present black upsurge would do well to consider the superficiality of the damage done by previous generations of political zealots. Undoubtedly, all the signs of the disease are once again manifest. At their worst, the more shrill ideologues of the black liberation movement recapitulate the totalitarianism of the Left of the 1930s and, in inverted form, of the Right (which, let us recall, included an army of liberals) of the 1950s: a white novelist must not write about a slave rebel, at least not in the first person; whites cannot understand "soul history" and must not teach it; all white criticism of the black experience constitutes "racism"; and so forth *ad nauseam*. We ought not to underestimate the importance of these recurrent manifestations in both the white and black community of moral terror, nor ought we to deflect attention from the duty to combat them vigorously whenever they appear. But their importance must not be exaggerated or allowed to obscure the much deeper and decidedly healthy impact that the black political revolt is having on American historical scholarship.

The ill-fated Moynihan Report illustrates the limited impact of direct political concern on historical scholarship. Moynihan attempted to put social science at the service of social policy. In so doing, he combined historical with sociological analysis and created a sketch of the "Negro family" or at least of a major historical tendency within the totality of Negro families. We need not here enter into a discussion of the main features of the report nor of the criticism it evoked, especially since the relationship between theoretical and applied sociology and policy-making obviously raises a different set of problems. The historical dimension of the report does concern us, for, although it covered only a few pages, it properly assumed a large place in the ensuing acrimonious discussion.[2] Moynihan drew on a few standard sources to try to show that slavery and Reconstruction had destroyed black family life or rather had prevented its development. The studies in question, notably that of the outstanding sociologist, E. Franklin Frazier,[3] had not, however, been based, in their historical dimension, on extensive research. Not surprisingly, therefore, the counterattack is already on. Forthcoming studies, independent of each other, will argue forcefully that a sufficient degree of family cohesion existed among slaves to have laid the foundations for greater stability under freedom and that, in fact, considerable family cohesion was in evidence during and after Reconstruction. Lower-class black family patterns approximated those of lower-class whites at least until World War I and the beginnings of the great trek north.[4] Evaluations of these historical investigations will have to await their publication and the criticism of opposing scholars. When they do appear, they are almost certain to be taken as reactions to the Moynihan Report and as deliberate interventions into the disputes it occasioned. As a matter of fact, they will be nothing of the kind. Each will have arisen from its author's long-developing concern with the culture of the lower classes and in response to the older scholarship of Frazier, Stampp, and others. The controversy over the Moynihan Report may give some form to the new work, may increase popular interest, and may introduce a sharper polemical cutting edge; despite appearances however, the origins and fundamental content of these forthcoming studies, except perhaps for an occasional opportunistic and short-lived intellectual gambit, are to be sought elsewhere.

We should resist the temptation to overestimate the impact of immediate political concerns on the course of historical scholarship. There has never been a shortage of academic and political careerists to rush into print at every juncture and to proclaim some new truth to accommodate the latest ideological fad. Happily, such efforts usually disappear with a rapidity that matches their appearances. The ideologically conditioned works leaving a deep impression are generally those that reflect a historical moment that is in itself a culmination of a long process and that represents the crystallization of a "climate of opinion." When, for example, Kenneth M. Stampp published *The Peculiar Institution* in 1956 and stood the racist work of Ulrich Bonnell Phillips on its head, he caught the temper of the mid-1950s, but only in a limited sense.[5] Stampp, a serious and responsible historian, had been at work on his book for many years and could hardly have known that it would appear in the midst of a new wave of problack feeling and civil rights agitation. Whatever criticisms one might make of the book, it is anything but an attempt to capitalize on a mood or a political moment. The critique of Phillips's views and of those from the Big House generally had been building for twenty-five years or more.

It is doubtful that many professional historians had accepted Phillips's viewpoint on the day before Stampp's book appeared; rather, most seem to have been so thoroughly prepared for a new interpretation that they simply breathed a sigh of relief when a substantial alternative finally arrived. Those twenty-five years had been marked by such books as Charles Sydnor's *Slavery in Mississippi,* which built on Phillips's work while quietly departing from it in many essentials; Herbert Aptheker's *American Negro Slave Revolts,* which challenged Phillips's paternalistic treatment of slavery at its most vunerable point; W. E. B. Du Bois's *Black Reconstruction,* which even a profession overflowing with white racism could not wholly ignore; and disturbing methodological assaults on Phillips by Richard Hofstadter and by Stampp himself. These provided only the most visible and widely read items; the literature pointing toward a new departure was in fact greater.[6]

To lay bare the relationship between the evolving climate of opinion and this historical revisionism would require a full-length intellectual history, but certain features stand out immediately. The anthropological assault on racism gained momentum during the 1920s, but its impact on the historical profession was minimal. It remains an open question how much the new anthropology prepared historians to resist doctrines and how much the revulsion against Hitlerism and the attraction of New Deal liberalism and its urban political coalition forced them to take seriously a body of thought they had deftly ignored. What is clear enough is that the power of the new viewpoint lay precisely in the conjuncture of a decade or so of serious scholarship and the force of political circumstances. One or the other alone might have generated a revisionist history, but the conjuncture guaranteed a sweeping victory. By the time that *The Peculiar Institution* appeared —and this observation in no way slights Stampp's formidable accomplishment—it was virtually an ideological anticlimax.

Not surprisingly, the reaction against Stampp's neoabolitionism began almost immediately. Stanley M. Elkins's *Slavery: A Problem in American Institutional and Intellectual Life*, probably the most vigorously contested book yet written on the subject, in effect took the discussion in a new direction by demonstrating that Stampp had remained on the terrain staked out by Phillips even while opposing him.[7] Elkins chose to take the evils of slavery as given and to pose the question of the system's psychological effect on its victims. Historians' reactions to the book were generally hostile, at least initially, whereas those of social scientists were appreciable and even enthusiastic. For our immediate purposes the disquiet it occasioned among the black intelligentsia is more to the point, although black historians of varying political complexion have generally been fair and measured in their appraisals.

What is not often appreciated is that Elkins's *Slavery* represents one of the highpoints of the New Conservative scholarship of the 1950s. That it has not gone the way of most of the efforts of that transitory movement is a tribute to Elkins's intellectual gifts, but it also demonstrates that Stampp had closed an old chapter rather than opened a new one. As Elkins wrote, once Stampp had replied adequately there was little else to be accomplished within the old framework. If Elkins's defense of the Sambo stereotype disturbed blacks and white liberals, it also reinforced some of their own major arguments. There has hardly been an outstanding leader of any faction of the black liberation movement who has not called upon his people to renounce the legacy of slavery and to assert manhood. Had Elkins's main thesis been offered with adequate qualifications, in slightly different language, without so many debatable secondary theses, and perhaps in different ideological terms, it is likely that the reception would have been entirely different. In any case, in view of the hostility of historians in general to his bold use of psychological models and historical analogy, and in view of the shivers occasioned by the Sambo thesis itself, the rising respect for the book, even among its determined opponents, deserves comment.

It seems to me that Elkins's achievement, like that of Stampp, resulted from a convergence of internal and external circumstances.[8] (I, of course, take for granted the talent of the authors, which, as a long line of able, but ignored black historians could testify, would hardly have been enough to gain a respectful hearing). The staying power of the works of both Elkins and Stampp has resulted from their having heightened and crystallized long developing trends within the academic profession and simultaneously having illuminated important political trends. We have here an illustration of the point that S. Lilley makes for the history of science. Between those who argue for the centrality of social forces and those who argue for a self-propelling history of scientific ideas, Lilley insists that the source of major advances must be sought in the conjuncture of both.[9] Far from being a plea for a spiritless eclecticism, this viewpoint represents an attempt to take full account of the power of material conditions, broadly defined, while it appreciates the role of intellectual labor in giving substance as well as form to those material conditions.

The second half of the 1950s exhibited a growing concern for civil rights and for the integration of the black man into American life and yet continued to display strong evidence of neoconservatism and Cold War liberalism. The works of Stampp and Elkins fit well into this complex setting. They did not in any way reflect the more vulgar political impulses of the time, but neither did they directly challenge prevalent commitments. For our purposes the politically dominant mood can be seen as extending in two directions—it prepared the ground for a positive public reception of certain lines of thought and also prepared the historical profession itself. In this respect the works of these historians bridged the gap between the prevailing national sensibility and the cumulative and developing understanding of the academic intelligentsia. Therein lies its significance and its power. In short, the question of the effect of politics on scholarship must be understood primarily as the intersection of two derivatives of a common source that is at once political and scholarly since it shapes the thinking of the intelligentsia, in itself an artistic and scientific establishment and a political force of considerable consequence.

The political developments of the second half of our decade must be assessed in these terms, for, although superficially pointing one way, ultimately they point another. The abrupt shift of SNCC in the mid-1960s may serve as an adequate illustration of the more general shift of the black liberation movement. From radical integrationism and nonviolence SNCC moved to "Black Power" and a defense of revolutionary violence. The content of Black Power remains obscure, but there can be no question of its separatist and nationalist overtones. That SNCC has largely disappeared as a political organization is beside the point. The desperate about-face in its point of view signaled a change in the temper of the entire black liberation movement albeit to new forms that the older leadership has had trouble mastering. The black political landscape in the last few years has been dominated by such leftwing, revolutionary nationalist groups as the Black Panther Party, such rightwing nationalist groups as Ron Karenga's US, and such vacillating groups as a revamped CORE under Roy Innis, which combines radical rhetoric with a shamefaced espousal of black capitalism.

Whatever the forms of black militancy in the 1970s, certain intellectual advances seem destined for consolidation. I do not refer to the appearance of black nationalism as such, for that is a story as old as the struggle of black people against oppression and white racism in America. Previous waves of black nationalism left few traces in the intellectual life of white America and, for that matter, only a weak if nonetheless discernible and pregnant legacy for black America. The current wave, on the other hand, should cast a long shadow over both for discrete but intersecting reasons.

Previous waves of black nationalism were almost entirely a product of the counsel of despair. They generally represented a defensive reflex in periods of defeat, desertion by white allies, and paralysis of the national conscience. Without disparaging the integrity of their fundamental content, they may be viewed as rear-guard actions in an overpowering and hostile environment. An insensitive, not to say racist, intellectual milieu virtually drowned their intellectual products. These are increasingly known and respected in black America, but until recently their message even there was severely circumscribed by white intellectual hegemony. W. E. B. DuBois, of course, could not easily be ignored, but how many white scholars even today appreciate the nationalist side of his complex thought? Yet, the present generation of black-nationalist scholars and, more to the point, the generation that is clearly on the way, represent a new intellectual as well as political force, not necessarily because they are or will be more talented than their predecessors but because they are emerging at a historically propitious moment.

Politically, the Black Power movement marks a new stage, for it combines cultural and social separatism with a sober appraisal of the realities of an integrated national and international economy. The shape of a future united black liberation movement, if one ever develops, may be left to those directly concerned, but the implications of the persistent combination of separatist social and integrationist economic demands must be understood as an embryonic program rather than as some new rhetorical incoherence.[10] In these terms, the insistence of the younger black intelligentsia on a nationalist interpretation of Afro-American history has special force, for it corresponds—at least up to a point—with that temper of the new realism among both blacks and whites which has been generated by the collapse of the integrationist dreams of the 1950s. The singular failure of liberal integrationism has demonstrated, if nothing else, the extent to which blacks are perceived and perceive themselves as a people apart—a people with a separate history, culture, and national sensibility. The first point of conjuncture, then, arises from a new and determined effort by a rising black intelligentsia to delineate a separate national history for black America. Obviously, this effort would have poor prospects were it not in accordance with historical reality. We shall return to an evaluation and try to demonstrate, among other things, that the nationalist thesis presents an unusually complex set of problems.

Thus far we have glanced only at the external side of the problem—at the emergence of black and white politics in relation to the unfolding receptivity among both blacks and whites to a black-nationalist standpoint in historical interpretation. But what of the internal condition, by which we understand the intellectual preparation of the black intelligentsia and of the dominant white elements of the historical profession? The nationalist stream in black thought, as has been suggested, is long standing and runs deep. If we bracket for a moment the question of its intellectual legitimacy (its inherent truth), there can be no doubt about its social authenticity (its roots in the intellectual history of the black community). Yet, in the past white America has ignored or rejected this line of thought. Even liberal and antiracist scholars have treated it as a pathological projection of a people whose only hope, ostensible desire, and practical destiny lay in integration. The collapse of liberal integrationism, which may or may not spell the end of all integrationism, and the burgeoning of a variety of militant and apparently anti-integrationist Black Power movements have shaken the white intelligentsia and opened the way to its giving black nationalism a hearing, both in its political and intellectual manifestations. But even within the white-dominated academy of historical scholarship, quite different forces have been at work, and their intersection with those just reviewed promises to reinforce the tendency toward a more sympathetic hearing for a nationalist black history.

I refer to the growing emphasis on cultural history in general and on the history of the lower classes in particular. Although the history of Afro-Americans might be thought to form one dimension of a cultural history of the lower classes, until recently such has not been the case. First, until less than ten years ago, Afro-American history held little or no interest for white historians. Books and articles in learned journals were few and far between. Since the white intelligentsia has controlled the main accesses to publication the blacks have had to wage a bitter struggle with meager resources to develop and present their own points of view. Second, the black experience in America has generally been viewed as the history of what Anglo-Saxon barbarism has done to a passive and helpless people. There are a few ironies here. The exclusive concern with race, in contradistinction to class, has inhibited rather than sharpened a concern with black ethnicity, so that even avowedly antiracist scholarship has unwittingly deprived black people of their own heritage. To this day, despite a library full of books on slavery, we do not have more than a few fragmentary studies of slave life, of the activity of the quarters, of slave religion (understood as something other than the religion that masters thought they were imposing on slaves), or on slave folklore. Slavery and the black experience have been one subject—and a subject usually mauled by the treatment of blacks as objects rather than subjects; lower-class white and immigrant history has been another; labor history, usually interpreted to mean trade-union history, has been a third; and "cultural history," by which is generally meant an account of high culture, has been a fourth. Rarely, if ever, do we find the kind of history in which, say, the lives of black workers are studied as points of intersection among black history per se, the interaction of the various ethnic components of the working class, and the relationship of popular to high culture. During the last ten years, however, this intellectual insanity has finally come under sustained attack. The New Left upsurge, with its renewed populism, and the impressive intellectual history of the 1950s—one thinks especially of Perry Miller's work—have combined to create favorable conditions for, and have in fact demanded, that synthesis of popular and elite thought and behavior which only an integrated cultural history could make possible.

Scholars, especially black scholars, have long explored the cultural dimension of Afro-American history. Everyone reads Du Bois's *Souls of Black Folk,* but only a handful of scholars (mostly black) have appreciated the elements of a cultural history that it contains. The promise of lasting results comes from the intersection of this renewed black effort with two other developments: parallel work by white scholars in the cultural history of the lower classes and those political conditions converging to guarantee a more sympathetic hearing for black nationalism to which we have already referred.

The insistence of black scholars on the centrality of popular as well as high culture for an understanding of the black experience corresponds to the insistence of a growing number of white historians on the centrality of culture to the American experience generally. This line of thought has recently been applied directly and indirectly to Afro-American history by a wide variety of scholars, notably David Brion Davis, Winthrop D. Jordan, and Herbert Gutman.

Davis and Jordan treat primarily white and especially Anglo-Saxon culture in attempting to account for the origins, force, and extent of racism.[11] Among many outstanding contributions, both identify the problem of racism as a product of a long and complex historical evolution and yet avoid obscuring the functionality of racism within systems of class oppression. Davis's work, moreover, represents a high point in the development of a comparative approach to the study of slavery. This postwar trend, initiated by Frank Tannenbaum, has been continued by such diverse scholars as Sidney Mintz and Marvin Harris in anthropology; Harmannus Hoetink and Arnold A. Sio in sociology; and Stanley M. Elkins and Herbert S. Klein in history. The participation of both historians and social scientists has helped guarantee that slavery must henceforth be treated both internationally and cross-culturally—precisely as Tannenbaum had insisted. Black scholars in the United States have not yet contributed much to this trend, but black and colored scholars in the Caribbean and Brazil have; and their influence is bound to be felt sooner or later.

The introduction of the comparative and cross-cultural dimension has led American historians away from their famous provincialism and into a confrontation with anthropology and popular culture. So, for example, serious students of American slavery can no longer avoid learning something about Brazilian and Cuban slavery. Accordingly, they must come to terms with the broad cultural history of Gilberto Freyre, Fernando Ortiz, and Roger Bastide, to mention only a few outstanding figures. Bastide's *Religions africaines au Brésil* may serve as an illustration. With slave revolts and resistance an important and popular subject in the United States, Bastide's provocative analyses of the role of religion in the *quilombo* (runaway slave camp) of Palmares and in the massive Bahia risings can no longer be overlooked. Vincent Harding's essay, in which he insists that the slaves could and often did bend their masters' religion to their own subversive purposes, therefore intersects with similar concerns and theses being advanced elsewhere.[12] One should expect more serious study of these various theses if only because of the way in which they reinforce each other and reflect common origins in a growing concern with the politics of culture in many countries. Even if we take full account of the desire of many black scholars to go their own way and to minimize white influence, we can hardly expect major success in an attempt at intellectual self-isolation; and the new concerns of white scholars themselves are likely to result in an increased attention to the product of black scholarship for reasons quite apart from the course of the racial crisis.

Gutman has set out to reinterpret the history of the American working class and in so doing has come to emphasize the process by which various immigrant groups, especially those from pre-industrial settings, became acculturated in the double sense of "Americanized" and integrated into an advanced industrial economy.[13] This concern has naturally led him toward a critical appraisal of the intersection of peasant migrations, the growth of the working class in its particular ethnic manifestations, and the black experience. This new approach to the history of the black and white working class points toward an appreciation of culture as politics.

It would, therefore, be tragic to allow the inevitable but momentary incoherence of these tumultuous years to interfere with a cool appraisal of the long-term potential contributions of the new black militancy to the development of historical studies. The genuine and probably lasting work by black scholars, including the most politically committed and militant, are those which point toward a re-evaluation of black culture and its relationship to the problem of nationality. The most striking achievement so far is perhaps LeRoi Jones's

Blues People, which traces the development of a distinct black music from slavery to freedom in a fresh and incisive way.[14] Jones examines the African roots of black music and ingeniously explores the relationship of the slave and ghetto culture to the musical expression of black people. Here, as in such essays as Sterling Stuckey's "Through the Prism of Folklore: Black Ethos in Slavery,"[15] black scholars are attempting to write a responsible history of the inarticulate masses. In view of the appearance of this trend at the moment in which so many white intellectual historians are passing over to cultural history and in view of the political pressures toward a pronationalist position, this trend is likely to gain strength.

The positive response to Harold W. Cruse's *Crisis of the Negro Intellectual*[16] suggests a new receptivity to the explorations of this theme. Ironically, Cruse's bitter indictment of the American intelligentsia for its insensitivity to the cultural dimension of politics and historical process comes at the very moment in which that insensitivity seems on its way out. (But of course, Cruse's book itself is helping to bring this about.) He comes down with special severity on Marxists, whose alleged intellectual hegemony in Harlem during the 1930s and 1940s he deplores, and charges them with being imprisoned by an ideology that waives culture as mere "superstructure" in favor of a primary concern with "economic base"; yet, these strictures appear when the long-term influence of William Appleman Williams and the steadily gaining awareness of the work of Antonio Gramsci are combining to reorient serious American Marxists in just the way Cruse demands. These objections aside, *The Crisis of the Negro Intellectual* has undoubtedly affected the thinking of both white and black intellectuals in an altogether positive way.

So, we might add, has Eldridge Cleaver's *Soul on Ice.*[17] Another irony lurks here, for Cleaver's book has also helped to demonstrate the cultural dimension of politics and history despite Cleaver's being the leading black-nationalist opponent of the "cultural nationalist" trend in the movement. If Cleaver is hostile toward specific manifestations of Afro-American culture, and if he is particularly suspicious of attempts to make cultural-nationalist concerns a substitute for politics, he still devotes most of his space to the cultural dimension of what he considers to be the essentials of a revolutionary political point of view. In other words, the emphasis on cultural questions in the black movement is not likely to recede even if the leftwing Panther tendency gains ascendancy; for all its hostility to cultural nationalism, it too finds it difficult to avoid doing battle on this terrain.

Although the new phase of the black revolt, in its direct political form, will continue to make an impact on scholarship, it is unlikely to have any more lasting effects than earlier white movements. In the short run, of course, anything is possible. Undoubtedly, we are witnessing the rise of a new type, the House Honkey, who is replacing the House Nigger of bygone days. In the intellectual arena, these honkeys will do their best to preserve and extend the romantic interpretation of black history, with all its supposed political advantages to this or that movement. However irritating, they present no serious threat and ought to be regarded with no more fear or misgivings than any other wave of opportunist mediocrity.

The danger, rather, lies in the subtle encouragement of reactive history that these tense and difficult circumstances produce. The shrill and insistent demands that whites get out of black history could not be met even if whites were inclined to meet them: The history of America can no longer be written without a full account of its black element; and that element cannot be isolated for discrete analysis since it penetrates and has been penetrated by everything else. This lesson has been taught us by the effective blows delivered against the racism of white intellectuals by the black intellectuals themselves. What may occur (and there are already ominous signs) is a steady, barely visible retreat by white scholars into a historical study that merely reacts—whether positively or negatively is of little importance—to the supposed exigencies of the political struggle and the real or imagined provocations of the more militant black intellectuals. Blacks have justly complained that for too long their best historians have wasted much of their time and energy reacting to biased and ignorant white scholarship and refuting one or another fashionable interpretation. The damage done to black scholarship by this tendency has probably been as great as its black critics suggest, but it at least has had the excuse of reflecting the exigencies of the social and political balance of power in racist America. A white version of the same thing would have no excuse at all, unless we count an adolescent compulsion to respond to every expression of hostility from people who are not exactly without commanding reason to be hostile.

I have so far tried to show that the black political revolt, with its increasingly nationalist and separatist influence among the youth and especially the young intellectuals, has generated a major concern for culture as politics and history, and that this concern will probably be consolidated as a contribution to both American and Afro-American history since it occurs at one of those fateful conjunctures of external and internal events. Beyond this general achievement lies another one of a different but no less important order: the development of an Afro-American nationalist history. So far we have bracketed the question of the legitimacy of the nationalist interpretation of Afro-American history. It is time to remove the brackets.

In the past black nationalism has made little impact on American scholarship and left only scattered traces in the much ignored Afro-American scholarship. Previous black scholars of a nationalist bent have generally had to work in isolation or at least without much material support. Black nationalist movements, especially the large ones of Garvey and Elijah Muhammed, never attracted many intellectuals and generally left little or no direct historical interpretations of the black experience, however much they may have contributed to the formation of one by successors.[18] Perhaps the most striking and far-reaching feature of the black nationalism of the 1960s has been the unprecedented identification of young intellectuals with a mass movement. It seems safe to say that if the nationalist movements coalesce and endure, their success will be due in a large measure to this achievement. The adherence of so many talented black intellectuals —Harold W. Cruse, Julius Lester, LeRoi Jones, Eldridge Cleaver, Vincent Harding, A. B. Spellman, and many others —to one or another wing of the nationalist movement in itself creates a new situation with overtones of a self-fulfilling prophecy. If, as could be demonstrated, the black experience in America has yielded a common body of interest, strong elements of a discrete culture, and a general sense of being a distinct people, then the creation of a separate nation—although not necessarily a nation-state—is within the grasp of the black intelligentsia as an act of will: All that has been missing in the attempt to forge such a nation has been a unifying ideology capable of commanding the respect of the intelligentsia and the political allegiance of the masses.

I cannot here do more than to assert, without adequate elaboration and defense, what seems to me to be the central theme—to borrow the term Phillips made famous in Southern history—of Afro-American history: the duality of the black presence as a vital and inseparable part of the national American experience and yet a national experience unto itself. As August Meier has convincingly argued in *Negro Thought in America, 1880–1915*,[19] and as the apparently zigzag ideological course of the great W. E. B. Du Bois perfectly illustrates, the history of black America may be viewed, on one level of analysis, as a record of alternating and simultaneous integrationist and separatist responses to white oppression. Meier plausibly suggests that integration has prevailed among blacks during those periods when for one reason or another whites needed and sought black support for national purposes and were prepared to make some concessions toward the realization of black aspirations; alternatively, he adds, separatism and nationalism have shown great strength during periods of defeat, despair, and acute and open white hostility.

The question of the legitimacy of the nationalist political tendency might be left right there, but it would be a mistake to do so. David Potter maintains, in his brilliant essay, "The Historians' Use of Nationalism and Vice Versa,"[20] that it would be naive and dangerous to proceed as if the only psychological basis for nationalism lies in the evolution of a common culture. Potter suggests that a nationalist psychology has a second and often stronger basis in a perceived common interest. Where such an interest exists over a long period of time, a strong national feeling may develop among a people even in the absence of a separate culture. Potter is concerned with the Old South, not Afro-America, and insists on the paucity of evidence of a distinct Southern culture until the slaveholding intellectuals, cognizant of the threat to their social system, set out to create one. In an analogous way one might judge the nationalist response, which has always had manifestations in the black community, as a defensive rationale rather than a legitimate projection of a national life. I doubt that Potter means to propose so mechanical a formula for any national movement. If I understand him correctly, he is suggesting that even weak elements of a separate culture can be wielded into a powerful force under the whip of a politically well situated intelligentsia, which, in response to a threat to a genuine community of interest, deliberately bends its efforts toward the formation of a coherent nationally based world view.

The black intellectuals, especially the younger ones, today are doing just that. Their insistence on a nationalist interpretation of black culture and black history may be one-sided, but it is by no means irresponsible, as is so often charged. The elements of a separate culture, however weak, are there and are capable of being raised to the dignity of a discrete social and ideological formulation. Slavery, for example, did create conditions within which there developed a particular religion (the African and distinctly Afro-American features of which are yet to be analyzed adequately), folklore, music, dialect, and group sensibility, and postwar conditions in both the rural South and the Northern ghettos reshaped and fortified the product. Thus, we hear much of a "Negro subculture." Left there, perhaps that is all we would ever see—disparate and even pathetic manifestations of a people who are trying to be part of the American nation and yet who can never quite win acceptance. But, that body of common interest—that perpetual threat to existence—has given special meaning to those cultural manifestations. Until recently, however, the forces have not existed to wield them into a single ideology, to relate them coherently to a perceived common interest, to blend the folk elements with an embryonic high culture, and to unite a vigorous intelligentsia to the masses. Now they do. The emergence of a black intelligentsia, conscious of the historical evolution of a community of interest, has within itself the power to forge a separate culture out of a tradition that has been both of America and a thing apart. In view of the white-racist resistance to integration, the victory of this tendency seems probable. The current group of black historians may or may not write the comprehensive nationalist interpretation of Afro-American history for which it calls, but it is at least laying the ideological and organizational basis for it.

We may expect to arrive, therefore, at a new view of Afro-American history, whatever the political outcome of the present turmoil. If the nationalist movement scores substantial gains, this view will be immensely strengthened; if it is crushed or substantially beaten back, the strategic position of the young nationalist intelligentsia is still likely to guarantee the consolidation of a considerable portion of its interpretation of the historical record. Are we then at the threshold of a new mythology and a new version of history-as-ideology? Yes and no. The tendency toward myth-making and ideological interpretation will certainly grow stronger—directly, if the nationalists can deliver a major political victory; indirectly and nostalgically, if they cannot. But such a tendency has always pervaded the histories of white and black peoples alike. It represents a persistent threat to intellectual integrity, but one that can be contained if never wholly defeated.

Those who fear that an idelogical-mythical history will triumph in black studies display a droll underestimation of white racism and professional conservatism in American life and a grave misunderstanding of the position of the black man within and without our national society. Large sectors of the historical profession and the secondary teaching profession for the best and worst of reasons will continue to oppose the romantic and mystical interpretation of the black experience. So long as this interpretation encounters opposition among respected and serious historians, white and black, and so long as there is no danger of a reactionary black ascendancy within the professional institutions themselves, prospects for the growth of a sane and empirically balanced view will remain bright. The young black intelligentsia and especially the students might defect *en masse* to mythology, but their defection is certain to be arrested and reversed if it generates—as it probably will—political defeats in place of the promised victories. A brief consideration of the position of the blacks in American life will show the improbability of a sustained and consolidated defection.

Were black Americans to secede from the American Union and to get those five states they demand, then a fairy tale history could become government policy and the only tolerated viewpoint in a black state. But even so—and such totalitarianism would by no means have to accompany separation—black history would continue to be studied in quite a different way in white-dominated America. If, as is the overwhelming probability, black Americans will find some kind of halfway house between integration and separation, then there will be little likelihood of insulating a romantic interpretation from withering criticism.

Without enforced insulation the majority of even the most militant black youth could not be expected to remain ideologically imprisoned for long. A mystique may imprison some men forever, but to imprison most men for long it must accompany real political victories. Many black youths today openly defend a romanticized and mystified history by reference to the exigencies of revolutions like the Algerian. Even if we could admit that ideological mystification helped rather than retarded the Algerian or other national revolutions, an extrapolation to black America would be nonsensical. In black America the prospects for the secession of a contiguous colonial area are nil, and so are the prospects for the forcible overthrow of the American national state. Under these conditions the struggle for black liberation will have to be a protracted one that can combine both integrationist and separatist advances. Hence, only an objective history is likely to be politically useful for the long haul, and the black intelligentsia would sooner or later have to come to terms with this reality or face an interminable series of defeats. In any case, the prospects for intellectual and ideological insulation in so complex a social setting are, to say the least, poor.

The permanent and invaluable contribution rendered by the new nationalist militancy to historical scholarship rests on its ability to compel attention to the genuine duality of the black experience, even if it chooses to stress the side it prefers. In that duality lies most of what is essential to an understanding of black history in the United States as well as to the probable ideological shape of a viable black liberation movement. If so, then the impact of the current political disorder on historical scholarship will be judged, in some calmer future, to have been on balance wholesome, constructive, and long overdue.

NOTES

1. For an elaboration of the remarks on Marxism, see Eugene D. Genovese, "Marxian Interpretations of the Slave South," in Barton J. Bernstein, ed., *Towards a New Past: Dissenting Essays in American History* (New York, 1968), pp. 90–125; for a critical and yet sympathetic critique of conservatism from a leftwing point of view, see Allen Guttman, *The Conservative Tradition in America* (New York, 1967).

2. Cf., Lee Rainwater and William L. Yancey, *The Moynihan Report and the Politics of Controversy* (Cambridge, Mass., 1967), which includes the text of the report.

3. E. Franklin Frazier, *The Negro Family in the United States* (Chicago, 1939).

4. Prevailing notions of slave family life are challenged in Bobby F. Jones, "A Cultural Middle Passage," unpublished doctoral dissertation, University of North Carolina, Chapel Hill, N.C., 1965. The argument for greater stability and cohesion than has been generally appreciated will be made in my forthcoming study of black slave life; the argument against the matrifocal thesis and the idea of general family disorganization before World War I will appear in forthcoming studies by Herbert Gutman.

5. Kenneth M. Stampp, *The Peculiar Institution: Slavery in the Ante-Bellum South* (New York, 1956).

6. Charles S. Sydnor, *Slavery in Mississippi* (New York, 1933); Herbert Aptheker, *American Negro Slave Revolts* (New York, 1943); W. E. B. Du Bois, *Black Reconstruction* (New York, 1934); Richard Hofstadter, "U. B. Phillips and the Plantation Legend," *Journal of Negro History,* 29 (April 1944); Kenneth M. Stampp, "The Historian and Southern Negro Slavery," *American Historical Review,* 57 (April 1952). It should be noted that black historians had attacked Phillips sharply and responsibly from the start but were ignored in white academic circles. After all, being black, how could they be objective!

7. Stanley M. Elkins, *Slavery: A Problem in American Institutional and Intellectual Life* (Chicago, 1959).

8. By internal I mean internal to the historical profession and the mainstream of intellectual work; by external I mean the political and social setting and those intellectual currents affecting professional historical work from the outside. Needless to say, the political and social milieu impinges quite differently on the black and white intelligentsia in many ways. I have had to do some homogenizing in a short paper but have at least tried to keep the distinction in mind.

9. S. Lilley, "Cause and Effect in the History of Science," in Lilley, ed., *Essays on the Social History of Science* (Copenhagen, 1953), pp. 58–72.

10. For an elaboration of this argument see "Class and Nationality in Black America," *supra*.

11. David Brion Davis, *The Problem of Slavery in Western Culture* (Ithaca, 1966); Winthrop D. Jordan, *White Over Black: American Attitudes toward the Negro, 1550–1812* (Chapel Hill, 1968).

12. Vincent Harding, "Religion and Resistance among Ante-Bellum Negroes, 1800–1860," in August Meier and Elliott Rudwick, eds., *The Making of Black America*, 2 vols. (New York, 1969), 1: 179–197.

13. Professor Gutman has read several papers at recent conferences in which he has developed this line of thought. He will soon publish a lengthy version.

14. LeRoi Jones, *Blues People* (New York, 1963).

15. Sterling Stuckey, "Through the Prism of Folklore: Black Ethos in Slavery," *Massachusetts Review*, 1968.

16. Harold W. Cruse, *The Crisis of the Negro Intellectual* (New York, 1967). For an excellent critical extension of Cruse's argument on the relationship of culture and politics, see Christopher Lasch, *The Agony of the American Left* (New York, 1969).

17. Eldridge Cleaver, *Soul on Ice* (New York, 1968).

18. On black nationalism in its many facets the literature is large and growing, but see especially E. U. Essien-Udom, *Black Nationalism: The Search for an Identity in America* (Chicago, 1962). Basically a study of the Muslims, it contains an excellent discussion of the earlier movements as well.

19. August Meier, *Negro Thought in America,* 1880–1915 (Ann Arbor, 1963).

20. David M. Potter, "The Historians' Use of Nationalism and Vice Versa," *The South and the Sectional Conflict* (New York, 1969), chap. 3.

Part Three

THE SOUTH IN A WIDER WORLD

Chapter 13

ULRICH BONNELL PHILLIPS: TWO STUDIES

These two studies, with their ungrudging admiration for the South's most famous racist historian, upset some people. Together with my essay on George Fitzhugh (part two of The World the Slaveholders Made*), they have been interpreted in some quarters as evidence of perversity, a penchant for trying to shock, and various other forms of game playing. I am compelled to reply that I have better things to do with my time.*

Although the essays speak for themselves—at least to those willing to read them with a decent degree of care—an introductory word might be in order. I have been amused but not surprised that almost all of the howling has come from white liberals and from certain types of white radicals, neither of whom is famous for a willingness to respect and learn from adversaries. Since the whole point of the first study is that Phillips's racism undermined his performance, it would be pointless to reply to the charge that I minimize or am indifferent to his racism. I do, however, plead guilty to the charge that I believe his racism to have sharpened some of his genuine insights. My job is to note and to try to explain the ironies of my subject matter, not to assume responsibility for them.

The harsh truth is that racists like Phillips, until recently, have taught us much more about the South, and the Southern black man too, than their Northern liberal detractors have ever been able to do. I am sorry about that. It is terribly annoying. But there is not much to be done about it. In my opinion liberal assimilationist historians would have long ago ruined us, had it not been for the opposition of Southerners, white and black, racist and antiracist, who could not stomach the ideological cant we have been served up as "scientific" history.

If, for example, one wishes to study the development of black culture in slavery, one must go to two sources: the blacks themselves and the white-racist planters. The latter, despite their inability to understand much of what they were describing, nevertheless had no need to pretend that black people were sunburned whites, and they therefore could and did describe many of their "peculiarities." Their negative judgments may safely be put aside. They at least told us something about black religion, language, and music, among other things. Unlike the black man's abolitionist friends—always excepting a few like the great Thomas Wentworth Higginson—they had no need to deny him a culture, a tradition, and a personality of his own.

Phillips came out of that white-racist Southern tradition, which in his case manifested itself positively, not so much in the realm of black culture as in other realms I have sought to explore. In particular, I have argued that he must be understood as a conservative whose social viewpoint allowed him to penetrate deep into Southern life even while it imposed its own limits on his understanding. For reasons that I hope are made clear in the second study—and in some other material in this book—I have learned much more from conservative Southerners (or from Southern liberals like C. Vann Woodward, Willie Lee Rose, and Paul Gaston, who understand and can transcend the conservative tradition) than I have ever been able to learn from smug outsiders who see nothing but racism and reaction in everything Southern. More generally, I have tried to show that conservatives, with a sense for the organic and traditional, have generally been especially attuned to the essential qualities of Southern life.

Having had to read Phillips for one of my classes, a black student remarked, "Professor, he was a son-of-a-bitch, but he was a smart son-of-a-bitch." Whether or not Phillips deserves the name is beside the point, although no one could seriously deny a black man's right to see any racist that way. My student's essential point was nonetheless sound. Here as elsewhere, there is infinitely more to be learned from one smart son-of-a-bitch than from an army of well-meaning fools.

I

Ulrich Bonnell Phillips & His Critics

SINCE WORLD WAR II increasing numbers of American historians have been reading Ulrich Bonnell Phillips with hostility, suspicion, and even contempt; worse, they have not been encouraging their students to read him at all. This negative reaction is not difficult to account for although it stands in the starkest contrast to Phillips's enviable reputation in his own day. David M. Potter spoke for the historical profession when, at the time of Phillips's death in 1934, he wrote of "his conciseness, his remarkable accuracy of expression, his avoidance of the trite and inane, and his profusion of fruitful suggestions" and then added, "He never set pen to paper without expressing cogent ideas."[1] Times have changed. Racism and a patronizing attitude toward the Negro have gone out of style since they began to embarrass United States foreign policy. What could be more natural than that Ulrich Phillips, a Georgian who loved the Old South and never could take the Negro seriously, should have gone out of style too?

This essay was originally published as a foreword to Ulrich Bonnell Phillips, *American Negro Slavery* (Baton Rouge, La., Louisiana State University Press, 1967). Reprinted by permission of the publisher.

Phillips came close to greatness as a historian, perhaps as close as any historian this country has yet produced. We may leave to those who live in the world of absolute good and evil the task of explaining how a man with such primitive views on fundamental social questions could write such splendid history. Let there be no mistake about it: Phillips was a racist, however benign and paternalistic. Some historians have argued that he was gradually moving away from racist doctrines as he began to catch up with the new anthropological and biological researches making their appearance in the last decade or two of his life. Between *American Negro Slavery* (1918) and *Life and Labor in the Old South* (1929) he is supposed to have shifted away from a view holding the Negro to be biologically inferior to one holding him to be culturally backward. The shift, in my judgment, was merely one of emphasis, for Phillips held both views simultaneously. But, in any case, it is difficult to become enthusiastic about a shift from a less to a more sophisticated racism that could not have stood critical examination even in his day.[2] If we dwell on this weakness now, it is neither to establish our own superior virtue (it is not especially difficult to be verbally an integrationist in 1966, especially if one lives in New York City), nor even to try to provide a balanced estimate in deference to the academic niceties. It is rather to suggest that this racism cost him dearly and alone accounts for his lapse from greatness as a historian. It blinded him; it inhibited him from developing fully his own extraordinary insights; it prevented him from knowing many things he in fact knew very well.

We may begin with chapter one, "The Early Exploitation of Guinea," which is easily the worst in the book and is close to being worthless. The kindest thing that could be done with it would be to burn it, for its discussion of African society was foolish and incompetent when written and is embarrassing to have to read today. The student who wishes to learn anything about the range of problems discussed must begin elsewhere—with J. D. Fage's *Introduction to the History of West Africa,*

J. Spencer Trimingham's studies of African Islam, Basil Davidson's *Black Mother* and *Lost Cities of Africa,* or with the researches of R. S. Rattray and other anthropologists, especially the British. I doubt that there is an important point made in Phillips's opening chapter that could stand critical examination. We may hurry past this clumsy beginning, but the bias which led him so far astray will return to plague him elsewhere.

In chapter two we meet Phillips the historian. Much work has been done on the African slave trade since Phillips wrote, and no advanced student could be content with his sketch, but it stands up surprisingly well as an introduction to such important questions as the rise of the trade within the context of European rivalries or even the corrupting effects of European penetration on African culture. The most remarkable part of the discussion, however, concerns tribal differences. Phillips was apparently convinced that these differences somehow affected life in the New World. His discussion is halting, unsure, speculative, but it does mark the way forward. Unfortunately, his insight has not been developed by his successors, apart from some discussion in the work of Melville J. Herskovits. Here as elsewhere, Phillips grasped the complexity of his subject and indicated the need to probe on many fronts.

Chapter three, "The Sugar Islands," again confronts us with a tantalizing collection of insights and hypotheses that ought to make us wonder what historians have been doing for the last half century. Long before Frank Tannenbaum, not to mention Stanley M. Elkins, Phillips drew attention to the different kinds of New World slavery, to the importance of divergent cultural traditions, and to the separate developments of the ruling classes. His remarks on the bourgeois quality of the British West Indian slaveholders, in contrast to the American, still need to be pursued and extended. In short, even in his background explorations, if we leave aside those which succumbed completely to his racist bias, he asked more and better questions than many of us still are willing to admit, and he carried on his investigations with consistent freshness and critical intelligence.

The chapters on the tobacco colonies, rice coast, Northern colonies, and many others, remain peerless introductions to their subjects. His treatment of the revolutionary era will still stand up. The appearance of Robert McColley's *Slavery and Jeffersonian Virginia* (1964), for example, deepens and complements much more in Phillips than it upsets. The account of the closing of the African slave trade, the westward movement, and the domestic slave trade, however much they need to be qualified, corrected, or supplemented by the work of later historians, may still be read with the assurance that they are rarely wide of the mark. I find it incredible that Kenneth M. Stampp should write: "It may be that his most durable monument will be the vast amount of new source material which he uncovered."[3]

I have so far not discussed the heart of the book, chapters ten to thirteen, against which his critics have struck their most telling blows. Since Richard Hofstadter and Stampp have led the attack we shall have to examine their arguments in some detail. We may quickly dispose of the attack on Phillips as an economic historian. Chapters eighteen and nineteen of this book are still worth reading after decades of the most severe criticism. Undoubtedly, they suffer from some confusion and hasty generalization; undoubtedly they contain mistakes.[4] Their central notions retain force and value: that slavery "was less a business than a life"; that its economics cannot be understood apart from politics, social structure, and prevailing values; that the system struggled against a tendency toward unprofitability in the narrow sense of the term; and that even when it was profitable in that narrow sense for the slaveholders it seriously retarded regional development. Not everyone agrees with these and other conclusions; the debate has been unusually vigorous and will continue. What is astonishing is how well Phillips presented his case and how much of it remains respectable interpretation worthy of continued exploration and discussion. Harold D. Woodman has demonstrated Phillips's continued relevance for the debate on the economics of slavery and not surprisingly has given Phillips unusual attention and space in his anthology *Slavery and the Southern Economy*.[5]

To appreciate Phillips as an economic historian, one needs to go beyond the impressive discussions in his book. His ground-breaking work in the formation of the black belts (1906) stressed the concentration of wealth and economic power and laid the basis for a social history of the constituent classes. His study of the plantation under slave and free labor (1925) developed several of the themes presented here and is still useful as an introduction to ante-bellum and post-bellum Southern society.[6] These and many other specialized articles deserve to be studied with the greatest care; much of the analysis they contain has yet to be surpassed. This side of Phillips's work received considerable praise at one time but no longer receives the attention it deserves. Perhaps the most striking illustration of how easy it is to slight his accomplishment may be found in a generally appreciative and sympathetic essay by Wood Gray. He evaluates *A History of Transportation in the Eastern Cotton Belt to 1860* (1908) as "essentially a straight forward factual narrative . . . ."[7] On the contrary, the book is an impressive contribution to political economy and economic history. Phillips carefully traces the development of a quasi-colonial transportation system, which arose in response to special kinds of economic needs and then reinforced not merely a particular economy but an entire structure of political and social power. Phillips's modesty, unwillingness to resort to an unnecessarily technical vocabulary, and cautious presentation of generalizations ought not to cause us to underestimate his achievement. That book like this one and the whole body of his lifetime's work might well serve as required reading for students of colonialism—or as we politely call it today, "the economics of underdevelopment."

Hofstadter's critique pertains, as he himself cautions us,

to four chapters: twelve, "The Cotton Regime"; thirteen, "Types of Large Plantations"; fourteen, "Plantation Management"; and fifteen, "Plantation Labor." It consists of two main points: Phillips's data are inadequate and misleading, for they are drawn only from plantation-sized estates; and they are not even a good sample of plantation-sized estates, for they are overwhelmingly drawn from the largest. Hofstadter adds a third point, which is, however, a corollary of these: that the vast majority of slaves did not live on large plantations. He adds that Phillips nowhere made a serious effort to compare large and small plantations or plantations and farms but observes, "The precise importance of this failure . . . cannot be stated until much more investigation has been done in the great realm that Phillips chose to ignore . . . ."[8]

Hofstadter recognizes the paucity of data for small units but says that we should at least suspect generalizations based only on larger units. He shows that Phillips cited manuscript material pertaining to units averaging two hundred slaves—virtually a handful of estates and certainly only those forming the extreme top of society. The states of Maryland, Missouri, Kentucky, and Tennessee, with a small-slaveholders' economy embracing eighteen per cent of all Southern slaves, virtually went unnoticed by Phillips. Hofstadter notes that the task of studying the Deep South absorbed Phillips's energies but properly adds that consideration of the border states might force important revisions in his findings.

Hofstadter raises fair questions but hardly touches the value of Phillips's work. Phillips drew his illustrations from the largest plantations because they provided the fullest accounts, but his lifelong researches undoubtedly brought him into contact with the records of smaller units. He clearly believed that in certain essential respects the largest plantations did not vary significantly from the "average" ones. The real question concerns the units below the plantation rank. There is no evidence that treatment of slaves, for example, varied dramatically between units of twenty and two hundred. Since half the slaves lived on plantations (units of twenty or more) Phillips's work would be of great importance even if it could be shown that conditions did vary dramatically on the farms.

As a matter of fact, there is no reason to believe that data from small farms would upset Phillips's generalizations. Hofstadter admits that Phillips might have used Olmsted's work to advantage, for he thought slaves better treated on the smaller units. Stampp, in *The Peculiar Institution,* argues strongly for this view, although on little evidence. In short, after fifty years we still could not demonstrate that a consideration of smaller units would in itself shake Phillips's main contentions. Similarly, the work of specialists on slavery in the border states has not supported the common assumption that treatment there varied much from Deep South patterns. When, therefore, Hofstadter tells us that Olmsted offers us "a fuller and more accurate knowledge of the late ante-bellum South"[9] than Phillips, he is well wide of the mark.

All of this "scientific" and statistical refutation of Phillips does not get us anywhere, but we soon do get to the heart of the matter. At the beginning we note the charge that Phillips slights the smallholder in favor of the great planter. Thus appears his class bias. Later, we note that he could not take the Negro seriously and that he hardly did him justice. Thus appears his race bias. The two together provide us with the perfect white Southerner: "The way of thinking which underlay Phillips's work needs no elaboration here. He was a native of Georgia, to whom the Southern past always appeared in a haze of romance . . . . His books can best be placed in the course of our intellectual history when it is realized that they represent a latter-day phase of the proslavery argument."[10] I do not find these *ad hominem* thrusts helpful. Phillips's concern with the small ruling class of slaveholders was altogether proper: that class dominated the economy, politics, and social life of the South; it imposed its visions and values on the humbler men in society; it in fact ruled more completely than many other ruling classes in modern times. Even its notions of master-slave relationships set the tone for society, and for that reason alone an emphasis on its practices has been justified. Thus, Hofstadter even misses the point when he attacks Phillips for stressing "ideal rules" of treatment, instead of actual practice. Phillips did look closely at practice, but did not err by considering carefully those "ideal rules," for the standards men publicly set for themselves tell us much of the quality of the men and tell us something of the practice.

We are finally brought to the last complaint: Phillip's race bias made him a prisoner of the slaveholders' viewpoint and blinded him to much of the record. Hofstadter scores heavily when he remarks with barely restrained sarcasm that Phillips's "great powers of intellectual resistance" are attested to by the avoidance of the enormous problem of miscegenation. The charge is unanswerable, but the conclusion of Hofstadter's argument is another matter: "Let the study of the Old South be undertaken by other scholars who have absorbed the viewpoint of modern cultural anthropology, who have a feeling for social psychology . . . and who realize that any history of slavery must be written in large part from the standpoint of the slave . . . ."[11] Since there is no "viewpoint of modern cultural anthropology"—only contending schools of thought, as in every discipline—the criticism is hard to take. Most anthropologists today reject racism, but we might reflect on the development of this rejection, for Adolf Hitler probably had more to do with it than Franz Boas. A theory of racial inferiority could no more be debated calmly and tested scientifically today than could the virtues of communism under the watchful eye of the late Senator McCarthy. Phillips had an anthropological view of his own. It was certainly primitive, but it is not certain that his neoabolitionist critics today defend views that will stand up forever or that have been more objectively arrived at. Phillips's racism needs to be rejected firmly, for it condemns a people to inferior status without evidence of inherent inferiority, but the task facing us is to evaluate its effects on his work, rather than to assume that it automatically ruined everything by its pervasive sinfulness.

The stage has been set for a re-evaluation of Phillips's view of slavery by the publication of Stanley M. Elkins's *Slavery: A Problem in American Institutional and Intellectual Life* (1959), which was originally prepared as a dissertation under Hofstadter's direction. Elkins pays handsome tribute to Phillips in his excellent survey of the literature on slavery and then identifies and criticizes Phillips's view of the Negro. Elkins argues that Phillips's work has been surpassed by Stampp's *The Peculiar Institution:* "There is now little that Phillips did with the plantation regime that has not been done with greater thoroughness by his Northern successor." Elkins hails Stampp's greater scholarship and wider research. He is entitled to his opinion, just as we are entitled to dissent on each count without denying the immense value of Stampp's work, which permanently and positively destroyed some of the worst features of the older scholarship. The irony in Elkins's enthusiasm for Stampp, as he himself at least once seems to glimpse (p. 83), is that Phillips's view of the Negro slave, with its racist underpinnings, comes out close to the Sambo whom Elkins seeks to explain. His views of slavery present a firmer basis for Elkins's social-psychological analysis than do those of Stampp, whose emphasis on brutality fits into Elkins's controversial and dubious concentration-camp analogy. Phillips's view of a patriarchal plantation dominated by a spirit of paternalism, which of course may be either benign or cruel, should be taken into full account by any theory of infantilization of the dependents.

Stampp published his critique of Phillips in 1952 and presented his alternative account in 1956. If we examine his 1952 effort in relation to that of 1956 we get a clearer notion of the difficulties inherent in the subject, for Stampp was not able to do in his own book much that he, like Hofstadter, had criticized Phillips for not doing.[12]

Stampp agreed with Hofstadter that Phillips erred in sampling only the largest estates and insisted that travelers' accounts, which Phillips used sparingly, and the manuscript census returns and court records uncovered by Frank L. Owsley and his students could provide a satisfactory picture of slavery on small units. Stampp himself noted that the results of such investigations would be unpredictable since logic suggested that slaves on small units would be treated better than those on large in some respects and worse in others. When Stampp faced these problems in *The Peculiar Institution,* he insisted that small slaveholders generally demonstrated greater paternalism and treated their slaves better than did large slaveholders. This conclusion hardly does violence to Phillips's main contentions, but the more interesting feature of Stampp's argument is that it is thinly documented and consists of little more than vague impressions. The difficulties of arriving at a more precise view of difference between large and small units plagued Stampp quite as much as they plagued Phillips.

Stampp looked suspiciously at Phillips's generalizations about the kindness of masters and insisted that slaveholders ranged from kind to cruel with any master being both to some degree and in some circumstances. These observations make good sense so far as they go, but they miss the main point. Phillips repeatedly shows his awareness of cruelty and the harsher side of master-slave relationships, although he is open to severe criticism for understatement. The essential contribution he makes is to the notion of Southern paternalism, which Stampp and many others too often confuse with kindliness. Paternalism necessarily involves harshness and may even involve cruelty so long as it is within the context of a strong sense of duty and responsibility toward those in dependent status. A father may be cruel to disobedient children and yet be deeply concerned with their material and moral welfare. Phillips also argues that the slaves' standard of material comfort rose steadily during the nineteenth century, and Stampp, in *The Peculiar Institution,* comes to a similar conclusion. The difference is that Stampp sees economic interest dominating the master-slave relationship and therefore treats the improvement as a matter of small importance, whereas Phillips describes a process of deepening patriarchal commitment as the slave society matured. Phillips does so in a somewhat contradictory or inconsistent way, for he is loathe to dwell too much on the harsher side of eighteenth century slavery and blunts the very point he is making for the later period. His obsession with the problem of racial hegemony prevents him from developing his insights into the class character of patriarchal ideology. Notwithstanding these objections, his viewpoint is decidedly more fruitful than that of his critic and permits him, for example, to treat the improvement in the slaves' conditions of life as an illustration of the advance of a distinct world view.

Stampp repeatedly strikes blows at Phillips, some of which are on the mark, but rarely transcends his performance. He takes Phillips to task for insisting on the Negro's docility and argues that the slave population had its share of active rebels, who in any case constitute a minority in any society. Thus, Phillips's pleasant judgment is replaced by an unpleasant one (or vice versa), but the principal historical questions remain unanswered: What accounts for the extent of docility? Under what conditions does individual and collective rebellion occur? What are the specific historical forms of accommodation, docility, and rebellion, and what is the significance of these forms for Southern culture? So long as we remain on the level on which Phillips placed the discussion and Stampp chose to keep it, we cannot get much further along, but if we must choose between two one-sided views, it is difficult not to regard Phillips's as closer to the norm.

Similarly, whereas Phillips stresses the lighter side of slave life, Stampp brushes the singing and dancing aside as unworthy of close attention. One may and should criticize Phillips for not analyzing these activities more closely to see the extent of group consciousness as well as of ordinary diversions and for not seeing how deeply they penetrated the life of the master in a thousand subtle ways. Yet, Phillips gives us food for thought with his descriptions, anecdotes, and sense of plantation community life; Stampp pictures a prison camp peopled by jailers and inmates. Whereas Phillips sees only the bare outlines of the road ahead, Stampp would take us in the wrong direction.

The difference may be perceived most sharply in Stampp's discussion of so narrow a question as investment in slaves: "And what is to be made of the oft-repeated argument that the planters got nowhere because 'they bought lands and slaves wherewith to grow cotton, and with the proceeds ever bought more slaves to make more cotton'? If this is the essence of economic futility, then one must also pity the late Andrew Carnegie who built a mill wherewith to make steel, and with the proceeds ever built more mills to make more steel."[13] The economic consequences of reliance on direct investments in labor and therefore on a labor-intensive path to economic growth were grasped by Phillips but elude his critic. Beyond economics, the social relations inherent in the two cases cited by Stampp are diametrically opposed and give rise to different ways of life and thought which themselves have profound consequences for the economy; this Phillips understood and stressed.

How then does Phillips's racism return again and again to plague him? And why have his successors, friendly and critical, not done better? Phillips willingly displayed the many-sidedness of plantation life and presented it as a community of white men and black struggling to find a way to live together. Yet, he stopped short precisely where he ought to have begun. Because he did not take the Negroes seriously as men and women he could not believe that in meaningful and even decisive ways they shaped the lives of their masters. After discussing the impact of the white man on the black he adds: "The Caucasian was also changed by the contact in a far from negligible degree; but the negro's conversion was much the more thorough, partly because the process in his case was coercive, partly because his genius was imitative."[14] How easily he dismisses the subject! If he believes his own words, why should he have to introduce a silly theory from Gabriel Tarde to tell us that masters do not learn from slaves but that slaves do learn from masters? Throughout this book Phillips demonstrates how well he knows better. On page 296 he tells us that "the relation of planter and slave was largely shaped by a sense of propriety, proportion and cooperation." All that without significant impact on their respective personalities! Or again on page 327: "The plantations were homes to which, as they were fond of singing, their hearts turned ever; and the negroes, exasperating as they often were to visiting strangers, were an element in the home itself . . . . The separate integration of the slaves was no more than rudimentary. They were always within the social mind and conscience of the whites, as the whites were in turn within the mind and conscience of the blacks." And yet again a few lines further along, Phillips quotes a "sagacious" slaveholder as saying that the Negro understood the white man better than the white man understood the Negro. To which Phillips adds: "This knowledge gave a power of its own. The general régime was in fact shaped by mutual requirements, concessions and understandings, producing reciprocal codes of conventional morality."[15] Now, if such was the case—as indeed it was—how absurd to deny the profound impact of the Negro on every aspect of the white man's being. Phillips brings us to the brink of profound insight only to call a retreat made necessary by the poisonous demands of white supremacy. Yet, his critics have done no better. They have in fact not done so well, for his perceptive descriptions and flashes of insight are a beginning, whereas their sermons on the guilt complexes and sadism inherent in slave ownership tell us no more than the obvious.

To supplement Phillips's work the student must certainly read Stampp's passionate *The Peculiar Institution,* which is so rich in insights and which for all its faults brings to the surface much that Phillips obscures. He must read other works as well, particularly Gilberto Freyre's great essay on Brazilian slavery *The Masters and the Slaves,* which takes us into the kitchen and the bedroom, explores architecture and folklore, and slides from black to white and back again. He must read Frank Tannenbaum's *Slave & Citizen,* which in little more than one hundred pages brings the contrast between Hispanic and American slavery into unforgettable focus. And he must read Frantz Fanon's *The Wretched of the Earth,* which provides all the answer one needs to Phillips's curious suggestion that a slave revolt ought to be discussed under the rubric of "crime." If our tender sensibilities choke on Fanon's notion that the colonial (read: slave) comes to manhood through the act of violence against his tormentors, so much the worse for our sensibilities. The point is not that this road to manhood is the best road, nor even a "good" one; the point is that it is better than none, and that a society which provides no other has no right to complain.

Phillips's racism blinded him, corroded his enormous talent, and kept him short of the greatness he approached. Our revulsion at it ought not to blind us to the wisdom that constantly breaks through his work: "For him . . . who has known the considerate and cordial, courteous and charming men and women, white and black, which that picturesque life in its best phases produced, it is impossible to agree that its basis and its operation were wholly evil, the law and the prophets to the contrary notwithstanding."[16] Those who see in these words merely the nostalgia of a latter-day proslavery writer may be left to contemplate their own moral virtue. The South, white and black, has given America some of its finest traditions and sensibilities and certainly its best manners. These were once firmly rooted in the plantation way of life and especially in the master-slave relationship. Their preservation does not require the preservation of the injustice and brutality with which they were originally and inseparably linked, but it does require a full understanding and appreciation of those origins. In this sense Phillips, despite his bias, still has much to say to us, however much more remains to be said by a new generation. *American Negro Slavery* is not the last word on its subject; merely the indispensable first.

NOTES

1. David M. Potter, "A Bibliography of the Printed Writings of Ulrich Bonnell Phillips," *Georgia Historical Quarterly,* 18 (September, 1934), 271.

2. See the criticism of Phillips's racial views in Melville J. Herskovits, *The Myth of the Negro Past* (New York, 1941), chaps. 1 and 2; Kenneth M. Stampp, *The Peculiar Institution* (New York, 1956), chap. 1; and Eugene D. Genovese, *The Political Economy of Slavery* (New York, 1965), chap. 3.

3. Kenneth M. Stampp, "The Historian and Southern Negro Slavery," *American Historical Review,* 57 (April, 1952), 613.

4. For example, in his discussion of the profitability of slavery, Phillips makes much of the relationship between slave and cotton prices but fails to consider labor productivity. As a result, he neglects the factor that might have offset the unfavorable spread between the two sets of price data.

5. Harold D. Woodman, "The Profitability of Slavery: A Historical Perennial," *Journal of Southern History,* 29 (August, 1963), 303–25; Woodman, ed., *Slavery and the Southern Economy* (New York, 1966).

6. Ulrich Bonnell Phillips, "The Origin and Growth of the Southern Black Belts," *American Historical Review,* 11 (July, 1906), 798–816; "Plantations with Slave Labor and Free," *American Historical Review,* 30 (July, 1925), 738–53.

7. Wood Gray, "Ulrich Bonnell Phillips," in *The Marcus Jernegan Essays in American Historiography,* William T. Hutchinson, ed. (Chicago, 1937), p. 361.

8. Richard Hofstadter, "U. B. Phillips and the Plantation Legend," *Journal of Negro History,* 29 (April, 1944), 110.

9. *Ibid.*, p. 121.

10. *Ibid.,* 121–22.

11. *Ibid.,* p. 124.

12. Stampp, "The Historian and Southern Negro Slavery."

13. *Ibid.,* p. 623.

14. Ulrich Bonnell Phillips, *American Negro Slavery,* (Baton Rouge, La., 1967), p. 291.

15. *Ibid.,* p. 327.

16. *Ibid.,* p. 514.

II

Race and Class in Southern History: An Appraisal of the Work of Ulrich Bonnell Phillips

DURING THE LAST FEW DECADES the reputation of Ulrich Bonnell Phillips has swung from an extreme positive to a decided negative. At present he is probably read apologetically and uneasily in much of the South and read not at all in much of the North. The charges are familiar: Phillips was a racist; he concerned himself with the upper classes; he held a nostalgic latter-day proslavery view of Southern history, and of course, unlike the rest of us, he was biased. I would suggest, nonetheless, that his work, taken as a whole, remains the best and most subtle introduction to ante-bellum Southern history and especially to the problems posed by race and class, and that his social viewpoint was neither nostalgic, nor unreconstructed, but was cautiously forward looking, humanely conservative, and deeply committed to social and racial justice.

This essay was originally published in *Agricultural History,* 41, Oct. 1967, 345–358. It is reprinted here by permission of the Agricultural History Society.

One of the earliest and most persistent comments on Phillips's work has described it as being largely free of generalization. Apart from his primitive statements about Negro traits, which were mere assertions, and his interpretative essays on the origins of the secession crisis, he deliberately shied away from drawing conclusions. As he observed in his own special manner, "A lover may generalize his lady, to be startled by her individualization after marriage."[1] Yet, he did generalize about method and content and in so doing provided us with a rich harvest of insights into the history and nature of class rule in the South, as well as into the history and nature of the race problem. In the accents of Frederick Jackson Turner, to whose influence he paid high tribute, Phillips interpreted the history of the Old South as the product of frontier and plantation, which together "shaped the general order of life without serious rival."[2] On a more general plane he asserted in the accents of a historical materialism with which much of Turner's work, like so much of his own, is compatible:

> If made inclusive enough, the study of industrial society may touch all phases of human life; but its concern is, primarily, with the grouping and activity of the people as organized in society for the purpose of producing material goods, and secondarily, with the reflex influence of the work and work-grouping upon life, upon philosophy, and upon the internal and external relations of the society.[3]

Phillips opened *Life and Labor in the Old South* by discussing the weather and attributing to it that set of human responses which produced the plantation, staple crops, slavery, regional controversy, and the race question. He carefully avoided treating the plantation regimes as a uniform entity but did not shrink from describing its essence as "the matter-of-course habituation of all the personnel to responsible and responsive adjustments between masters and men of the two races."[4]

For him, the Negro constituted an essential element in "the distinctive Southern pattern of life." The regime, he observed in one of his sensitive though infrequent passages on miscegenation, facilitated concubinage "not merely by making black women subject to white men's wills but by promoting intimacy and weakening racial antipathy."[5] Slavery he conceded, emerged as a system of class exploitation. "No prophet in early times could have told that kindliness would grow as a flower from a soil so foul, that slaves would come to be cherished not only as property of high value but as loving if lowly friends."[6] Perhaps his saddest failure, which flowed directly from his racist assumptions and sensibilities, was his refusal to develop his most pregnant insight—that the plantation produced a community in which the lives of master and slave became inextricably blended.

Professor Frank Tannenbaum has taken Phillips severely to task for failing to appreciate, in the manner of Gilberto Freyre, that plantation slavery bound master and slave together and made of them a single people with a shared culture to which they both contributed. Tannenbaum's criticism is fully justified, and yet Phillips repeatedly showed his awareness of this process so long as he could discuss it in general terms; only when he had to face its specific implications did his white supremist sensibilities command a retreat.[7] Thus, he could write of tasks he himself could never even try to accomplish:

> "The Negro in American civilization" may some day be the theme of an epic whether in verse or prose. It will involve African folkways and American vestiges thereof, gang labor and slave discipline, abolition chaos and latter-day repression, concubinage, quadroons, and "passing for white," rural isolation and urban congestion, dialects and manners, caste and caste within caste, songs and prayers, sermons and schisms—the nonchalance and bewilderment, the very human hopes

and fears, the protests and acquiescences of a somewhat peculiar people through cataclysmic changes in a very complex land.[8]

For Phillips, the nonplantation whites, too, felt the plantation influence in countless, decisive ways. It is not true, as is so often charged, that Phillips ignored the lower- and middle-class whites, much less that he showed them no sympathy or understanding.[9] His early work on Georgia politics and on the southeastern transportation system demonstrated considerable awareness and sympathy. If he slighted these classes, in his later, more mature work, it was because he correctly saw the plantation regime as having penetrated every part of Southern life and consciousness and as having directly commanded much of what it penetrated. The Negro, who never long slipped from his mind, provided an integral part of the regime. For the humbler white men of the black belt and the mountains, he insisted that their economic life, which he saw as of primary importance for their cultural and political life, was ultimately shaped and limited by the plantation regime. Astride society as a whole stood the slaveholders and especially the planters. If he centered his attention on them, it was not so much because they had his heart, although they did, as because they exercised hegemony and, to an important degree, molded the lives of all. For this reason, among others, he insisted that the essential features and tendencies of Southern society could be most readily grasped through the study of the plantation regime where it was most mature.[10]

Phillips began and ended with race relations, which he saw as extruding particular class formations. He affirmed the economic impulse to slavery and to the plantation system, which he considered prior to slavery, but he insisted that, upon establishment of both, social rather than economic considerations prevailed. Specifically, the presence of large numbers of Africans, whom he regarded as primitive, if not savage, required the maintenance of a regime capable of disciplining them and of preserving social order. The plantation proved the best vehicle; slavery served only as the necessary basis for the plantation regime in its early phases. For Phillips, "a realization of the race problem as a persistent and often paramount factor in shaping political orientation is the beginning of wisdom in any general study of the South."[11] The determination of the Southern whites to preserve white supremacy constitutes, in this sense, the central theme of Southern history and, indeed defines a Southerner.[12] Yet, so much of Phillips's work concerns class structure and especially the quality and decisive influence of the ruling class that Professor Stephenson has plausibly, if not altogether convincingly, described him as a historian of aristocracy and only incidentally of slavery.[13]

Phillips opened himself to this criticism by denying that slavery provided the basis of Southern identity. A review of his argument reveals it to be surprisingly weak. He began by noting that during the eighteenth century slavery had legal sanction everywhere on the continent but during the twentieth century nowhere. He concluded by maintaining that if slavery, rather than race, had shaped the South, we could not account for the loyalty of the non-slaveholders to the regime. It is, of course, true that slavery was general in the eighteenth century and has been absent in the twentieth, but this observation tells us nothing. Slavery in the North was an incidental arrangement, tangential to society and the economy; slavery in the South was the heart of the regime. The difference lay precisely in the notion of class that repeatedly breaks through Phillips's historical writing, though it is obscured in his specifically theoretical statements. A slave society, not merely slavery, emerged in the South, and it emerged on the basis of the formation of a dominant slaveholding class, which was nowhere to be found in the North, despite considerable occasional slaveownership. Phillips described that class and its society in almost everything he wrote but did not face its ultimate implications.

The loyalty of the nonslaveholders to the regime presents an exceptionally difficult problem. That race played a great role in shaping such loyalty, none would deny, but there were many other forces at work. Phillips, in any case, made the careless error of assuming that lack of class consciousness proves lack of class antagonism, but the advocates of a class view of history and of the doctrine of class struggle are not so naive as to equate consciousness with interest. Phillips simply failed to meet the argument.

Despite this unimpressive excursion he did have something to say on the problem of lower-class consciousness: "For reasons common in the world at large, the Southern whites were not to be divided into sharply antagonistic classes . . . . Habitat grouping, it is clear, had a cementing force great enough to overcome the cleaving tendency of economic stratification."[14] In this passage he perceived the difference between objective antagonism and subjective response but chose, as always, to emphasize community cohesion and therefore historical continuity, much as he did when he recognized the injustices to and the frustrated aspirations of the slaves, but chose to emphasize their submission. Implicit here is not so much racism nor even upper-class snobbery (although elements of both are present) as a profoundly conservative notion of social change. We shall return to this problem further along. For the moment we may observe that, notwithstanding Phillips's obsession with the race question, he repeatedly returned to the dimension of class. Thus, after referring to the prevalence of slavery among the Greeks and Romans, he added, "In later days the peoples and powers of Europe . . . . employed other means of maintaining a safely stratified social order."[15]

The duality in Phillips's thought between a primary concern for racial hegemony and the persistent reassertion of a class hegemony does not necessarily imply contradiction but does raise strong suspicions. If slavery, whether or not seen primarily as a means of racial control, threw up a ruling class of the power Phillips described, then the relationship between class and racial hegemony needs to be firmly established; yet, he repeatedly shied away from this confrontation and thereby introduced considerable ambiguity into his work. This ambiguity may be overcome by recapitulating the main lines of his analysis with one major alteration: whereas he consistently held the class question to be subsidiary to the race question, we may view the race question as the prevailing social form of the class question. If this procedure alters Phillips's intent, it simultaneously rescues his work from insoluble logical and empirical difficulties without doing violence to its spirit.

From this point of view, the entire body of Phillips's work emerges as the history and sociology of the slaveholding class and of the regime to which it gave rise. In his remarkable early essays—the more remarkable because he was still in his twenties—he laid down several lifelong themes: that the plantation system was a capitalistic enterprise, in the sense of being highly competitive, heavily capitalized, and oriented toward commodity production; that it nonetheless took on the primary characteristics of a paternalistic community; and that it suffered severe economic disadvantages, such as overcapitalization of labor and a tendency toward unprofitability.[16] More to the point, he drew attention to "the tendency of slavery as a system of essentially capitalistic industry to concentrate wealth, such as there was, within the hands of a single economic class and within certain distinctive geographic areas."[17] Virtually all of Phillips's economic writings focused on the origins and growth of this class and its regime. Thus, in his splendid book, *A History of Transportation in the Eastern Cotton Belt to 1860,* he combined careful economic and political analysis with social insight:

In the larger aspect, that [railroad] system was a source of

> weakness and failure. Transportation is not an end in itself, but when rightly used, is a means to the end of increasing wealth, developing resources, and strengthening society. And in the South these greater purposes were not accomplished. The building of railroads led to little else but the extension and the intensifying of the plantation system and the increase in the staple output. Specialization and commerce were extended, when just the opposite development, towards diversification of products and economic self-sufficiency, was the real need.[18]

He skillfully demonstrated that the stakes included much more than a dangerously one-sided economic growth and that the economic process solidified an entire social system, which reacted to strengthen the economic one-sidedness and which carried with it grave political implications. The slaveholding class and the regime it spawned traveled those rails and subdued everything in their path. The experience of the Virginia Piedmont was recapitulated in the cotton belt. A social, not merely an economic system conquered the South—a system of class rule, not merely of economic inequality or racial control.[19]

Throughout his life Phillips offered descriptions of and rendered judgments on the quality of the slaveholders and their interaction with other social classes. A typical plantation owner, in his view, had "the faculty of unruffled response to the multitudinous calls of slaves upon the attention and the tolerance of slack service."[20] The slaveholders, he insisted, relished and exalted their calling, and this exaltation fell to the advantage of the slaves, for it reflected a "genuine self-respect, of which an essential ingredient is respect for others."[21]

Phillips attributed these sterling qualities of the ruling class to the plantation, rather than to slavery. Contrary to what even some of his fairest and most professionally scrupulous critics have suggested, he found slavery distasteful; he defended it only as a means of introducing the Negro into the plantation culture but damned it as an increasingly dubious institution once the breaking-in process had been completed. He praised it as a civilizing school but condemned it for failing to produce graduates; he noted with sorrow the unwillingness to provide for the development of the talents of the intelligent and the eager among the slaves; he expressed disgust at the refusal to protect black women against sexual exploitation by masters and overseers; and he commented frequently on the stultifying effects of slavery on economic growth and intellectual freedom.[22] Those Southern qualities which he admired he attributed to the plantation way of life, to which slavery was, in his opinion, incidental. The plantation he viewed as a homestead, the spirit of which was neighborliness.

When we reconsider those qualities of personality which he singled out for praise, the emphasis on the plantation rather than on slavery appears more than dubious. The plantation "made for strength of character and readiness to meet emergencies, for patience and tact, for large-mindedness, gentility and self-control."[23] These and other qualities may be attributed to the plantation only in the sense that the plantation housed a series of human relationships. The personal qualities engendered by the system arose from the manner in which men faced men, specifically the manner in which masters faced slaves. When Phillips separated the house from its inhabitants, he offered, implicitly and on occasion explicity, a vision of other inhabitants. He spoke of plantations with free labor, but it never took him long to get to the point, which was a frank admission of dependent status within a system of paternalistic control. If we use as our model Hegel's extraordinary analysis of the way in which one man comes to self-consciousness through confrontation with a dependent other, then slavery represents the perfect case of the general phenomenon of lordship and bondage. Phenomenologically, Phillips's alternative to slavery appears as an imperfect variation, capable of recapitulating some or perhaps most of the effects of the old regime. But historically, it was another matter. The plantation and slavery grew up together and "the plantation product of men" of which Phillips spoke so glowingly was, in fact, the slaveholding product of men. Even the postwar plantation largely carried on a regional tradition and preserved a revered sensibility rather than raising an old product on a new soil. When Phillips lamented the threat to the old values and called for their restoration, he refused to place his trust wholly in a restored plantation system: he stressed instead "the impress of the old regime" and hoped that "those who cherish its memory will zealously propagate the qualities it fostered . . . ."[24]

In any case, there can be no dispute over his admiration for the men the regime produced. On the strength of his estimate of their qualities, he penned his striking dedication to *A History of Transportation in the Eastern Cotton Belt*, the opening lines of which read: "To the Dominant Class of the South, who in the piping ante-bellum time schooled multitudes, white and black, to the acceptance of higher standards . . . ."

Phillips's notion of the central theme of white supremacy came most nearly to grief in his discussion of the secession crisis. From the political writings on Georgia and South Carolina with which he began his career, to the interpretive lectures on Southern political history with which he closed it, he displayed little patience with the state rights ideology and insisted that fundamental social questions lay beneath it. In "The Central Theme of Southern History" and *The Course of the South to Secession,* which included that essay, he argued for the primacy of the race question, but his evidence at best raises other possibilities and at worst is irrelevant to his thesis. Phillips quoted Robert Barnwell Rhett and Elijah F.

Nuttall to illustrate his point, but their remarks offer questionable support. "A people owning slaves," said Rhett in 1833, "are mad or worse than mad, if they do not hold their destinies in their own hands."[25] In 1849, Nuttall replied to Cassius M. Clay by saying: "Kentucky, sir, will be ready for emancipation when she is ready to cut loose all her feelings for the South . . . then she will be ready to unite with our northern friends, and not until then."[26] These statements are not incompatible with a racial interpretation, but, if anything, they suggest an awareness of a separate Southern civilization.

Phillips's resistance to such an interpretation plunged him deep into trouble, as a review of the evidence he arrays will show. He cited an 1822 pamphlet by Edwin C. Holland as evidence of a concern for racial hegemony. The pamphlet urged the expulsion of the free blacks but not of the free mulattoes, "for he said that many of the mulattoes were slaveholders themselves and watchful of slaveholding interests."[27] If this is not a class view, I cannot imagine what would qualify. With noticeable discomfiture Phillips passed rapidly over the work of men like Henry Hughes and George Fitzhugh and finally offered us two clear, well developed contemporary statements of the sectional question as a race question. The first was by the English-born scientist, Thomas Ewbank, the second by the lawyer and absentee slaveowner, Sidney G. Fisher. Phillips noted, apparently without appreciating the irony, that both men lived in the North. Then he turned to Edward A. Pollard's *The Lost Cause Regained,* which appeared during 1868. In it, Pollard castigated Southerners for having defended slavery per se instead of having taken a stand on the race question. One wonders what Phillips thought Pollard could or should have said in 1868. It was surely too late to say anything else.

Finally, Phillips dogmatically asserted that the argument for Southern rights was nothing more than the demand that the South be left alone to handle the race problem. This view is unworthy of his splendid assessment of the slaveholders and of the plantation's powerful effect on human personality. If, as he never tired of reiterating, the plantation system conditioned all of Southern life, and if the slaveholders were its ultimate product, then surely the demand for local and regional autonomy must be understood as the political expression of lordship and as the projection of the plantation ethos into the wider social arena.

The regional divergence on the race question did not, in Phillips's view, have to end in secession and war. Although in his early work he admitted the possibility that the conflict might have been irrepressible,[28] he increasingly spoke of the tragedy of political blundering and sectional insensitivity.[29] Southerners might have conceded the injustices of slavery and the need for a better system of racial control, he argued, had not the abolition agitation pushed them into intellectual and political rigidity.[30] All this is standard fare, which is objectionable not because it is standard, nor because it is intrinsically unworthy of respect, but because it fits so poorly into Phillips's thought.

He asserted that abolition blinded Southerners to their own best interests and thereby kept them from disestablishing slavery voluntarily.[31] He held, in general, that the slave system tended toward unprofitability, had reached the limits of expansion, and would have yielded to a system of plantation wage-labor. Having told us, in virtually all his writings, that the Southern regime produced men of a special, high-spirited type, he proceeded to insist that their ultimate decisions would flow from economic calculation of the crassest sort. The most serious difficulty with this view is that it does violence to the manner of men we have been offered so lovingly, and that this violence is the worse for its being predicated on a mechanical economic process.

It was one thing for Phillips to insist that the slave economy manifested a tendency toward unprofitability, however defined; it was another for him to assume that the economy was approaching zero profitability. The assumption is palpably absurd and without a hint of empirical verification. If, on the other hand, he meant only to imply that the average rate of profit was falling below the interest rate and that the slaveholders would accordingly wish to switch to free labor, then he would have fallen into another calamitous difficulty. The whole burden of his life's work rejected the idea that the planter could be understood as economic man and affirmed the roles of patriarchal ideology and the achievement of status through slaveownership. The very definition of a planter used by Phillips turned primarily on slaveownership and only incidentally on landownership. Phillips could not have argued that masters bought and sold slaves, when it was economically irrational to do so, in order to do their part in controlling race relations. There are limits to altruism beyond which even the flower of the ruling class of South Carolina could not be expected to go. The only explanation for such behavior, as Phillips repeatedly demonstrated in *American Negro Slavery* and *Life and Labor in the Old South,* is to be found in an ideology of status through the extension of the patriarchal plantation family and its attendant ownership of human labor. Here, as almost everywhere, Phillips's reiteration of the theme of racial hegemony, attractive, enticing, and deceptively simple as it was, proved hopelessly encased in a pyramid of dubious assumptions and less useful for historical analysis than would appear at first glance.[32] His uneasiness may be gleaned from his remarks on the fire-eaters, whom he could and often did call reckless extremists but whom he had to accept as "products of plantation life, exalting the system which had bred them . . . self-chosen guardians of rural gentility . . . as conservative as any men have ever been."[33]

Phillips's revisionist view of secession flowed from a tenacious commitment to a racial interpretation of Southern society and from a faith in history as a process of resolving resolvable antagonisms. The Northerners failed to understand the race question because they lacked enough experience with it. Their hostility caused Southerners to turn from needed reforms to reactionary intransigence. Yet, Phillips himself demonstrated that Southerners gradually did reform their slave practices during late ante-bellum times. The steady improvement in the conditions of slave life and the steady growth of paternalistic feeling constituted two of the main themes of his magnificent social histories. It was, to say the least, arbitrary of him to decide that abolition agitation barred those reforms which might have compromised the sectional crisis but spurred, or at least did not inhibit, those which intensified it. The history of reform predated the post-dated Garrison's onslaught and had one outstanding feature: it displayed a growing tendency to confirm slavery as the Negro's natural and permanent state while making him more comfortable within it. Phillips's racial interpretation offers a few clues to this process, but the class analysis implicit in his work offers a solution. This process may properly be understood as part of an ascent by the slaveholders to self-consciousness and to the formation of a slaveholders' world view. George Fitzhugh, not the postwar Edward A. Pollard, presented its logical outcome. Phillips described the slaveholders as a very special kind of men, which they certainly were, and he attributed to them qualities which were anything but bourgeois. If he failed to draw the necessary conclusions from his extraordinary lifetime efforts, we are under no compulsion to follow suit.

To criticize in this way Phillips's notion of the central theme of white supremacy is not to reject it; the thesis contains too much painstaking observation, sound reflection, and good, hard sense for that. The notion of white supremacy as the prime mover of Southern history, independent of and superior to all class struggles, breaks down at many points, but its modification into the persistent form of those struggles retains great vitality. All societies are rent by class antagonisms, the depth and violence of which may vary enormously, but Southern society has, to a remarkable degree, disciplined its potentially explosive antagonism in an unusual and, in some respects, unique way. The history of race relations in the South, as Phillips so clearly saw, has been the history of that process.

Phillips's interpretation of the Old South was informed by his vision of a New South in a Progressive America. The most serious error committed by his detractors has been their oft-repeated and widely accepted charge that he looked back nostalgically to a romantic age of moonlight and magnolias. On the contrary, as C. Vann Woodward has pointed out, Phillips's racial attitudes reflected much of the ideology of the Progressive era.[34] This insight might properly be extended to include the whole range of Phillips's social thought. He did not pine away over the loss of the golden age of slavery, much less desire in the slightest its restoration. Phillips accepted without hesitation the industrial-commercial civilization of the United States and sought actively, as a journalistic reformer as well as a historian, to ease the South toward it.

Phillips harshly criticized the Bourbon-inspired agricultural regime of the New South and strongly urged the restoration of the patriarchal plantation. He decried the tendency toward smallholdings and hoped it could be reversed. The small farm, especially when worked by tenants and sharecroppers, could only foster economic and cultural backwardness and mediocrity. A restored plantation system, with resident owners and wage workers would provide the vehicle for economic rationality and a proper balance between staple-crop production and diversification. He urged a state tax on cotton to drive out marginal producers and the application of the proceeds to encourage industrial and agricultural development.[35]

His social goals may be gleaned from a passage written in 1903, in which he combined an acquiescence in the modern capitalist order with a demand for the preservation and extension of some of the older values: "Any modern system must take a tone from the active, pushing world of today; but in essentials the plantation of old could again look with hope to the system which produced the fine type of the Southern gentleman of the old regime."[36] He attacked the impersonality of the modern industrial system and lamented the loss of individual and family interest in the fate of the working classes.[37] In a brief but revealing review-essay on *I'll Take My Stand,* the Mitchells's *Industrial Revolution in the South,* and Odum's *American Epoch,* he noted the persistence of conflict and peacemaking in the "social process" and pitted the Agrarians against the Yankeefying Mitchells. Between the demands of the past and those of the present he yielded to the latter, but his love and flights of lyrical rapture went to those who would preserve from the past what could safely be preserved.[38]

Phillips particularly criticized the agricultural regime of the New South for gravely weakening the relationship between white and Negro. Absentee owners and tenant or sharecropping arrangements divided the races to the cost of both.[39] He drew an analogy between the old plantation and the settlement house, comparing the master and mistress to social workers whose duty was to guide their Negroes toward full participation in American life.[40] A new plantation regime on a free-labor basis would, he argued train and educate the great mass of the blacks, who must still be subject to racial control. Absentee owners would not do: nothing short of the restoration of a resident planter class and especially the restoration of the prestige and influence of the plantation mistress would do.[41] The patriarchal feature was decisive:

The average negro has many of the characteristics of a child

> . . . . The presence of the planter and his wife and children and his neighbors is required for example and precept among the negroes. Factory methods and purely business relations will not serve; the tie of personal sympathy and affection is essential to the successful working of the system.

The old plantation had molded whites and blacks into one community, and its passing had opened the way for racial antipathy and for a segregation which he deplored.[42]

A new plantation regime would avoid the worst evils of the old. On the economic level it would escape dependence on a one-crop system and would not suffer from the overcapitalization of labor. On the social level it would avoid the most depressing and unjust feature of slavery by providing for the graduation of apt pupils to supervisory positions as well as to industrial and other tasks. In this way the Southern ruling class could complete its historic task of bringing the Negro into our national life without the risk of social disorder.[43]

It would not be difficult to criticize this vision on either economic or social grounds. Phillips himself observed, for example, that if the plantation integrated the Negro with the most culturally advanced and socially responsible whites, it simultaneously separated him from the great mass of whites. He did not seem to appreciate that this segregation provided social cohesion under the slave regime only because of the special power of the slaveholders over society, but that it invited social upheaval and terror under a regime from which this special power was removed. The gradual promotion of apt Negroes into such a society would have been, and indeed has been, fraught with all the ingredients of disorder and hatred. Apart from many other problems, it never seems to have occurred to Phillips that an oppressed class or race is not likely to agree to be guided forever by a benevolent paternalism. Those apt Negroes of his were supposed to be grateful for their new opportunities and to help guide their more stupid brethren. What ingrates they have turned out to be! Granted that we have the wisdom of hindsight, Phillips's inability to realize that many of them would use their acquired privileges and culture to lead their people in a more rapid, if disorderly, advance, stemmed from his conservative ideology, not from his historical studies.[44]

The significance of Phillips's vision lies not in the value of his specific political or economic proposals, for he had little influence in these spheres, but in the light it sheds on his historical sensibility. His sympathetic and appreciative portrayal of the plantation regime of the Old South—a portrayal I think largely accurate—must be understood not as a defense of slavery but as an appeal for the incorporation of the more humane and rational values of prebourgeois culture into modern industrial life. Those who argue that the United States lacks a conservative tradition stumble badly when they consider the Old South and its heritage. Of course, if one is willing to see only the competitive, capitalistic side of the slave regime, then one is left free to declare it a tortured, guilt-ridden, hypocritical child of bourgeois liberalism and to let it go at that. If, on the other hand, one follows Phillips into an appreciation of the patriarchal and paternalistic side of the regime, then one must necessarily follow him into an appreciation of the authenticity of the world view it engendered. How ironical, therefore, that Phillips should have been betrayed by his own effort weak and uncertain as that effort was—to prove the Old South a capitalist society. Yet, he had to make it, for how else could he have established an ideological rationale for his defense of its values in the world in which he lived? His effort suggests that he was concerned not with defending the Old South but with reforming the New and with guiding it safely toward a respect for conservative values and racial justice. It suggests also the dilemma of the conservative critics of liberal society, who would restore the world view of a dead world without even the wish to bring the world itself back to life.[45]

The particular difficulty with Phillips's humane vision

was that those values and that halting and contradictory start toward racial justice were products not of the plantation per se but of the master-slave relationship and were specifically the contribution of the slaveholding class. Every element of paternalism and of the patriarchal ethos necessary to make Phillips's modern plantation function properly would have undercut economic rationality. Many post-bellum planters may have tried, even with some local successes, to preserve the older way of life, but for the South as a whole, they were fighting a losing battle. And just where Phillips expected to find enough good bourgeois willing to live down on the farm just to take care of the darkies is beyond my powers of imagination. The old world died with the Confederacy, and if its values and manners have lingered on, they have done so with diminishing force. Phillips, by 1918 at least, began to face this fact and to appeal to ideals and sentiments rather than for the creation of a new material basis in a restored plantation:

> The plantation is largely a thing of the past, and yet it is of the present. We do not live in the past, but the past lives in us. Every man and woman is the product of his or her environment and of the environment of his or her forbears, for we are controlled by tradition. Our minds are the resultant of the experience of those who gave us birth and rearing; and this plantation regime of which we speak was a powerful influence in the lives of millions of men and women.[46]

This retreat into a fanciful idealism could not save him but might remind us of the extremity of the task facing those who would accept the world of the cash nexus and yet try to defend the ideals of social responsibility, legitimate authority, and a regime of liberating discipline. Toward the end of his sadly shortened life, when he prepared to meet an expected death with a dignity and manliness that would have done honor to the most splendid representatives of the old ruling class he so deeply admired, he spoke less (or at least less surely) of the possibilities for a new plantation regime and more of the need to keep the spirit alive. He accepted the industrial order but would not quit the fight for the preservation of something of the older ethos.

Today we may reread his work for its understanding of slavery as a social system; for its appreciation of the plantation as a community of unlike men trying to live together decently; and for its brilliant descriptions of a proud and tough people who forged themselves into a ruling class and imposed their values as well as their will on society at large. We may consider that his notion of white supremacy as a central theme remains an extraordinary insight, even if it requires modification. And we may profit too from the profound critique of our national culture that informed his life's work. Living as we do amidst a world-wide civil war in which new heights of personal liberty are accompanied by the unspeakable degradation of millions of colored men throughout the world, and in which the revolutionary alternative seems incapable of coming to fruition without the crucifixion of whole generations, we might well take heart from his example. He knew he had to make hard choices, and he made them. But he knew too that if much of the old were not preserved, nothing of the new would be worth the battle; that if much of the new were not accepted, nothing of the old could long be endured. Without tears, or pretense, or whining, he demonstrated how one could accept, while refusing to surrender to, that melancholy wisdom so trenchantly offered us by Santayana: "The necessity of rejecting and destroying some things that are beautiful is the deepest curse of existence."[47]

NOTES

1. Ulrich Bonnell Phillips, *Life and Labor in the Old South,* paperback ed. (Boston, 1964), p. viii. (All references in this chapter are to work by Phillips, unless another author is indicated.) For a discussion of Phillips as being in the tradition of Ranke, see Sam E. Salem, "U. B. Phillips and the Scientific Tradition," *Georgia Historical Quarterly,* 44 (June 1960), 172–185. See also Phillips's early claims to eschew historical imagination for "thorough scientific treatment," *Georgia and State Rights,* Annual Report of the American Historical Association for 1901, 2 (Washington: 1902), 6.

2. Introduction to *Plantation and Frontier (1649–1863),* vols. 1 and 2 of J. R. Commons, *et al., History of American Industrial Society,* 10 vols. (Cleveland: 909), 1: 72.

3. *Ibid.*

4. *Life and Labor,* p. 304.

5. *Ibid.,* pp. 138, 205.

6. *Ibid.,* p. 214.

7. Frank Tannenbaum, *Slave and Citizen: The Negro in the Americas* (New York: 1947).

8. "The Perennial Negro," review-essay, *Yale Review,* 21 (Autumn 1931), 202.

9. For this viewpoint in the context of a warm and generous critique, see Wendell Holmes Stephenson, "Ulrich B. Phillips, Historian of Aristocracy," *The South Lives in History: Southern Historians and Their Legacy* (Baton Rouge: 1955), pp. 58–94, esp. 93.

10. Cf. "The Slave Labor Problem in the Charleston District," *Political Science Quarterly,* 22 (Sept. 1907), 416. How astonishing then that he should choose to study the African not in West Africa, which supplied most of our slaves, but in primitive east-central areas, which supplied few or none. He argued that he wanted to see the Negro in his natural state, where contact with whites had been minimal. It never occurred to him that those particular Africans had never approached the level of pre-European West Africa. See e.g., "Azandeland," *Yale Review,* 20 (Winter 1931), 293–313.

11. "A Quest of the Common Man," review of J. T. Adams, *The Epic of America,* in *Yale Review,* 21 (Dec. 1931), 402–403.

12. "The Central Theme of Southern History," originally published in the *American Historical Review,* 34 (Oct. 1928), and added as a final chapter to *The Course of the South to Secession,* ed. E. Merton Coulter, paperback ed. (New York, 1964). All references to this article will be from the latter work.

13. Stephenson, *The South Lives in History,* p. 93.

14. *The Course of the South to Secession,* p. 155.

15. *Ibid.,* p. 83.

16. Cf. esp. "The Economic Cost of Slaveholding in the Cotton Belt," *Political Science Quarterly,* 20 (June 1905), 257–275.

17. "The Origin and Growth of the Southern Black Belts," *American Historical Review,* 11 (July 1906), 798.

18. *A History of Transportation in the Eastern Cotton Belt to 1860* (New York: 1908), pp. 19–20.

19. *Ibid.,* p. 396; *Life and Labor,* pp. 24–25, 110, 111, 148. For Phillips's assessment of the political side of this process, see his *Georgia and State Rights,* and *The Life of Robert Toombs* (New York: 1913), esp. pp. 25–28; "The South Carolina Federalists," *American Historical Review,* 14 (April 1909), 529–540, esp. 531, and 14 (July 1909), 731–743; and *The Course of the South to Secession.*

20. "Plantations with Slave Labor and Free," *American Historical Review,* 30 (July 1925), 744.

21. *Ibid.*

22. See, e.g., "Racial Problems, Adjustments and Disturbances," *The South in the Building of the Nation,* 4: 240; "Conservatism and Progress in the Cotton Belt," *South Atlantic Quarterly,* 3 (Jan. 1904), 2.

23. "The Plantation Product of Men," *Proceedings of the 2nd Annual Session of the Georgia Historical Association* (Atlanta: 1918), pp. 14–15.

24. *Ibid.,* p. 15.

25. *The Course of the South to Secession,* p. 133.

26. *Ibid.,* p. 110.

27. *Ibid.,* p. 102.

28. *Life of Robert Toombs,* p. 102.

29. Some of his strongest statements were made in lectures. For a discussion see Stephenson, *The South Lives in History,* p. 90.

30. Cf. *Life of Robert Toombs,* p. 51.

31. "Conservatism and Progress in the Cotton Belt," p. 8; "Plantations with Slave Labor and Free," p. 748.

32. Phillips criticized William E. Dodd for emphasizing the purely economic rather than social side of the economics of slavery, but whenever he discussed the question with an eye on the larger political issues, he interpreted "social" as racial. See "On the Economics of Slavery", Annual Report of the American Historical Association for the Year 1912 (Washington: 1914), p. 151. In his less polemical efforts—i.e., his major writings on slavery—his notion of "social" comes close to the one I am defending here.

33. "Protagonists of Southern Independence," review-essay, *Yale Review,* 22 (March 1933), 643.

34. C. Vann Woodward, Introduction to *Life and Labor.*

35. "The Economics of the Plantation," *South Atlantic Quarterly,* 2

(July 1903), 231; "The Overproduction of Cotton and a Possible Remedy," *South Atlantic Quarterly,* 4 (April 1905), 148–158.

36. "The Economics of the Plantation," p. 236.

37. "The Plantation Product of Men," p. 13; "Plantations with Slave Labor and Free," p. 745.

38. "Fifteen Vocal Southerners," *Yale Review,* 20 (Spring 1931), 611–613.

39. "Plantations with Slave Labor and Free," p. 752.

40. "The Plantation Product of Men," p. 13.

41. "The Decadence of the Plantation System," *Annals of the American Academy of Political and Social Science,* 35 (Jan. 1910), 40–41; "The Plantation as a Civilizing Factor," *Sewanee Review,* 12 (July 1904), 266.

42. "The Decadence of the Plantation System," p. 38; "The Plantation as a Civilizing Factor, p. 266.

43. "The Economics of the Plantation," p. 232; "The Plantation as a Civilizing Factor," p. 265; "The Black Belt," review of Carl Kelsey's *The Negro Farmer,* in *Sewanee Review,* 12 (Jan. 1904), 73–77.

44. "Origin and Growth of the Southern Black Belts," p. 815.

45. I am indebted to Professor Warren I. Susman of Rutgers University for an opportunity to study his brilliant paper on the conservative tradition in America. The paper was presented to the first annual Socialist Scholars Conference (1965).

46. "The Plantation Product of Men," p. 12.

47. George Santayana, *Character and Opinion in the United States* (New York: 1920), p. 130.

Chapter 14

POTTER AND WOODWARD ON THE SOUTH

had the South not existed: what regional mysteries would there have been? Until the blacks themselves demonstrated that racism has been a national, not merely a sectional, disease and that Northern liberalism had little left to offer their liberation movement, the South served splendidly as the American scapegoat. The black revolt has shattered the hypocrisy and undermined the smugness; we may now expect a serious reappraisal of Southern history and culture in the years ahead. In this, as in so many other ways, black militancy, in both its directly political and its intellectual manifestations, has already contributed substantially to the positive reorientation of American life.

In the past, Southern history and culture have been the special province of white Southerners; with a few important exceptions—most recently and notably, William Freehling and Winthrop Jordan—Northern white scholars have been

This essay was originally published in *New York Review of Books,* Sept. 11, 1969, pp. 27–30.

blinded by self-righteousness whereas blacks have largely restricted themselves to those problems which bear most directly on their own people. It is now only a question of time, however, before we will get studies of, say, planter-poor white relations or of the economics of the plantation by black writers, who will bring their own points of view to the wider subject matter of history—that is, they will follow the path already opened by John Hope Franklin and a few other black historians who have refused to limit themselves to "black" subjects.

That Southern history has been largely dominated by white Southerners has been unfortunate only to the extent that we have needed to hear other voices as well. Contrary to the slanders of professional South-baiters, the level of scholarship of the best white Southern historians has been unusually high. The volumes of interpretive essays under review[1] represent years of work and thought by two of the best minds in the historical profession. Together with Ulrich Bonnell Phillips, whose productive life ended more than thirty years ago, David Potter and C. Vann Woodward are the greatest of Southern historians. Both are from the Deep South—Potter from Georgia, Woodward from Arkansas; both attended Emory University in Atlanta; both have lived and taught in the North for many years; both are now close to sixty; both have won the admiration of their profession. Ideologically, Potter is the more conservative whereas Woodward combines a strong Populism with liberal political views. Both are notable for their willingness to take ideological opponents seriously.

Taken together, these books represent the culmination of several decades of white Southern scholarship, which left the racism and regional chauvinism of Phillips far behind and sought to reinterpret Southern experience in a sympathetic but uncompromisingly critical spirit. Whether future historians, black and white, succeed in explaining the paradox of the South will largely depend both on their willingness to absorb what Potter and Woodward have written and on their ability to transcend those formidable performances.

Both books are rich but necessarily uneven. Each covers a great deal of ground, and every essay deserves lengthy discussion. One cannot do them justice in fewer pages than they themselves contain. Potter's book is a new collection of essays, whereas Woodward's is an old collection revised and enlarged. If I treat them together briefly, my purpose is to try to demonstrate the limits imposed on the best scholarship when it avoids the central role of class.

Both books wrestle with the question of distinctiveness of Southern identity. Potter's *The South and the Sectional Conflict* consists of eleven essays, grouped in three sections: "The Nature of Southernism," "Three Historiographical Forays," and "The Crisis of the Union." The first section lays down his point of view, and the second and third apply it. We shall therefore concentrate on the general ideas spelled out in the beginning although this procedure obscures important contributions to many particular historical questions. A word on the second part is, however, essential. Potter's review of the historical literature on the South and the nation during the nineteenth century is not only useful, it is unique. No other historian in the United States has his ability to present the arguments of others, including his opponents, with such conciseness, scrupulousness, and sensitivity to nuance.

Potter and Woodward center their analyses on the abrasive relationship between the South and the rest of the nation; Potter stresses the material foundations of the antagonism, whereas Woodward makes a point of the irony inherent in the antagonism itself. To Woodward, for example, the South has generally been out of step with the rest of the country, but this eccentricity has brought it closer to the experience of the rest of the world. In this and in other respects, the points of view of Woodward and Potter are complementary. For Potter, the South has provided the focus for two great national problems: it has represented distinctiveness and combative sectionalism in a republic undergoing consolidation; and it has upheld racial caste in a society committed in principle, if not in practice, to equality.

Irony is a theme running through Woodward's book, from the first essay, "The Search for Southern Identity," to "The Irony of Southern History" and "A Second Look at the Theme of Irony," an essay which has been added to this collection. The seven other essays take up specific problems in this spirit. The United States, Woodward argues, is unique in the world, but the South has not shared in this uniqueness. He too seeks the roots and quality of the Southern heritage. What makes the South distinctive, he argues, is its collective historical experience, in which it developed both as part of a larger nation and yet as an entity that has taken a road different from that of the nation.

If the United States has had—within limits and with qualifications—unparalleled prosperity, the South has suffered from a persistent as well as a cyclical poverty. If Americans have been imprisoned by the notion that nothing is beyond their power to accomplish, Southerners have borne too many failures to entertain such illusions. If America has stood rigidly by its legend of innocence and moral superiority, the South has had a long, painful inner struggle to reconcile its democratic and egalitarian inheritance with the exigencies of slavery and racial caste. If America has won—by its own reckoning at least—all its wars and become convinced of its invincibility, the South lost the one that counted most and came to know the shock of defeat, humiliation, and the hardship of survival. (There is another irony here, by the way: the fate of occupation and Reconstruction taught the white South how to survive in defeat and thereby sharpened its sensitivity in a way analogous to that experienced by the black South during and after its bitter years of enslavement.) If America has been supremely optimistic in its world outlook, the South has long tended toward pessimism and conservatism. If Americans have little sense of the past, Southerners traditionally have maintained a strong historical sense.

Southerners have long known, Woodward concludes, what other Americans have always been intent on not knowing—that they have been caught up in history and cannot stand outside it. Hence the irony: It is not so much the South but the North that is distinctive when considered along with the experience of other nations. But as Woodward warned during the 1950s and restates forcefully now, the string has about run out. The war in Vietnam and the black revolt in the cities have brought the rest of the country face to face with defeat and with problems that stubbornly resist solution. History is now happening to us. Thus Woodward believes that the Southern intelligentsia—by which he means both blacks and whites—has a special, positive contribution to make in easing America into the new era, because Southerners are heirs to those traditions and experiences which can link American culture and sensibility to those of the rest of the world. That many of these traditions and experiences have been reactionary and even brutal does not at all upset his argument; it merely underscores the irony he sees as being so deeply embedded in the duality of Southern life.

Woodward's concern for a sympathetic reappraisal of the Southern experience is double edged. On the one side, he extols the radicalism of Southern Populism and draws attention to its absorption of the aristocratic Southern ethos at the same time as it sharply attacked the bourgeois values and policies of the New South. On the other side, he dispassionately examines the aristocratic and conservative tradition itself, with its roots in slavery and plantation exploitation, and traces some of the ways in which its inherent injustice has been attended by valuable patterns of community relations and resistance to commercial values. From this Southern vantage point, he can attack much in American life, and call for a radical re-evaluation of the national commitment to capitalism; but he never allows himself to be uncritical toward the South itself.

Woodward's argument is internally sound and convincing but, as Potter sees, it does not go far enough. In a review of the first edition of *The Burden of Southern History,* Potter approves of Woodward's views on Southern distinctiveness, but observes, ". . . though Woodward discusses these factors [summarized above] as experiences impinging upon the Southern culture, we still need a dissection of the culture itself on which they impinge."

In his opening essay, "The Enigma of the South," Potter attempts to do this. The essay begins with a convincing attack on the legend of Southern agrarianism, and then proceeds to analyze Ulrich Phillips's thesis that the central theme of Southern history is the determination to preserve a white man's country. Potter observes that, ironically, it took a racist, Phillips, to restore the black man to the center of the Southern stage: Phillips's liberal critics, who logically should have embraced his thesis, allowed themselves to be sidetracked by their revulsion against his prejudices. They could never see that one could readily reverse Phillips's approbation of white supremacy and yet agree to the fact that it is the central theme in Southern history.

Potter strives to transcend the views of Phillips and Woodward on the origins of Southern distinctiveness by examining the folk culture of the South. Southern folk culture, he argues, has tenaciously resisted the onslaught of urbanization and industrialization. Potter is not as specific as one might wish about the content of Southern folk culture; but it is clear that when he refers to it he has in mind such elements as the sense of family, the stress on formal courtesy, and the intense awareness of local community that have characterized Southern life. "It was an aspect of this culture," he writes,

> that the relation between land and people remained more direct and more primal in the South than in other parts of the country. (This may be more true for the Negroes than for the whites, but then there is also a question whether the Negroes have not embodied the distinctive qualities of the Southern character even more than the whites.)

It seems to me that this is a brilliant insight but that Potter leaves it undeveloped. Were he to relate his analysis of Phillips's thesis to this part of his discussion, he would have to shift the locus of his concern with Southern distinctiveness from the fact of racial domination—as important as that question will remain in its own right—to the duality of Southern culture and from the category of race to that of class. If, as I believe, the "central theme" of Afro-American history has been its duality as at once a part of the general American national experience and simultaneously a national experience in itself, then that duality has imparted to the South a folk culture separately black and white and yet both black and white. The northward movement of black people has been therefore—another wonderful irony for Woodward to add to his list—the vehicle for the extension of certain aspects of Southern culture as well as of a distinct Afro-American culture.

Like Woodward, Potter never allows his sympathetic presentation of the Southern experience to descend to apologetics. Far from hiding the naked and brutal economic exploitation at the base of this tradition of community relations, he exposes it to full view and examines the paradox it implies. No other American historian, with the possible exception of Frank Tannenbaum, has so clearly seen the contradictory nature of the slave plantation as a force that on some levels bound two classes and races together in an organic community and yet on other levels, which he seems to regard as decisive, guaranteed their bitter estrangement.

Potter, like Woodward, adds much of our understanding of Southern history, but ultimately the problem he set out to examine eludes him. The difficulty, it seems to me, lies in the failure to face the class question. Both historians discuss class forces and make decisive contributions to a social history of the South; but neither will concede the central role of those class forces which nevertheless constantly break through in their work. As a result, their respective analyses spend their force at the very moment when they are most incisive.

The cultural question that Potter and Woodward raise cannot be understood apart from its class character. This alone, I would suggest, explains the dual nature of Southern society as a reflection of the patriarchal ethos of the ante-bellum ruling class on the one hand, and, on the other, the patterns by which black slaves and white non-slaveholders both resisted and accommodated themselves to those who had power over them. The origin of those Southern cultural elements to which both authors draw attention is unintelligible apart from the plantation setting, at the center of which was the relation between master and slaves. The social and economic forces drawing the non-slaveholders into the widening circle of paternalism and the planters to lordship require a separate and extended analysis, but their roots in plantation life are clear.

Woodward's singular achievement in his great book, *The Origins of the New South,* was to lay the foundations for a coherent and faithful history that brings together economic, cultural, and political forces; but we still need much more work on the persistence of the ante-bellum tradition to the present day, and the intimate relationship between this tradition and the development of class. I fail to see how Southern culture can be explained satisfactorily apart from the character of the slaveholding planters, their dealings with black slave labor, and their hegemony over the white small farmers throughout the countryside. The contradictory elements of Southern culture (those aristocratic-democratic, patriarchal-egalitarian juxtapositions which both Potter and Woodward so valuably describe) are the result of confrontations between classes: on the one hand between masters and slaves, and, on the other, between masters and enfranchised non-slaveholders.

These class relations crystalized as the plantation owners became more powerful and assured in their sense of "lordship"; their persistence must be sought in the nature of the post-bellum ruling class, understood as a new quality; in the emergence of a socially disaffected but racist white yeomanry; and in the continuity and transformation of certain antebellum cultural patterns among the blacks, who passed from one form of dependent labor (slavery) to others (sharecropping, tenancy). Potter and Woodward do not face all the implications of their astute analyses and do not relate Southern culture to its discrete class roots, but they do appreciate fully the positive side of the culture that resulted—a side that has combined the aristocratic sensibilities of the master class with the staying power of the black and white lower classes, each of which learned, in different and often tragically opposed ways, how to survive and preserve considerable social cohesion in a world of exploitation, oppression, and domination.

If Potter and Woodward end by being somewhat vague about the class character of Southern culture, their radical critics are in no position to criticize them. Until recently Marxists have interpreted class forces in American life in an ahistorical (that is, anti-Marxian) way by insisting on the existence of classes of farmers, bourgeois, workers, etc. Yet, the experience of both North and South—not to mention that of the rest of the world—ought by now to have made it clear that social classes are determined by particular national and cultural circumstances. The American working class, as Herbert Gutman demonstrates in several papers on working-class history, soon to be published, cannot be understood apart from a careful study of the diverse cultural origins of the quite different immigrant groups composing it. Black America, as Harold Cruse is forcing the rest of us to see, cannot be understood apart from a painstaking cultural analysis of its constituent classes. But Gutman and Cruse are raising new questions that have yet to be explored adequately.

Thus scholars like Potter and Woodward are, or ought to be, an embarrassment to the Left. Not being imprisoned by arid formulas and dogmas, they have been free to see, with the utmost clarity, the decisive importance of national (and regional) culture for the solution of diverse historical and political problems. Without a serious Marxism to challenge them, however, they have not had to confront what I think is fundamental to a full appreciation of their own work—that the culture they have been dissecting must be understood as part of the class question itself.

One feature of both books requires comment, even if we must pass over many others. The distance traveled by these greatest of Southern historians from the point at which Phillips left off may be measured by their respectful concern with the place of the black man. Woodward treats the black experience in two essays, "Equality: The Deferred Commitment" and "What Happened to the Civil Rights Movement." In both essays he advances a cautious optimism. The first sees a genuine commitment to equality in the Reconstruction period, but recently Woodward has added new doubts and qualifications to those which he originally expressed.

The second essay contrasts the Reconstruction period with the "Second Reconstruction" of the 1950s and early 1960s. Woodward stresses the elements of the predominance of blacks and youth in the Civil Rights Movement and makes some penetrating observations on the conflict of generations in the struggle—and by extension, on current white student radicalism as well. In spite of its power, the essay founders on its integrationist optimism, which is not saved by a grim postscript on Dr. King's assassination. Woodward, himself a courageous veteran, along with many other much abused Southern liberals, of the struggle against racial segregation, cannot accept black separatism in any form. It is his one blind spot and prevents him from confronting black history as an experience that embraces both the information of an ethnically conditioned class and the growth of a separate nationality. As a result, Woodward, whose work, including *The Strange Career of Jim Crow* as well as the essays under review, contains so much of value for a study of Afro-American history, falls short of that mastery of the black Southern experience which he so elegantly demonstrates in his analysis of the Southern experience of the whites.

Potter discusses the role of the blacks in the South only sporadically and seems almost to shy away from it. Yet his discussion of the forces behind the Confederate movement implicitly sheds much light on the black experience. If Potter's book contained nothing but the essay, "The Historian's Use of Nationalism and Vice Versa," it would be worth the price. The argument here is subtle and runs deep, and a quick summary risks distortion. The burden of the argument is that historians have been easily misled into exaggerating the cultural attributes of nationality and generally underestimate the extent to which nations arise from a perceived or real common material interest. He agrees that an awareness of both a common culture and common interests must exist for a nation to take shape. But, he insists, historians must understand that nationalism has two psychological roots, not one, or they will attempt to find a national culture every time they find a growing community of interest.

Antislavery writers more than others, Potter believes, ought to see the extent of the division between the North and South; but their liberal commitment to the notion of national self-determination forces them to deny their own viewpoint. Pro-Southern writers have a similar problem since they must rest their claims for a separate Southern nation on a distinct culture, the elements of which they are hard pressed to describe. Potter, in my view, slights the genuine cultural difference, but his main point—that common material interests generated a conscious effort to develop a separate culture—

is well argued and, by extension, speaks directly to the current black scene. Nationalism, for him, must be understood as an ideological process arising out of both culture and material interest, either of which may be initially feeble but which may grow powerful under the stimulation of the other. His judgment on the Confederacy, even if arguable, might well serve as a critical standpoint from which to assess the sharpening debate between revolutionary black nationalists (especially the Panthers) and cultural nationalists (Karenga, Jones, *et al*):

> The Southern sympathizer finds that his view of the separateness of Southern culture cannot be formed on the merits of the question without reference to his conviction that the South enjoyed a full national identity, which finds its ultimate sanction in the possession of a full-fledged culture. The attribution of culture is evaluative for the question of nationality, just as the question of nationality, in turn, is evaluative for the justification of the acts of a group claiming the right to exercise autonomy.

Potter has much to say about the problem of the nationalism of the Old South and perhaps even more to say about black nationalism. Since the South adjusted quickly to a new place in the Union after Appomatox, Potter reasons that its nationalism could not have been so deeply rooted as, say, that of Poland. What drove the South forward in the 1850s, he suggests, was less a separate national culture than a shared sense of threatened common interests. The North, he adds, fought to overthrow "a vast property interest." But Potter cannot so easily reduce slavery to a matter of "interest," and indeed throughout these essays he provides abundant evidence that the material interests generated by the plantation system were strongly complemented by the slave-master relationship itself. His sudden disparagement of the cultural question therefore appears strained. More to the point, the elements he so trenchantly dissects had their basis in the slave system and most particularly in its ruling class, which commanded that "vast property interest" and necessarily attempted, both consciously and unconsciously, to grasp the moral and intellectual implications of its own existence. All these ingredients Potter gives us. What he does not make explicit is the one thing that holds the discrete parts of his cogent analysis together—the central role of class and its economic, ideological, and political power.

A short while ago a young black nationalist, selected to head a black studies program at a large Eastern university, told *The New York Times* that he might invite one or two whites to participate but that historians like Woodward were another matter. More recently, a leading liberal magazine called upon a learned gentleman from the University of Georgia to review Potter's book, and he wrote that Potter was a Southern apologist and a no-account thinker. This ideological hatchet work has its counterpart in a sharpening attack on the growing number of leftwing historians who unashamedly admit to having infinitely more admiration for the work of these "bourgeois" scholars than they do for most of their radical critics. No one has a right to complain, not even those who do not regard rough polemics as a welcome relief from the boredom of academic life. In fact, if the most one suffers these days in the ivory tower is verbal or written assault, one should be grateful. Without complaint, I should like to exercise the reviewer's prerogative of ending on a personal note.

Not surprisingly, I was recently treated to a dose of the inanity to which Woodward and Potter (not to mention William Styron, Stanley Elkins, and many others) were subjected. At the risk of seeming self-serving, I think the following incident is relevant to the difficulties in establishing a rational line of criticism about Southern matters. The leftwing scholarly journal, *Science & Society,* which enjoys a well-deserved reputation for factionalism and an easy attitude toward the truth, published a lengthy series of falsehoods designed to show that I equate the slave South with the Union and that I am ethically neutral, if not downright pro-Confederate, in my views on the War. The details of the attacks on Styron and Elkins as racists, on Potter as a Southern apologist, on Woodward as the Lord knows what, and on me as soft on Jefferson Davis—are unimportant. What is serious in this familiar scenario of ideological malice is the persistent unwillingness of so many radicals, as well as liberals, to confront conservative criticism of their assumptions.

Potter and Woodward have argued that Southern history has been deeply paradoxical and that its most gruesome features have engendered powerful qualities worthy of respect and preservation. If I read them correctly, they would accept the view that even slavery—that most foul of modern social systems—bequeathed, in spite of itself, important achievements to future generations. How many Americans, for example, including the most radical, continue to admire the personal quality, political ideals, and historical legacy of the early generations of Virginia slaveholders? Somehow everything reactionary in Jefferson, Madison, and Washington, is supposed to have emanated from their slaveownership, but everything noble and wholesome is supposed to have been a gift of God. Such a view is not serious, and the paradox it obscures presents precisely the kind of problem to which Potter and Woodward have applied their exceptional talent. If they had done no more than to force us to think about the contradictory nature of the Southern legacy, we would owe them much.

Are they then, after all, and are their radical admirers, apologists for Southern reaction or indifferent to the moral issues in the struggle between slavery and freedom? Hardly. They take the immorality of slavery racism as undeniable but recognize that much of lasting value had its roots in the original injustice. Those folkways to which Potter draws attention, for example, today represent an important and potentially radical force against capitalist values; that they were once organically linked to a reactionary social order provides Woodward with further irony but is not his responsibility.

The critical position Potter and Woodward share is the opposite of any apologetics, for it provides a base from which to attack the reactionary origins of the Southern heritage and simultaneously transforms that heritage into a weapon of criticism against prevailing national values. If anything, they ought to be criticized for not going far enough. I have argued elsewhere and at some length that the slaveholders were deeply committed to slavery as a way of life, not just as a way of making money, and that they were essentially men of principle. There has been no shortage of idiots, or even of scholars who should know better, to conclude—contrary to the evidence and all reason—that I equate the Union and Confederate causes and remain ethically neutral.

In fact—as conservative critics have had no trouble in understanding—the point is the reverse: Since they were men of honor and subjective morality, and since they defended an objectively immoral system for which they must be held responsible, the slaveholders could not have been frightened into submission or bought off. If a radical regional revolution and the genuine liberation of black people were to be effected, the slaveholders as a class would have had to be exterminated. As Southern apologetics go, I am not aware that these have ever been received with enthusiasm by their ostensible beneficiaries.

Woodward and Potter do not see the issue in such terms; as anti-Marxists who reject the idea that class confrontation is of central importance, they cannot do so and would probably recoil at such conclusions. But in their own terms they have brilliantly faced, and compelled their honest opponents to face, the problems of class power, with all the irony and tragedy contained therein. It ought then to be obvious why they find an increasing number of admirers on the Left. For all their ideological disagreements, they have set an example for us by rising far above their biases to pose the major problems; by paying respectful attention to opposing points of view; and by bringing strong understanding and scholarship to bear on burning questions. Historians on the Left have a long way to go to match, much less transcend, their performance.

NOTE

1. David Potter, *The South and The Sectional Conflict* (Baton Rouge, 1969); C. Vann Woodward, *The Burden of Southern History,* rev. ed. (Baton Rouge, 1968).

Chapter 15

MARXIAN INTERPRETATIONS OF THE SLAVE SOUTH*

A science which hesitates to forget its founders is lost.

—ALFRED NORTH WHITEHEAD

Je ne suis pas un marxiste. —KARL MARX

AMERICAN MARXISM has had a curious history; in a sense, it has not so much had a history as a series of aborted births. In the political realm the experience of the last half-century has been unpleasant: the large and promising Socialist party of the World War I era went to pieces and the impressive stirrings of the Communist party during the 1930s have culminated in the pathetic exhortations of a beleaguered sect kept alive by government persecution and a franchise from the slight remains of a world movement. The political record, however disappointing, constitutes a history; the same could only be said for the intellectual record if one were determined to display Christian charity. In the early period Marxian thought, typified perhaps in the historical writing of Algie M. Simons, rarely rose above the level of economic determinism. In the 1930s the economic determinism remained

This essay was originally published in Barton J. Bernstein, ed., *Towards a New Past: Dissenting Essays in American History* (New York, Pantheon Books, 1968), pp. 90–125.

but was encased in the romanticization of the lower classes. The workers, farmers, and Negroes increasingly became the objects of affection and adulation. In both periods the political movement was on the upswing, and the prime function of theory, and especially of the interpretation of history, was assumed to be to provide a justification for the revolutionary cause by uncovering roots in American experience and to give the intellectuals and the masses a sense of a common and inevitably victorious destiny.

Most American Marxian historians of any reputation came out of the generation of the 1930s. The depression helped forge them as Communists, but the advance of fascism and the threat to the survival of the world's only socialist state in some ways had a more profound impact. The racist doctrines of the German fascists led Marxists, as well as others, to reaffirm their commitment to racial equality and to view with intense hostility any critical comment on Jews, Negroes, or other peoples. The possibility of a fascist victory led them to to seek allies in a defensive Popular Front, which despite rhetoric and appearance generally produced ideological as well as political capitulation to New Deal liberalism. The Communist party's search for an alliance with liberals, from Roosevelt to the Kennedys, has stressed the possibilities of working with the "progressive" sections of the bourgeoisie against the "reactionary" sections. In practice this policy has meant support for those who have been willing to accede to a modus vivendi with the U.S.S.R. in return for the sterilization of the revolutionary forces in the world generally and the underdeveloped countries in particular. For American Marxian historiography it has meant a lack of concern with class forces and the process of capitalist development in favor of the pseudo-radical division of historical categories into "progressive" and "reactionary," which has generally been translated into the glorification of the Jefferson-Jackson-Roosevelt liberal tradition and the denigration of the evil men of the Right. This parlor game, so reminiscent of liberals like Parrington and Josephson, spiced with leftist jargon and a few words about the masses and the revolutionary heritage, has passed for Marxism.

Popular Front liberalism has by no means been merely a product of the political exigencies of the 1930s; it has deep roots in the history of the American working class. From the beginning the working class has held full political rights within a bourgeois-democratic republic that has been one of the modern world's great success stories. Presided over by a powerful, confident bourgeoisie, which has had to face serious internal opposition only once in its life and which crushed that opposition during the war of 1861–1865, American capitalism has generally been able to divert, placate, and buy the potentially troublesome sections of its working class. Without much possibility of building a revolutionary working-class movement in the near future, more and more Marxists have turned in despair to an illusory "people's movement" against entrenched privilege and have taken this alleged movement to be the principal manifestation of the class struggle in America. For the specific subject at hand—the slave South—the results were predictable. The slaveholders naturally and wonderfully qualify as reactionaries and defenders of an entrenched privilege, which of course they were, and important sections of the bourgeoisie qualify as candidates for membership in a progressive coalition, which they, in the same sense, also were. All that is missing from this viewpoint is an awareness of the process of capitalist development and of the metamorphosis of the bourgeoisie—that is, all that is missing is the essence of a Marxian analysis.

For Popular Front Marxists—that is, for liberals with radical pretensions—the slave South constitutes a nightmare. It is not so much that it conjures up the full horror of white supremacy and chattel slavery, although the emotional reaction to these has been both genuine and understandable; it is rather that the slaveholders presented the only politically powerful challenge to liberal capitalism to emanate from within the United States. It was they, especially in the brilliant polemics of George Fitzhugh but also in the writings of Calhoun, Holmes, Hughes, Hammond, Ruffin, and others, who questioned the assumptions of liberal society, denounced the hypocrisy and barbarism of the marketplace, and advanced a vision of an organic society and a collective community. That their critique was self-serving and their alternative reactionary need not detain us. As in the European tradition of feudal socialism, the self-serving and reactionary can prove illuminating and, in the most profound sense, critical. The commitment of American Marxists to Popular Front liberalism has prevented them from taking the ideology of the slave South seriously. As a result, they have been unable to reconstruct the historical reality and have been unwilling to admit that certain elements of the slaveholders' ideology deserve the attention and respect of those who would build a socialist order. It is no accident that the one American socialist historian to glimpse these possibilities, William Appleman Williams, is more of a Christian than a Marxist.

Even the strongest proponents of Marxism must admit that Marxian historical writing in the United States has been something less than a cause for rejoicing and that it has not approached the level attained by such English Marxists as Christopher Hill, Eric J. Hobsbawm, and E. P. Thompson. Marxian writing on the slave South and the origins of the secession crisis looks especially weak when ranked alongside work done on Brazilian slave society by such Marxists as Caio Prado Júnior, Octávio Ianni, and Fernando Henrique Cardoso.[1] The record is so poor that we would be justified in ignoring it, if it had not become so curiously influential in traditional circles and if Marxism did not have so much to contribute to the interpretation of American history.

The paradoxical juxtaposition of ostensible Marxian influence and the low level of Marxian performance arises in part out of the widespread confusion of Marxism with economic determinism. American historians, especially the most harshly anti-Marxian, generally confuse the two and then, since economic determinism is easy to refute, dismiss Marxism as being of no value. This game would prove entertaining, were it not that these same historians so often retreat into banal economic explanations to suit their convenience. How often does one find discussions of the profitability of slavery embracing the assumption that one or another accounting result would explain the course of political events? Or that the idea of an irrepressible conflict between North and South has to stand on proof of an unnegotiable economic antagonism? Or that proof of natural limits to slavery expansion would constitute proof that the slave system, left to itself, would evolve into something else? These and even cruder notions run through the literature, and their equivalents infect much of American history. The fountainhead of this tendency has been the work of Charles Beard. When his line of thought has proven useful for conservative or liberal purposes, his arguments have been appropriated and his name more often than not dropped; when it has proven an obstacle, his name has been remembered and linked with Marxism in order to discredit him. Yet, a concern for "economics," and more to the point, for "classes," has been irresistible even for his most caustic critics. Marxism has both fed the stream of economic interpretation and been contaminated by it.

Of greater importance is what Marxism, shorn of its romanticism and superficial economic determinist trappings, might offer. That it has not accomplished more has been due to many things, not the least of which have been the periodic purges of Marxists from our universities and the venal treatment meted out by professional associations and learned journals. (It would be wonderful fun to list the respected and influential historians who have protected their jobs and their families by eschewing the Marxist label while writing from a Marxian viewpoint and even greater fun to recount the multitude of ways in which the profession has misunderstood what they are in fact doing and saying.) More fundamental, however, has been the misrepresentation of Marxism by our official Marxist historians—that is, by those who have written with the blessings of the more important, if also the most morally discredited, political organizations. These blessings have proven a double joy: to the writers in question, generally although by no means always men of little talent, they have provided high status in a limited but adoring circle; to the profession as a whole, ever anxious to identify Marxism with imbecility, they have provided the perfect straw men. They have converged—I almost said conspired—to present Marxism on the general level as economic determinism and on the level of specific analysis as some variation of moralistic fatalism. We may properly suspect that Herbert Aptheker's grand pronouncement would simultaneously have convulsed Marx with laughter and raised his temper to the boiling point: "There is an immutable justice in history, and the law of dialectical development works its inexorable way."[2] For the liberals, statements such as this prove Marxism's uselessness; for the illiterates among the political faithful of the Left, they offer consolation in a period of defeat. All they fail to do is to present Marxian thought seriously and therefore to provide the slightest genuine utility for a political movement that seeks to alter the existing order.

Perhaps the strongest indication of the power of Marxian analysis, even its more vulgar forms, has been the extent to which class analysis has intruded itself into American history despite the contempt poured out on "Marxian economic determinism." For this reason alone a careful review of Marxian interpretations of a defined portion of American history has its uses. If vulgar Marxism and simplistic economic interpretations have, as is generally conceded, somehow illuminated the subject, Marxism, purged of its adolescent cravings for neat packages and the easy way, ought to be able to do much more. The first task is to see clearly and specifically what has gone wrong.

Would it not be incongruous for Marxists to believe in original sin, we might trace our embarrassment to our fathers, for, in truth they are guilty; but it is incumbent upon us to be charitable, for their guilt is less than that of their descendants. Marx and Engels restricted themselves to journalistic pieces on the secession crisis and never attempted that kind of analysis of class dynamics which we have come to call Marxian. As political journalism their writings are of a high order and ought to give their admirers no cause to blush.[3] As Professor Runkle, hardly a friendly critic, has shown, their writings display remarkable insight into a wide variety of political and military problems and still repay careful reading.[4] It is not their fault that later generations of epigoni have canonized them and insisted on the value of every word, have mistaken political commitment for historical analysis, and have done violence to Marxism by defending positions taken by Marx and Engels on matters to which they devoted little study. Marx and Engels probably had not read much more than Olmsted's travel accounts and J. E. Cairnes's *The Slave Power*, which is hardly unimpeachable even as a secondary source; their writings show little special acquaintanceship with Southern life and history. Political journalism, even at its best, often breathes passionate commitment, which rarely facilitates sober historical analysis. We need not side with those who would transform Marx into a nonpartisan sociologist—those who would draw his revolutionary teeth in the manner of the European Social Democrats—to recognize that his burning hatred of slavery and commitment to the Union cause interfered with his judgment. It need not have been so, for as Karl Kautsky observes, if the socialist movement genuinely believes that history is on its side, it can profit only from the truth, no matter how disadvantageous in the short run, and can only lose by politically expedient fabrications.[5] It was proper for Marx to hate slavery and to throw his efforts into organizing the European proletariat against it; it was neither proper nor necessary for him to permit his partisanship to lead to a gross underestimation of the slaveholding class and to an ambiguous assessment of the origins of the war.

It would be comfortable to account for the weakness in the performance of Marx and Engels wholly by reference to their political engagement and thereby, in a sense, to acquit them at the expense of their successors. There is, however, a deeper difficulty. The Marxian interpretation of history contains an undeniable ambiguity, which creates a dangerous tendency toward economic determinism—that vulgar and useless historical dogma. Even Marx's preface to *The Critique of Political Economy,* which remains the best brief statement of the Marxian viewpoint, may be reduced to economic determinism, not to mention such politically serviceable if historically simplistic notions as the unilinear theory of history.[6] As a general and preliminary statement, the preface[7] leaves little to be desired, but it does, by its necessarily schematic form, lend itself to economic, unilinear, and other deterministic interpretations. To be understood properly—I refer not to what Marx "really meant" but to what is meaningful in his thought—passages such as this must be understood in the context of his life's work. The Hegelian and dialectical side of Marx's thought cannot be introduced and dropped at will; it constitutes an integral part of its core and renders, on principle, all forms of mechanism foreign to its nature.

Marx and Engels tell us that ideas grow out of social existence, but have a life of their own. A particular base (mode of production) will generate a corresponding superstructure (political system, complex of ideologies, culture, etc.), but that superstructure will develop according to its own logic as well as in response to the development of the base. If, for example, the crisis of ancient slave society produced the Christian religion, the development of its theology would still depend—and in fact has depended—significantly on its own internal logic and structure as well as on social changes. The staying power of such a religion would depend, therefore, on the flexibility of its leaders in overcoming unavoidable contradictions between internal and external lines of development.[8]

If ideas, once called into being as a social force, have a life of their own, then it follows that no analysis of the base is possible without consideration of the superstructure it engenders since the development of that superstructure is determined only partially by its orgins, and since any changes in the superstructure, including those generated by its inner logic, must modify the base itself. If, from the Marxian point of view, classes and class struggles are at the center of historical transformations,[9] then economic determinism, in any of its forms, can have no place in Marxism. The confusion between Marxism and economic determinism arises from the Marxian definition of classes as groups, the members of which stand in a particular relationship to the means of production. This definition is essentially "economic" but only in the broadest sense. Broad or narrow, there is no excuse for identifying the economic origins of a social class with the developing nature of that class, which necessarily embraces the full range of its human experience in its manifold political, social, economic, and cultural manifestations. That the economic interests of a particular class will necessarily prove more important to its specific behavior than, say, its religious values, is an ahistorical and therefore un-Marxian assumption. Since those values are conditioned only originally and broadly by the economy, and since they develop according to their own inner logic and in conflict with other such values, as well as according to social changes, an economic interpretation of religion can at best serve as a first approximation and might even prove largely useless.

On a more general level the distinction between "objective" and "subjective" forces in history, which so persistently fascinates dogmatic Marxists, ends by making a mockery of dialectical analysis. As the great Italian Marxist, Antonio

Gramsci, observes after noting Marx's more sophisticated statements on the role of ideas: "The analysis of these statements, I believe, reinforces the notion of 'historical bloc,' in which the material forces are the content and ideologies the form—merely an analytical distinction since material forces would be historically inconceivable without form and since ideologies would have to be considered individual dabbling without material forces."[10] The decisive element in historical development, from a Marxian point of view, is class struggle, an understanding of which presupposes a specific historical analysis of the constituent classes. Such an analysis must recognize the sociological uniqueness of every social class as the product of a configuration of economic interests, a semi-autonomous culture, and a particular world outlook; and it must recognize the historical uniqueness of these classes as the product of the evolution of that culture and world outlook in relation to, but not wholly subordinate to, those economic interests. If certain kinds of economic threats sometimes shake a society more severely than do other kinds of threats, it is only because they ordinarily strike more closely at the existence of the ruling class. Most ruling classes have been wise enough to know, however, that particular ideological challenges can be quite as dangerous as economic ones, and that no challenge need be taken seriously unless it presents itself, at least potentially, on the terrain of politics.

If Marxism is misrepresented as economic determinism by friends as well as foes, Marx and Engels are partly responsible. As Gramsci observes, Karl Marx, "the writer of *concrete* historical works," was not guilty of such naiveté,[11] but as the statement implies, Karl Marx, the journalist and essayist, cannot always be acquitted. With a tendency toward economic interpretation and an intellectually undisciplined political passion, Marx and Engels left us nothing close to a coherent and comprehensive critique of the slave South. In view of how hard our official Marxists have been working to conceal this fact, one would suppose they think Marxism too fragile to withstand the revelation.

Nowhere do Marx or Engels examine systematically the origins, history, ideology, or character of the slaveholding class; yet without such an examination no "Marxian" analysis is possible. Instead, they resort to ridicule and charge hypocrisy and cynicism. At times their writings come close to demagogy. "The Confederate Congress," writes Marx, "boasted that its new-fangled Constitution, as distinguished from the Constitution of the Washingtons, Jeffersons, and Adamses, had recognized for the first time slavery as a thing good in itself, a bulwark of civilization, and a divine institution."[12] These sentiments he branded as "cynical confessions." He cheered signs that the North was ready to deal with these upstarts and to return the Union "to the true principles of its development."[13] Marx and Engels denied the legitimacy of Southern claims. North and South, they wrote, form one country. "The South, however, is neither a territory strictly detached from the North geographically, nor a moral unity. It is not a country at all, but a battle cry."[14] These assertions could do very well to rally support to the Union, which is what they were supposed to do, but they go down hard as serious assessment.

In a more sober moment they wrote: "The present struggle between the South and North is, therefore, nothing but a struggle between two social systems, the system of slavery and the system of free labor."[15] If we are to admit of two social systems in the country and if, as we must, we recognize that they occupied substantially different territory, what are we to make of the contemptuous rejections of Southern claims to legitimacy? When the Confederates proudly proclaimed the defense of slavery, they were being neither cynical nor hypocritical but honest. The corresponding values, ethos, and standards of civilization represented their social system as properly as those of the bourgeoisie represented Northern capitalism. Between the Revolution and the War for Southern Independence, the slaveholders took long strides toward the perfection of a world view of their own. In their political, social, and economic thought they steadily sloughed off those liberal-bourgeois elements of the Virginia Tidewater tradition, which had, in any case, never struck deep social roots. Even in the early national period, John Taylor of Caroline and John Randolph of Roanoke, not to mention the lesser lights of Virginia and South Carolina, advanced, in however a contradictory way, essential ideas for a conservative Southern philosophy. Step by step, from Thomas Cooper to Thomas Roderick Dew to John C. Calhoun to George Fitzhugh, we may trace the formation of a political and social philosophy singularly appropriate to the defense of the plantation regime. On another level, several forces combined to generate a peculiar ethos among the slaveholders. With the closing of the African slave trade in 1808, slave prices rose sharply, and slaveholders had to depend on the natural increase of their labor force or on purchases in the older areas, which was the same thing once removed. Improvement in the material conditions of slave life became the order of the day and with it a growing rationale of paternalistic responsibility. At the same time these very conditions slowly generated an almost wholly American-born slave force and narrowed the cultural gap between master and slave and between white and black. When the abolitionist onslaught began, the slaveholders, reigning as resident lords over dependent human beings, had only to look about them and into their own souls to discover that they held values and social attitudes at variance with those of their Northern contemporaries, and that they and the abolitionists did not speak the same language or live in the same world. The slaveholders, in short, matured as a ruling class and with increasing self-consciousness came to stand for a social system of a distinct type. If the legitimacy of their ideology is not understood, it will not be possible to estimate the strength of their system and its peculiar forms of class rule. Marx and Engels badly misjudged these men and their society, but then so have virtually all the liberal historians and not a few conservatives. So appalling is the idea of slavery to our historians, as to Marx and Engels, that they vigorously resist crediting it with the formation of a respectable and authentic ideology and way of life. In their insistence on treating the slaveholders' ideology as a rationalization for plunder, as something unworthy of attention and analysis except as mere apologetics, Marx and Engels assume a liberal stance. The correspondence between their view and the view of the liberals and vulgar Marxists on this question stems less from the positive influence of Marxism over our liberal historians than from the retreat of Marx, Engels, and too many Marxists into liberalism. Ironically, to criticize Marx and Engels on this particular question, as on some others, means to criticize certain features of American liberal dogma. Marxism, however, necessarily brings into historical analysis a central concern with the process by which ruling classes arise and establish their hegemony and offers an indispensable framework for the study of the civilization of the slave South.

The denial of Southern legitimacy had a more serious effect than an underestimation of the slaveholders; it introduced a curious ambiguity into the notion of "social systems" itself. Rather than admit the territoriality of these systems, with everything it implies, they interpret the struggle strictly as a class struggle within the Union as a whole.[16] The concentration of the slave system in one part of the country is not considered of great importance. Most subsequent Marxists, as well as the Beards and their followers, insist on the same point and thereby sacrifice historical reality to the need to fit the conflict into a unilinear model of world development. Marx and Engels, followed somewhat more cautiously by the Beards, argue that the South desired not an independent existence but the reorganization of the Union on a slaveholding basis. A Confederate victory, they insist, would have eventually detached the Northwest from the Union: "In the

Northern states, where Negro slavery is in practice unworkable, the white working class would gradually be forced down to the level of helotry."[17] In more strident terms Marx wrote Lincoln on behalf of the International Workingmen's Association:

> Counterrevolution, with systematic thoroughness, gloried in rescinding "the ideas entertained at the time of the Old Constitution," and maintained "slavery to be a beneficent institution, indeed the only solution of the great problem of the relation of labor to capital," and cynically proclaimed property in man "the cornerstone of the new edifice"; then the working classes of Europe understood at once, even before the fanatical partisanship of the upper classes for the Confederate gentry had given its dismal warning, that the slaveholders' rebellion was to sound the tocsin for a general holy crusade of property against labor . . . .[18]

That a Confederate victory would have strengthened reaction internationally and confronted the working classes with new dangers cannot be denied, but Marx's exaggerations open the way for a series of dubious assertions. The fear that the South might conquer the Union for slavery deserves to be taken only slightly more seriously than Marx's charge in 1863 that Union military reverses suggested treason. Certainly, the Confederates would have liked to take Chicago and New York—why not?—but few thought it remotely possible. Confederate imperialist ambitions extended to the South and Southwest. Yet, so bound are Marx and Engels to this notion that without a shred of evidence they proceeded to this astounding appraisal of the outbreak of hostilities: "The secessionists resolved to force the Union government out of its passive attitude by a sensational act of war, and *solely for this reason* proceeded to the bombardment of Fort Sumter . . . ."[19]

The worst feature of this nightmare is its negation of an excellent insight on the role of the Northwest. Marx and Engels were among the first to realize that the agrarian Northwest, contrary to all simplistic notions of an irreconcilable struggle between agrarianism and industrialism, would stand with the Northeast against the South and would be much more militant about it. They write, in terms economic determinists are not likely to appreciate, that the Northwest was "a power that was not inclined by tradition, temperament, or mode of life to let itself be dragged from compromise to compromise in the manner of the Northern states."[20] This judgment, based on newspaper and other ordinary sources of information, flows from their profound grasp of the process of capitalist development; it is neither mere guesswork nor hasty but lucky extrapolation. Their study of the history and economic theory of capitalism enables them in this case to project their data legitimately and to excellent effect. Their analysis of the course of American development corresponds to their brilliant treatment of the agrarian origins of capitalism in Europe and of the revolutionary role of the small producers.[21] It is, therefore, discouraging to watch them tremble at the danger that the Confederates would win the Northwest by threatening to close the Mississippi.[22] This retreat into economic interpretation might have been a politically useful gambit, but does not reflect well on their analysis. Apart from its dismissal of those traditions and sentiments which ought to have led the Northwestern classes to other solutions, it overlooks the central economic point. The Northwest, as Marx and Engels say, formed part of a developing national economy; hence, theoretically and in fact, its economic ties with the Northeast were steadily tightening at the expense of those with the South. Railroads east to west, not the Mississippi River north to south, proved decisive, and if they had not already been built, no economic law or Southern economic aggression could have prevented their being built. The argument of Marx and Engels makes sense only on the crude economic-determinist assumptions that they so contemptuously and rightfully toss aside.

The discussion of slavery expansionism, for which they owe a considerable debt to the liberal economist J. E. Cairnes's influential book *The Slave Power,* constituted the most impressive part of their historical analysis, if we put aside their acute observations on military and international affairs:

> By force of circumstances South Carolina is already transformed in part into a slave-raising state, since it already sells slaves to the states of the extreme South and Southwest for four million dollars yearly. As soon as this point is reached, the acquisition of new Territories becomes necessary in order that one section of the slaveholders may equip new, fertile landed estates with slaves and in order that by this means a new market for slave-raising, therefore for the sale of slaves, may be created for the section left behind it. It is, for example, indubitable that without the acquisition of Louisiana, Missouri and Arkansas by the United States, slavery would long ago have been wiped out. In the secessionist Congress at Montgomery, Senator Toombs, one of the spokesmen of the South, has strikingly formulated the economic law that commands the constant expansion of the territory of slavery. "In fifteen years more," said he, "without a great increase in slave territory, either the slaves must be permitted to flee from the whites, or the whites must flee from the slaves."[23]

This passage contains a clause that sets it apart from many contemporary ideas and from such well-known theses as those of Weber, Ramsdell, and Phillips: that in Virginia and Maryland ". . . slavery would long ago have been wiped out." For Marx and Engels the political, not the economic, side of the process would have been decisive, the implication being that acute economic distress in the midst of a society with warring ideologies would have generated a new relationship of class forces. They ridicule the idea that economic laws would lead to the extinction of slavery. As Marx observes, those economic laws were understood perfectly by the slaveholders, who were using their political and military power to stay them. In discussing the origins of slavery expansionism, they stress three things: economic pressure, the balance of political power in the Union, and the exigencies created by an uneasy rule over the non-slaveholders. Each of these represents an aspect of the class rule of the slaveholders. What is most clearly missing is an adequate treatment of the ideological side and therefore of the problem of hegemony.[24] The omission in part results from and in part causes their exaggeration of the place of the yeomanry in the strategy and tactics of the ruling class.[25]

The hegemony of the slaveholders extended over urban and rural classes but has been little studied. In particular, we need to examine the specific economic, political, social, and psychological relationships between each of these quite distinct classes and strata and the ruling slaveholders. If we take the industrialists as a case in point, their supine loyalty to the regime becomes no mystery when they are studied as a specific historical class rather than as a historical abstraction of such classes. Much of their capital came from surpluses accumulated by the planters; many of the industrialists themselves were planters or from planter families; their corporate charters and political existence were dependent on planter-dominated legislatures; and much of their market consisted of the plantations. These and other ties bound the industrialists, as individuals and even as an economic stratum, narrowly considered, to the regime, although their class interests, which might hypothetically be constructed as a program for the expansion of the South's industrial base and of the power of its industrialists, clearly required the overthrow of slavery. Marxian economic historians, notably Maurice Dobb in his groundbreaking *Studies in the Development of Capitalism,* explore the reasons for and mechanisms by which the commercial bourgeoisie normally serves the existing order instead of trying to overthrow it. As a class that profits from existing arrangements and stands to lose everything by social disruption, their prime ambition normally is to expand their share of the profits being siphoned from the productive mechanism. Any abrupt change in that mechanism threatens them with disaster. Dobb demonstrates, in particular, the conservative and at times reactionary role played by the commercial bourgeoisie during the revolutionary upheavals that accompanied capitalism's rise as a social system. Eric Hobsbawm, in his work on the seventeenth century, questions the rigid dichotomy that Dobb, following Marx, makes between industrial and commercial capitalists, and suggests the need for closer analysis of particular strata within these classes. Thus, he argues, important entrenched sections of industrial capital can, and during the seventeenth century did, play a similarly reactionary role. So, we may add, did the industrialists of the slave South. These questions, which concern the notion of class and class rule, ought to be at the center of all Marxian historical analysis, but like most liberals who write on slavery and the Negro, American Marxists have generally been preoccupied with narrow economic analysis or, worse, with the romanticization of the submerged classes.

Marx and Engels themselves exaggerate the degree of class conflict in the South. Secession, they argue, was a *coup d'état* against the non-slaveholders. In particular they insist that the masses of the border states were pro-Union and held down only by their political inexperience. Their discussion is marred by contradictory judgments and ignorance. Nowhere do they analyze the class structure to distinguish among such groups as self-sufficient upcountry farmers, black-belt yeomen, agricultural laborers, and poor whites. When convenient, they are "poor white trash," good only for brigandage and for frightening the slaveholders by their nihilism. In general, we are offered a two-class white South.[26] The potentially revolutionary masses of 1861 become the white trash of

1865. Thus, Engels to Marx on July 15, 1865: "The mean whites, I think, will gradually die out. With this stock there is nothing to be done; what is left after two generations will merge with the migrants into a stock entirely different.[27] We need not inquire into the accuracy of such judgments, based as they are on little more than a few tendentious books, but we cannot ignore the total failure to confront the problem of hegemony—to try to discover the economic, political, social, cultural, and psychological bonds binding the masses to the ruling class.[28]

The other side of their misunderstanding, or lack of curiosity, about the essentials of the slaveholding rule is their assessment of Northern society. It all depends on mood and the vicissitudes of battle. Thus, "The manner in which the North wages war," writes Marx to Engels, "is only to be expected from a *bourgeois* republic, where fraud has so long reigned supreme."[29] Thus, Engels to Marx: "I must say that I cannot work up much enthusiasm for a people which on such a colossal issue allows itself to be continually beaten by a fourth of its own population and which has achieved nothing more than the discovery that all its generals are idiots and all its officials rascals and traitors. After all, the thing must happen differently, even in a bourgeois republic, if it is not to end in utter failure.[30] Marx replies ten days later that Northern corruption and stupidity serve some purpose, for at least "the bourgeois republic exposes itself in thoroughgoing fashion, so that in future it can never again be preached on its own merits but solely as a means and a form of transition to the social revolution . . . ."[31] And again in 1864, when predicting Lincoln's re-election, Marx writes to Engels, "In the model country of the democratic swindle this election time is full of contingencies . . . ."[32] In the light of these hard but not unfair judgments, what are we to make of some other pronouncements, except to suspect a combination of wishful thinking and political opportunism?

In the "Address of the International Workingmen's Association to Abraham Lincoln" Marx refers to the Northern workers as "the true political power of the North."[33] Not content with this excursion into fantasy, he adds that the international workers' movement considers "it an earnest of the epoch to come that it fell to the lot of Abraham Lincoln, the single-minded son of the working class, to lead his country through the matchless struggle for the rescue of an enchained race and the reconstruction of a social world."[34] This would seem quite a feat to expect from the leader of a bourgeois republic in which fraud reigns supreme and which has thoroughly exposed itself. Yet, this obviously self-serving cant is taken at face value even by so sober a Marxian historian as Philip S. Foner, who labors to save the "proletarian" character of the struggle. Marx puts himself in a box. If the South represented the counterrevolution of property, why should the Northern bourgeoisie be its most determined adversary? It is, accordingly, necessary to invent a labor-based antislavery movement and then to attribute to it a major share of regional power or at least a decisive role in pushing a reluctant bourgeoisie to the left.[35] Foner, who did excellent work on the New York merchants, comes close to judging the Northern bourgeoisie by its most vacillating and Southern-oriented section.[36] Most Marxists continue to write in this way, although William Z. Foster, in his superficial but occasionally shrewd *Outline Political History of the Americas,* after a verbal bow to the heroism of the Northern workers, places the leadership in the hands of the industrial bourgeoisie.[37] Foner flirts with improper extrapolations from his conscientious but limited study and does not attempt a full analysis of the Southern regime. In his *History of the Labor Movement in the United States,* the first volume of which has much to say about the conditions and attitudes of labor, he does not discuss the nature of the war itself. In *Business & Slavery* he explicitly presents a modified Beardian thesis. Marx and Engels, for their part, limit themselves to political exhortations when publicly discussing some of the most important questions.[38]

In the end Marx and Engels regain their balance. During the early phase of Reconstruction, Marx writes: "The American Civil War brought in its train a colossal national debt, and with it the pressure of taxes, the rise of the vilest financial aristocracy, the squandering of a huge part of the public land on speculative companies for the exploitation of railways, mines, etc., in brief, the most rapid centralization of capital. The great republic has, therefore, ceased to be the promised land for emigrant laborers."[39] Gone is the working class that supposedly constituted the real power. Marx and Engels normally do not idealize the working classes or exaggerate their virtues, although their claims, and those of their successors, that the British working class prevented intervention, are unwarranted. As Royden Harrison convincingly demonstrates, the British workers did not mobilize in defense of the Union until other forces had already compelled the government to abandon any idea of intervening on the Confederate side.[40]

The opportunism is more disturbing. On February 2, 1862, writing in *Die Presse,* they praise the workers' "obstinacy" in resisting, by silence or open hostility, efforts to panic them into interventionism.[41] Later in the same year, Marx writes to Engels: "During this recent period England has disgraced herself more than any other country, the workers by their christian slave nature, the bourgeois and aristocrats by their enthusiasm for slavery in its most direct form. But the two manifestations supplement one another."[42] Between the mechanistic tendencies in their thought and these opportunistic and uninformed assertions they badly cluttered the legacy they left their successors, but there is no excuse for surrendering the class analysis of history, which was the highest product of their genius, in order to embrace what is tangential and superficial in their remarkable life's work.[43]

The response of avowed Marxists to these writings of Marx and Engels is drearily revealing. Somehow, there is not a critical word in sight; the masters' writings apparently contain no mistakes. We shall consider only Herbert Aptheker's review and Richard Enmale's introduction to *The Civil War in the United States.* Aptheker, writing in *New Masses,* insists that Marx and Engels were right about everything, including the details of the role of Northern wheat in the British economy, the central contribution of the British working class in preventing intervention, and various other judgments that no longer seem flawless to everyone. Finally, Aptheker asks how Marx and Engels could have seen so much and predicted so well: "Marx and Engels brought into their analysis of the present their historical materialism—their theory of the fundamental significance of the forces of production in explaining human events, and the shaping of these events in the cauldron of class struggle . . . . This book is one more evidence of the scientific nature of Marxism, for it passes the ultimate test of science—accuracy of prediction, and significance for the future."[44] Of such is the Kingdom of Heaven.

Enmale presents the official Marxist version which, despite years of professional advances and the development of Marxian thought, still somehow survives as the only version acceptable in party circles. It is a version that shares everything essential with the liberals while it berates them for ignoring the workers and Negroes. As such, it constitutes a perfect illustration of how the notion of Popular Front can and generally does end in ideological as well as political capitulation to those being courted. Since more and more liberals in this field are coming to study the Negroes with an attention and sympathy equal to those of the Marxists, the gap between the two groups of historians is steadily narrowing, and we may soon look forward to open concubinage—the liberals, of course, would never hear of marriage.

Enmale praises Charles Beard—it is astonishing how easily

poor Mary disappears—and Arthur C. Cole for recognizing the war as a conflict of two social systems, but adds:

> The work of Beard and Cole, though containing much useful material, suffers from certain limitations inherent in the liberal bourgeois approach . . . . Failing to appreciate fully the dynamics of historical development, liberal bourgeois historians do not clearly distinguish between the class forces at work. This leads them to ignore some of the most significant revolutionary phenomena of the period. Not least is the part played by the American working class in bringing the Civil War to a successful conclusion.[45]

We have seen how Marx and Engels treat the working class. As for the Negroes, to whom Enmale subsequently refers in a similar way, Marx and Engels say little or nothing beyond suggesting the psychological, as well as military, need to use Negro troops against the Confederacy. Despite attempts to make them say other than what they do say, they recognize significant passivity in the slaves: "Thanks to the slaves, who perform all productive labors, the entire manhood of the South that is fit to fight can be led into the field."[46] Their tendency to view the slaves more as objects than subjects—that is, to see them as a potential weapon in the hands of the North rather than as an independent force—is consistent with the realistic view of slave classes in evidence in their scattered writings on the ancient world. In this instance they raised questions that their followers might have profitably pursued, had not short-run political considerations influenced them.

Like Marx and Engels, the early American socialist Algie M. Simons is ambiguous about the origins of the war because he is ambiguous about the quality of the slave South. For Simons the war grew out of a clash between two expansive social systems—a Northern capitalism and a Southern "semi-feudal" slavery. Each economic system (the shift from "social" to "economic" comes easy to Simons, as it does to Beard) needed control of the federal government to advance and protect its interests; since they both needed the same territory to exploit, a clash was inevitable. Simons is never clear about the reasons for the inability of the two systems to compromise their differences, even at someone else's expense. Yet, if only economic interests were at stake, joint imperialist projects ought to have appeared as a solution. Simons's Marxism here, and in general, was never more than simplistic economic determinism. Yet, in some ways his analysis is superior to the fuller, more knowledgeable treatment of the period by the Beards, who stress Southern opposition to homesteads, tariffs, and bounties, and minimize the territorial question. For them, the rapid and disorderly growth of divergent economic systems and the interests they created generated the war. They come close to a Marxian standpoint when writing that slavery provided the basis for the Southern aristocracy and merged its economic interests and ethical standards, but the burden of their treatment centers on the clash of economic interests, narrowly defined. They are well behind Marx, who properly dismissed the tariff question as a matter of little substance.[47]

The Beards, for all their apparent concern with class forces, see little more than economic interests. Like some Marxists after them, they write:

> Merely by the accidents of climate, soil, and geography was it a sectional struggle. If the planting interest had been scattered evenly throughout the industrial region . . . the irrepressible conflict would have been resolved by other methods and accompanied by other logical defense mechanisms.[48]

Thus are the world outlooks of ruling classes reduced to "logical defense mechanisms"—that is, to the rationalization of particular interests. Despite occasional general statements, the Beards never see ideology as something partially autonomous and capable of affecting material interests profoundly. Their insistence that a scattered slavocracy would behave no differently from a geographically compact one substitutes a consideration of ostensible economic interests for an analysis of a specific social class and thereby reduces itself to idealism, for it becomes a concern for abstract economic models instead of for the actual historical process within which all class interests develop their own content.

As a result the Beards are unable to deal adequately with many other questions, especially those raised by the notion of a "Second American Revolution." In their terms the Northern farmers and capitalists grew stronger during the war and shaped events in their own interests. They badly underestimate the capitalist quality of the farmers and have great difficulty explaining their subsequent defeat at the hands of their former capitalist allies. Rather than examine the problems associated with the developing hegemony of the bourgeoisie, they remain, as usual, narrowly tied to an analysis of economic interests and therefore end by seeing conspiracies everywhere.[49]

Many Marxists, as well as non-Marxists, extricate themselves from difficulty only to plunge into greater ones by treating the slave South as a "feudal" society. The definitions of feudalism used by non-Marxists make little sense here, for the medieval European political and juridical arrangements that loom large in such definitions clearly did not exist in the South. Consciously or unconsciously, some variation of Marxian categories has come to be applied. For Marxists the term feudal refers to a mode of production within which property is privately owned, the laborer retains claims to the means of production, and the laborer owes the lord an economic yield, whether in money, kind, or service.[50] Definitions being tools, not religious tenets, they must be judged by their usefulness; at issue here is not the usefulness of the definition, with which I have no quarrel, but its applicability to the slave South. If the Marxian notion of mode of production is as valuable as the steady retreat into its framework by ostensibly anti-Marxist historians would suggest, there is all the more reason to avoid blurring lines. In Marxian terms the slave South was prebourgeois in essential respects, but it was far from being feudal. That is, the South rested on a distinct mode of production that was as different from the feudal as from the capitalist. At the same time the slave mode of production arose anachronistically and as a hybrid during the epoch of capitalism's world conquest. As such, the full autonomy of the slave mode of production could never be achieved; it functioned as part of the capitalist world and could not separate itself from the bourgeois economy or ideology. It was a system perpetually at war with itself, struggling to perfect its own spirit and simultaneously to remain part of a world foreign to that spirit. It helps not at all to label it feudal and then to think that by doing so some problem has been solved.

That the world market bent the slave economy to its own ends is incontrovertible. In this sense capitalism certainly did make its appearance in Southern agriculture; in this sense the South certainly was part of the capitalistic world. Slavery did something else, which those who would write Southern and nineteenth century American history cannot avoid: it raised to regional power a prebourgeois ruling class of formidable political strength and military potential. Capitalism may be able to absorb and use prebourgeois economies, but it cannot readily digest prebourgeois ruling classes that are proud and strong enough to reject the roles of comprador and retainer.

There have been two obstacles to the development of the Marxian viewpoint along these lines. First, the obsession of Marxists with the unilinear theory of history has compelled them to view Southern slavery as a form of feudalism—a formulation that plays loose with the principal categories of the Marxian interpretation of history—and to treat it as a general American rather than a sectional question. In these terms the problem of "two social systems" reduces itself to one of internal class struggle between anachronistic and modern formations. Unilinear Marxists find incomprehensible the notion that social stages may be reversed or that archaic modes of production may reappear in modern forms with considerable political independence. History, it seems, may not go backwards.

Second, most Marxists suffer from their passionate commitment to the cause of Negro liberation and from their hatred of slavery.[51] They identify politically and morally with abolitionism and sacrifice much of their historical sense and even their political acumen. Marxists understand morality as a class question; they reject absolute values. They see process in history and class struggles at the center of that process. Accordingly, they judge slavery, in its modern phases, to be immoral and to represent a fetter on the development of human freedom, which during the seventeenth and eighteenth centuries, and even to some extent the nineteenth, cannot be separated from the development of bourgeois social relations. Their class morality is proletarian and insists that the secular interests of the working class, and the cause of its liberation, requires the abolition of bourgeois social relations. From this point of view it is possible to read history in such a way as to separate "progressive" from "retrogressive" forces: the former are those which revolutionize the economic base of society and create conditions for the advancement of human freedom. This viewpoint has its problems. The rise of ancient slavery, for example, must be interpreted as progressive and revolutionary since the enslavement of one portion of mankind made possible the development of the productive forces of civilization, and therefore of a much more extensive and meaningful freedom.[52] Modern slavery presents an easier problem because it provides valuable support for the rise of capitalism but was far from indispensable. The main problem concerning modern slavery arises from the duality inherent in a class approach to morality. It is at least one-sided to judge Judah P. Benjamin, Jefferson Davis, and J. H. Hammond by the standards of bourgeois society or by the standards of a projected socialist society. These men were class conscious, socially responsible, and personally honorable; they selflessly fulfilled their duties and did what their class and society required of them. It is rather hard to assert that class responsibility is the highest test of morality and then to condemn as immoral those who behave responsibly toward their class instead of someone else's. There is no reason, unless we count as reason the indignation flowing from a passionate hatred for oppression, to withhold from such people full respect and even admiration; nor is there any reason to permit such respect and admiration to prevent their being treated harshly if the liberation of oppressed peoples demands it. The issue transcends considerations of abstract justice or a desire to be fair to one's enemies; it involves political judgment. If we blind ourselves to everything noble, virtuous, honorable, decent, and selfless in a ruling class, how do we account for its hegemony? The people cannot long be held down by force alone, especially since so much of this force must be recruited from the lower orders of society, nor are the people so cowardly as to accept arbitrary dictation forever. Ruling classes must develop a comprehensive world outlook that transcends its immediate and particular interests and that, however partially, identifies itself with the values and aspirations of the people as a whole. Such hegemony could never be maintained without some leaders whose individual qualities are intrinsically admirable. There is a firm link between the doctrinaire inability of many Marxists to appreciate the positive qualities of the best elements of the slaveholding class, and their common tendency to underestimate the hegemony of the bourgeoisie in our own day by merely seeing in it the deception or corruption of the working class.

On another level, Marxists avoid the embarrassment of analyzing the Southern world outlook because it is so patently antibourgeois. It would be difficult for a Marxist not to agree with much of George Fitzhugh's criticism of bourgeois society. Rather than admit as much, and proceed to delineate the differences between reactionary and socialist criticism, they usually charge hypocrisy. We may doubt that a ruling class could stand a year with an ideology based on nothing more than hypocrisy and deception.

The one Marxian writer who tries to take the South on its own terms, with the partial exception of Du Bois, is William Appleman Williams. That Williams is a Marxist in any meaningful sense is open to question, but he speaks as one, and it would be unjust, to say the least, to quarrel over his credentials. As a socialist whose views have been influenced by Marx, he offers many fruitful suggestions that might profitably be integrated into a Marxian analysis.[53]

In its weaker manifestation Williams's argument recapitulates that of the Beards, although with greater sophistication. Here again we have a conflict that might have been avoided had America's economic growth been less disorderly. Here again is an expansive North aiming primarily at the containment of a South that presents itself essentially as an economic rival. Here again we find the South largely as victim.[54] This side of Williams's analysis displays little originality and is not even especially suggestive. The other side displays a good deal more.

For Williams, American history has been a struggle between "mercantilism" and "laissez faire," with the former to be understood as an effort "to retain and adapt an original Christian morality during the dynamic secularization of a religious outlook as an agrarian society was transformed into a life of commerce and industry."[55] Within this struggle Williams sees the South as offering much to the "mercantilist" (i.e., socially responsible) tradition he admires. He speaks well of the planters, especially those of the early national period, and admires their style of life, their architecture, and their sense of community. At the same time he assumes a critical stance toward what he calls the "physiocratic" tendency in their thought (the attempt to build a feudal utopia within the context of a laissez faire world), which he regards as a defense of purely agricultural and local interests against the common good. Before long he must defend Calhoun, the "mercantilist," against John Taylor, the "physiocrat." What begins as a suggestive dissection of the conflict in Southern thought between bourgeois and antibourgeois values, albeit a conflict translated into a strange language, ends back with Beard as an account of alternative economic policies.

Williams comes to grief over the question of slavery. For him, the best representatives of the Southern school during the early national period were antislavery or at least moving in an antislavery direction. So far does he press this dubious notion that he declares the three-fifths clause of the Constitution to have antislavery implications. He insists, contrary to all fact and reason, that the provision shows the Southerners to be intent on effecting the eventual freedom of the slaves. The disorderly onrush of laissez faire capitalism generated new economic pressures for the preservation of slavery, and the attacks of the abolitionists convinced Southerners that the defense of slavery was the defense of their community values against the ideology of the marketplace. "Perhaps the greatest, if unplanned, strategic triumph of the laissez faire antislavery campaign was its making the slave system a hero in the eyes of Southerners."[56] Williams misses the essential thrust of Southern development: the rising self-consciousness of the planters and their growing knowledge that Southern community values rested wholly on the plantation-slave nature of their regime. Williams's idealism misleads him at the very moment of his keenest insight, for he fails to ask the main question: On what kind of material base did the slaveholders' ideology arise? His dichotomy between "mercantilist" and "physiocratic" tendencies is beside the point. The particularism he laments went hand in hand with the sense of community, for each reflected conditions of locally rooted lordship.

Williams's treatment of the abolitionists is unfair and wrong on principle. Since he sees only one national society, with the South a particular set of local interests, he is appalled at abolitionist fanaticism and narrow-mindedness. In his view they ought to have concentrated on ameliorating the conditions of bondage and thereby setting the institution on the road to extinction. He does not appreciate the conflict of worlds, not just interests, underlying the conflict of ideologies. Were he to see the slave system as a social system in itself, he might be able to see that amelioration and reform would have strengthened it, much as liberal reformism has strengthened capitalism.[57] His view is unjust both to the slaveholders and to the abolitionists. It is unjust to the slaveholders because it implicitly makes their ideology a defensive afterthought, instead of appreciating its legitimacy—in Williams's terms, its place at the center of Southern "mercantilism." It is unjust to the abolitionists because it denies their fundamental insight—that no compromise was either possible or desirable. By glossing over the problem of divergent social systems, Williams retreats even from the Beards, but it is in part a useful retreat, capable of preparing for new advances, for it reopens in a serious way the question of rival world outlooks.

The most successful attempt at a Marxian analysis of the South and the coming of the wars is Barrington Moore's "The American Civil War: The Last Capitalist Revolution."[58] Since Moore discusses a great number of European and Asian societies, a critique of his chapter on the United States in isolation risks some distortion, and since he makes no pretense to specialized knowledge, and relies on a relatively slim literature, some allowance needs to be made for a confessed tendency to generalize beyond the data presented. His analysis is nonetheless impressive and unintentionally reveals how banal most Marxian interpretations have been.

Moore sees the war as the last revolutionary offensive on the part of the urban or bourgeois democracy. He rejects simplistic economic interpretations but insists on the ultimate importance of the economic impulse which generated slavery and therefore provided the basis for a divergent social order in the South. In this way Moore develops a two-civilizations thesis without surrendering an "economic" interpretation. As he observes, the numerical balance between free and slave states could be understood as "something that mattered . . . only if the difference between a society with slavery and one without mattered."[59]

Moore's rejection of the thesis of economic rivalry reveals the fundamental weakness in his discussion. Plantation slavery did not rival industry capitalism, he argues, but arose as an integral part of it. Slavery was a spur, not a fetter, to industrial growth. In this form the argument is unexceptionable, but it does obscure the class issue. Slavery simultaneously extruded a ruling class with strong prebourgeois qualities and economic interests that did conflict with Northern capitalism. Moore himself notes the probability of an expansionist tendency in the Southern economy and society, but he pays insufficient attention to it and to the extraordinary expansionism of Northern capitalism, and thereby minimizes the economic aspect of the collision. (If it is not presumptuous to suggest it, I think he would have benefitted from careful concern with Williams's work here.) Moore is so anxious to repel crude economic interpretation that he concedes far more ground than is necessary or safe. The development of national capitalism, he says, transformed the Western farmers into petty capitalists and tied them to the East. The existence of free land muted the class struggle in the Eastern cities. Without a major threat from the Left, the bourgeoisie had no need of Southern *Junkerism* and every need for a democratic alliance with Western farmers in order to expand and deepen its home market and to strengthen its position in the world market. With slavery's generating an antidemocratic ethos in the South, the two sections pulled further and further apart. Slavery, in Moore's view, did not inhibit industrial capitalism but did inhibit the democratic, competitive capitalism from which the bourgeoisie stood to profit most and to which it was increasingly committed ideologically.

Moore returns, in this manner, to the question of two civilizations and to the nature of Southern society. He begins weakly by drawing a parallel between the slaveholders and the *Junkers* in whom he sees a class of "not quite slaveholders." In the end, however, he surrenders this part of the argument by noting that the Northern bourgeoisie could only absorb the planters into a conservative coalition when slavery was gone and Northern capital was conquering the South. In general, he exaggerates the prebourgeois quality of the post-Napoleonic *Junkers* and underestimates the prebourgeois quality of the slaveholders.

Moore pays little attention to Southern ideology and weakens his two-civilizations argument. His notion that slaveholders were too "ashamed" to justify slavery on economic grounds and sought elaborate rationales does him no credit. He does recognize certain genuinely prebourgeois and aristocratic features in the Southern world outlook but insists, on balance, that they were largely a fraud. After all, did not the Southern social system rest on commercial profits? He does not consider the possibility of a social system and ethos at war with itself, much less one in which the old was prevailing over the new—the prebourgeois over the bourgeois—because nowhere does he analyze the plantation as community and way of life. Despite a framework that places social classes at the center, he never analyzes the slaveholders as a class; he merely describes certain of their features and interests in a tangential way. Finally, he settles for the extraordinary formulation: "The South had a capitalist civilization, then, but not a bourgeois one. Certainly it was not based on town life."[60]

Thus, with much greater skill and subtlety than can be apparent in this short account, Moore tries to bridge the gap between the notion of the South as agrarian-capitalist and the notion of it as aristocratic or prebourgeois. The implications of this point of view are beyond the scope of this paper, but they clearly represent the beginnings of a serious class analysis and of a viable Marxian interpretation. I have elsewhere presented, somewhat schematically and one-sidedly, the case for the prebourgeois thesis,[61] but no one would argue that a strong dose of capitalism did not exist in the South. The argument turns on the proportions and their significance. Ultimately, the task of Marxian interpretation is the analysis of the constituent social classes, their interests and ideology, and especially of the ruling slaveholders. The advantages of Moore's model or some other can only be definitely established in a broader context, such as the one Moore offers in his learned book. Unable to pursue this subject here, we may welcome Moore's effort as a new departure, which, if taken seriously by the developing generation of American Marxists, may finally bring us out of the wilderness of dogmatism, romanticism, and humbug.

The suggestions of Moore and Williams will hopefully constitute a beginning; that neither is part of the orthodox Marxian movements is its own comment on those movements. This beginning means, above all, a break with naive determinism, economic interpretation, and the insipid glorification of the lower classes, all of which ends as some form of fatalism. There are at least three reasons for retreating into fatalism—cowardice, laziness, and simple-mindedness—and probably many more for resorting to political formulas instead of proceeding with honest research. Marxism and the socialist movement have no need for fatalism or formulas. Marxism has already contributed much to the history of the slave South by bringing a class focus to a subject that historians increasingly recognize as a special case of class rule. Freed of dogmatism and special pleading, it has infinitely more to bring to an empirical analysis of the rise, course, and fall of the slaveholding class and of its relationship to other classes in society. The advance of such an analysis should help practical socialist work, no matter how many treasured theories and prejudices fall away, for it should tell us a great deal about the way in which a ruling class rules. Marxists have only begun to study the hegemonic mechanisms of bourgeois society. Without suggesting easy and probably false analogies to contemporary problems, we might expect that a study of such mechanisms in a society displaying so many typically American and Western European political and institutional forms ought to illuminate some features of present problems. At least it ought to serve as a check against oversimplification and the exaggeration of the place of purely economic and material forces. In view of this promise and potential, those who would defend Marxian socialism by protecting its founder from just criticism do an immeasurable disservice. They would do well to recall Marx's preface to the first German edition of *Capital:* "Every opinion based on scientific criticism I welcome. As to the prejudices of so-called public opinion, to which I have never made concessions, now as aforetime the maxim of the great Florentine is mine: *'Segui il tuo corso, e lascia dir le genti.'* "[62]

NOTES

* I shall not define "Marxian" too closely here. The works considered are those by professed Marxists, by certain writers like Beard who acknowledge a strong influence from Marx, and by those whose analysis centers on essential Marxian categories. I received a copy of Raimondo Luraghi's *Storia della guerra civile americana* (Turin, 1966), too late for inclusion in this discussion. Luraghi's analysis of the origins of the war and his treatment of the South are important contributions toward the development of a class analysis of American history and will hopefully secure the attention they deserve from Marxists and non-Marxists alike.

1. *Cf.,* Caio Prado Júnior, *Formação do Brasil Contemporâneo: Colônia,* 7th ed. (São Paulo, n.d.); Fernando Henrique Cardoso, *Capitalismo e Escravidão no Brasil Meridional* (São Paulo, 1962); Octávio Ianni, *As Metamorfoses do Escravo* (São Paulo, 1962) and *Raças e Classes Sociais no Brasil* (Rio de Janeiro, 1966), esp. part 2.

2. Herbert Aptheker, *American Foreign Policy and the Cold War* (New York, 1962), p. 291. This book is a leading illustration of the uses to which Popular Frontism can be put in trying to effect "an open-

ing to the right." Cf., my critique "Dr. Herbert Aptheker's Retreat from Marxism," *Science & Society,* 27 (Spring, 1963), 212–26.

3. Marx's articles for the *New York Daily Tribune* and those of Marx and Engels for the Vienna *Die Presse,* together with relevant correspondence, have been collected and translated as *The Civil War in the United States,* first published in 1937 and edited by Richard Enmale and reprinted in 1961. In the latter paperback edition, to which all page references here refer, the editor's name is dropped; obviously it was a pseudonym. For convenience, however, I shall use the name Enmale when referring to the editor's own remarks in his introduction.

4. Gerald Runkle, "Karl Marx and the American Civil War," *Comparative Studies in Society and History,* 6, no. 1 (1963–64), 117–41.

5. Karl Kautsky, *The Foundations of Christianity* (New York, 1953), foreword.

6. For an illuminating discussion of some phases of this pseudo-revolutionary juggling see Eric J. Hobsbawm's introduction to Karl Marx, *Pre-Capitalist Economic Formations* (New York, 1965), which traces the fate of Marx's pregnant notion of an "Asiatic mode of production" in later Marxist writing.

7. Karl Marx, *A Contribution to the Critique of Political Economy* (Chicago, 1904), pp. 11–13.

8. In the history of science Marxists have generally stressed the social impulses to theoretical advance, whereas others have stressed the theoretical impulses internal to the science. But as S. Lilley says: "Any scientific development, I suggest, becomes possible only when both internal and external conditions are ripe. So much can be demonstrated by considering conspicuous cases in which, for a considerable period, one set of conditions, *either* external *or* internal, was favorable to an advance, but the other was not." "Cause and Effect in the History of Science," *Essays in the Social History of Science,* ed. S. Lilley (Copenhagen, 1953), p. 59.

9. I mean fundamental transformations in the way in which human beings face each other in society. To trace all historical events and changes to class structure and class struggles is to convert Marxian analysis into a childish formula worthy of a particularly fanatic and simple-minded religious cult.

10. Antonio Gramsci, *Il Materialismo storico e la filosofia di Benedetto Croce, Opere,* 2 (Turin, 1949), p. 49.

11. Quoted by John M. Cammett, *Antonio Gramsci and the Origins of Italian Communism* (Stanford, Cal., 1967), p. 191. This book is an invaluable introduction to Gramsci's political and intellectual work.

12. Marx and Engels, *Civil War,* p. 4.

13. *Ibid.,* p. 7.

14. *Ibid.,* p. 72.

15. *Ibid.,* p. 81.

16. Runkle is therefore wrong to accuse them of inconsistency. He

argues that if their historical viewpoint were valid, the main struggle would have been within the South itself. In their terms, however, the Union as a whole was the relevant entity. Beyond this formal matter, Runkle's distinction between internal and external contradictions ignores the first principle of dialectics—the interrelatedness of all phenomena—and is a false problem. See Runkle, *Comparative Studies in Society and History,* 6, no. 1 (1963–64), 117–41.

17. Marx and Engels, *Civil War,* p. 81. Cf. Charles and Mary Beard, *The Rise of American Civilization,* 2 vols. in 1 (New York, 1944), 2: 33 and esp. 56.

18. Marx and Engels, *Civil War,* p. 280.

19. *Ibid.*, p. 60; original emphasis.

20. *Ibid.*, p. 70.

21. In addition to Marx, *Capital,* 3 vols. (Moscow, n.d.) see Maurice Dobb, *Studies in the Development of Capitalism* (New York, 1947), esp. chaps. 1 and 2, and Dobb, ed., *The Transition from Feudalism to Capitalism* (New York, 1963), esp. the essay by H. K. Takahashi.

22. Marx and Engels, *Civil War,* p. 80.

23. *Ibid.*, pp. 67–68.

24. I use the term hegemony in its Gramscian sense—the seemingly spontaneous loyalty that a ruling class evokes from the masses through its cultural position and its ability to promote its own world view as the general will. For an introduction to Gramsci's ideas see Cammett, *Antonio Gramsci,* chap. 10, and Gwynn A. Williams, "Gramsci's Concept of *Egemonia,*" *Journal of the History of Ideas,* 21 (October–December 1960), pp. 586–99.

25. For an alternative view of Southern expansionism, which nonetheless owes much to their lines of inquiry, see my *The Political Economy of Slavery* (New York, 1965), chap. 10. For the discussion that follows, part 3 of this book examines the position of the industrialists and tries to account for their conservatism.

26. See, e.g., *Civil War,* p. 190.

27. *Ibid.*, p. 277.

28. No Marxist writer has yet dealt adequately with this question. For some it is not even a question since the lower-class whites were ostensibly moving not only into opposition to slavery but toward an alliance with Negroes. Those wishing to pursue these fairy tales may consult Herbert Aptheker, "Class Conflicts in the South, 1850–1860," *Toward Negro Freedom* (New York, 1956), pp. 44–67.

29. Marx and Engels, *Civil War,* p. 255.

30. *Ibid.*, p. 259.

31. *Ibid.*

32. *Ibid.*, p. 271.

33. *Ibid.*, p. 281.

34. *Ibid.*

35. Philip S. Foner, *Business & Slavery* (Chapel Hill, N.C.), 1941.

For an alternative view see Bernard Mandel, *Labor: Free and Slave* (New York, 1955).

36. Foner, *Business & Slavery, passim.*

37. William Z. Foster, *Outline Political History of the Americas* (New York, 1951), chap. 17.

38. The worst illustration is the "Address of the International Workingmen's Association to President Johnson," *Civil War,* pp. 283–85, which is embarrassing in its pompous rhetoric and sentimentality.

39. Marx, *Capital,* 1: 773.

40. Royden Harrison, "British Labor and American Slavery," *Science & Society,* 25 (December 1961), 291–319.

41. Marx and Engels, *Civil War,* p. 141.

42. *Ibid.,* pp. 261–62.

43. I therefore find puzzling the assertion of Melvin Drimmers, in his review of my *Political Economy of Slavery* in the *William and Mary Quarterly,* that I had applied and updated Marx on the Civil War.

44. Herbert Aptheker, *Toward Negro Freedom,* pp. 84–85.

45. Richard Enmale in Marx and Engels, *Civil War,* pp. xviii–xix. Aptheker makes the same points.

46. Marx and Engels, *Civil War,* pp. 199–200, 252. The recent work of Brazil's outstanding Marxists is refreshingly free from the dogmatism and romanticism of American Marxian writing on the Negro. Octavio Ianni, especially, is ruthlessly objective and places the Negro contribution to the abolition of Brazilian slavery in realistic perspective without the slightest tendency to exaggerate. Cf. *As Metamorfoses do escravo,* pp. 232–35.

47. Beard and Beard, *Rise,* 2, chaps. 17–18. For another example of essentially economic interpretation by a Marxist see Herman Schlüter, *Lincoln, Labor and Slavery: A Chapter from the Social History of America* (New York, 1913), chap. 1. Thomas J. Pressly, *Americans Interpret their Civil War* (New York, 1962), pp. 238 ff., does a good job in showing just how narrowly economic the Beardian viewpoint is. Pressly does, however, exaggerate the critical side of Marxian writings in an apparent attempt to show how far the Beards are from Marxism. He does not seem to appreciate how close most of these Marxists are to being Beardians.

48. Beard and Beard, *Rise,* 2: 53.

49. *Ibid.,* 2: 99, 106. Among the Marxists who follow Beardian lines is George Novak, but some of his generalizations are well balanced and suggestive: see esp. his discussion of the stages of the development of American slavery. *Marxist Essays in American History* (New York, 1966), pp. 10, 34.

50. Cf. Dobb, *Studies in the Development of Capitalism,* pp. 35–36.

51. The closest any avowed Marxist has come to an appreciation of the strength and quality of the slaveholding class is W. E. B. Du Bois, *Black Reconstruction in America* (New York, 1935), chap. 3, but even

he retreats into moralizing and mystification.

52. Many Marxists nevertheless gag and try to interpret the rise of ancient slavery as a reactionary phenomenon. See, e.g., Kautsky, *Foundations of Christianity.*

53. Williams's understanding of Marxism comes out most sharply in his book, *The Great Evasion: An Essay on the Contemporary Relevance of Karl Marx and on the Wisdom of Admitting the Heretic into the Dialogue about America's Future* (Chicago, 1964). I have criticized this book and its interpretation of Marxism at length. See "William Appleman Williams on Marx and America," *Studies on the Left,* 6, no. 1 (1966), pp. 70–86.

54. William Appleman Williams, *The Contours of American History* (Cleveland, 1961), see esp. pp. 285–99.

55. *Ibid.,* p. 33. Williams's categories are his own and owe nothing to Marx. For a discussion of mercantilism from a Marxian viewpoint see the relevant chapter in Dobb, *Studies in the Development of Capitalism.*

56. *Ibid.,* p. 299.

57. Barrington Moore, Jr., on the other hand, sees the point clearly and criticizes Stanley M. Elkins on just this point: "These [reform] measures seem to me highly reactionary, a form of tokenism within the framework of slavery." *Social Origins of Dictatorship and Democracy: Lord and Peasant in the Making of the Modern World* (Boston, 1966), p. 132, n. 47.

58. *Ibid.,* chap. 3, pp. 110–55. Moore's categories are basically Marxian, and I shall treat his work as such. He writes, nevertheless, in a manner calculated to divorce himself from Marxism. At times he descends to something close to red-baiting. Thus, on Philip S. Foner: "The author is a well-known Marxist but in this study seems quite undogmatic" (p. 125, n. 29). That a scholar of Moore's quality should pander to prejudices in this way is sad.

59. *Ibid.,* p. 120.

60. *Ibid.,* p. 121.

61. Genovese, *Political Economy,* esp. chap. 1, "The Slave South: An Interpretation." For an incisive critique by a conservative who shares some important ideas with Moore see Stanley M. Elkins's review in *Commentary,* July 1966, pp. 73–75. I would not deny having exaggerated my case and having opened the way to Elkins's strictures, but I would insist on the main lines of the argument, which will have to be developed in future efforts. Elkins's thoughtful attempt to come to terms with the argument demonstrates that a mutually useful dialogue between Marxists and anti-Marxists is possible even in cold war America. Since the present essay was first published I have attempted a refined statement in *The World the Slaveholders Made.*

62. ["Follow your course, and let people say what they please."] Marx, *Capital,* vol. 1 and 2.

Chapter 16

STAUGHTON LYND AS HISTORIAN AND IDEOLOGUE

THE PUBLICATION, almost simultaneously, of two books[1] by Staughton Lynd provides an opportunity to assess his position both as a historian and as an ideologue of the New Left. Normally, it would be bad manners to confuse the two roles, but Lynd has argued forcefully that they ought not to be separated, and both books, especially *Intellectual Origins of American Radicalism,* are plainly meant to serve direct political ends. As a contribution to American radical historiography, Lynd's work must be evaluated as part of the present effort of scholars, most of them under forty, to establish an ideological foundation for their political movement. These men and women have been in revolt against a vulgar-Marxist tradition based on economic determinism, a glorification of the lower classes, and the self-defeating tendency to read the past according to the political demands of the moment. Historians like W. A. Williams, Aileen Kraditor, and Christopher Lasch, starting from such different ideologies as Christian socialism, orthodox Marxism, pragmatism, and existentialism,

This essay was originally published in the *New York Review of Books,* Sept. 26, 1968, pp. 69–74.

have recently converged in an attack on the economic determinism and romanticism of the earlier tradition and, especially, the assumption that myth-making and falsifying in historical writing can be of political use. It is ironic that even historians who do not consider themselves Marxists are steadily building a genuine American version of Marxism by the very act of destroying the caricature to which they fell heir. Lynd speaks as part of this current, but, as these books reveal, he might more properly be placed in the tradition being overthrown.

Class Conflict, Slavery, and the United States Constitution, by far the better of the two books, contains excellent empirical work on a number of important questions, but also reveals much methodological and philosophical confusion. Its value lies in its painstaking analyses of local responses to the political and social crises of the Revolutionary and Constitutional eras. By making careful studies of selected areas in New York State, Lynd tests the familiar theses of Beard and Becker, with their strong suggestion of a counterrevolution by large property owners. In particular he writes well about the position of the artisans and lower-middle-class radicals who played an important part in the Revolution and the constitutional crisis. When, for example, he demonstrates, with impressive skill, how foreign policy considerations played a major role in the radical thinking of the lower classes, he begins to discuss class positions as a complex mixture of material interests, ideologies, and psychological attitudes, and implicitly comes close to replacing economic determinism with a sophisticated class analysis of historical change. The four essays in part one of his book, together with Lynd's other published work on the revolutionary period, justify his reputation as a thoughtful scholar of early American history.

In "Beyond Beard" the introductory essay, however, Lynd seems unable to pull the threads of his empirical work together into a coherent theory that would in fact go "beyond Beard." The narrow economic analysis characteristic of so much of Beard's work is based upon an investigation of the role of interest groups, the most important of which he defined as holders of real and personal property. Today, the best radical scholars agree that such forms of vulgar Marxism should be replaced with serious research on the nature and role of social classes, considered not only as representative of specific material interests but as complexes of goals, cultural assumptions, and social and psychological relationships. In this way, these scholars are moving from a concern with mechanistic details to the mainsprings of social and political behavior. Lynd has no trouble in destroying Beard's crude class analysis—in any case, the criticism of Forrest McDonald and others has prepared the way—but in this introductory essay he never breaks with economic determinism itself. Thus we are left with a view only slightly different from that of the older, admittedly sterile one; the broader implications of Lynd's diligent empirical work are forced into a theoretical frame too narrow to encompass them.

In Parts Two and Three Lynd turns to the slavery question, which he sees as a decisive importance for an understanding of the Revolution and the Constitution, and it is here that his agreement breaks down. He attempts to demonstrate that the antagonism between the slaveholders and the Northern middle classes helped to shape the early national period, but he fails to identify the significant conflicts of interest. That the interests of the two emerging classes diverged in some important respects is beyond doubt, but for the most part that divergence arose from different expectations of the future and from different ways of thinking. Lynd fails to analyze the slaveholders as a class and seems to gag on the notion that they could have been developing their own system of morality, reflecting their particular social system. Thus he cannot explain the nature of the antagonism between them and the Northern middle class, and consequently he overestimates the immediate political and economic conflict. His argument is finally no more than an indictment of the Founding Fathers for having failed to take a moral stand against slavery. He refuses to see the ideology of nascent American capitalism as a process that had not yet matured to the point of regarding slavery as morally and materially incompatible with its own assumptions, and he insists on holding up to it moral standards abstracted from any time and place.

In short, Lynd moves from the economic determinist view of the first part of his book to a subjective and ahistorical one in the second. Unable to justify his moralistic condemnation of slavery according to his materialist theory, he asserts a moral absolutism that contradicts the theory itself.

We may perhaps account for the contradiction between the two parts of *Class Conflict* in its origin as a collection of separate essays written over a period of five years or more. In any case, that contradiction disappears in *Intellectual Origins,* which abandons all attempts at a materialist interpretation. The book is based on carefully selected statements from Lynd's favorite English theorists, Revolutionary War heroes, philosophical anarchists, and other middle-class radicals—from Cartwright and Paine through the Abolitionists to writers like Henry George—and is designed to establish certain of their ideas as the core of the radical tradition. The intellectual tradition of radicalism Lynd describes in this way:

> The tradition I have attempted to describe made the following affirmations: that the proper foundation for government is a universal law of right and wrong self-evident to the intuitive common sense of every man; that freedom is a power of personal self-direction which no man can delegate to another; that the purpose of society is not the protection of property but fulfillment of the needs of living human beings; that good citizens have the right and duty, not only to overthrow incurably oppressive governments, but before that point is reached to break particular oppressive laws; and that we owe our ultimate allegiance, not to this or that nation, but to the whole family of man.

Lynd views the Declaration of Independence as the most relevant expression of these ideas, and makes large claims on its continuing fascination for some American radicals. He does not mention that many American radicals have disagreed—imagine Daniel De Leon peddling such stuff! Still less does he tell us anything about the role of class or the historical setting of the debates among radicals. For Lynd, this moralistic version of radical doctrine is all that matters; he seeks merely to trace its history and its relation to conservative thought—which is, by the way, more abused than presented or criticized.

The book is, therefore, not history at all—how could one write a history of "self-evident truths"—but a political testament with historical references added to establish a pedigree. Leaving aside possible disagreements with Lynd's particular readings, we find little surprise or controversy in his account of how the English Dissenters developed Lockian doctrine in a democratic direction, or of the importance of the inner light in egalitarian movements during the seventeenth century, or of the link between radical Protestantism and Abolitionism. The historical record is familiar. The claims of the book rest on Lynd's interpretation, or, rather, on his assumption, that moral absolutism is what the radical tradition has to offer radicals today.

The uses to which Lynd puts moral absolutism reveal much about his attitude toward history itself. We are told that the "great truths" are intuitively accessible to the average man and that conscience, not constituted authority, must be the ultimate arbiter of political good and evil. Lynd has no trouble in showing that these and related "Inner-Light" doctrines served revolutionary ends in the European peasant wars or the English Revolution, but somehow he thinks that this demonstration, now standard fare, proves his case for their contemporary importance. Previous revolutionary movements were millenarian or bourgeois, and hence these doctrines could serve a revolutionary purpose, but Lynd seeks to graft them on to a socialist revolution, the content of which he never discusses. He merely asserts that they form the kernel of revolutionary socialist thought, although no important socialist movement has ever been built on such an ideology; indeed the history of modern Western society suggests that the working class would laugh its exponents off the political stage.

Since Lynd never discusses the relation of these ideas to the social groups that hold them, he is freed from a concern with unpleasant questions. Writing as a historian, he nevertheless denies the importance of the social context in which ideas occur—the "great truths" are to him self-evident and absolute—and he thereby denies the usefulness of history except for purposes of moral exhortation. He frankly asserts an antirationalist position:

> Therefore, the neo-Lockians of the eighteenth century, like the neo-Marxists of the twentieth, were obliged to reintroduce the ethical dimension. They insisted on the reality of the good and on man's ability to recognize it, defended the intuitions of the heart against the paralyzing analysis of the head.

It is difficult to know where to begin criticism, all the more so since Lynd's hippie neo-Marxists go unnamed and we are not told just whose (or which) heads become paralyzed by analysis. Lynd seeks to prove that the essence of radicalism is something akin to obscurantism. The countertendencies and opposing view of the left are ignored; the book is therefore a travesty of history.

Lynd describes various strains of radical thought in English and early American history, and invokes the formidable authority of E.P. Thompson's masterpiece, *The Making of the English Working Class,* which also seeks to find the roots of modern radical thought in preindustrial and early industrial bourgeois and petit-bourgeois currents. Regrettably, Lynd omits a decisive step in his argument and thereby inverts Thompson's method. He establishes a pedigree for his favorite radical ideas, among which are the right of revolution, the right to disobey personally obnoxious laws, and the primacy of human over property rights, and he seeks to relate the ideas of the New Left to the ideas of the American Revolution and Abolitionism.

This procedure has its problems. One of Thompson's most valuable contributions was to show how utopian and radical religious doctrines passed into the working-class and socialist movements and prepared the way for, and helped to shape, English Marxism and Fabianism. Lynd, on the other hand, completely omits the working class, the socialist movements, and everything else that does not fit his formula. Since he deals with early American history, he cannot be expected to analyze those currents closely; but if he is to convince us, he should show how the tradition he has "attempted to describe" relates to such main currents of twentieth century American radicalism as Populism or Marxism. Instead, he implies that the New Left, which in fact embraces many tendencies, is a new manifestation of an earlier philosophical radicalism, and that the rest does not matter. To exorcise the past in this way he must reduce Marx to a European version of Thoreau, ignore the actual history of the American Left, and identify his own particular position within the New Left as the sole embodiment of a relevant radicalism.

Lynd opens *Intellectual Origins* with a statement by poor Stokely Carmichael, who seems to have enough trouble these days without having to bear the full burden of this cross: "There is a higher law than the law of government. That's the law of conscience." Lynd proceeds, "The characteristic concepts of the existential radicalism of today have a long and honorable history." We are spared an explanation of why an existential anything needs any history at all, but are told, however, that today's radicals speak of inalienable rights, a natural higher law, and the rights of revolution. It is clear enough that bourgeois revolutionaries of previous epochs were encumbered by these ideas; that today's revolutionaries need any of them remains to be demonstrated.

Lynd sees the special contribution of Abolitionism to radicalism as the extension of the right of revolution, understood as a majority movement, to the right of anyone on grounds of conscience to break the law. The reactionaries among us may be permitted some questions as to how one man's conscience may justify this right and not another's; once again we need not ask for evidence for "self-evident truths." Let us grant that "good citizens" have a right to overthrow an oppressive regime; but if we are to speak of such a "right," what shall we do with the right of self-defense? Officials of the state and men of property, who must also have hearts with intuitive knowledge of the good, surely have a right to shoot down those who threaten them. If we have a right to break any law that outrages our conscience, do not those who feel the need for the protection of that law or of the legal system in general have the right to take their own measures? It does not occur to Lynd that even fascists—it is enough to recall Giovanni Gentile—may be men of strong principle, love of humanity, and clear conscience.

For those who regard the existing order as intolerable and barbarous, revolution may legitimately appear as a necessity and a duty, but he who chooses revolutionary confrontations or defies the law cannot easily pretend that he is not appealing to force. There is only one justification for a civilized man's doing either: the existence of irreconcilable antagonisms, each of which has its claims and neither of which can or will be compromised. When, for example, slaves rose in revolt, they advanced simultaneously their claims to individual freedom and with varying degrees of consciousness, a notion of a just social order; when the slaveholders moved to crush them, they advanced simultaneously the claims of property and a commitment to the existing arrangement as the foundation of the only social order they could see as just.

The interests of the two were irreconcilable. But this view cannot appeal to the heart or the intuition of the common man; it can only appeal to a developing social consciousness based not on some abstract common sense but on that sense of duty and responsibility to humanity which can only be defined in a specific time and place through disciplined, collective ideological and political effort.

Among the difficulties with Lynd's appeal to self-evident truths and absolute values is an implicit right of counter-revolution. After all, why cannot proslavery, profascist, and other reactionary forces also consult their consciences and discover their own self-evident truths? And what, one wonders, would be the fate of a small revolutionary country, faced with the hostility of a super power, if it were simply to adopt Lynd's position and grant the right to appeal to individual conscience against the law? It would not last a day, and neither, we suspect, would anyone advocating this doctrine in such a country.

Lynd scores a point when he notes that the experience of twentieth century man under totalitarian regimes gives reason to trust the toughness and self-renewing qualities of the human spirit, and, no doubt, until recently Marxists have not paid sufficient attention to this. But whereas Hannah Arendt, to cite only one example, can write with eloquence, power, and reason on this matter, Lynd merely announces an Absolute Spirit in everyman and its self-evident right to stand against society. He buttresses his assertion by the second, arrogant assertion that the first is self-evident. If we are obliged to admit, and indeed to glory in the evidence of a human spirit reaching toward freedom, we are not thereby justified in rejecting the counterclaims offered us by Dostoevsky's Grand Inquisitor. The problem of that celebrated parable remains with us, even if Lynd prefers to ignore it. Freedom, too, is a historically determined process and the outcome of a persistent tension between rival claims. The problem of our day, which no nihilism can remove for us, is to expand individual freedom, conventionally defined, as far as possible by so ordering society as to reduce steadily its constraints in a manner consistent with the general safety. From this view, which Lynd ignores, the problem is specific and exists in general only as an abstract ideal shared by all decent men. It is to be solved, however momentarily, in each historical context, and it is likely to remain with us in any social order we may devise.

Lynd's view leads him to do violence to almost every historical question he touches. It is enough for him that Anabaptists or Diggers or primitive rebels here or there raised the banner of equality and inalienable rights. In this way he ignores history itself and also ignores (but never refutes) both conservative and Marxist criticism. Conservatives do not, as Lynd naïvely supposes, generally defend property rights as more important than human rights; they argue, with considerable justification for most of historical time, that, without property, freedom would have collapsed into anarchy, demagogic manipulation, and loss of freedom. Marxism sees freedom as a historical process, not an absolute: it admires early radical movements for their vision of human brotherhood and their war against exploitation, but it also criticizes them for their irrationalism and for their manifestly reactionary side. If it is true that only under modern economic and technological conditions has much individual freedom been possible without the sacrifice of basic material needs and the opportunity for a widespread leisure and culture, then it is also true that the early peasant revolts, however noble and admirable in some respects, were backward-looking and, in the strictest sense of the word, reactionary, when they sought to establish a primitive agrarian communism.

Lynd praises the Abolitionists for raising the question of conscience in a special way: "A minority, even a minority of one, had the duty of living on the basis of God's law in defiance of all man-made authorities." This doctrine is respectable for those who believe in God and His law. Their concern is with the individual soul, and they might argue that every other man will have to attend to himself. If the judgment proves wrong, at least their good intentions might commend them to their Lord's mercy. But once secularized, the doctrine reduces itself to mere egotism and expresses contempt for the collective judgment of mankind. Lynd cannot get around this obvious fact by arguing that an appeal to conscience is an appeal to the judgment of the common man. Common men, like uncommon men, often disagree and kill one another.

Lynd's argument collapses totally when he discusses Marx and Marxism. For Lynd, Marx "paralleled" Thoreau and other American radicals and is of only passing interest. Lynd's Marx, as might be expected, is the early Marx; and although elsewhere in *The Dissenting Academy* he says that he knows of and rejects the mature Marx, nowhere does he give the slightest evidence of study or understanding. His readers are left with a wholly misleading impression. Gone are all the essential contributions which, for better or worse, have shaped the thinking of much of the Left for a hundred years: the theory of exploitation, the materialist interpretation of history, and the class analysis of the state. We are offered, instead, quotations from Marx's early writings carefully selected to show that Marx took only one step beyond the Abolitionists—by attacking private property itself. Since this attack also had American parallels, it is of only academic interest. Thus, we are treated to grotesque assertions, such as: ". . . Marx, whose concepts of alienation and fetishism can be paralleled in the pages of *Walden*." If his discussion of Marx is worth examining, it is only to reveal Lynd's shallow scholarship:

> For Marx, responsible social action presupposed a rational survey of the economic situation in which one planned to act. Inevitably the required analysis fell to an elite which had the leisure and training to make it. Despite his emphasis on the

> dependence of theory upon practice, Marx felt considerable distrust for workingmen who sought to change society from the basis of their own experience and perceptions. In this he somewhat resembled those American Founding Fathers who considered moral outrage against slavery premature and utopian, and placed their hope for its eventual abolition in long-run economic trends. [*Intellectual Origins*]

It has been a long time since Marx was so absurdly caricatured by someone who professes respect for him. Lynd does not footnote his statements, nor could he, and the whole weight of Marx's life, his political and historical writing, and the efforts of generations of Marxists—communists, Trotskyists, and Social Democrats—are sufficient refutation. If only Lynd's ignorance were at stake we could let it pass; other aspects are more serious. Marx certainly did not celebrate the alleged goodness of the working class and the oppressed, but neither did he "distrust" them. Rather, he affirmed that they must make themselves over by collective effort, that they must frankly assess the effects of the degradation the ruling classes have imposed on them, and that they must overcome the banality, brutality, and corruption in their own lives. For this reason he saw the movement as a disciplining force and as decisive for the success of the revolution, understood as something other than a *coup d'état,* and for this reason he saw an intelligentsia and a leadership as decisive if the movement was to develop. Marx's view, like that of subsequent serious Marxists, displays a far greater subtlety and sophistication than Lynd imagines. In any case, whatever its political and intellectual value, it deserves to be presented fully and fairly.

Lynd's glorification of the "common man"—the words sound strange since the passing of Henry Wallace—is something quite different from that essential respect for and identification with the oppressed which every revolutionary must feel; and it is more than mere sentimentalism. It is in his hands an intellectual device necessary to sustain an egocentric view of the world, and as such, it descends into demagogy: "The characteristic exponents of the revolutionary tradition were poor workingmen who did not go to college and rarely held public offices, such as Paine, Garrison, George, and Debs." Lynd might have told unwary readers that, during the lives of these men, most Americans, including Rockefeller, Carnegie, and almost all the robber barons, did not go to college either. Lynd's flattering of the poor, here and elsewhere, disguises the real point, which is a contempt for and distrust of the intelligentsia. The outcome of his line of thought is the cry now being heard that radical intellectuals must leave the university for the redemptive atmosphere of the ghetto.

The most valuable contributions being made by the young radicals of today stem from their revolt against the totalitarian interpretation of Marxist political doctrine. They have reasserted the claims of the led against would-be leaders, for the experience of the twentieth century revolutions has clearly shown how easily Marxist notions of class and party can pass over into bureaucratization, dictatorship, and cynical manipulation. Recognition of these dangers and a determination to oppose them hardly justify the obscurantist retreat Lynd proposes, and, in fact, there is encouraging evidence that much of the New Left is now groping in its own ways toward more rational solutions. However, heroic "confrontations," such as occurred in Chicago during the recent [1968] Democratic party convention, are hardly new. What is at issue is the theoretical framework in which they are set. The old problems are still with us: How do we consolidate such impressive actions? How do we integrate them into a long-term struggle that must also embrace the older and more settled elements in society? So long as the goals are unclear and so long as a rational program for the restructuring of society remains obscure, we have every reason to fear the outcome.

Lynd presents himself as a spokesman for the New Left, but he has only the right to present himself as a spokesman for a particular tendency of it. If there is a "New" Left, it is a many-sided movement, and it deserves to be called new principally for its insistence on bypassing old factional quarrels and for its unwillingness to submit to the discipline of one or another of the older organizations, most of which have discredited themselves by pronounced totalitarianism. It is not new by virtue of its activism, for the Left of the 1930s was nothing, if not activist. Its nihilist qualities are not new either, as Lynd implies, for these are very old tendencies, which have everywhere led the Left to defeat and slaughter. Susan Sontag, in one of her more spirited moments, tells us that nihilism is our contemporary form of moral uplift. No doubt. But if it is the best that Staughton Lynd can offer us, either as a revolutionary political ideology or as an attitude toward history, then we shall have to look elsewhere.

NOTE

1. *Class Conflict, Slavery, and The United States Constitution* (Indianapolis, 1967); *Intellectual Origins of American Radicalism* (New York, 1968).

Chapter 17

A QUESTION OF MORALS

ACCORDING TO SOME of my critics, I refuse to make a moral judgment on slavery; I consider moral judgments out of place in all historical writing; and I take a relativist position on morals, if indeed I bother to take any position at all. This interpretation was presented honestly by Irwin Unger in the *American Historical Review,*[1] to which I replied with the following communication (slightly abridged).[2] The reply has not prevented the charge from being repeated by other, politically motivated critics who cannot seem to understand that opposition to moralizing does not imply indifference to morals and that opposition to a doctrine of absolute truth does not imply relativism.

To the Editor of the American Historical Review (February 1968).

Professor Unger raises too many questions for brief reply, and his particular arguments ought properly to be answered by different individuals. I should like to consider one general question and illustrate it with reference to his generous but mistaken remarks on my work on slavery. I agree with him that a radical politics does not require repudiation of the consensus view of American history; that such a view must be examined empirically and without bias; and that present-mindedness mars much of the new leftwing historiography, just as it marred much of the old. I see no principled objection to the consensus view in its more sophisticated versions, although if the bloody years 1861–1865 formed part of that consensus, we need a new vocabulary. In general, no Marxist ought to be embarrassed if the consensus view withstands the attacks of its critics: We should then have before us the particular history of the process by which the American bourgeoisie established its hegemony. We would not thereby be required to join the celebration. If such has been the true history of American capitalism, it would be incumbent upon radicals to study the secret of its success so as the better to oppose it. Radicals need a proper understanding of class dynamics and social forces, not a "usable past." Even if there had never been a viable radicalism in America, only Philistines would argue that therefore there never could be or should be. Professor Unger is, on these questions, shrewd and to the point. But for just this reason he ought to reconsider his notion that *The Contours of American History,* whatever its specific merits or demerits, "gives aid and comfort to the enemy."

Professor Williams in his way, and others (by no means all) in theirs, are trying to interpret American history in class terms. We know very well that a class interpretation does not imply an emphasis on class confrontation and struggle; it may reveal a process by which a given ruling class successfully avoided such confrontations. It was Marx himself, after all, who first pointed out that Asia had nothing like a social revolution until the advent of imperialist penetration. Professor Unger, therefore, makes too sharp a distinction between the Old and New Left: both have had a tendency to exaggerate confrontation and have, accordingly, failed to see the processes by which ruling classes may avoid such confrontation. It is no accident that such striking problems as the loyalty of the yeomen to the slave regime have received virtually no attention from the Left.

Contrary to Professor Unger, I should be prepared to argue—and have in detail in the essay "Marxian Interpretations of the Slave South"—that Marxists, beginning with Marx, have made a mess of their interpretation of the Old South and of the origins of the war. Two strains in Marxist and non-Marxist radical historiography account for this: the crude economic determinism into which even Marx and Engels sometimes retreated, and the tendency to adjust historical analysis to immediate political pressures. These, contrary to Professor Unger's implications, have plagued the historiography of the Left as a whole (and not only the Left) for a century. The philosophical idealism of some of the New Left historians has not enabled them to correct these weaknesses; it has at best led them to repeat past mistakes and at worst to compound them.

The best of the new radical scholarship is groping toward a class interpretation, as Professor Unger astutely observes, but for just that reason it marks the first stage of a resurgent Marxism. It forms a counterpart to the reassertion of an undogmatic Marxism in Europe and will, sooner or later, have to wed itself to the neo-Marxism most closely identified with the work of Antonio Gramsci. To Marxists being raised in this spirit, a class interpretation is at once economic, political, ideological, and moral; it is, by its very nature, opposed to economic determinism, which it regards as being not only wrong but silly, and in fact to determinism in general, except in a special sense of the word.

Let me illustrate the point with reference to Professor Unger's treatment of my essays on slavery and the War for Southern Independence, which, being a Yankee, he insists on calling a "civil war." Professor Unger sums up my viewpoint as follows: "Slavery, at least by implication, caused the war, not because it aroused the moral indignation of the Western world, but because it isolated the South from the progressive economic currents of the day." He defends me against the charge of economic determinism—for which I am grateful—

but nonetheless misses the point. I never intended to slight the moral question; without it there probably would have been no war, however sharp the political and economic antagonism. My point, at the risk of oversimplification, is that the South and North developed different systems of morality just as they developed different systems of economy, and that they did both because the classes rising to power in each section diverged fundamentally, that is, diverged in their elemental relationship to other human beings. For this reason I stressed the total antagonism of the free and slave labor systems. I do suggest a moral relativism here, but only on one level of historical analysis. In doing so, nothing prevents me from taking sides politically, in part as a response to the moral question. In arguing that the moral defense of slavery was an authentic and legitimate expression of the world view of its ruling class, and not a vulgar rationalization, I say that it therefore deserves to be treated with care, respect, and seriousness; I do not argue that the issue of North versus South did not present itself in part as a fundamental moral antagonism—quite the contrary—and I do not argue that the resolution of that moral antagonism was a matter of little or no importance for the development of modern civilization. Surely, Professor Unger, of all people, knows that an attempt at sympathetic understanding does not imply approval or moral neutrality. (If he will permit me to lecture him on one point: in irreconcilable confrontations, as Comrade Stalin, who remains dear to some of us for the genuine accomplishments that accompanied his crimes, clearly understood, it is precisely the most admirable, manly, principled, and, by their own lights, moral opponents who have to be killed; the others can be frightened or bought.)

Were Professor Unger to review his essay, he would have to reconsider the link between the old radical historiography and the new, but more important, he would have to reconsider future prospects. The class analysis he sees emerging and the greater restraint and objectivity for which he pleads are likely to converge in a way his essay fails to notice: in the re-emergence of a Marxism that is purged of its economic determinism and its naive romanticization of oppressed classes and peoples—a Marxism capable of doing for the United States what Lenin, Gramsci, and Mao, in radically different ways, did for their respective countries.

I have tried to demonstrate that the slaveholders could be and in fact were deeply committed to their defense of slavery and subjectively moral and socially responsible in their commitment to a world view of their own, but that their morality conflicted with that of the North and, more significantly, of Western civilization at large. What I have opposed is the—to me—fantastic notion that the slaveholders should be judged hypocrites or men without honor because they adhered to an archaic moral code, which authentically reflected the archaic social order in which they lived. In short, I have tried to suggest that the historian must take an objective and interior view if he is to understand the men about whom he is writing.

But of course that same historian can and should express relief that the slave South and its morality were defeated. In doing so, he does more than state a personal preference; he renders an affirmative moral judgment on historical process. The advance of human society has had, among other manifestations, an advance in the respect for the dignity and value of human life, and the unacceptability of slavery has formed part of that advance.

If we try to transcend these two levels of moral judgment, we arrive at a historical (not a relativist) view that permits us to commit ourselves wholly to the war against an evil institution (and to be able to judge it to be evil) and yet not moralize or assume a self-righteous pose. On the contrary, it is only through an appreciation of the duality of historical judgment that we can appreciate the tragic dimension of all human history. And at the risk of doing unintended violence to my radical critics and their assertion of absolute values, I must confess to believing that a man who cannot understand the inherent tragedy of history is not likely to be able to tell us much about the past, the present, or the future.

One of the amusing sidelights of this argument came forth in Staughton Lynd's remark:

> Overall the exchange between myself and Eugene Genovese may have generated more heat than light. But I believe it to have been worthwhile for the following sentence alone:
>
>> Lynd must necessarily declare slavery and servitude evil and immoral for every time and place; I [Genovese] would argue that at certain times throughout history they contributed to social development and that the moral case against modern slavery must rest on its being a historical anachronism.
>
> I accept this as a fair summary of our respective positions. I plead guilty to thinking slavery and servitude evil and immoral for every time and place. If this be demagogy and obscurantism, make the most of it. (*New York Review of Books,* Feb. 27, 1969.)

Now, it could be, and generally is, argued that the development of slavery and other forms of servitude propelled human society from a primitive existence, which, in Hobbes's famous phrase, was "nasty, brutish, and short," toward civilization. How else could ruling strata, including those who were freed from manual work and could engage in art and science, emerge? Without those strata, how could civilization have developed, and with it the present possibilities for a long and full life for the masses themselves? The tragedy inherent in this ironical historical process has been lost on few who have reflected on history at all; it was certainly not lost on Marx. Thus, Lynd tells us that we may put forward as morality—and absolute morality at that—the view that the human race should have been condemned to permanent savagery or, alternatively, that conditions necessary to bring the human race out of savagery must be judged immoral. But he fails to explain the criteria by which an advance needed to end a life that is "nasty, brutish, and short" can be judged immoral.

(He might get out of the difficulty by invoking God and original sin, but the great theologians have handled that problem rather nicely without invoking anything like Lynd's version of moral absolutism, which is so clearly flawed and open to so many diverse challenges.)

But the historical view implied in an appreciation of the positive role of class exploitation in the early stages of man's history implies a harsh critique of slavery in the modern world, especially in the nineteenth century. However much we may appreciate the internal integrity of the South's decision to defend an older social (and moral) order, it must also be judged by the historically developed moral sensibility of the larger Western world of which it was a part. On these grounds, it had to be condemned by those who took the higher ground of Western civilization's most developed values against the provincial ground of the slaveholders. The war certainly was a moral issue and a moral crusade, although it was many other less admirable things also. The value of a historical, as opposed to either an absolutist or relativist, treatment of the moral question lies in its ability to appreciate the tragic position of the slaveholders and the personal decency with which they could assert their own moral position, and yet to be free to condemn the world for which they stood and to justify a struggle to the death against it.

NOTES

1. Irwin Unger, "The 'New Left' and American History: Some Recent Trends in United States Historiography," *American Historical Review,* 72, no. 4 (July 1967), 1237–1263.

2. Letter from Eugene D. Genovese and reply by Unger, *American Historical Review,* 63, no. 3 (February 1968), 993–995.

Chapter 18

THE COMPARATIVE FOCUS IN LATIN AMERICAN HISTORY

There are at least two reasons for United States and Latin American historians to bring their work together into a comparative focus, the first being the need to maximize control of generalizations, and the second being the need to write the history of the social process by which a single world community has been developing since the sixteenth century. Recently, considerable progress with the first task has been made in the study of slavery and race relations, but little progress can yet be reported with the second.

One result of the work on slavery and race relations ought to warn and encourage us. Without entering here into a discussion of the specific points of view advanced by Frank Tannenbaum, Marvin Harris, Sidney Mintz, Stanley Elkins, Gilberto Freyre, Herbert Klein, and so many others, it could be demonstrated that the comparisons of slavery in the United States, South America, and the Carribbean have so far proven enormously important in clarifying issues and stimulating

This paper was read to the annual luncheon meeting of Latin Americanists at the December, 1969, meetings of the American Historical Association, Washington, D.C. Reprinted from *Journal of Inter-American Affairs,* 12, July 1970, pp. 317–327.

new research and yet have failed to yield some of the most sought-after generalizations.[1] Specifically, it is now clear that such factors as the closing of the African slave trade and the advent of commercial specialization in the slave economies affected the treatment of slaves according to a definite pattern although within that pattern the effects depended on a wide range of cultural, social, and political factors. As a result, we can now make much sounder generalizations about the nature of the slaveholders and their regimes, considered over time in historical evolution, in any particular slaveholding country.

But the one great generalization sought by so many of the participants in the discussion—that generalization which would bring the various patterns of race relations together within a single explanation—has proven elusive. It may be, of course, that such an explanation will emerge from future research, but we may be permitted some doubts. Pierre van den Berghe has used the comparative method to argue that no general theory of race relations is possible and that racial patterns are a function of class and other social relations.[2] But this conclusion, which I suspect will stand up over time, hardly negates the effort, for it can lead directly to new and more fruitful hypotheses about the social structure and the cultural systems of each society in which slavery was embedded.

Similarly, not long ago historians and sociologists felt certain that racial discrimination in the Southern United States would recede with the advance of urbanization and industrialization. Now we must come to terms with the complex findings of Roger Bastide, Florestan Fernandes, Octávio Ianni, Fernando Henrique Cardoso, and others who have been discovering quite different correlations in Brazil.[3] Until scholars in the United States can absorb this research and integrate it into their own, they cannot hope to make out a plausible case for their own favorite theories. If exhaustive comparative studies do not yield a single explanation for the advance or decline of racism as a pervasive ideology, they must, at the very least, shed a great deal of light on the various cultural systems.

The first problem is that the comparative method is a treacherous business, and we have yet to learn to recognize all its pitfalls or to understand its limits. This problem may be illustrated from the exciting new work on Cuban slavery. Herbert Klein opened the discussion with his *Slavery in the Americas* and took the risks that inevitably accompany an initial attempt to define the appropriate method and content of a new procedure—in this case, the comparison and contrast in depth of two slave societies.[4] Klein's bold thrust helped to clarify the methodological issues both by its direct attack on the problem and by the alternative viewpoints and criticism it called forth. Whatever the merits of its particular theses, it demonstrated the limits of one kind of comparative focus. I fear, however, that Klein, like Stanley Elkins before him, ran afoul of a problem destined to plague us all with untold misery. He had to choose between an intensive contrast of Virginia and Cuba in the same period and, alternatively, a contrast of Virginia and Cuba at different dates but at comparable points in their economic development. He chose the former and thereby ran the risk of confusing the specific effects of Virginia's secular economic decline and Cuba's secular economic advance with the other institutional factors he wished to isolate. I think he made the wrong choice and suspect that Richard Corwin, Franklin Knight, Roland Ely, and Manuel Moreno Fraginals—none of whom directly applies the comparative method but each of whom implicitly applies controls derived from it—are closer to the target.[5]

Yet, Klein has a few laughs in reserve, for it will not be easy to translate these efforts into a specifically comparative analysis without running risks quite as great as the ones he did. Knight, for example, in his forthcoming book on Cuban slave society on the eve of abolition, pays close attention to the social and cultural revolutions wrought by the sugar boom. He does not overthrow Klein's work, but he does show that its main theses are only valid for the eighteenth century, and he then traces the dissolution of those institutional arrangements during the nineteenth century, the alleged continuity of which formed an important part of Klein's argument. Knight restricted himself to Cuba, but his vision has clearly been in a comparative focus, as his present work attests. The problem with which he, like the rest of us, must sooner or later wrestle comes to this: If the sugar boom revolutionized Cuban society in the nineteenth century, as it had Barbadian in the seventeenth and Jamaican and Saint-Domingan in the eighteenth, how do we go about comparing and contrasting nineteenth century Cuba with seventeenth century Barbados or eighteenth century Saint-Domingue since, obviously, the experience of the former did not and could not recapitulate those of the latter, not only because of different social, political, and cultural settings, but also because the human beings who brought the sugar boom to Cuba could and did learn from the experience of their predecessors and because structural changes in the world economy and the international relationship of political forces confronted each new wave of sugar planters with drastically altered conditions?

The magnitude of the implied task has led some historians to give up at the start and to suggest that the writing of a comparative history of slave societies ought to be left to God. This frustration can be overcome once we accept the limits of the comparative method and realize that its promise falls far short of a grand synthesis of all human history or an even grander first principle of historical causation. Within its proper limits it will help us to shed false generalizations by providing much better controls than insulated studies can, and it will therefore help, as it already has, in forming richer hypotheses. One would think that these advantages would be quite enough.

The pursuit of Latin American history has much more to

gain from a comparative focus than better controls and richer hypotheses. To begin with, we ought to keep in mind that a comparative focus need not express itself in a comparative study; it may simply inform a particular study and thereby transform it, however imperceptibly, from being one more monograph into being a major historical work. A recent and outstanding example is John Womack's *Zapata and the Mexican Revolution*.[6] At first glance it appears that Womack concerns himself only with a certain phase of Mexican history and with a particular revolutionary movement. Yet, a careful reading of his book makes it clear that it was written with one eye on the experience of peasant rebellions throughout modern history and especially during our own century. Had he not been so informed, Womack could not have posed so sharply the theoretical implications of the intersection of a peasant with a bourgeois revolution. To appreciate his accomplishment one need only compare his book with Eric Wolf's recent comparative study, *Peasant Wars of the Twentieth Century.* Wolf takes up Russia, China, Algeria, and Vietnam, in addition to Mexico and Cuba. With his customary skill and learning, he shows that in each case the peasants rose in defense of familiar values and arrangements but ended by advancing causes that were not initially theirs and yet represented a possible response to the dilemmas posed by the encroachments of capitalism on the countryside. With due respect to Wolf's cogent analyses, once must admit that he brings nothing to the study of the Mexican revolution that cannot be found in Womack's book. If there is a criticism to be made of Womack's effort, it is the same one that might be made of Wolf's more directly comparative one: The decidedly reactionary and regressive features of the peasant movement are described without adequate comment and reflection. But in both cases this weakness probably results from the strong, sympathetic attitude toward the protagonists rather than from the absence or presence of a comparative focus. In any case, Womack's book will likely stand the test of time and become required reading for anyone interested in the great social tranformations of the modern world, whether in Europe, Asia, Africa, or Latin America. Had the book been written in ignorance of the general history of modern peasant wars, it could hardly have come close to offering the penetrating insights it in fact does.

A comparative focus has much more to offer than a general enriching of national, regional, and topical histories, but to date it has offered little of general importance despite the early prodding of Herbert E. Bolton and his students. Bolton's own work, which essentially looked toward a world perspective for national histories, came to be interpreted rather narrowly by his critics, who generally concerned themselves less with his breadth of vision than with his admittedly dubious secondary thesis of a common history for the Americas. The ensuing debate has always been a bit depressing and has sometimes seemed little more than a series of ideological gambits. Bolton saw that United States historians had been provincial and chauvinistic; he was surely right in suggesting that a United States historian who knew little of European history and virtually nothing of Latin American was no historian at all. But, it was one thing for him to argue that a historian must bring a sympathetic understanding of the history of other peoples to the study of his own, and it was quite another to project a common history for peoples of diverse Old World cultures and diverse New World experiences. Bolton's interest and contribution lay in the broadening of our perspective, and it is regrettable that so much attention has been directed toward the refutation of his weak specific thesis of a common history. On that specific question Edmundo O'Gorman appears to have had the better of the argument. However much we may admire Bolton's vision and constructive labors, we ought to conclude that his more limited thesis was a somewhat premature, if praiseworthy, attempt to overcome the narrow-mindedness and national exclusiveness against which he devoted so much of his time and work.

He and his followers have nonetheless scored points, and we cannot leave matters with O'Gorman's critique, which clearly had its own ideological bias. O'Gorman pushed his argument beyond all reasonable limits when he insisted that the common element in the history of the Americas was merely the common element in all human history. But if we are to speak of something more viable, we shall have to delineate our subject with much greater rigor than has so far been done.

At present the comparative focus in Latin American history has been fragmented into the debate over the so-called Bolton Thesis;[7] the rapidly unfolding comparative work on slave systems; the models of economic development advanced in the work of Sanford Mosk, Celso Furtado, Raul Prebisch, and Maurice Halperin and some others; and any number of other lines of inquiry into social, political, intellectual, and economic history. Implicit in these seemingly discrete discussions has been a new point of departure.

Since the sixteenth century, if not earlier, increasing sections of the world have been absorbed into a single international economy. The rise of the world market represents the essential aspect of what has come to be called capitalism—that is, a mode of production based on private ownership of the means of production within which labor-power has itself become a commodity to be bought and sold like any other. From this point of view, all New World colonies represented particular responses to the claims of the world market as manifested in particular national political economies. Similarly, the world history of Asia and Africa, in contradistinction to the purely local history of their component tribes, nations, and empires, begins with European penetration. Let us again recall the observation by Marx that Western expansion brought about the only revolution Asia ever experienced

—that is, the only profound upheaval in its relationship of class forces. The same comment could be made for Africa, if we qualify it to take account of the effects of Islamic penetration, and of the indigenous Indo-American highland societies.

There are unpleasant ironies here, for the condemnation of Western colonialism and imperialism has generally been advanced by those who adhere to a linear view of history and who sing the praises of the Gospel of Progress. I fear, however, that one cannot have an unqualified anticolonialism, a unilinear view of history, and the Gospel of Progress all at the same time without inducing schizophrenia. It ought to be clear, in any case, that no one can seriously study the history of colonialism and the impact of the West on Africa, Asia, or Indo-America without paying the closest attention to the vigorous debate raging in France and Eastern Europe over the "Asian mode of production" or, for those who prefer Karl Wittfogel's terminology, "oriental despotism."

It may be objected that this line of attack links Latin American history to Asian and African through a unified history of modern imperialism but does not demonstrate that a comparative focus within New World history itself has much to offer. This objection has merit, which ought not to distress us, but it is also much too sweeping. If we speak of the New World experience as a series of variations on the theme of European expansion, we do indeed in some ways relate, for example, the history of Brazil more closely to that of China than to that of the United States. Naturally, this view creates concern among those who confuse the writing of history with the propagandistic exigencies of Pan-Americanism, the State Department, Standard Oil, or the United Fruit Company—to the extent that it is ever useful to separate these weighty categories. These problems, however, may be safely left to plague ideologues and need not concern us further.

Nor need we fear that such an approach will yield a new version of ideology and myth-making masquerading as history in the form of some proposed unity of the experience of the so-called Third World or some comparable political swindle. Rather, what is proposed is a recognition that the steady expansion of the world market during the last four hundred years or more has drawn almost every people into its orbit. The elements of unity in the experience of the several American countries, which Bolton and his followers sought to delineate, prove to be essentially manifestations of the process by which the expansion of commodity production and the attendant rise of a single international economy has created a genuinely world history.

The Americas do, nonetheless, display common experiences that set them apart from Asia and Africa. Always leaving room for exceptions in South Africa, Australia, or where you will, it was the New World that bore the brunt of Europe's massive export of settlers and Africa's forced export of slaves. Richard Morse has drawn our attention to the importance of a comparative study of these population movements for any meaningful attempt to find a common denominator to the New World experience.[8] It would take little effort to demonstrate that these movements, unlike such previous ones as those of the Mongols or Arabs, were functionally related to the rise and expansion of European capitalism, with all that that implies for culture and ethos as well as for politics and economics. Similarly, however much New World slavery had in common with the labor systems introduced by Europeans into Java or Ceylon, plantation slavery and the formation of distinct Afro-American peoples represent, for better or for worse, specifically New World experiences which, as Tannenbaum so eloquently and tirelessly argued, altered fundamentally and permanently the lives, culture, and destiny of everyone, black or white, who touched them.[9]

Then, too, those who, like Professor Whitaker, have urged attention to the developing intellectual and moral bonds among the American peoples, have in their own way reminded us that the irreversible development of an all-embracing world market has steadily eroded the possibilities of spiritual isolation. If, for example, Mosk was correct—as he certainly was—in suggesting that diverse paths of institutional development led Anglo- and Latin America into radically different relationships to world capitalism, it nonetheless remains true that in an increasingly commercial world the exploited, underdeveloped, and colonial countries can and generally do import modern ideas, styles, and values a good deal more rapidly and successfully than they can duplicate the economic performance of the cosmopolitan powers.[10]

We end, therefore, with the need for a synthetic history of world capitalism and with the expectation that the Americas have participated in that history in ways which have combined shared and diverse responses. It would, however, be a mistake to leave matters there, for if the history of the Americas has anything at all to contribute to an understanding of European history, it is precisely in the necessity for a reconsideration of capitalism itself. The United States, after all, lacked a feudal past and was spawned by the most advanced of European capitalist countries. The history of its place in the development of capitalism has therefore been no less theoretically uninteresting than it has been politically momentous. In Latin America we find traditional societies conquered by Iberian countries that had only dubious claims on the label "capitalist" at all. Having outlined my views in a recent book, in which I have argued that Spain and Portugal were commercial but essentially not capitalist societies in the early modern period, I shall not pursue the matter here.[11] But whether or not one characterizes Incaic and Aztec societies as oriental despotisms, feudal empires, or traditional communes; whether or not one characterizes Spanish and Portuguese colonization as a bourgeois or a seigneurial process—the questions must be debated, and the answers ought to tell us a great deal about the content and significance of European capitalist development.

A brief consideration of a recent book will illustrate the

problem and illuminate the possibilities. Andre Gunder Frank, in *Capitalism and Under-Development in Latin America,*[12] argues that Chile, Brazil, and by extension the rest of Latin America were, from the beginning, drawn into the capitalist orbit in a condition of colonial-satellite dependency. For Frank, the entire history of Latin America must be seen as the steady absorption of subject peoples into a world market and specifically into one or another system of metropolitan exploitation. Hence, he speaks of Latin American backwardness not as the result of the bypassing of peoples and regions in the process of economic development, but as the planned and incidental effects of colonial-capitalist evolution—of what he calls the "development of under-development." Frank's abilities as a historian, not to mention a logician, leave something to be desired: his evidence from the colonial period will not pass muster, is crudely interpreted, and does not prove a thing. It could even be demonstrated that this professed Marxist either did not read or did not take seriously Marx's *Capital* before he set about to discuss its interpretation of history. The fact remains that Frank, for all his idiosyncracies and special pleading, has forcefully raised the question of the integrative nature of the developing world market and has plausibly suggested that any modern history which is written without this dimension is simply beside the point. Yet, apart from the books of Sergio Bagú, the brilliant speculations of José Carlos Mariátegui, and the contributions of one or two others, historians of the colonial period of Latin American history have gone to extraordinary lengths to avoid the theoretical implications of their own work.

What Frank cannot understand—and this failure stems from his singular concern with economics and not at all from his ostensible Marxism—is that it is one thing to argue that European capitalism has intruded itself into every part of the world and has exploited and subjugated the most diverse peoples, societies, and social systems; but that it is quite another thing to argue that therefore every such people, society, and social system has become one more variant of bourgeois culture.

When Frank explicitly suggests that a significant portion of Indian village economy has in fact become absorbed into external exploitative market relations, he at least provides a hypothesis worth investigating. When he implicitly dismisses subsistence and nonmarket economic relations as either insignificant or one more manifestation of colonial capitalism, he ceases to make sense. But more serious is his implicit equation of economics—of the penetration of market relations—with culture and therefore specifically with ideology. But then, it is hard to talk to people who think that the history of the Catholic church, the formation of a Catholic ethos, and the development of Catholic theology can be understood as reflexes of Vatican property ownership.

If we stand back from the polemics and the special pleading, what comes into view is not merely the possibility of a dual economy within a single nation-state, but of a dual society. In a forthcoming interpretation of the course of French history, Professor Edward Whiting Fox will argue that the rise of the Atlantic economy in the early modern period split France into two societies—the one interlocked with the world market and reflecting its developing world view; the other bypassed and largely self-sufficient and retaining, as best it could, an increasingly strange and dangerous world view of its own. Professor Fox posits two parallel societies, two parallel class structures, two parallel ethos and derived political principles, at war with each other on one level and intersecting at other levels. It seems to me that some such model must be developed by Latin American historians to explain the elusive character of their subject. Professor Tannenbaum used to remark that a sophisticated citizen of Lima was more likely to know all about New York or Paris than about the nearest Indian village.

The major theoretical problem here—the extent and specific quality of this duality in different times and countries—

must lead us to a redefinition of capitalism. From being understood as merely a system of economic relations, it must be understood as a social process. European capitalism penetrated Brazil, Mexico, Peru, and the United States in radically different ways and created special conditions in each case. Those conditions and national or regional responses necessarily fed back into the mainstream of capitalist development and thereby helped shape the culture as well as the economy of the center of the capitalist world. Seen from this angle, the comparative study of the Anglo- and Latin American experiences ought to contribute to a general history of world capitalist society in its many national variations, so that we may begin to appreciate the full extent to which capitalism has profoundly and irreversibly altered the life and consciousness of all peoples and has begun to generate an international society and not merely an international economy. But it in no sense implies a homogenizing of Latin American or any other history and in fact must be predicated on the assumption that each national response is in part a result of a particular precapitalist culture, which alone guarantees each a unique historical status.

The comparative focus in Latin American history will probably prove most fruitful as a way of integrating Latin American into world history and as a way, more specifically, of contributing to a synthetic history of modern capitalism. It may also reveal some evidence of shared experience in the history of the Americas, but we need not be discouraged if these prove less important than the evidence of divergence, for ultimately the links will have to be sought at the higher level of analysis. Those who would seek a general and integrated history of the Americas will not be happy. Yet, a synthetic history of modern capitalism, in its full cultural dimension, and of the place of Latin America within it ought to be enough work for several generations, and I frankly doubt that we shall ever be able to do much more. But if this secular age objects to leaving the pet task of writing an inclusive American history to God, then we should remember that a comparative focus can help us here too. After all, it was the Mexicans who taught us that even a confirmed atheist is not without celestial recourse. Those of us who do not believe in God are at liberty to believe in the Virgin of Guadalupe, into whose compassionate hands we may thrust our most painful dilemma.

NOTES

1. For a collection of leading points of view on slavery in the Americas, with selections from these and other authors and appropriate bibliography, see Laura Foner and Eugene D. Genovese, eds., *Slavery in the New World: A Reader in Comparative History* (New Jersey, 1969).

2. Pierre L. van den Berghe, *Race and Racism: A Comparative Perspective* (New York, 1967).

3. Cf., e.g., Fernando Henrique Cardoso and Octávio Ianni, *Côr e mobilidade social en Florianópolis* (São Paulo, 1960).

4. Herbert S. Klein, *Slavery in The Americas: A Comparative Study of Cuba and Virginia* (Chicago, 1967).

5. Arthur Corwin, *Spain and the Abolition of Slavery in Cuba 1817–1866* (Austin, 1967); Franklin W. Knight, *Cuban Slave Society on the Eve of Abolition* (Madison, 1971); Roland T. Ely, *Cuando reinaba su majestad el azúcar* (Buenos Aires, 1963); Manuel Moreno Fraginals, *El Ingenio* (Havana, 1963).

6. John Womack, *Zapata and The Mexican Revolution* (New York, 1969).

7. Lewis Hanke, ed., *Do The Americas Have a Common History?* (New York, 1962).

8. Richard Morse, "The Heritage of Latin America" in Louis Hartz, ed., *The Founding of New Societies* (New York, 1964), pp. 123–177.

9. See Frank Tannenbaum, *Slave and Citizen: The Negro in the Americas* (New York, 1947).

10. The views of Whitaker and Mosk may be found in brief form in Hanke, *Do The Americas Have a Common History?*

11. Eugene D. Genovese, *The World the Slaveholders Made* (New York, 1969).

12. Andre Gunder Frank, *Capitalism and Under-Development in Latin America* (New York, 1967).

Part Four

THE POINT OF VIEW RESTATED

Chapter 19

ON ANTONIO GRAMSCI

THAT THE WORK and indeed the name of Antonio Gramsci remain virtually unknown to the American Left provides the fullest, if saddest, proof of the intellectual bankruptcy of "official" Marxism and its parties, old and new. Every sect, no matter how trivial or tiresome, will spend its first few dollars to publish some cant labeled theory. After all, without a revolutionary theory there can be no . . . . Even more appalling, the franchise holders of what was once a Communist movement continue to be financially well endowed if morally and politically moribund and hardly know what to do with their money. Publishing houses, schools, and institutes abound, and—if my talent for estimating bureaucratic expenditures does not fail me—annually cost tens and hundreds of thousands of dollars. The barely literate party hack has come into his own. Like the associate professor at Useless U. who finds himself in the paperback market, he will be published. All of which would not be without its delights were the cost not so dear. As it is, it is nothing short of a disgrace that the greatest

This essay was originally published in *Studies on the Left,* 7, March–April, 1967, pp. 83–108. Reprinted by permission.

Western Marxist theorist of our century remains untranslated, unread, and undiscussed.[1]

Professor Cammett's excellent book, *Antonio Gramsci and The Origins of Italian Communism,* brings this shabby game to a close, although not until a significant portion of Gramsci's *Quaderni del carcere* (*Prison Notebooks*) are in English will the full extent of the shabbiness be appreciated. The few intellectuals surviving in the Communist party, with an occasional exception, recite from dated texts of minimal relevance to current problems; their counterparts in the Leftist sects, who at least have the excuse of youth and of political *élan,* diligently search the writings of recent theorists of societies unlike our own.

While these charades are being played out, the books of the one theorist of genius who posed and faced Western socialism's most difficult problems lie unopened. It is no accident. Gramsci challenged the best of the bourgeois intellectuals on their own ground, but no less did he challenge their social-democratic imitators and especially their dogmatic, simple-minded and mediocre opponents in the revolutionary camp. Gramsci's thought represents the maturation of Marxism and its restoration to the high level of its founders; as such, it exposes the degeneracy of much that has passed for Marxism in our day.

Professor H. Stuart Hughes takes some liberties when he writes that compared with the theoretical work of Gramsci that of Lenin appears "crude indeed."[2] The assertion is exaggerated and unjust, but it is not absurd or indefensible. Its plausibility constitutes the highest compliment to the richness and depth of Gramsci's thought. And there is no higher compliment to Lenin's intellectual achievements than that Gramsci sincerely considered himself a Leninist and did not merely strike a Leninist pose to facilitate his leadership of the Italian Communist party (PCI). For Gramsci, Lenin was the man who revitalized Marxism by purging it of determinism and economism, by restoring the element of will and by grasping the role of consciousness. Gramsci did for European Marxism what Mao Tse-tung did for Asian: he continued Lenin's effort to liberate Marxism from the mechanism that has plagued it from the beginning.

Cammett explores briefly but suggestively the intellectual kinship of Gramsci and Mao. Gramsci early saw the backwardness of Italy and the attendant weakness of its social order as providing especially good soil for a revolutionary movement. He was the first Italian Marxist political leader to stress the agrarian question in general and the question of the Mezzogiorno (the underdeveloped South) in particular. If he insisted that only the working class could solve those questions, he also insisted that the success of the proletarian revolution was bound up with them. Cammett sees a parallel between Gramsci's work on the Mezzogiorno (1926) and Lin Piao's celebrated thesis as presented in *Long Live the Victory of a People's War!* (1965). "In [Lin's] theory the whole underdeveloped world becomes a vast Mezzogiorno. The principal difference is that for the Italian theorist of 1926, the revolutionary impulse originated in the cities, though its success depended on support from the rural areas. For the Chinese theorist of 1965, the revolution has its primary center in the countryside, and support from the cities may even be unnecessary." Cammett examines the relationship between Italian and Chinese Marxism on several levels but stresses the peasant question. This emphasis, although justified by today's most pressing practical questions, should not obscure the deeper link between the two—that concern for the dialectics of historical development which Cammett elsewhere discusses with considerable sophistication. Gramsci's remarks on revolutionary thought represent, although obviously not so intended, the firmest defense of the "Marxism" of a Chinese revolution with a peasant rather than proletarian base: "Revolutionary thought does not see time as a factor of progress . . . . To pass through one stage and advance to another, it is enough that the first stage be realized in thought."

II

ANTONIO GRAMSCI came from a petit-bourgeois family in Sardinia—perhaps the most economically and culturally wretched section of Italy. Despite his achievements as a pupil he had to leave school as a boy to help support the family. Supported by the efforts of his mother and sisters, he finally managed to study at the University of Turin, which was then beginning to feel the powerful cleansing wind of Croceian idealism and to slough off its superficial positivism. There is much about Gramsci's youth we do not know, but Cammett's painstaking scholarship gives us enough. His biographical sketch shows us a sensitive, physically deformed, brilliant boy who, in his own words, "had known only the most brutal aspects of life." Cammett shows two great and lasting influences in his life: the experience with personal and class harshness, which steeled him for the life of a revolutionary and for an eleven-year confinement in a fascist prison, and the serious study of Hegelian and Croceian thought, from which he proceeded to Marxism and because of which he became implacably hostile to economic determinism and mechanism of all varieties.

The outcome was the making of an unusual Communist, who like his long-time collaborator and successor to the leadership of the PCI, Palmiro Togliatti, remained an intellectual deeply concerned with the quality of man's spiritual and cultural life and who simultaneously had the qualities necessary to win the support of the Comintern and to prepare the PCI to survive the long years of fascist repression. In 1926 the fascist secret police reported that the PCI alone among the opposition parties, retained links with the masses and had prepared itself for underground struggle. Gramsci himself was arrested and spent the last eleven years of his life in prison, where he read whatever the authorities would let him have and where he wrote his greatest works—prison notebooks on political theory, Italian history and culture, philosophical criticism (most notably his critique of Croce), and on an astonishing assortment of other subjects. Prison, he observed, is a poor place to study, but he made it do and by this act of will alone exemplified that selflessness and heroism which has brought socialism into the world.

If the American Left has not appreciated the significance of Gramsci's thought, the Italian fascists were not so backward. This "Sardinian hunchback," remarked Mussolini, "has an unquestionably powerful brain." More to the point were the words of the fascist prosecutor at Gramsci's trial in 1926, "We must stop this brain from functioning for twenty years."

As a party leader Gramsci had a difficult time on two counts. First, he and his fellow students from the University of Turin had to organize their own socialist faction around the journal *L'Ordine nuovo (The New Order)*. Their position as intellectuals and their concern with cultural questions as well as with bread-and-butter issues made them suspect in the PSI generally and in proletarian Turin especially. It was a long road to leadership first of the Turin proletariat and then of the new Communist party, in which they were originally only secondary and uncomfortable allies of the ultra-leftist Amadeo Bordiga. Their success depended less on factional political maneuvering, for which Gramsci had great distaste, than on the wisdom of their course in the specific circumstances of the Turin labor movement. This side of the story can only be noted here, but its telling is one of Cammett's special achievements. Rarely has the relationship between a man's political thought and action been explored so specifically and shrewdly as is Gramsci's in this indispensable book.

The second front on which Gramsci had to fight was against the Comintern itself. His arrest in 1926 might have saved him from being deposed as a party leader. Although he had no special admiration for Trotsky—Cammett even suggests that he had put forward the idea of socialism in one country before anyone in Russia—he spoke up in opposition to excessive and administrative measures against the Left opposition and warned of the dangers of bureaucratic degeneration. An early advocate of the united front, he received news of the "Third Period" (the Comintern's period of ultra-leftism in which the social democrats were seen as the main enemy) and its attacks on "social fascism" with foreboding. Had he been a free man and effective leader of the party at the time, his fate would have become problematical. The subsequent turn to the popular front, long foreshadowed in his own work, removed the pressure. Gramsci's life's work came to political fruition in the postwar rise of the PCI under the brilliant leadership of Togliatti.

III

THE GREAT QUESTION absorbing Gramsci's attention and intruding itself into everything else was the nature and role of the party. Even his lengthy and painstaking examination of the historical role of the intelligentsia represents a special case of his more general concern. I suspect that he would have found nonsensical, or at least trivial, the question of "agency of change" now agitating the American Left and would have found incomprehensible the dispute over the relative merits of class and party as agency. One of his most striking ideas was that a class is hardly worthy of the name until it comes to self-consciousness—an idea that veers dangerously close to idealism and that nonetheless is hard to turn aside. The party of the working class therefore has tasks beyond that of providing leadership in daily battle; it is charged with the transformation of the working class itself into a body worthy to rule. The "cultural" task of the party is to win the working class to a world view capable of absorbing and transcending the culture and accomplishment of the past.

Professor Hughes is mistaken when he writes, "What interested him was the character of the new culture that would develop *after* the proletarian assumption of power."[3] The reverse is true. Gramsci had no faith in the triumph of a working class that had not already begun to think and live in a new way. To the party fell the task of completing that transformation in the working class which was immanent in capitalist society itself. To accomplish this task the party needed to find its own way—to establish an authentic, autonomous world view purged of all fatalism and mechanical determinism. It is in this context that Cammett's penetrating remark on Serrati and Gramsci must be evaluated: "Serrati thought of the possession of power as the culmination of the general elevation of the masses whereas Gramsci believed that the masses could be elevated only by possessing power. The principal difference between the Second and Third Internationals is contained in this contrast." The possession of power, however, means in the first place the building of an autonomous party and movement: The "elevation of the masses," therefore, begins with the struggle for control of civil society as well as the state and reaches its climax when the state has been conquered and turned to that purpose.

Nothing irritated Gramsci more than the mechanical side of Marxism. For him the genuine doctrine of Marx was one "in which man and reality, the instrument of labor and the will, are not separated but come together in the *historical act*. Hence [Marxists] believe that the canons of historical materialism are valid only after the fact, for studying and understanding the events of the past, and ought not to become a mortgage on the present and future." He scoffed at reliance on such "objective conditions" as economic depression. The objective conditions for proletarian revolution, he once observed, had existed in Europe for fifty years or more.

It seems to me that Cammett stresses unduly the relationship between Gramsci's concern for superstructural problems, in contradistinction to those directly connected with the economic base, and the postrevolutionary situation in the 1920s and 1930s. Cammett is correct in pointing out that Gramsci himself saw the cultural front as especially important during such periods, when the direct confrontation of classes recedes, and that Gramsci, unlike so many others in the Comintern, understood the defensive character of the period in question. Yet, this emphasis on superstructure—in Cammett's words, on "the whole complex of political, social, and cultural institutions and ideas"—had even deeper roots in his awareness of the dependence of revolution, even in periods of dramatic confrontation, on consciousness rather than on economics. (There is in Cammett's book a tendency to avoid a frank discussion of the markedly idealist cast of Gramsci's thought, and this tendency, I suspect, accounts for his insistence on reading Gramsci narrowly on this question.) Simple as it is, Gramsci's observation that capitalism has been objectively ready for burial since the late nineteenth century—that, if I may put it this way, the Leninist theory of a general crisis in society and not merely the economy deserves to be taken seriously—ought to render permanent the concentration on the ideological struggle.

Unlike the simpletons who insist that the desire for liberation flows from the innate qualities of oppressed classes and peoples, Gramsci saw that desire as a function of specific social processes: "Men, when they feel their strength and are conscious of their responsibility and their value, do not want another man to impose his will on theirs and undertake to control their thoughts and actions." It was precisely the struggle to bring the working class to a sense of its strength, responsibility and value that provided his main concern. He obliquely criticized Marx for lapsing on occasion from his own insight and for stressing in an abstract way the predominance of material over ideological forces. Gramsci pointed out that the principle of unity of form and content calls into question the validity of such a dichotomy. Material forces as "content" and ideologies as "form" necessarily comprise a "historical bloc" since material forces are unthinkable without form and ideologies merely individual chattering when not expressive of such forces.

The instrument favored by Gramsci in the ideological struggle for the working class was the workers' council or soviet. He did not borrow this idea directly from Russian experience. It arose from several sources, not the least of which was the American journal, *The Liberator,* and especially the writings of Daniel De Leon. For Gramsci the socialist state already existed in the potentiality of working-class social institutions. To create such a state the first task is to bring the working class as a whole within such institutions.

Gramsci rejected the trade unions as organs of revolutionary transformation and preparation, and Cammett's account of his critique ought to be required reading for American socialists, especially those in the Marxist parties. The seriousness with which Gramsci viewed the role of the councils may be gleaned from his insistence that the working class must "educate itself, gather experience, and acquire a responsible awareness of the duties incumbent upon classes that hold the power of the state."

For him the worst error committed by the party in relation to the unions was the tendency to regard the economic struggle as an activity essential to the social revolution. The trade union, in its very origins, organized itself in response to hostile and imposed conditions, rather than as an autonomous expression of the working class. The trade union struggle was contingent, not permanent, and its organization was, accordingly, incapable of embodying a revolutionary movement. Unionism, being a form of capitalist society, brings the worker to see labor as a means for gain, not as a productive process, but it is consciousness of the latter that alone can raise the working class to an appreciation of its historic responsibilities. The council, on the other hand, effected the collaboration of skilled and unskilled workers, the technical strata and the clerical personnel within a notion of the unity of the industrial process. Whereas the unions exist to prevent the class war from being unleashed, the council threatens to unleash it at any moment. Long before the corporate state in Italy or the perception by radicals of a growing corporate liberalism in the United States, Gramsci observed that the detachment of the union bureaucracies from their rank-and-file constitutes the movement's strength, not weakness. The detached bureaucracies, isolated from the tumult of the masses, guarantee stability in the negotiation and enforcement of contracts. This guarantee establishes the "legitimacy" of the unions in the eyes of the bourgeoisie and makes possible those union-inspired advances in living conditions which have occurred under capitalism.

Gramsci's thinking on these questions, even apart from his critique of trade unionism, should prove unusually suggestive in our country. In his view the councils could educate the Italian workers in the political process and prepare them to wield state power. The English and American workers, however, have long been practiced in the exercise of political power, at least in the ordinary sense of the word. Certainly, he meant something deeper—the instillation in the working class of a sense that it stands for a culturally, economically, politically and socially superior order. Yet, it does seem to me that as a practical matter the two meanings were necessarily inseparable in the thought of a man concerned with one of the weaker and more backward capitalist states of Europe. Cammett cites the view of the distinguished Marxist historian, Giuliano Procacci, that the backwardness of the Italian labor movement prevented its being trapped like those of the more advanced countries into a primary concern for economic issues. The struggle for democracy and for the reorganization of civil society became indissolubly linked to the economic struggle.

Thus does the Marxism of Italian communism part company with the superficiality of its official American counterpart. One of the more banal themes of American Marxist historiography has been the allegedly wonderful advantages to the working class provided by the gift of bourgeois democracy. From this philistine viewpoint, the movements associated with St. Thomas of Monticello and Andrew Jackson graciously bestowed upon the working class the full benefit of their battle to broaden the base of American capitalism. The victory of the "people" over Tories, Federalists, and Whigs produced a broad franchise; by the time the working class matured it found itself enfranchised free of charge. Those on the Left who have celebrated this circumstance have substituted a retrospective popular frontism for Marxian analysis and have thereby missed the duality of the process and its significance. On the one hand this bourgeois-democratic political process did present the working class with extraordinary opportunities for improving its material conditions under capitalism; on the other hand this same process drew the revolutionary teeth of the proletariat and helped extend over it the hegemony of the bourgeoisie. We should let the bourgeoisie do the celebrating. For American socialism it ushered in a debacle, albeit one retaining some long-range positive possibilities. At least it has generated a level of culture and political practice among the workers on which a movement not sterilized by dogmatism or liberal shibboleths may someday build.

Gramsci's central concern with the working class and its changing composition led him to consider the metamorphosis of the bourgeoisie as well. He noted that technological developments were eliminating the master craftsmen and were rendering the workers increasingly capable of carrying on without technical supervision. With a self-disciplined working class, the technicians were being "reduced to the level of the producer," connected to the capitalists by a nakedly exploitative relationship. Cammett notes that Gramsci regarded this shift as carrying with it an attendant shift from a petitbourgeois to a proletarian consciousness.

In relatively underdeveloped Italy this attendant shift may

well have taken place according to Gramsci's expectations, but in the United States the reverse has apparently occurred: the technicians have shifted from a petit-bourgeois to a bourgeois psychology. They have proceeded from shopkeeper individualism to team consciousness within the framework of bourgeois values and assumptions; they have proceeded from consciousness of personal economic and social interests to consciousness of class responsibilities, which unfortunately have been the responsibilities of the present rather than the future ruling class. Yet, the potentialities foreseen by Gramsci remain and provide considerable hope for a future socialist movement.

Finance capitalism, Gramsci observed, separates the owner from the factory and therefore renders him parasitic and superfluous; he no longer has a role to play in production. The consequences of this process, about which bourgeois theorists talk such self-serving nonsense, are as ominous as they are ludicrous:

> The owner of capital [writes Gramsci] has become a dead branch in the field of production. Since he is no longer indispensable—since his historical functions have atrophied—he has become a mere agent of the police. He puts his interests immediately in the hands of the state, which will ruthlessly defend them.

These circumstances—increasing parasitism and increasing reliance on an authoritarian state—create favorable conditions for a working-class movement sufficiently broad to include the technical strata and the so-called new middle class. The rationalization of the economy proceeds hand-in-hand with the intensification of the system's higher level irrationalities, which have their primary manifestations in war, racism, ghetto poverty and moral decay. The process as a whole threatens to destroy the very security it offers the affluent sections of the upper and middle echelons of the technical and proletarian strata. When Staughton Lynd told the First

Annual Socialist Scholars Conference in 1965 that the irrationalities of capitalism might soon force the American people as a whole to consider a socialist alternative as a matter of survival, he departed less from a class analysis than would appear on the surface.

Gramsci's popular frontism must be understood in this context. Early in his career he stressed the national character of the proletarian revolution and spoke of the need to explain the advantages of socialism to the middle classes. At the same time he had the utmost contempt for the revisionists and would have roared with laughter at the slogan, "Socialism is not on the agenda." The autonomy of the party and the unceasing agitation among the masses for socialism were among his life-long themes. For him tactical alliances with other parties and classes, especially defensive ones, could never be an excuse for hiding the face of the party, or for advancing only bourgeois-democratic demands, or for sowing illusions about "progressive" sections of the bourgeoisie.

Gramsci initially fought for unity in the PSI, although he sharply criticized the reformists, but the failure of the party's nerve during the revolutionary crisis of 1919–1920 convinced him of the need for a split. He may have been influenced in this course by his assessment of the rise of fascism, which he analyzed with a depth and clarity setting him apart in Italy and, with the exception of Trotsky and a few others, in the Comintern as well. After the split in 1921 he worked unceasingly to win the new Communist party away from Bordiga's ultraleftism and to create an apparatus capable of guiding the workers through a rapid ideological transformation.

In Gramscian terms a political party is an agent of education and civilization—a school in which one studies the life of the state. Parties represent the adherence of élites to particular forms of class rule; they educate their followers in the principles of moral conduct, the duties and the obligations appropriate to that social order. A party justifies its historical existence when it develops three strata: (1) a rank-and-file or ordinary men whose participation is characterized by discipline and faith; (2) a leadership, which provides cohesion; and (3) cadres, which mediate morally, physically and intellectually between the other two. Of these three strata he stressed leadership:

> We speak of captains without an army, but in reality it is easier to form an army than to find captains. It is surely true that an already existing army will be destroyed if it lacks captains, whereas a group of captains, cooperative and in agreement on common ends, will not be slow in forming an army where none exists.

To this view he added two observations. Contrary to the Social Democrats, he argued that a socialist party must be an autonomous entity, not one dependent on the larger movement of bourgeois democracy; it must reject the existing order and work relentlessly for its overthrow. It must also be monolithic in the sense that is formed on principle and essentials, not on secondary considerations. As in so many cases, his verbal acquiescence in the line of the Stalinist Comintern hid fundamental differences. A monolithic party, for Gramsci, meant one without factional organizations but with room for dissent. A socialist party must have enthusiasm and good will from its members, neither of which can be coerced ideologically or by administrative measures. To grasp the full significance of his ideas on these subjects we need to consider his groundbreaking work on the role of the intellectuals.

IV

CRITICAL SELF-CONSCIOUSNESS, wrote Gramsci in *Il Materialismo storico,* means historically and politically the formation of an intellectual élite, for the masses cannot achieve ideological independence through their own efforts. They first must be organized, but there can be no organization without intellectuals. By intellectuals, Gramsci meant more than artists and scholars; he meant also technicians, industrial managers, and administrative personnel. The first, he called "traditional intellectuals"; the second, he called "organic intellectuals." Cammett's last chapter summarizes concisely and impressively the ideas on both strata that Gramsci scattered in the *Quaderni*.

The outstanding feature of the traditional intellectuals is their sense of representing, in Gramsci's words, "historical continuity uninterrupted even by the most radical and complicated changes of social and political systems." These men consequently consider themselves an autonomous group, independent of the ruling class. They are tied to the Establishment indirectly and in ways sufficiently subtle to permit them to maintain illusions. If this indirection fosters illusions, it also creates room for independent thought and action.

The organic intellectuals, being more directly bound to the Establishment, rarely escape awareness of their place in the economic process. These men share the interests of the ruling class. For this reason the working-class movement must create its own organic intellectuals—must train its own technical strata. Here again the party looms as the indispensable instrument. Gramsci apparently had in mind primarily one section of the organic intellectuals—the administrative personnel capable of commanding the state and the organs of political society. The changes of the last few decades have not lessened the urgency of this task, but the growing importance of technical strata capable of commanding the economy cannot be ignored. In Gramsci's day it was still possible, if not wholly realistic, to urge the technical training of workers under autonomous auspices in order to prepare them for the tasks of class rule. The technological revolution through which we are passing has enormously widened the gap between these organic intellectuals and the most intelligent, skilled and politically advanced workers. It appears, therefore, that our tasks are today much more complex and include a determined effort to break the hegemony of the bourgeoisie over these, its most pampered servants.

The two groups of intellectuals parallel those two aspects of society which Gramsci analyzed in terms reminiscent of Vico and Hegel. The organic intellectuals, as part of the ruling class, provide the personnel for those coercive organs constituting "political society." The traditional intellectuals, in contrast, staff the organs of "civil society"—the church, schools, social clubs, political parties, etc. Their task is to reason with the masses, to persuade, to convince; they are the essential element in the hegemony of the ruling class.

Gramsci's notion of hegemony is perhaps his most important contribution to Marxian political theory and forms a necessary counterpart to Lenin's development of the Marxian theory of the state. Gramsci's notion has been summarized by Gwynn Williams:

> [Hegemony is] an order in which a certain way of life and thought is dominant, in which one concept of reality is diffused throughout society in all its institutional and private manifestations, informing with its spirit all taste, morality, customs, religious and political principles, and all social relations, particularly in their intellectual and moral connotations.[4]

Hegemony, therefore, is achieved by consent, not force, through the civil and ostensibly private institutions of society. Marxists as Cammett observes, usually think of "the state" simply as political society whereas, he argues, the state (or as I should prefer to say, the system of class rule) ought to be understood more broadly as an equilibrium between political and civil society. Cammett observes further, "In its general sense, hegemony refers to the 'spontaneous' loyalty that any dominant social group obtains from the masses by virtue of its social and intellectual prestige and its supposedly superior function in the world of production."

It follows that hegemony depends on much more than consciousness of economic interests on the part of the ruling class and unconsciousness of such interests on the part of the submerged classes. The success of a ruling class in establishing its hegemony depends entirely on its ability to convince the lower classes that its interests are those of society at large—that it defends the common sensibility and stands for a natural and proper social order.

It is nonsense to think that an economic depression or devastating war could alone revolutionize consciousness. For the masses to be able to attribute their particular woes to the social system they must be more broadly convinced that the interests of the ruling class are at variance with those of society in general and of their own class in particular. To bring the masses to such a point we must recognize that such an identification between bourgeois and general interests exists and has existed, with the exception of the ante-bellum South, throughout American history. Too often our Marxists have assumed that economic deprivation, political repression, or socially retrogressive actions could rouse the exploited classes to anger and resistance. Even today we witness the absurdity of allegedly "vanguard" movements tying their hopes to some future depression or alternative catastrophe. Apathy, however, is not necessarily a product of fear, much less of indifference to discomfort and oppression; it may flow from a failure to identify the source of the discomfort and oppression.

Every organ of civil society labors to cloud the issue, to misdirect the anger and to produce resignation. If all we had to contend with was the force of political society, as so many of our ultraleftists as well as dogmatic revisionists like to believe, our prospects would now be much brighter. If, as is the case, we have to contend with a pervasive world view that identifies exploitation and social injustice as minor concomitants of the defense of a proper order, of religious and moral truth and of elementary decency in human relationships, then we had better begin doing our homework in philosophy, sociology, political theory and even theology. It is the totality of the bourgeois world view—the enormous complex of prejudices, assumptions, half-thought-out notions and no small number of profound ideas—that infects the victims of bourgeois rule, and it is the totality of an alternative world view that alone can challenge it for supremacy.

Socialists, as Gramsci said, must overcome the reluctance of the masses to risk the chaos inevitably accompanying the transition to a new society, but one of our hardest tasks seems to be to convince our own ultras that the masses, even the most wretched and desperate sections of them, normally do fear such chaos and must be made to see order and discipline during the most tumultuous transformations. The only elements that welcome choas are those among the masses whom the bourgeoisie has degraded into nihilism or those among our most dedicated and courageous cadres who have been tragically misled into desperation. In bourgeois-democratic societies the hegemony of the bourgeoisie masks its dictatorship. As Gramsci noted,

> In countries where open conflicts do not take place, where fundamental laws of the state are not trampled on, where arbitrary acts of the dominant class are not seen, the class struggle loses its harshness, the revolutionary struggle loses its drive and falters . . . . Where an order exists, it is more difficult to decide to replace it with a new order.

Fascism, therefore, is a sign of great weakness on the part of the bourgeoisie, and it is exasperating inanity to speak, as so many of our official Marxists do, of the "drive" of the bourgeoisie toward fascism.

The trouble with those who anxiously pore over the lessons of China and Cuba, or of Russia for that matter, is not that all those great revolutions do not have much to teach us, but that the gulf separating all of them from the experience of

Western Europe must always be kept in the forefront. In each of those societies, civil society had come apart and hardly existed as a hegemonic force any longer; the struggle could therefore be opened on the terrain of political society. The central fact of our own experience has been the enormous power of civil society even when the state power has faltered momentarily; we cannot hope to topple the state until we have fought and won the battle for civil society.

In the Western capitalist countries the hegemony of the bourgeoisie creates especially painful difficulties. Gramsci noted the contrast to Russia: "In the East the state was everything, and civil society was primordial and gelatinous; in the West there was a correct relationship between the state and civil society." A robust civil society can support an apparently shaky state and can carry it through difficult moments. Under this condition, the seizure of power is unlikely until civil society has been substantially transformed.

The war for position on the cultural front and the allegiance of the intellectuals is consequently vital to the struggle for socialism. As Cammett adds,

> The fundamental assumption behind Gramsci's view of hegemony is that the working class, before it seizes power, must establish its claim to be a ruling class in the political, cultural, and "ethical" fields. "The founding of a ruling class is equivalent to the creation of a *Weltanschauung*." . . . For Gramsci, a social class scarcely deserves the name until it becomes *conscious* of its existence as a class; it cannot play a role in history until it develops a comprehensive world view and a political program.

Bourgeois sociologists are, from this point of view, not entirely wrong to deny the existence of a working class in the United States. Leftist dismissal of the working class as "corrupt," or "irrelevant" or "just another part of the Establishment" nonetheless constitutes a superficial response to a problem that may be defined as the search for ways to develop such consciousness among those strata of the population capable, immediately or potentially, of forming a new ruling class.

V

I HAVE TRIED in the foregoing sections to present Gramsci's ideas, as outlined by Cammett, with a minimum of extension and interpretation; at least I hope that it is clear where Gramsci ends and Cammett begins and where Cammett ends and Genovese begins. The following section is, however, wholly interpretive and polemical and consists of loosely related thoughts suggested by Cammett's book and Gramsci's voluminous writings, parts of which I have studied carefully, parts casually and parts not at all.

The Role of the Working Class

Pretenses aside, the great Communist revolution in China has been based on the peasants. Admitting some exaggeration, we might say that instead of the proletariat's making the revolution, the revolution has been making the proletariat. For a revolution to pass from one stage to another, to recall Gramsci's dictum, it is enough to realize the first stage in thought. Socialism traditionally has been a proletarian demand and program; as a major political movement it was the creation of the working class, defined to include those intellectuals openly attached to it.

For more than one hundred years socialism has been a living idea; as such it has embraced the aspirations of all who value the humane and egalitarian traditions of Western society but who recognize that capitalism is unable to preserve the best in its own revolutionary heritage. If the idea of socialism, with its proletarian origins and its intentions of raising the working class to power, could seize hold of the peasants of

China, there is no reason that it cannot seize hold of the "new middle class" in the United States. The Chinese revolution was prevented from degenerating into a peasant-based social order by the commanding position of the party. With a small working class with which to staff the organs of political society, the party has to create a civil society of its own—to persuade, to convince, to win the battle for the minds of the peasant masses. The "proletarian" character of the Chinese revolution has rested on its commitment to a socialist order and has been determined in the realm of ideology—of thought. The assertion that only the working class can establish socialism is dogmatic nonsense.

I do not suggest that American socialism turn away from the working class, for I cannot imagine where else it could turn. I do suggest that we recognize the extent to which the question of socialism has become a matter of urgency for our people as a whole, and the extent to which the psychology of our workers, at least of our organized workers, has become indistinguishable from that of the "new middle class" of which so many of them in fact form a part. In view of the unprecedented strength of American capitalism, the power center of world imperialism, the prospects for resolving the old class questions—depression levels of unemployment, hunger, acute deprivation, insecurity in old age—within the present system are excellent.

Capitalism's inherent irrationality and immanent contradictions have not been overcome, but their social and phenomenal manifestations have changed drastically. The great issues facing the working class today are only indirectly those suggestive of economic exploitation. Principally they are the issue of survival (war or peace), elementary security to enjoy those material advantages which high capitalism has generated (protection against race riots, urban congestion, rampant hooliganism, and crime and the rest of the familiar items from Senator Goldwater's demagogic but by no means irrelevant speeches), the preservation of an adequate degree of stability in the face of pressures to dissolve the family without providing an adequate replacement, and in general the crisis in ideals and values that has descended in personal as well as social relationships. These are problems facing society as a whole; they grip all social classes, although not to the same degree, and are not class questions in the traditional sense. The solution, however, is very much a class question, for nothing short of the hegemony of the working class, broadly defined to include most of the producing elements of our society, can establish a viable alternative social order.

Two conclusions follow: First, the most oppressed sections of our society can, in various ways too complicated for summary discussion, play an important part in the formation of a new movement but cannot serve as its basis since they cannot possibly form the basis of a new ruling class. Second, under present conditions the working class can be won and the hegemony of the bourgeoisie broken only through a struggle that includes but does not rely on the bread-and-butter issues. The measures necessary to win the workers are essentially the same as those necessary to win the technical strata and the intelligentsia as a whole.

To reach the workers, especially the most socially conscious workers, we need to frame appeals to a much broader section of our population. The spectacle of dock workers refusing to load ships that trade with communist countries is especially instructive. These workers are not motivated primarily by the desire for personal gain; such stoppages might even cost them a good deal of money. However much we may deplore their reactionary stance, we ought to realize that their action connotes a strong social consciousness and a sense of their responsibility as workers in the formulation of social policy. Their willingness to move from economic to political and social issues opens the way to their radicalization and provides a suitable terrain on which to struggle for their ideological allegiance.

The position of the new technical and administrative strata may be approached in one of two ways. We might, with some justice, place them in the bourgeoisie, which certainly holds their allegiance at present. In this case, we would, even under the best of circumstances, have to concentrate on winning the working class alone since the agrarian classes no longer are numerically significant. Among the several objections to such an approach is the obvious one that a large and perhaps decisive section of the working class itself shares the outlook of these strata for the good reason that its social and economic position is only quantitatively distinct. The second approach would be to consider these technical and administrative strata as part of the working class, and in traditional Marxian terms, a good case can be made out for the identification.

This solution would, however, be mere sleight-of-hand and self-deception were it not for that degradation of all these strata alluded to by Gramsci. The technicians and administrators are well-paid servants, but they in fact run the plant and have usurped the functions of the capitalists. As a result the system hardly gives full rein to their talent or, worse, prostitutes it. They are, moreover, victims of the same general insecurities plaguing the population as a whole. If the working class has become part of the middle class, in a psychological sense and even to some extent as an income stratum, it is no less true that the new middle class is part of the working class. As such, its members have personal bourgeois interests but not a bourgeois class interest. Together with the traditional working class, they are the ones most capable of ruling society and of undergoing a revolution in consciousness. The ghetto populations may prove to be invaluable allies, but the construction of a new ruling class must come from the stable elements of our society.

The Struggle for Hegemony

If we were to pose the question of hegemony in Gramscian terms and ask which sections of the American Left have addressed themselves to it, we should have to confess that the answer would be the New Left. In a country and at a time when the idea of workers' councils and a mass party seems remote, the New Left's notion of countercommunities and counterinstitutions has considerable freshness and a certain plausibility. Measured against this notion the traditional insistence of the Communist party and other groups on working within existing institutions might seem not only old-fashioned but counterrevolutionary. Would that life were so simple! The overwhelming fact is that all attempts to replace the universities, for example, with "free universities" of "people's schools" are doomed to failure. The concentration of wealth and the level of institutional integration and sophistication being what they are, the most we could hope to accomplish would be supplementary activities, which might prove politically invaluable, but only within narrow limits. Free universities can do important work in helping to train political and intellectual cadres, but can hardly be expected to replace the academic institutions.

The problem we face is how to steer between two equally futile courses. To orient ourselves to work in existing universities, unions, and political organizations in the way in which the Communist party urges would merely repeat past defeats and add up to the pathetic efforts of well meaning individuals who objectively work to strengthen the hegemony of the bourgeoisie. To withdraw, to go it alone, to spend our strength trying to build counterinstitutions would be to surrender the possibilities of practical and meaningful work and to replace it with activities designed to save our individual souls from sin and corruption. The course demanded is to work within the institutions of civil society openly as socialists, despite the risks, with the avowed aim of transforming them into organs of transition to socialism. They must be made the battleground on which we transform the consciousness of the intelligentsia and the masses and therefore instruments for the structural reform of society. What separates a revolutionary from a reformist notion of structural reform, as Togliatti pointed out in his brilliant postwar articles in *Rinascita,* is the commitment to the socialist goal—the insistence that every advance must be integrated into the life of the party, the incessant struggle against bourgeois ideology, the adherence to the responsibilities of internationalism and the unfailing attention to the conquest of state power.

The state of and prospects for international relations present favorable opportunities for a struggle within the existing institutions—within civil society. So long as the world movement, even in its present state of crisis and disunity, remains sufficiently powerful and responsible to prevent the United States from unleashing a general nuclear war, the prospects for American imperialism's retaining its informal empire are not bright. The retreat from a position of world-wide looting must necessarily bring the United States face to face with itself. Even if armaments expenditures have largely usurped the place previously held by capital exports in the structure of imperialist economics, the bourgeoisie is headed for trouble. The Cold War is needed more and more to support domestic war programs, instead of vice versa, but the imperialists' growing difficulty in maintaining a Cold War psychology threatens them on all fronts. There is no reason, except one, to assume that our people will forever tolerate a regime which cannot cope satisfactorily with the most pressing problems of the day despite unprecedented resources. The one reason, of course, is the continued absence of a movement capable of advancing alternatives.

If the primary task at the moment must be a Gramscian "war for position on the cultural front" and if that war must be fought within the existing unions, universities, and social organizations, a variety of problems present themselves for urgent attention. Without attempting here even a suitable preliminary analysis of these complex problems, we may for the moment restrict ourselves to a few questions posed in the universities.

As the citadels of the traditional intellectuals, the universities are probably the institutions most convinced of their own autonomy, independence, and freedom of thought. Let us grant that the reality has always been something less; the fact remains that the myth of a community of disinterested scholars and the tradition, however often violated, of academic freedom ought to be central concerns for socialists. We may bypass for the present the problem of disinterestedness and partisanship in scholarship. It ought to be clear that the development of a humane and just social order requires maximum freedom of thought and expression, and that the universities are the institutions in which the greatest latitude possible must be maintained.

Our task, accordingly, is not to cry over the prevalence of bourgeois sterility, much less to dream of the day when we will have control of these institutions and can settle old scores. The ideal of the university as a community of scholars constitutes one of the finest features of the civilization we inherit from the past. If the reality falls far short of the ideal, socialists ought to be the staunchest champions of the ideal; they ought to be easily identified as men who advance specific programs for bringing the reality closer to the ideal and who have definite ideas for narrowing the gap in a future society. The university as ideal is already a quasi-socialist institution; the struggle to uphold the ideal is or could be a struggle to educate its personnel and the people generally in socialist ethical and political standards.

An object lesson in what not to do came out of Stanford University recently. A young man—serious, dedicated, intelligent and morally responsible—undertook to campaign for the presidency of the student council on a radical New Left platform that included hostility to America's imperialist war in Vietnam. To everyone's surprise in so conservative a university, he won. After a while he resigned, arguing that he had made his point through the campaign and had no desire to be caught up in the Establishment's bureaucracy, in which he could only function more or less like everyone else. I cannot imagine a greater exercise in futility; enough such abdications and the Left will lose, and deserve to lose, whatever audience it has. I intend no personal criticism of this young man, for what else could he have done in a political vacuum? We have no party or organized movement to provide direction and purpose; we have no general strategy to apply to specific situations. Quite possibly he was, in a narrow sense, right: had he remained in office under such circumstances, he might have become merely another functionary.

The frustration and confusion with which we must contend are exemplified by the tendency to nihilism among some of our best young people in the universities. Unable to influence society as a whole and overcome with a sense of powerlessness, they confront the universities with unreasonable and dubious demands and charges: all administrations are necessarily class enemies; the professors are generally finks, sell-outs, and prigs; the students ought to control the curricula; students and professors have equal rights in the classroom; and only the good Lord knows what else. Let me make clear that these remarks are no veiled criticism of student behavior at Berkeley or elsewhere, where complicated issues require specific analysis. I speak here only of a mood that prevails over too large a section of our student radicals.

Nothing will come of all this thrashing because nothing can come of it. Certainly, students' opinions on most matters of educational policy ought to be sought; and with equal certainty, no professor worthy of the name would surrender his prerogative to teach his course as he and he alone sees fit. The university cannot supply the student with the sense of power and relevance that society denies him. It is an institution with specific purposes, not society in microcosm. Its administrators are generally weak, frightened careerists rather than conscious servants of a hostile power; it does them too much honor in most cases to regard them as class enemies.

It is, of course, easier to provoke a bitter quarrel with an administration than to organize a movement for peace and socialism—the students will support you much more readily—but this is the essence of opportunism. The only administrations worthy of being treated as enemies are those which deny the right of the faculty or the student body to pursue its legitimate intellectual interests and to organize itself politically. In a period in which the financial control of the universities is passing into the hands of the state, students and professors have a double duty; to organize opinion and action against the foreign and domestic policies of imperialism and to defeat every encroachment against traditional liberties on the campus.

What might a president of a student council do? He might, among other things, lead a movement to drive off the campus every agency threatening the institution's autonomy, and he might lead an effort to make his university an ideological battleground in which the problems of our society are debated and the outlines of a better society are explored. To do this does not require usurping the prerogatives of professors or destroying the structure of the classroom.

Much of the theoretical work of the international socialist movement came out of the universities, as the experience of Gramsci and his circle reminds us. They must be kept free to permit that work to continue and expand. The fight for the preservation of their freedom and for their transformation, through ideological work and persuasion, not self-defeating bullying and totalitarian measures, into authentic communities of scholars is the fight to prepare them for their place in a new socialist order. It is one of many battles that must be waged to overthrow the hegemony of the bourgeoisie.

The Party

Those on the Left who today call for a new socialist party generally stress the urgent need for a center to coordinate political action and provide ideological and organizational continuity. The editorials in *Studies on the Left* may be cited as a good example. That we do face such urgency and do need a party to cope with it could hardly be denied. The case for a new party rests, however, on a broader base, as the experience of the New Left makes clear.

The New Left has been primarily a moral rather than political (in the narrow sense of the word) movement. It has been a protest against a society wealthy and cynical enough to buy the silent acquiescence of its people in world-wide plunder and various forms of domestic barbarism. The answers of the New Left have been thin and sometimes so utopian or undesirable as to call forth ridicule and even contempt. This reaction, of which I among others have sometimes been guilty, has missed the most politically important contribution that the New Left has made: In its own terms it has raised the question of cultural hegemony and has insisted on its centrality. Its answers have been poor, and in some ways worse than nothing, but its instinct for the enemy's vulnerability and its sense of what constitutes a proper battleground have been much more impressive than anything coming from Marxist sources, old or new, official or independent.

The New Left has nonetheless been unable to proceed from its insight to a position from which it could effectively challenge the regime. The reasons are familiar, and the most thoughtful elements in the new movements have provided as good an analysis as have their critics. Those who have criticized them from a Marxist viewpoint have failed to impress them with the argument for a new party because that demand has been advanced as a political-administrative solution to what seems to them, quite correctly, to be a moral and broadly social problem. They deny a hostility to theory, but insist they have seen no theory worthy of their commitment. Marxists have been irritated and puzzled by this taunt because they know that Marxism, for all its roughness and incompleteness, offers a perfectly sound starting point for theoretical work, and they cannot understand the lack of attention from the New Left. There are many reasons for this lack not all of which are flattering to the New Left, but there can be no question about the intelligence, sincerity, and seriousness of many, who have remained aloof.

In part, the problem has been the unwillingness of the Marxist parties and tendencies to accept responsibility for waging a Gramscian struggle on the cultural level. The most profound questions have been reopened in the light of the negative side of the experience of the Eastern socialist countries: questions about the nature of man, of his responsibility to himself and to society, of a new and higher morality and of the proper relationship among students and workers, leaders and led, men and women. Our Marxists have given no answers, or answers the banality of which ought to embarrass them.

The New Left's indifference to Marxism[5] may, with supreme irony, finally do what the sterile Marxist parties have failed to do—lead to the restoration of Marxism to its rightful place in American intellectual and political life. By rejecting the mechanism and determinism of official American Marxism, not to mention its totalitarianism, the New Left may finally force American Marxists to come to terms with Gramscian thought and to prepare to make its own departure. American Marxists cannot hope to advance until they meet the ideologies of the New Left on their own ground; the thought of Antonio Gramsci does not provide ready-made answers but does provide the starting point for which we have been searching.

The need is for more than a dialogue; it is for a body of common experience in action. Until socialists have a party within which to test their doctrines, the doctrines must remain abstract and undeveloped. Until we have an organization capable of demonstrating that we can live and work as well as think in ways foreshadowing a better society, there is no reason for any skeptic, no matter how honest and conscionable, to believe us. The question of building a party can no longer be avoided. If the careful study of Gramsci's life and work does not guarantee our success, it will at least help us shape the kind of party in which we and our potential allies on a fragmented Left can live together.

VI

WE MAY HOPE that Cammett's book receives the wide reading it deserves; it is a model of meticulous scholarship and clarity of exposition. We might regret that Cammett does not develop his criticisms of Gramsci and that he restricts himself so much to the task of presenting Gramsci's case, but he is right in believing that the main problem at the moment is to tell the story. He will be writing other books in which the job of developing his critical insights, largely implicit or in passing in this book, can be undertaken. Until Gramsci's works are made available in English it will be difficult to exploit his accomplishment. Even then they would be incomprehensible without an understanding of their historical and political context. To provide this context Cammett had to proceed with painstaking care with the biography, the factional struggles in the PSI, PCI, and the Comintern and the intellectual origins of Gramscian Marxism. He has accomplished this task, to which he has selflessly devoted himself for more than a decade, with admirable intellectual depth, political judgment and scholarly responsibility. It now becomes possible to raise significantly the level of our theoretical work through the study of Gramsci's contributions, and for this we owe Cammett an immeasurable debt.

NOTES

1. There are two slim and inadequate volumes in English: *The Open Marxism of Antonio Gramsci,* translated and edited by Carl Marzani (New York, 1957). A brief selection from the *Materialismo storico,* much of which consists of the editor's extrapolations in editorial comments on American problems; *The Modern Prince and Other Writings,* translated and edited by Louis Marks, consisting of selections from several volumes of Gramsci's *Opere* with inadequate editing.

2. H. Stuart Hughes, *Consciousness and Society* (New York, 1958), p. 101.

3. *Ibid.,* p. 102. Original emphasis.

4. Gwynn Williams, as quoted by Cammett, *Antonio Gramsci,* p. 204.

5. Since these lines were written, much of The New Left has gone over to one or another form of dogmatic Marxism and some of it to a new Stalinism.

INDEX